Somewhere a Master

Elie Wiesel was born in Hungary in 1928. He was deported with his family to Auschwitz when he was still a boy, and then to Buchenwald, where his parents and a younger sister were killed. *Night* (Penguin, 1981), his first book, is the moving memoir of these experiences. After the war he moved to Paris, where he adopted the French language and assumed French nationality. His work as a journalist took him to Israel and finally to the United States.

Elie Wiesel has achieved an international reputation with such books as *A Beggar in Jerusalem*, which won the French Prix Medici for 1969. *Souls on Fire* is a collection of portraits and legends describing the Hasidic Masters who revitalized Judaism and of which Charles Silberman, writing in *The New York Times Book Review*, said, '*Souls on Fire* should be read by everyone concerned with the existential question, which is to say, by every sensitive and thinking human being ... It is a work of genius and of art – an extraordinary man's extraordinary effort to "humanize fate"'; *Somewhere a Master* is the sequel to that masterpiece. His other books are *Dawn, The Accident, The Town Beyond the Wall, The Gates of the Forest, The Jews of Silence, Legends of Our Time, One Generation After, The Oath, Ani Maamin: A Cantata, Zalmen, or the Madness of God, Messengers of God, A Jew Today, Four Hasidic Masters* and *The Testament* (Penguin, 1982), which was awarded the Prix-Inter for 1980.

Elie Wiesel is Andrew Mellon Professor in the Humanities at Boston University. He is also Chairman of the President's Commission on the Holocaust. He and his family live in New York City.

Elie Wiesel

===== Souls on Fire =====

and

===== Somewhere a Master =====

Translated from the French by
Marion Wiesel

Penguin Books

Penguin Books Ltd, Harmondsworth, Middlesex, England
Penguin Books, 40 West 23rd Street, New York, New York 10010, U.S.A.
Penguin Books Australia Ltd, Ringwood, Victoria, Australia
Penguin Books Canada Ltd, 2801 John Street, Markham, Ontario, Canada L3R 1B4
Penguin Books (N.Z.) Ltd, 182–190 Wairau Road, Auckland 10, New Zealand

Souls on Fire first published in France as *Célébration Hassidique* by Editions du Seuil
This translation first published in the U.S.A. by Random House 1972

Somewhere a Master first published in France
This translation first published in the U.S.A. by Summit Books 1982

Published in one volume in Penguin Books 1984

Souls on Fire copyright © Elie Wiesel, 1972
Somewhere a Master copyright © Elirion Associates, Inc., 1982
All rights reserved

Made and printed in Great Britain by
Richard Clay (The Chaucer Press) Ltd, Bungay, Suffolk
Set in 10/11 pt Monophoto Sabon

Contents

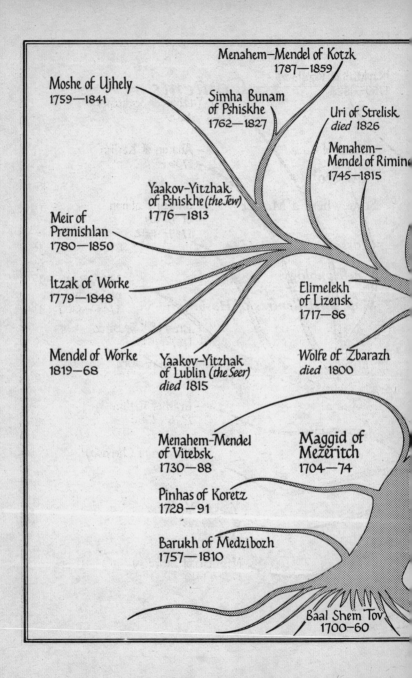

Menahem–Mendel of Kotzk
1787—1859

Moshe of Ujhely
1759—1841

Simha Bunam
of Pshiskhe
1762—1827

Uri of Strelisk
died 1826

Menahem–
Mendel of Rimino
1745—1815

Yaakov–Yitzhak
of Pshiskhe *(the Jew)*
1776—1813

Meir of
Premishlan
1780—1850

Itzak of Worke
1779—1848

Elimelekh
of Lizensk
1717—86

Mendel of Worke
1819—68

Yaakov–Yitzhak
of Lublin *(the Seer)*
died 1815

Wolfe of Zbarazh
died 1800

Menahem–Mendel
of Vitebsk
1730—88

Maggid of
Mezeritch
1704—74

Pinhas of Koretz
1728—91

Barukh of Medzibozh
1757—1810

Baal Shem Tov
1700—60

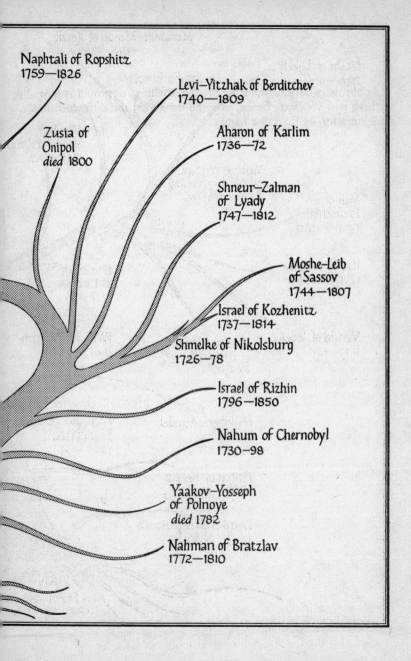

Naphtali of Ropshitz
1759—1826

Levi–Yitzhak of Berditchev
1740—1809

Zusia of
Onipol
died 1800

Aharon of Karlim
1736—72

Shneur–Zalman
of Lyady
1747—1812

Moshe–Leib
of Sassov
1744—1807

Israel of Kozhenitz
1737—1814

Shmelke of Nikolsburg
1726—78

Israel of Rizhin
1796—1850

Nahum of Chernobyl
1730—98

Yaakov–Yosseph
of Polnoye
died 1782

Nahman of Bratzlav
1772—1810

Publishers' Note

The publishers have retained the original spellings of proper names in these two volumes; hence, in some instances, the difference in transliteration of the same names.

Souls on Fire

Contents

Author's Note

The main chapters in this volume are based on lectures delivered at the Sorbonne in Paris and at the 92nd Street 'Y' in New York. The latter would not have been undertaken had it not been for the initiative of Lily Edelman, Director of Adult Education of B'nai B'rith, the cooperation of William Kolodney, former Educational Director of the 92nd Street 'Y', and the dedication of Herbert Reiman, also of B'nai B'rith.

My thanks to Professor Gerson D. Cohen for his valuable suggestions during the preparation of the Synchronology, and to Professor Abraham J. Heschel, my gratitude for sharing with me his own insight on Mendl of Kotzk.

The tales and sayings are translated from the original Yiddish and Hebrew texts, the languages used by the Hasidic Masters and their disciples. Their names and the names of their towns are spelled – arbitrarily – to approximate the way they were pronounced by the Hasidim I knew.

My father, an enlightened spirit, believed in man.
My grandfather, a fervent Hasid, believed in God.
The one taught me to speak, the other to sing.
Both loved stories.
And when I tell mine, I hear their voices.
Whispering from beyond the silenced storm,
they are what links the survivor to their memory.

Israel Baal Shem Tov

And it came to pass that the great Rebbe Israel Baal Shem Tov, Master of the Good Name, known for his powers in heaven as well as on earth, decided to try once more to force his Creator's hand.

He had tried many times before – and failed. Burning with impatience, he wanted to end the ordeals of exile forcibly; and this time he was but one step away from success. The gates were ajar; the Messiah was about to appear and console the children and old men awaiting him, awaiting no one else but him. The Diaspora had lasted long enough; now men everywhere would gather and rejoice.

The heavens were in an uproar. The angels were dancing. Red with anger, outraged, Satan demanded an audience with God. Brought before Him, he protested, invoking laws and precedents, history and reason. Look at man's impudence, he said, how dare he take things in his own hands? Does the world deserve redemption? And the conditions to warrant the Messiah's coming, have they been met?

God listened. And had to recognize the validity of Satan's arguments: *Lo ikhshar dara*, the Rebbe's gesture was judged premature; his generation was not yet ready for a miracle of such magnitude. Moreover, since the order of creation may not be disturbed with impunity, he and his faithful scribe Reb Tzvi-Hersh Soifer were deported to a distant uncharted island. Where they were promptly taken prisoners by a band of pirates.

Never had the Masters been so submissive, so resigned.

'Master,' the scribe pleaded, 'do something, say something!'

'I can't,' said the Baal Shem Tov, 'my powers are gone.'

'What about your secret knowledge, your divine gifts: your *yik-hudim*? What happened to them?'

'Forgotten,' said the Master. 'Disappeared, vanished. All my knowledge has been taken away; I remember nothing.'

But when he saw Hersh Soifer's despair, he was moved to pity. 'Don't give up,' he said, 'we still have one chance. You are here, and that is good. For you can save us. There must be one thing I taught you that you remember. Anything – a parable, a prayer. Anything will do.'

Unfortunately, the scribe too had forgotten everything. Like his Master, he was a man without memory.

'You really remember nothing,' the Master asked again, 'nothing at all?'

'Nothing, Master. Except . . .'

'. . . except what?'

'. . . the *aleph, beith*.'

'Then what are you waiting for?' shouted the Master, suddenly excited. 'Start reciting! Right now!'

Obedient as always, the scribe proceeded to recite slowly, painfully, the first of the sacred letters which together contain all the mysteries of the entire universe: '*Aleph, beith, gimmel, daleth . . .*'

And the Master, impatiently, repeated after him: '*Aleph, beith, gimmel, daleth . . .*'

Then they started all over again, from the beginning. And their voices became stronger and clearer: *aleph, beith, gimmel, daleth . . .* until the Baal Shem became so entranced that he forgot who and where he was. When the Baal Shem was in such ecstasy, nothing could resist him, that is well known. Oblivious to the world, he transcended the laws of time and geography. He broke the chains and revoked the curse: Master and scribe found themselves back home, unharmed, richer, wiser and more nostalgic than ever before.

The Messiah had not come.

This tale is characteristic because it contains most of the basic elements of Hasidism. The fervent waiting, the longing for redemption; the erratic wanderings over untravelled roads; the link between man and his Creator, between the individual act and its repercussions in the celestial spheres; the importance of ordinary words; the accent on fervour and on friendship too; the concept of miracles performed by man for man. It is also characteristic because it may well . . . not be true.

Like most of the stories about the Baal Shem – or the Besht, as he is called in Hasidic tradition – it describes events that may or may not have happened, and if they did, may or may not have happened in quite the way they are told. Viewed from the outside, all of these tales are incomprehensible; one must enter them, for their truth may be measured only from the inside. Whether accurately retold or invented outright by his admiring contemporaries, they must be passed on exactly as the narrator received them in his childhood. Clearly, it is to relive that childhood that he is telling them in his turn.

I would listen to them as night fell – between the prayers of Minha and Maariv – in the House of Study filled with the flickering shadows of yellow candles. The Elders spoke of the great Masters as though they had known them personally. Each had his favourite Rebbe and a legend he liked above all others. I came to feel that I was forever listening to the same story about the same Rebbe. Only the names of people and places changed. Motives, deeds, responses and outcomes hardly varied; just as there was always a person in need, there was always someone to lend him a hand. This apparent repetition troubled me, and so one day I discussed this with my grandfather: 'I don't understand. Is it possible there really was only one Rebbe?' – 'Yes,' said my grandfather, 'it is possible, and even probable. Every Rebbe has but one Hasid and every Hasid has but one Rebbe. One could not exist without the other.' – 'Isn't this a sign of weakness?' I asked. – 'No,' replied my grandfather, 'it is their very strength.'

In fact, he was that Hasid. Every Shabbat and every Holy Day, he would leave his village to come and celebrate with us. I would remain with him until he went back home. I accompanied him to the mikvah, the ritual bath; to services; to the Rebbe. He would sing and I sang with him; he would speak and I thrilled to every one of his words. He would say: 'A Hasid must know how to listen. To listen is to receive. The Jew who does not know how or does not wish to receive is not Jewish. Our people is what it is because it knew how to listen and receive the Law, right? Yet, though the Torah was given only once, each one of us must receive it every day.'

In his presence, the others in the House of Study kept respectfully silent. A fabulous storyteller, he knew how to captivate an audience. He would say: 'Listen attentively, and above all, remember that true tales are meant to be transmitted – to keep them to oneself is to betray them.' He knew how intently I listened; he must have known that I would remember, but he had no way of knowing how closely I would follow his advice. My very first Hasidic tales I heard from him. He made me enter the universe of the Baal Shem and his disciples, where facts became subservient to imagination and beauty. What difference did it make that events and chronological dates no longer matched? I surely didn't care. What mattered

*to me was not that two and two are four, but that God is one.
Better still: that man and God are one.*

*I can still hear my grandfather's voice: 'There will, of course,
always be someone to tell you that a certain tale cannot, could not,
be objectively true. That is of no importance; an objective Hasid is
not a Hasid.'*

He was right. The Baal Shem's call was a call to subjectivity, to
passionate involvement; the tales he told and those told about him
appeal to the imagination rather than to reason. They try to prove
that man is more than he appears to be and that he is capable
of giving more than he appears to possess. To dissect them, therefore, is to diminish them. To judge them is to detach oneself and
taint their candour – in so doing, one loses more than one could
gain.

And so it is not surprising that the Baal Shem should have fared
so poorly with the lay historians, who were, after all, 'outsiders'.
He eludes them. Historically speaking, the character barely
emerges, his outlines blurred by contradictions. Nothing about him
can be said with certainty. Those who claim to have known him, to
have come close to him or loved him, seem incapable of referring
to him in terms other than poetic. He has made them dream so much
that they describe him as in a dream. That is at least part of the
reason why so many rationalists study him with thinly veiled hostility. By becoming a legend, his life has slipped from their grasp.

There were scholars who made him the target of unrestrained
animosity, an animosity which went beyond any ideological stance.
He simply disturbed them in their roles of historians. They dismiss
him as a charlatan, a vulgar drunkard, an ignorant and greedy
quack, because they resent him.

Unable to draw a line – any line – between mythical and real
being, between fiction and testimony, they are embarrassed. Particularly since their subject is a man who, in a comparatively recent
past, shook the very foundations of Judaism, by revolutionizing its
thoughts, its perceptions, its way of life. A man who almost single-
handedly opened the soul of his people to a new creativity, a
creativity heretofore unexplored, of man come to grips with what
crushes or lifts him towards infinity.

The man who left his mark on so many survivors of so many
massacres in Central and Eastern Europe, the leader who not only
made survival imperative but possible, the Master who gave song
to despairing communities, managed – we shall never know how –

to disappear without leaving the professional seekers even a fragment of valid autobiographical material. Obsessed by eternity, he
neglected history and let himself be carried by legend.

The works attributed to him – *Shivkhei ha-Besht, Keter Shem
Tov, Tzvaat ha-Ribash* – really belong to others. His apocryphal
letters – to his children, his disciples – have been questioned more
than once. There remains of him no portrait, no document, no
signature constituting irrefutable evidence that behind the legend
there was a man, a face, a consciousness. Perhaps this was but
another way for him to emphasize his contempt for things written.
To the disciple who had transposed his verbal teachings to paper,
the Master said: 'There is nothing of me in your pages; you thought
you heard what I didn't say.' Also: 'I said one thing, you heard
another, and you wrote a third.' For the Baal Shem, imagination
gains in impact with each passing moment. Until finally its power
is perhaps greater than that of any testimony. The real and the
imagined, one like the other, are part of history; one is its shell, the
other its core. Not to recognize this is to deny art – any form of art
– the right to exist.
    Yet it is precisely on the imagination that the Baal-Shem plays –
even after his death. Each of his disciples saw him differently; to
each he represented something else. Their attitudes towards him, as
they emerge from their recollections, throw more light on themselves than on him. This explains the countless contradictory tales
relating to him.
    The historians may have been troubled, but not the Hasidim.
Hasidism does not fear contradictions; Hasidism teaches humility
and pride, the fear of God and the love of God, the at once sacred
and puerile dimension of life, the Master's role of intermediary
between man and God, a role that can and must be disregarded in
their I-and-Thou relationship. What does it prove? Only that contradictions are an intrinsic part of man.
    But not of historians. Frustrated by his elusiveness, they fight
him. Some go so far as to deny his very existence. They would like
us to believe that he was – quite simply – invented by his disciples,
whose own existence they fortunately do not doubt. Others, to
restore the balance, claim that ... there were actually two Baal
Shem Tovs and that the Hasidic movement was founded ... by the
other.
    Controversies, confusion of places and dates, paradoxes, the
Baal Shem's legend abounds with them. He who had the talent to

clarify ideas and concepts appears to have done his utmost to obscure the trails leading to his person.

The exact date of his birth has not been established: 1698 according to some, 1700 according to others – as though it made any difference. There seems to be no disagreement as to the place of his birth: a small village – a fortress perhaps – named Okop. Still, the scholars have some difficulty in agreeing on its precise location. Dubnov believes it to be near Kamenetz, Balaban moves it to the banks of the Dniepr, whereas Schechter prefers to see it in Bukovina. As for Mahler, he simply annexes it to Galicia. Evidently the Baal Shem succeeded in turning even geography into a mystery.

Mystery again in all references to his childhood, his education, his family life, his travels, his wanderings across mountains and valleys to come to the aid of anyone in need of help or love.

His parents – Eliezer and Sarah – were rich and generous, according to some; poor but generous, according to others. Their son – Israel – was given to them as a reward when they were almost one hundred years old. They had shown themselves hospitable and indulgent towards the Prophet Elijah, according to one version, and towards Satan, according to another. Their son was to be a symbol of promise and consolation, a guiding light to people in distress.

Eliezer, the father, was so kind, so generous a man, says legend, that it had been decided in heaven to put him to a test. And so, one Friday eve, a stranger dressed in rags, leaning on a staff, a bundle on his back, knocked at the old couple's door just as they were sitting down to celebrate the first meal of Shabbat. Without even the slightest hint of disapproval in their countenance, they warmly received the visitor, though he had transgressed the law. And because they neither offended nor embarrassed the poor prophet, he told them the news: the following year they would no longer be alone.

Another tale describes Eliezer as a victim turned hero. Captured and carried off by barbarians, he makes a career in the royal palace, counselling the sovereign and helping him plan and win his wars. Though the king showers him with honours, Eliezer privately continues to carry out the duties of a good Jew, obeying the laws of Torah. Of course, the king becomes so fond of him that he offers him his daughter in marriage. The marriage takes place, but to the princess's great chagrin, is not consummated. Pleading for her forgiveness, he confesses not only that he is married, but that he is a Jew. Reassured about her charms, she magnanimously helps him

leave the kingdom. And because of his faithfulness to his people
and to his wife, a son was born to him blessed with all gifts and
vested with all powers.

At his death, Eliezer told his heir: 'I leave before I can make you
into a man who fears God and loves those who fear Him. Remember one thing: God is at your side and He alone is to be
feared.' Later the Baal Shem was to add: 'God sees, God watches.
He is in every life, in every thing. The world hinges on His will. It
is He who decides how many times the leaf will turn in the dust
before the wind blows it away.'

Orphaned and destitute, without a friend, he practised all trades:
tutor, beadle, ritual slaughterer. Somewhat clumsy and absent-
minded, eccentric, he lived on a meagre subsidy from the community. He was still very young when the community took the first
opportunity to get him married. But soon after the marriage, his
wife died and he reverted to his former marginal, introspective
existence, and waited for a sign.

There are countless legends concerning the life he led before his
revelation. Some say that he saved schoolboys from were-wolves
and warlocks. Others, that he could bring mountains together.
And that during his walks through the forests, he spun dreams in
which ends found their beginnings and the world's song reverber-
ated in God's.

Some sources claim he was a saint who fled the limelight; others
describe him as a harmless dunce; still others endow him with
enough wisdom and learning to make him into a judge of the
rabbinical court: a *Dayan*, an arbiter of the community. It is as
such that he is said to have made the acquaintance of Reb Abraham
– or is it Ephraim? – Kitiver, who wished to arrange a suitable
match for his daughter Hannah. Her age at the time? A few months,
according to some texts, much more – since she was already
divorced – according to others. No matter, the engagement contract
was signed, showing the boy's name as Israel, son of Eliezer, and
mentioning no title whatever. Shortly thereafter Hannah's father
died.

Years went by, until one day the 'bridegroom', dressed in peasant
clothes, appeared in Brodi to see Reb Gershon Kitiver, Hannah's
brother, who took him for a beggar and offered him alms. 'No,'
said the visitor, 'that won't do. There's something I want to say to
you alone.' Then he added roughly: 'I want my wife, give me my
wife.'

Reb Gershon, one of the town's notables, did not take the jest lightly. Even after he had been shown the agreement signed by his father, he advised his sister against marrying this primitive, clumsy peasant. Hannah chose to obey her late father's wish and a date was set for the wedding. Before the ceremony, the Baal Shem drew Hannah aside and told her: 'I am not who you think I am, but you must tell no one.' He then described the road he had chosen and predicted the difficulties they would encounter, the obstacles still left to overcome. Hannah declared herself ready to confront them at his side.

Then followed hard, unrewarding days. Reb Gershon was ashamed of his brother-in-law and therefore persuaded the couple to go away, as far away as possible. He bought them an inn with a tavern, and then a horse and cart. Isolated in the Carpathian Mountains, Israel and Hannah lived in misery. They dug the soil and eked out a bare subsistence selling lime in the villages.

One day he was summoned by the local rabbi, who undertook to give him a lesson in Judaism. The Baal Shem, in quick succession, put on and removed his simpleton's mask. The rabbi was perplexed: how could the expression on a face change so rapidly? Stunned, he demanded his visitor tell him the truth.

'So be it,' said the Baal Shem. 'But you must keep what I tell you to yourself. For the moment.'

However, there lived in Brodi a woman who was mad. She saw through all men's masks. Brought face to face with the Baal Shem, she said: 'I know who you are and I am not afraid of you. I know that you possess certain powers; I also know that you may not use them before the age of thirty-six.'

'Be quiet,' he answered, 'otherwise I shall convene a court to evict the Dybbuk inside you.'

The frightened woman held her tongue – but she knew. The others found out much later. Seven lonely and ascetic years went by before the Baal Shem received the order to reveal himself and assume his destiny.

On that particular Saturday, a pupil of Reb Gershon interrupted a journey to spend Shabbat with Israel and Hannah. It was midnight when he awoke trembling with fright: a huge flame was rising from the hearth. Thinking to prevent a fire, he ran to extinguish it. When, instead, he saw his host flooded in light, he fainted. As he regained consciousness, he heard the Baal Shem scolding him: 'One does not look where one should not.' After Shabbat, the traveller hurried back to Brodi, where he stormed into the House of Study, shouting the great news: 'There is a new source of light close by.'

The men rushed to the edge of the forest and there built a throne with branches and leaves. The Besht took his seat. 'I shall open a new way,' he declared.

He was thirty-six.

The madwoman had seen right. She had known before anyone else. Strange: more than any of the town's devout and erudite men, she spoke the language of the young saint in the forest.

Strange, too, the Baal Shem's pilgrimage to the Holy Land. What had moved him to undertake it? Vague desire or well-defined project? One legend tells that bandits somewhere in the Carpathians revealed to him the existence of a tunnel leading to Jerusalem. Another legend claims that he reached the Holy Land by way of Istanbul, accompanied by his scribe Tzvi-Hersh Soifer or — alternately — by his daughter Udil. To simplify matters, a third version insists that he brought both — or then again, that maybe he made the trip . . . twice. A fourth version: his project came to naught; he never went at all.

More enigmas: did he or did he not participate in a public debate with Jacob Frank's followers in Lemberg? Did he or did he not practise healing, distribute amulets to influence fate and drive out demons? Opinions are divided. Even the date of his death is controversial. Some say he died the first day of Shavuot, others affirm it was the second.

Remember: all this confusion centres around a man who lived not in the Middle Ages, but in the eighteenth century. This contemporary of Voltaire and Kant, of Lessing and Diderot, built his empire not in a still far removed and backward Africa, but in the heart of Europe, where man in his quest for enlightenment had begun to reduce history to a human scale. People were striving to learn, to travel, to explore and experience. The word everywhere was becoming challenge, instrument of rebellion, heralding revolutionary changes. Men used it to smash idols and altars — and wanted to make certain that the rest of the world knew. Yet politicians and philanthropists, adventurers and preachers, conquerors and dreamers, all made their way into the chronicles, if not the history, of their times — all except the Baal Shem.

There remains of him nothing but legend, a legend whose profound and lasting reverberations paradoxically gained in strength with time. More than any other Jewish historical figure, with the exception of the Prophet Elijah, the Besht was present in joy as well as in despair; every *shtibl* reflected his light, his warmth. Every Hasid had two Masters: his own and the Baal Shem — each drew his strength from the other. The first was needed to live, the second to believe. Whoever disclaimed kinship with the Baal Shem found himself relegated outside the mainstream of the Hasidic community. The most hauntingly beautiful legends are those in which the Baal Shem is the central – or at least a major – character.

Perhaps then we should say that he was the sum of all tales that were – and still are – told about him and his work. More precisely: that he *is* the legend.

Yet the son of Sarah and Eliezer was not the first Baal Shem. There had been other Masters of the Name before him. Joel Baal Shem, Eliahu Baal Shem, Binyamin Baal Shem: wandering miracle-makers all, covering the countryside, visiting towns and villages, sometimes pushing as far as Worms and London. And then there was the mysterious Adam Baal Shem, considered the forerunner of Hasidism; he is the one rumoured to have entrusted his esoteric writings to his son for transmission to the Master of the Good Name. Saints or picturesque healers, depending on one's point of view, they were more or less proficient in their art; one came to see them to exorcize evil, chase away demons and make sterile women bear children. To distinguish the Baal Shem from the others, the word *Tov* was added to his name. Thus he became the Master of the *Good* Name, and all others receded into the background, if not oblivion. He remained alone, unchallenged.

Nor was he the first Hasid. Without going back as far as the Hasidim of the Talmud or of the twelfth century, there existed during the period immediately preceding the Baal Shem's appearance, Hasidic brotherhoods of a sort in Brodi, Bar, Kitev and Medzebozh. They brought together Kabbalists and noted scholars, among them Gershon Kitiver, Nahman of Horodenko, Nahman of Kossov, Wolfe Kitzes, Yitzhak of Drohobitch, Shabtai Rashkover. Theirs were closed circles – they wished to remain an elite. To discourage potential new members, they evolved rules for admission that required every candidate not only to display superior knowledge in Talmud and Kabbala, but also to pledge himself to the rigorous practice of asceticism and to 'abstain from indulging in prophecy'. It is said that the Besht himself tried to become one of them. He was refused, his knowledge being considered insufficient. Thus, there were Hasidim before the Besht, but Hasidism such as we know it was created – or re-created – by him. He gave an existing term new content and form.

It was not an easy task. Some of these early Hasidim were his worst adversaries before rallying around him as friends, companions and disciples. In the beginning they reproached him with having thrown open the gates too wide: they were weary of the masses. With a few exceptions, all submitted to his authority in the end, the small Hasidic brotherhoods absorbed by the new movement. Reb Nahman of Kossov was one of the exceptions; he refused even to meet the Baal Shem. Only after long and insistent urging by his disciples did he accept a face-to-face meeting. He started with a challenge: 'They say you can read other men's thoughts, is that true?' – 'Yes,' replied the Baal Shem. – 'Prove it. Tell me what I am thinking of this very moment.' – 'God, of course,' said the Baal Shem, taking no chances, since God must be present in every thought of every devout Jew. – 'Too easy,' was his guest's not unexpected comment. – 'True,' replied the Baal Shem, 'it is easy because in fact all men think of God. What varies is their way. If you like, I'll tell you yours.' Whether he did, no one knows. Though Reb Nahman did not become a Hasid, he thereafter forbade others to criticize the Baal Shem in his presence. He would say: 'This is an argument which concerns only him and me. It started before us; it has opposed David to Saul, Hillel to Shammai. I forbid you to become involved.'

The Baal Shem was more successful with other spiritual leaders of the region, such as Pinhas of Koretz, Yaakov-Yosseph of Polnoye and Dov-Ber of Mezeritch. The first he conquered with the intensity of his gaze; the second, with his tales; the third, with his fire.

To enlarge his following, the Baal Shem spared neither time nor strength. He was constantly on the roads, making sudden appearances here and there, in forests and in marketplaces; accosting strangers, rich or poor, learned or ignorant, making followers of them all. If someone caught his particular interest, he did not rest until he met him and, if possible, drew him into his intimate circle. To please Nahman of Kossov, he once subjected himself to the hardships of a long journey, proving thereby what little importance he attributed to distances if he could give pleasure to a friend. More than once did he travel night and day only to celebrate Shabbat with Yaakov-Yosseph of Polnoye.

For those he esteemed, he was generosity personified: kind, obliging, considerate. Learning that one of his followers was indulging in the mortification of his body, he took the time to write him a long letter, pleading with him to consider his health and even giving him a few practical suggestions, such as what to eat and what to drink and when.

Only when it came to the official rabbis did the Besht show himself merciless. 'One day they will be so many, they will prevent the coming of the Messiah!' Nor did he like physicians: 'They think they must explain everything, and yet they see nothing but the surface of man's ills.' His disciples, mostly simple and devoted men, he loved like a father or an older brother, showing interest in the activities of each, to the smallest detail. He wanted to know everything, understand everything. Each one of his disciples was convinced that the Master saw no one but him and gave to no one but him. One day, says legend, his disciples understood that in his eyes they were all equal – and 'they remained silent a long time'.

Still, even though he focused his attention on his followers, the Master was careful not to neglect those outside his immediate circle.

His frequent journeys through the fifty towns and villages mentioned in the *Shivkhei ha-Besht* were intended primarily to recruit followers, apostles as it were, destined to become community leaders. He gave of himself generously and without reservations to all who needed him, without any thought as to the future usefulness of the recipients; every human being deserved his attention. He simply appeared wherever he, or someone like him, was necessary, wherever utterly alone men and women, on the brink of despair, needed a sign, a messenger.

A man of contagious intensity, he changed all who approached him. The most mediocre of men vibrated at his contact; an encounter with him was the event of a lifetime.

To have his gaze rest on you meant feeling his fire run through you. An old peasant protects him from the cold – in return, the peasant will become rich and live for a hundred years. A boy recites his lesson with fervour – he will reap glory among his peers. A thief has the misfortune to cross his path. Discovered, he turns to the Master and says: 'Since you know how to look, why don't you rather try to see the good?' And so, even the thief enters the enchanted garden of Hasidic legend.

I can still hear my grandfather telling me: 'In the Besht's universe, no one felt left out.' That was true for his disciples as well. For Hasidim, no man is a stranger; for the Rebbe, no Hasid is unwanted. A Hasid who no longer practises remains a Hasid nevertheless; he will be saved in the end. By his companions who feel responsible for his fate. Beshtian Hasidism is founded on solidarity.

Unlike the Rebbes of succeeding generations, the Baal Shem had no permanent residence, maintained no court, kept neither servant nor secretary to screen visitors and act as a shield between himself and his solicitors. He wished to remain accessible to all who came to him to share their worries, their anguish. And he not only received them, he met them halfway. Always in motion, he granted himself no respite. Travelling sometimes with his coachman Alexei, sometimes with his scribe Tzvi-Hersh Soifer, he tried to be everywhere at once; what he wanted was to end all waiting, personify all hope. If one believes his legend, he succeeded. He belonged to all.

He addressed himself to men and women, some say more frequently to women than men, in synagogues and streets, at fairs and in taverns, at all hours, day or night. He needed to touch as many people as possible. No place was too far, no man too unworthy: 'As long as the branch is not cut from the tree every hope is justified,' he said. And also: 'To pull another out of the mud, man must step into the mud himself.' He is also supposed to have said: 'Small Tzaddikim like small sinners, a great Tzaddik likes a great sinner.' No wonder that, according to popular tradition, he tried to come to the aid of Shabtai-Tzvi's and Jacob Frank's damned souls. Not to judge others was one of the Baal Shem's principles; his function was to help, not to condemn.

And so it was with total unconcern that he moved in and out of suspect – not to say ill-famed – circles; he felt more useful there than among the just. Robbers sought him out to be their arbiter; criminals and outlaws asked for his blessing; and drunkards chose him as their confessor. He considered it an art and a virtue to listen to others.

One day he saw a man who had had too much to drink; he was stammering and singing sad songs. The Baal Shem listened attentively, and remarked: 'When a man confesses himself, the way he chooses to do it doesn't matter. One may not turn away.'

He loved to observe the peasants and ruffians who crowded the taverns drinking and singing their songs at the top of their lungs. He once introduced a young Jewish student to them: 'He sings better than you,' said he. Moments later they were all dancing to a new tune. Years passed, and a group of highwaymen were getting ready to kill a Jew, when suddenly their chief looked at him closely, and asked: 'Can you sing?' – 'Yes.' – 'Then sing!' And the Jew, too, remembered their encounter of long ago. He sang, and so was spared.

It is only natural that the Baal Shem was much talked about. People praised his powers and quoted his maxims. The Jewish world was in an uproar; it followed his astounding ascent with fear or hope, or both. To remain indifferent was impossible; one took a stand for or against this extraordinary personality who seemed to be everywhere at once, come and gone in a flash, leaving behind him a trail of wonder or anger. Both the traditional rabbinical and the rationalist emancipatory circles were in ferment. The first considered him too revolutionary; the second, too orthodox. All tried to find quick and efficient methods of fighting him before it was too late. It was already too late. The legend of the Baal Shem had fired Jewish imagination with such violence and in so many places, nobody could stop or even brake his momentum. He answered a need.

For the eighteenth century was not very kind towards these Jews who lived in the most ravaged parts of Central and Eastern Europe. They remained unaffected by the great liberating currents. The struggle against despotism and social injustice that was under way was not intended to alleviate *their* suffering. The Jews, mostly those from Poland and the Ukraine, were left to their own devices.

They had no rights whatever. They had to buy protection. Their freedom, their life hinged on the good will of local squires who exploited their commercial talents. Let the innkeeper or the superintendent present himself at week's end with a purse that was too light, and he would end up in jail savagely beaten. With no one to bail him out. This situation prevailed particularly in the small villages and isolated towns; none was to be pitied more than the Jew who lived in an out-of-the-way hamlet; he fled forgotten, forsaken by his brethren.

The larger communities had other kinds of problems; they were too divided. There were barriers between those with learning and those without, between the rich and the poor, the leaders and the craftsmen, the notables and the average citizens; the different classes watched each other with distrust, bitterness and rancour. At the top of the social ladder: the secular leaders (usually well-off if not rich), the rabbis named by them, the Talmudists, the devout, the teachers. Whoever possessed neither title nor fortune was ignored. Whoever showed neither knowledge nor piety belonged to the oppressed class and was doomed to impotence.

On a spiritual plane, Judaism went through a crisis that was no less serious: the existing rabbinical institutions were too rigid, too cloistered and inflexible. They allowed no digression, they tolerated no individual endeavour. Traumatized by the nightmare of false Messiahs of the seventeenth century, the rabbis looked askance at anything that seemed new, anything that was obscure. Whoever strayed from the strict interpretation of the Law or made too many promises was immediately suspected of heresy. They believed that Judaism had suffered too much at the hands of inspired visionaries and demagogues. And so, to protect tradition, they surrounded it with fences and obstacles; whoever tried to overturn them left himself open to fanatic, merciless repression.

The Jew, who has only his memory, remembers the dreams awakened and trampled by a Shabtai-Tzvi and his disciples. He knows that for man in exile, hope can become the most excruciating of tortures, the most cruel of dangers. To remain steadfast, one must know how to wait, how to be patient; to last, one must bend and follow the narrow but familiar paths and reject the call of the unknown.

But man cannot live indefinitely without a dream and without a legend. Tnerefore, if someone appears who brings them both – it is enough. He will impose himself and reign.

And yet the Baal Shem himself is said to have considered fame unworthy. The night he had the vision, and learned that the time had come for him to leave the mountain, to throw away his mask and assume the role and destiny of Israel's shepherd, his heart came close to breaking. In his anguish he fasted three days and three nights, praying to have the command revoked. He was thirty-six.

One day he sent his disciples to a distant village to meet a *Lamed Vavnik*, a Just Man, one of the thirty-six without whom the world could not survive. The Baal Shem told the disciples: 'This man resembles me like a brother, we are of the same age, we share the same origins, the same virtues and the same knowledge. Before coming down to earth, we decided jointly that we would, at the very first opportunity, observe the first commandment: that of *Kibud Em*, to honour our mothers. How? We would not cry. So as not to worry them. We kept our word. I never cried in my mother's presence, though as soon as she left the house to go to market or services, I could not hold back my tears. When the neighbours remarked on her apparent insensitivity, she naturally could not understand, and naturally she suffered. As for my friend, he controlled himself even when his mother was away. And that is why it was decided above that as a reward he would be allowed to remain a hidden Just Man, whereas I was condemned to fame.'

His admirers defended him against himself. Beneath the revealed Baal Shem, said they, there was another, hidden Baal Shem who was as great as he was intangible. They did not hesitate to rank him on a par with Moses. According to them, everything pertaining to him was bathed in holiness: his master was the Prophet Ahia of Shilo, the very same that David had as his instructor; Rabbi Yitzhak Lurie and Shimon Bar-Yohai – the most prestigious pillars in the history of Kabbala – were his peers; in his ascensions to the higher spheres, he would sometimes win victories over these distant forerunners and participate in study sessions at the patriarch's side; then, too, he frequently had occasion to converse with the Messiah.

In a letter to his brother-in-law, Reb Gershon Kitiver, the Baal Shem gives this account of one of these dialogues. To the question: 'But when, when will you come?' the Messiah answered: 'When your spring will run over, when your teaching will cover the land.' He even conversed with the Angel of Death, asking him: 'Why do you massacre so many innocent and helpless Jews?' – 'I do it for the sake of heaven, for the love of God and for His glory,' answered the Angel with disquieting humour.

Legend attributes his privileges to the 'root of his soul', to his so-called ancestral merits. Even so, the Baal Shem seems to have chosen to project the image of a man who cannot count on inherited gifts but must work hard for every victory. His charisma was of his own making. This is one of the appealing characteristics of Hasidism: everything is offered, yet everything remains to be done. Though powers may be given by God, it is for man to take them from Him.

The Baal Shem was a man of the people in the true sense of the word. He could not claim a notable ancestry, nor did he occupy an exalted social position; nothing linked him to the ruling class. He had no official titles, no influential friends, no powerful protectors. He had neither material possessions nor wealthy admirers. He could not even lay claim to vast Talmudic learning. On the contrary, he enjoyed playing the ignorant analphabet who stammers a few basic prayers unwillingly and with great difficulty.

This partly explains his immediate success among the less fortunate – they identified with him. Had he been a rabbi's son, or an *ilui*, a prodigy, he would have made less impact on people's imagination. His humble origins made it easier for the poor to approach him. In a way, he represented their sublimated selves. He told them what they wanted to hear: that every one of them existed in God's memory, that every one of them played a part in his people's destiny, each in his way and according to his means.

He assured them that a simple but sincere prayer has as much merit as a mystical incantation, that the fervour born in a pure heart is greater than the one born of a complex and unfathomable thought. He said: 'The coachman who kisses the holy scrolls of the Torah pleases God more than the angels who praise Him and do nothing else.' He warned them to be suspicious of anyone claiming to have all the answers: 'You want to know if a particular Rebbe is genuine? Go and ask his advice. Ask him if he knows a way to chase impure thoughts from your mind; if he says yes, you'll know he is a fake.' He told them that pride derived from knowledge is worse than ignorance, that to seek is better than to find. The greatness of man, he taught them, lies in his capacity for humility. Let him start by submitting to God: he will grow and he will be free. He taught them that sometimes it must be enough to *believe* there is a secret. And also that man requires little to elevate and fulfil himself, as long as that is what he longs for, longs for with all his heart.

He explained to them that abstract erudition is not the sole vessel of truth or the sole path leading to saintliness. And that saintliness is not the only link between man and the eternity he carries inside him. Song is more precious than words, intention more important than formulas. And since it is given to every man to acquire all the powers, why despair? Why give up the fight? One tear, one prayer can change the course of events; one fragment of melody can contain all the joy in the world, and by letting it go free, influence fate. And no elite has a monopoly on song or tears; God listens to the shepherd playing his flute as readily as He listens to the saint renouncing his earthly attachments. The prisoner's craving equals the wise man's: the one, like the other, has a bearing on the essence of man.

He taught them to fight sadness with joy. 'The man who looks only at himself cannot but sink into despair, yet as soon as he opens his eyes to the creation around him, he will know joy.' And this joy leads to the absolute, to redemption, to God; that was the new truth as defined by the Baal Shem. And Jews by the thousands let themselves be carried by this call, they needed it to live and to survive. Thanks to it, there was joy – following pain – and it brought together the dispersed and exiled. The joy of man no longer alone, the joy of the old sage waiting for the upheaval of time, the joy of a father wanting to talk and of children eager to listen. The Baal Shem was a moment of rapture and exaltation in times of mute lamentation. When he died in 1760, twenty-four years after his revelation, there remained in Central and Eastern Europe not a single Jewish town that was left unaffected. He had been the spark without which thousands of families would have succumbed to gloom and hopelessness – and the spark had fanned itself into a huge flame that tore into the darkness.

One day he promised his disciples to show them the prophet Elijah. 'Open your eyes wide,' he said.

A few days later they saw a beggar enter the House of Study and emerge clutching a book under his arm. Shortly thereafter they watched him leaving a ceremony, taking along a silver spoon. The third time he appeared to them disguised as a soldier on a horse, asking them to light his pipe.

'It was he,' said the Baal Shem. 'The secret is in the eyes.'

His disciple Rebbe David Leikes tells: 'After the last meal of Shabbat, our Master turned to me and asked me for a coin to buy a drink. Naturally, I had no money on me, but how could I disobey? I put my hand in my pocket, and when I brought out a coin – I was not surprised.'

In a dream, the Baal Shem glimpsed his future neighbour in paradise. Upon awakening, he decided to pay him a visit. He found a robust and earthy man. How well he disguises himself, thought the Baal Shem, and asked to be sheltered for a few days.

The Besht was convinced his host was leading a double life; that he was getting up at night to accomplish God knows what worthy deeds. Wrong: the man slept deeply and until the next morning, when he rose early, hastily said his prayers and gulped down a copious breakfast. At lunch he ate even more, and three times as much at dinner. And so it went for several days.

Let us wait for Shabbat, thought the Baal Shem. Perhaps his saintliness coincides with that of the seventh day. Wrong again: his host ate and slept even more than during the week. Unable to contain himself any longer, the Baal Shem spoke to him: 'When I came here, I had a question to ask you. I shall not ask it. But now I have another: why do you eat so much?'

'I'll tell you,' answered the man. 'It has to do with my father. Who was a good Jew, gentle and frail, aspiring only to please the Lord; nothing else interested him. Neither money nor honours, not even health. He lived only for and by the Torah. One day he was on his way to services when he was grabbed by bandits who tied him to a tree and ordered him to kiss a cross. He refused, of course. They beat him mercilessly; still he refused. They then poured kerosene over him and set him on fire. And because my father was so weak and thin, he burned only a moment; almost as soon as he was lit, he was burned out. And I, who saw him, who saw it all, swore that if ever I was put to the same test, I would not let them get away so easily. I would show them that a Jew does not go out like a miserable skinny candle. No. When I burn, I shall burn so long that they will burst with anger. That is why I eat so much; all my energy, all my passion is devoted to eating. Not that I am hungry, you understand . . .'

'Yes, I understand,' said the Baal Shem, smiling. 'Go on, continue; you must. What you are doing, you are doing well.' And, after a moment's silence: 'We'll talk about it again.'

One morning, accompanied by his disciples, he was walking through an uninhabited region.

'I am thirsty,' complained one of the young men, 'I am burning, I am dying of thirst.'

No sign of water anywhere. The countryside was like a desert.

'Don't worry,' said the Baal Shem, 'when God created the world, He foresaw your thirst as well as its remedy.'

Shortly thereafter they came upon a peasant balancing two pails of water on his shoulders.

'My lord has gone mad,' grumbled the peasant, 'this morning he sent me here to walk back and forth with this load of water; just like that, for no reason at all.'

'You see,' said the Baal Shem to the thirsty student, 'when He created the world, He arranged this madness solely so that you might quench your thirst.'

It happened during the High Holy Days. The Baal Shem had conducted New Year services with special fervour, concentrating on the prayers relating to redemption. Out of a common impulse, his disciples hurried to their secret retreat at the edge of the forest as soon as services were over – to wait together. Suddenly the youngest, who had stayed behind, had a frightening thought: the Messiah was about to come – and there would be no one to welcome him!

He ran to warn his companions. Out of breath, he burst open the door and saw them sitting around the table in solemn silence. He understood that they, too, were convinced that the so anxiously awaited saviour was on his way and that soon they would hear the pounding of his staff, announcing his presence.

The wait lasted late into the night. Then they went back to town, dejected. It is said that had the youth not interrupted their silent vigil, the awaited one would have appeared.

'Imagine a palace with an infinite number of doors,' said the Baal Shem to his disciples. 'In front of every door the visitor finds a treasure. Satisfied, he feels no urge to continue. Yet, at the end of the hallways, the king is waiting to receive those among his subjects who think of him rather than of the treasure.'

One morning he prayed longer than usual. Weary, the disciples left. Later, the Master commented sadly: 'Imagine a rare bird at the top of a tree. To reach it, men form a human ladder, thus allowing one of them to climb to the very top. But those at the bottom cannot see the bird and therefore lose patience and go home. The ladder falls apart, and up there the rare bird has flown away.'

During Simhat Torah the Baal Shem warned his followers that they were about to witness a peculiar service: 'Promise me you will not laugh!'

They promised.

And during the services the Master invited the Seven Shepherds of the world, including Adam, Abraham and David, to ascend the bimah and read from the Torah. At the end, he invited the Messiah. That proved too much for some of the disciples. They began to laugh. A shadow clouded the Master's face and – for what seemed an infinity – he refused to look at them.

'Do you want to know what Hasidism is? Do you know the story of the ironmonger who wanted to become independent? He bought an anvil, a hammer and bellows and went to work. Nothing happened – the forge remained inert. Then an old ironmonger, whose advice he sought, told him: "You have everything you need except the spark." That is what Hasidism is: the spark.'

What was Hasidism at its inception? A man. The Baal Shem. His was a powerful appeal to consolation, to unity. His Hasidism was neither philosophical doctrine nor system of social ethics and certainly not a new theosophy sprinkled with folklore and rebellion. Yet it was a combination of all of these; a desire to arrive at a synthesis. An acceptance of the fact that one may be a Jew in many different ways. For all paths lead somewhere, provided that God is present at the start.

This Hasidism has been erroneously compared to Spinoza's Pantheism. For the Baal Shem's followers, God is not neutral. Nor is

He an abstraction. He is at once ally and judge of man inside creation. The bond between them is irreplaceable, it is love. God himself needs love. Whoever loves God will be loved in turn, loved by man and loved by God. It is in man that God must be loved, because the love of God goes through the love of man. Whoever loves God exclusively, namely, excluding man, reduces his love and his God to the level of abstraction. Beshtian Hasidism denies all abstraction.

'God is the shadow of man' was commented upon by the Baal Shem as follows: just as a shadow follows the gestures and motions of the body, God follows those of the soul. If man is charitable, God will be charitable too. The name of man's secret is God, and the name of God's secret is none other than the one invented by man: love. Who loves, loves God.

It is in this sense that in Beshtian Hasidism, God is present even in evil, even in sin. He takes part in creation and chooses the side of man. For whoever creates affirms that the creative act has meaning, a meaning which transcends the act itself. And what is love if not a creative act, in which two beings fuse into a single consciousness scarred and healed a thousand times? Love's mystery resides in oneness, and so does God's. 'Whatever is above is also down below.' Between the present concrete world and the other, the one to come, there is a link as between source and reflection. God does not oppose humanity, and man, though vulnerable and ephemeral, can attain immortality in the passing moment. In man's universe, everything is connected because nothing is without meaning.

Thence the tolerance the Baal Shem exhibited towards sinners. He refused to give them up as lost. If need be, he could understand – though not accept – evil in others. But evil without consciousness of evil he deemed inadmissible.

That is why he never tried to convert non-Jews to Judaism. He preferred to 'convert' Jews to Hasidism, or in a wider sense, to Judaism.

To realize himself, the Baal Shem's Hasidism teaches us, man must first of all remain faithful to his most intimate, truest self; he cannot help others if he negates himself. Any man who loves God while hating or despising His creation, will in the end hate God. A Jew who rejects his origins, his brothers, to make a so-called contribution to mankind, will in the end betray mankind. That is true for all men.

'Beware, your coachman is dangerous and wicked,' said the Baal Shem to one of his followers. 'I saw him walk by the church without crossing himself. If he does not love his God, why then would he love you?'

The entire Hasidic concept is contained in this anecdote. The Baal Shem was concerned with people rather than theories. Theories could wait. His disciples – the Maggid of Mezeritch, Shneur-Zalmen of Ladi, Nahman of Bratzlav – could formulate them later. For the moment, what mattered was to communicate experience rather than scholarship, intuition rather than logic.

The Baal Shem's major concern was to create links at every level. To him, everything that brought people together and consolidated the community was good; everything that sowed discord was bad.

And so he turned a poetic image, the mystical concept of *likut nitzotzot*, the in-gathering of dispersed sparks, into concrete action. Man's role is to mitigate solitude; whoever opts for solitude chooses the side of death.

That is why, in all his tales, wandering nameless beggars play such a particular and important role. They too make people dream, they too are links between men. Every woodcutter may be a prophet in disguise, every shoemaker a Just Man, every unknown the Baal Shem. What is man if not a link between Adam and the Messiah, representing more than his own span, heralding more than he would wish to receive? A shepherd plays a tune – the Baal Shem relates him to King David. A stranger in rags provokes laughter – the Master refers to him as Abraham.

If the Baal Shem could have met Rabbi Haim Ben-Atar, who was awaiting him in the Holy Land, together the two men would have hastened the coming of the Messiah, or so says Hasidic tradition, with the stress on encounter. Every encounter quickens the steps of the Redeemer; let two beings become one and the world is no longer the same; let two human creatures accept one another and creation will have meaning, the meaning they will have imposed upon it. That is the new idea introduced into Jewish life by Hasidism. The individual is not a cog in a monstrous machine; it is within his power to modify the very laws which imprison him and the very relationship maintained by the Judge with the accused and witnesses. If it is true, as the Baal Shem says, that it is possible for man to hide the light of dawn emanating from the forest simply by shielding his eyes with his hands, still it is no less true that he can rediscover it by merely moving his hands. That is precisely what the Baal Shem accomplished. Thanks to him, thanks to this simple motion of a hand, the Hasid had discovered the world in all its awesome majesty and beauty.

And now let us speak of the miracles the Baal Shem is said to have performed in his lifetime and even after his death. The narrator did not evoke them earlier because, he readily admits, they trouble him; they flout his reason, his taste for rationality. Are we to believe that this awkward, retiring man, once having reached the prime of life, sought to amuse himself by rearranging the order of the universe? It is claimed that he brought learning to some, deprived others of their memory, recovered misplaced objects and horses that had lost their way. It is said that he earned total allegiance from men and beasts alike, and even from the angels up above; if an angel was not to his taste, he was replaced. It is said that he healed the sick – by gorging them with chicken soup – and that he prescribed a remedy against snoring. And . . . that he tried to persuade a priest that he should break his celibacy.

Naïve and childish, these tales are bound to make us smile. Written and transmitted without any literary purpose, could it be that they were meant to test our reason or our faith or perhaps our imagination? To prove that the Baal Shem is above and beyond anything man can even begin to imagine in his dreams? Did the Master encourage them? To his servant Reb Yaakov he entrusted the mission to travel and make his fortune by telling stories – about the Besht, of course. But did he wish Reb Yaakov or any of the others to add and embellish as they chose? Those exaggerations – did they originate with him? And to what end? To impress admirers who were already bound to him with their entire being? He who was so great and genuine in so many areas, why should he have felt the need to show his hold on the occult by resorting to miracles?

Perhaps he wanted to show the link – one more – between man's experiences and man's dreams, and how one may transcend the first with the help of the latter. We may contemplate such a hypothesis. We may even go one step further and say that while the Baal Shem indeed did not need miracles, his future followers did – they needed them to persevere, to take hold. They needed to believe that God took an interest in His creation, that He listened to all the voices; they needed to believe that miracles were still possible, even for them. That may be why he performed them.

All his prodigious deeds seem to spring from a desire to unite the people by offering it song and legend as refuge and shield. The

Jewish people, dispersed and decimated, needed new vigour – so the Master promised children to childless couples. If he moved with the 'speed of lightning', it was because he was freeing some innkeeper rotting in a dungeon – there was forever a Jewish innkeeper somewhere whom the prince had put in jail for not paying dues, for not doing well enough or, on the contrary, for doing too well. Was an enemy concocting a plan of persecution? The Master knew what prayer to recite, and where, in order to foil the plot. Was someone stumbling in the dark? With a mere look the Baal Shem set him back on the right road. The main theme remains constant: man owes it to himself to reject despair; better to rely on miracles than opt for resignation. By changing himself, man can change the world.

Thus it is possible for man to accept his contradictions. And to discover humility within pride, simplicity within generosity, charity within justice. There is no alternative: one must impose a meaning on what perhaps has none and draw ecstasy from nameless, faceless pain.

Certainly, by agreeing to follow the Baal Shem outside time, to the limit of perception, we run the risk of finding ourselves in a world which is not real. The Baal Shem himself had to pay the price. Towards the end of his life particularly, he displayed increasing signs of irritation and depression, expressing himself in ways 'defying the laws of language'. He who had worked so hard to make himself understood, no longer succeeded. Faces, words and incidents were forgotten; he was losing touch with his surroundings. He could be seen knocking his head against a tree or following what seemed to be a strange choreography with his body. He expressed regret at having used his powers; he was no longer himself.

One day he spoke longer than ever, and his words were more enticing than ever. His disciples were entranced, conscious of living privileged moments. Suddenly he stopped. And forgot what he had said. And forgot even that he had spoken.

Another time, during the same period, he felt himself sinking. One of his disciples saw him sway, and called out: 'Master!' and this outcry brought him back to the surface.

He had lived too fast and had made too many promises that God did not keep.

At the age of sixty he became ill; his insides were tearing him apart. It was Passover. Deviating from habit, he celebrated the

Holy Day far from other people, plunged into silent and un-interrupted meditation.

Seven weeks later, during Shavuot, feeling the end approaching, he gave his intimates detailed instructions for his burial. He requested them to sing at his bedside and invited a *minyan* for the last service. 'I have two hours to chat with God,' he said. Seeing tears on the faces of his faithful, he added: 'Why do you cry? I am leaving by one door only to enter by another.'

Rebbe Pinhas of Koretz began to pray, pleading on his behalf. 'Too late,' the Master told him, 'what is done is done; what is done will not be undone.'

When he died, the two clocks in his house stopped.

Symbolic break, dividing time and the fate of Hasidism. The end of an era. And the birth of another: the movement was to continue its work, expand its reign, go from conquest to conquest, from triumph to triumph, bring fresh air into stifling huts, surprise into routine lives, accompany the sick into their very anguish and the condemned into their resigned or questioning silence.

In the course of the next two centuries, his legend surfaced in many trials his followers endured: it helped people stay alive and sometimes to prepare for death. It appeared even in the kingdom of night. In the vision of a Jewish poet, the Baal Shem visits Jews massacred somewhere in the East. Their corpses fill the trenches to the very top. Suddenly their arms stretch up towards their illustrious visitor and a cry is heard: 'Welcome, Rebbe Israel Baal Shem Tov, thank you for your miracles, Rebbe Israel, son of Eliezer.'

And so, in the kingdom of Hasidic legend, the Baal Shem follows his disciples to the end of night. Another miracle? Certainly not. Death negates miracles, the death of one million children negates more than miracles.

What cannot help but astound us is that Hasidim remained Hasidim inside the ghetto walls, inside the death camps. In the shadow of the executioner, they celebrated life. Startled Germans whispered to each other of Jews dancing in the cattle cars rolling toward Birkenau: Hasidim ushering in Simhat Torah. And there were those who in Block 57 at Auschwitz tried to make me join in their fervent singing. Were these miracles? Some of those that failed? Perhaps.

Yet there is something else. There is the spark lit in the Carpathian Mountains which has refused to go out. On the contrary, it rekindles our own wavering flame. Consolidated in Jerusalem, Hasidism reappears in the Diaspora everywhere. It would be difficult to imagine a more curious phenomenon: with almost the totality of its followers lost in the Holocaust, Hasidism today is throbbing with newly found vigour. At the Lubavitcher court in Brooklyn, you can see hundreds of youths from every corner of the land. I met Hasidim in Leningrad, Kiev and Moscow, and I was deeply moved by their hidden faith.

And all of them define themselves in relation to the old Masters long dead. They live in America but they belong to Lizensk, Mezeritch or Rizhin. There are no more Jews in Wizsnitz, but there are Wizsnitzer Hasidim on both sides of the ocean. The same is true for the other Hasidic branches or dynasties. Ger, Kossov, Sadigor, Karlin — these kingdoms have but transferred their capitals. Lubavitch is everywhere except in Lubavitch; Sighet and Satmar are no longer in Transylvania but wherever Satmarer and Sigheter Hasidim live and remember. And then there are the tales the Besht has left us, for us to relive as though they were our own. That is the most striking, the most moving of his miracles.

Are we worthy of these tales and legends? It all depends. Are we still able to repeat them without impairing their innocence? It all depends. Are we still able to recite, with fervour and gratitude: *aleph, beith, gimmel, daleth,* the way he once did, a long time ago, to free us from exile by the word? Are we still capable of beginning all over again?

Disciples I

This is how Rabbi Yaakov-Yosseph of Polnoye found his way into the Hasidic fold:

One morning he arrived at the Sharogrod synagogue and found it empty.

'Where are the faithful?' he asked the beadle.

'At the market.'

'All of them? At this hour, when they should be praying?'

'Well, you see, there is this stranger there, telling stories. And when he speaks, one doesn't want to leave.'

'What impudence! Go and bring him here at once!'

The beadle had no choice, he obeyed as was his duty. He ran to the market, made his way through the crowd and transmitted the order to the storyteller.

'Fine,' the stranger said calmly, 'I am coming.'

The rabbi did not get up to receive him: 'Who are you and how dare you divert this community from the ways of the Lord?'

'Don't get angry,' said the visitor, 'a rabbi like you ought never to give in to anger. Instead, listen to a story.'

'What! More stories! Your insolence seems to have no limits! You'll pay for this!'

'Anger is something one must learn to control,' the visitor said gently. 'Listen to me . . .'

And there was in his voice a certain quality that troubled the rabbi and he fell silent. He could not keep himself from listening, never before had he felt such a need to listen.

'This is a story that happened to me,' said the Baal Shem. 'I was riding in a coach drawn by three horses, each of a different colour, and not one of them was neighing. I could not understand why. Until the day we crossed a peasant on the road who shouted at me to loosen the reins. And all at once, the three horses began to neigh.'

In one blinding flash the rabbi of Sharogrod understood the meaning of the parable. For the soul to vibrate and cry out, it must be freed; too many restrictions will stifle it.

And he began to cry. He cried as he had never cried before: freely, spontaneously, without apparent reason. What happened later is well known: Rebbe Yaakov-Yosseph became one of the pillars of the new movement.

'Man is not alone,' said the Baal Shem to his companion Rebbe Pinhas of Koretz. 'The past is heavy with meaning; it fills our solitude. You and I, all of us must be aware of it. Long ago, in Egypt, every one of us strove for the preservation of the holy language, the names of our ancestors and the memory of the Covenant. Every one of us was at the prophets' feet to receive their teachings. Every one of us followed Yohanan Ben-Zakkai into exile and every one of us heard the terrifying words of Shimon Bar-Yohai. And that is why we must stay together.'

And they stayed together.

Brilliant and humble but a fierce individualist, Rebbe Pinhas of Koretz was intent on finding his own path rather than following a Master – any Master. That is what kept him from declaring himself the Baal Shem's disciple, though he was and remained his friend.

A Hasidic tradition says that Rebbe Pinhas of Koretz learned three things from the Baal Shem; it does not say what they were. It adds that, in exchange, Rebbe Pinhas taught the Baal Shem three things; perhaps they were the same.

He regretted not having a voice. 'If I could sing,' he said, 'I would force God to live among men.'

He had no use for honours and riches. Though he was poor, he would say: 'I have never yearned for anything I did not already have.'

When he became a Master – against his will – he said: 'Everything I know I learned before, sitting in the last row near the hearth, out of sight. And now, here I am, occupying the place of honour – and I don't understand.'

His many admirers disturbed him so much that he asked God to make him repulsive in the eyes of the people. His wish was granted. Thereafter he was shunned. But the resulting solitude weighed heavily on his wife. Later it affected even him. So he begged God to restore his gifts to him, confessing: man must not try to be what he is not.

His passion: to bring back into the fold the Jewish converts to Christianity. His discussions with them were open; he never tried to evade issues. He would explain the merits and possibilities of repentance and then appeal to them to recite the *Sh'ma Israel* with him, saying: 'It doesn't cost you anything!' To please him, some consented.

One day, having been told that a group of atheists was demanding proof of God's existence, he rushed to the synagogue, opened the Holy Ark, seized the scrolls of the Torah and shouted: 'I swear that God exists, isn't that proof enough? What more do they want?'

Truth to him was the highest virtue of all. He said: 'If all men spoke the truth, there would be no further need to wait for the Messiah; he would have come long ago.'

During the preparations for his journey to the Holy Land, Rebbe Pinhas of Koretz became ill. Trembling with fever, delirious, he spoke only of death. Never had his faithful seen him so dejected, so anguished. Over and over he called for his friend Rebbe Haim of Krasna, begging him not to leave him: 'If you stay, I shall be less afraid of the Angel of Death.'

When the end came, Rebbe Haim was in a neighbouring village and it was Shabbat. A rabbinical council, convened in emergency session, authorized the dispatch of a messenger to summon him. Reb Haim arrived the next day. Too late.

Though he was rich, learned and covered with honours, Rebbe Nahman of Kossov nevertheless belonged to a Hasidic brotherhood practising asceticism.

His was a rebellious spirit; he opposed everybody. To the Hasidim, he presented the anti-Hasid; to the enemies of the Baal Shem, he was his supporter.

When people drew his attention to the fact that the Hasidim, contrary to ancestral tradition, had adopted a new version of the prayer book, he became vexed: 'Why do you care? What makes you so sure that all our ancestors reached paradise?'

From the very beginning of their friendship, the relationship between Rebbe Nahman of Kossov and the Baal Shem was ambiguous, and so it remained to the end. Once the Baal Shem let slip a rather strange statement: 'Rebbe Nahman of Kossov seeks to catch me, nay, kill me; but he won't succeed.'

'Do you know who rescinded the celestial decree that would have unleashed catastrophe unto our people?' the Baal Shem asked Rebbe Nahman of Horodenko. 'I'll tell you. Neither I nor you, nor the sages, nor the great spiritual leaders. Our litanies, our fasting were all in vain. We were saved by a woman, a woman of our people. This is how it happened: She came to the synagogue, tears running down her face, and addressed the Almighty: "Master of the Universe, are You or are You not our Father? Why won't You listen to Your children imploring You? You see, I am a mother. Children I have plenty of: five. And every time they shed a tear, it breaks my heart. But You, Father, You have so many more. Every man is Your child, and every one of them is weeping and weeping. Even if Your heart is made of stone, how can You remain indifferent?" And,' the Baal Shem concluded, 'God decided she was right.'

Rebbe David Kitzes was an enthusiastic traveller. On a faraway island he met a man dressed in oriental clothes who questioned him at great length about the situation of the Jews in Central Europe.

'They're all right,' answered Rebbe David. 'Thanks to God.'

'Wretch,' the Baal Shem later reprimanded him, 'you should have told him of our suffering! You should have cried out our distress! Do you have any idea *who* was asking you all those questions?'

Rebbe David Leikes cried only one time in his life: the day the Baal Shem died.

Rebbe David was known and liked for his exuberant, contagious joy. Prayer sent him into rapture; he turned even the lamentations into song.

He outlived his wife, four sons and three daughters. At seventy-three he was alone and in mourning. Yet he did not give in to sadness. To praise God, one must live, he said, and to live, one must enjoy life; one must enjoy life in spite of life.

And he remarried. An innkeeper, who bore him three sons and a daughter. He lived on contentedly to become president of the local rabbinical court, and remained lucid to the end. He was one hundred years old and on his deathbed when, hearing the court deliberating in the next room, he complained: 'Why do you leave me out? All my life I was God's associate in His work down here; is this the time to push me aside?'

And so he listened to witnesses, noted contradictory depositions and pronounced his verdict. A moment later his countenance was serene: 'Here I am, leaving one court for another,' he whispered.

His last words.

*

Rebbe Leib, surnamed the Grandfather of Shpole, was fond of saying: 'If I had seen the Baal Shem Tov a second time, I would have become somebody.'

He was somebody.

Known for his kindness, simplicity and warmth, his surname suited him perfectly. He played with children and he loved stories. He had a talent for making people happy. He was also the first Rebbe to turn dance into a ritual. Watching him sway and turn, the son of the Great Maggid of Mezeritch exclaimed: 'Your dancing counts for more than my prayers.'

Like most Hasidic Masters of his generation, he had led a turbulent existence before he made himself known.

He had been a member of a troupe of wandering beggars, roaming from village to village, provoking laughter or anger, earning applause or lashes for doing the very same thing, just barely managing to escape whenever an established Tzaddik came close to uncovering his true identity.

His adventurous past even included a two-month stay in prison. Before escaping from it, he succeeded in coaxing a horse thief into repenting. And it became a joint escape. Only when the future Rebbe became a beadle, did he and his accomplice part ways.

'Before I was born,' he said, 'I refused life. What's the good of toiling among mortals who are prey to their own weaknesses? To entice me into accepting, I was permitted to set certain conditions. I made four: that I would never forget anything; never be sick; beget only children who would become honest and simple Jews; and one more condition which I have neither the wish nor the right to divulge.'

This story has a sequel:

'Do you know who finally made me change my mind? A peasant with a shovel in his hands who accosted me as though I were an old acquaintance. "Hey, you," he said, "take a good look: I work without respite to give a little joy, a little rest to people who sorely need it, and what do you do? You lie around here as if creation had no human purpose. Why do you refuse to help me?" You see,' added the Grandfather of Shpole, 'I could resist the angels but not him. Because, well . . . Do you know who he was? Yes, it was the Baal Shem himself.'

Rebbe Leib was on the side of man, defending him even against God:

'Lord, You are unjust. You filled books with hell and hearts with desire; is it surprising then that man permits himself to be seduced by evil? Now, if it were the other way around ...'

Another time: 'If You think You can bring Your people back into the fold by making them suffer, then I, Leib, son of Rachel, swear to You that You will not succeed. So why try? Save Your children by giving them joy, by delivering them. By doing it that way, You have nothing to lose and everything to gain.'

And again: 'Lord, save Your people before it is too late. Otherwise there may be no one left to save.'

Famine was devastating the country. The Grandfather of Shpole convened a tribunal of ten Talmudic scholars: 'I need you to sit in judgement. I am accusing Him who kills His children.'

And he quoted texts and commentaries, decrees and decisions as evidence that God was in the wrong; that He was not fulfilling His duties toward man.

The trial lasted three days. Isolated from the outside world, the court deliberated without fear or prejudice, examining the problem from all angles, weighing all arguments, and finally reached a verdict: 'Whereas the Father of all creatures is responsible for their sustenance, let Him put an end to the famine.'

During New Year services, it was the Grandfather of Shpole's custom to retire to his room for an hour or two before the blowing of the shofar. Why? To speak to God in a language which is not that of prayer books:

'Don't think of man's sins, I beg of You. Think rather of his good deeds. They are fewer, I agree. But You must admit, they are more precious. Believe me, it isn't easy to be good in this world. And if I didn't see with my own two eyes that man, in spite of all obstacles, is capable of kindness, I would not believe it. And so I ask of You: don't be harsh with Your children; rare as it may be, it is their kindness that should surprise You.'

When Rebbe Nahum of Tchernobil came to see the Baal Shem, the latter said to his wife: 'Hannah, look at this man; he is a thief.'

'A thief, he? He is a saint!'

'A thief, I tell you. He wants paradise all to himself.'

To a guest he said: 'You want me to take you with me? Very well. On one condition: tell me what distinguishes the nocturnal litanies referred to as *Tikun Leah* from the ones called *Tikun Rachel*?'

Rachel and Leah: Jacob's two wives. Their prayers are recited at midnight, and it is also at midnight that one laments the destruction of the Temple and the exile of the Shekhina.

'I think I know the difference between them,' whispered Rebbe Nahum. 'What Leah accomplished with tears, Rachel, who was more beautiful and happier too, accomplished with joy.'

Why must the Just Man concern himself with earthly matters, with men of every station?

'Imagine a man on a roof,' explains Rebbe Nahum. 'He sees a pearl lying in the dust. Were he not to come down from his roof, how would he pick it up?'

One day he stopped abruptly in the midst of a sermon: 'Brothers, listen to my words, even if you don't understand them. A day will come when the Messiah will speak to you, and you will not understand him either. You may as well get used to it.'

He also said: 'I am much more afraid of my good deeds that please me than of my bad deeds that repel me.'

He led a humble and austere life: 'I like poverty,' he said. 'It is God's gift to man, a treasure.'

Rebbe Mikhal of Zlotchev was asked an embarrassing question: 'You are poor, Rebbe. And yet every day you thank God for taking care of your needs. Isn't that a lie?'

'Not at all. You see, for me poverty is a need.'

He said: 'Man's consciousness is in perpetual motion. Mine follows great men in their rise and attracts the lowly, to lift them up with me.'

And also: 'Saintliness is sometimes nothing but impure temptation.'

One of his prayers: 'I have but one request; may I never use my reason against truth.'

Before Rebbe Mikhal's revelation in Yampol, where he shared a miserable hut with his family, people thought him mad. Mad because he habitually prayed knocking his head against the wall until he drew blood.

The Baal Shem had to persuade him to accept a post of preacher-rabbi. People were afraid of him. They claimed that he could see through them. He needed only to look at a man's forehead to guess his sins. One day the faithful appeared at the synagogue with their caps pulled way down to their eyebrows. His wry comment: 'You really believe that a garment can prevent my eyes from seeing?'

Like all of the Baal Shem's disciples, he dreaded pride. He said: 'When I shall meet my Maker, I will be asked why I did not learn all that man can and must learn during his passage on earth. I shall reply: Don't blame me, I wasn't intelligent enough, that is hardly my fault.' – 'Then why didn't you give up earthly pleasures and devote yourself to serving the Lord?' – 'You mustn't blame me, I shall say, I lacked the physical strength for that. Then the court will examine my humanitarian activities and I shall be forced to admit that here too I failed to do my duty. My excuse? That I myself led a destitute existence. In the end, I can foresee it, one of the judges, unable to restrain his anger, will cry out: "One thing I cannot understand. You neither lived nor prayed as you should have, why then are you so proud?" And to that,' said Rebbe Mikhal, 'to that argument I shall have no answer.'

Infinitely naïve and pious, Rebbe Wolfe of Zbaraj repeated every night before going to bed: 'I revoke my rights on all I possess; whatever belongs to me is no longer mine. In this way, no matter what thieves may carry away, they will not have violated the law.'

One day his wife quarrelled with their servant in his presence. Seeing the two women leave for the rabbinical court, he got up, put on his Shabbat clothes and followed them there.

'Why did you take the trouble?' asked his wife. 'I don't need your help.'

'You don't, but the servant does. You, they know; but she is a poor orphan. No one will help her, no one will plead her cause.'

To his coachman, he said: 'Please throw away your whip. Even if a horse does deserve punishment, what makes you think it is up to you to inflict it?'

People came to him to denounce some Jews who were playing cards late into the night.

'And you want me to condemn them?' he cried out. 'Why me? And in the name of what? And for what crime? They stay up late? It's a good thing to resist sleep! They concentrate on the game. That is good too! Sooner or later they will give up card-playing – what will remain is a discipline of body and mind. And this time they will place it in the service of God! Why then should I condemn them?'

He was attending a circumcision. Stepping outside for a moment, he noticed the coachman shivering with cold:

'Inside it is warm,' he told him. 'Go in, warm yourself, have a drink and something to eat.'

'Who will watch the horses?'

'I will.'

The coachman did as the Master wished. Several hours later people saw Rebbe Wolfe, half frozen in the snow, jumping from one foot to the other, at a loss to understand why the guests were making such a fuss.

Rebbe Hersh, son of the Baal Shem, is depicted by legend as a shy, rather insignificant man. While his father lay dying, he was asleep. He had to be awakened and taken to the sick Master's bedside – who spoke to him, but Rebbe Hersh did not understand.

Called upon to take over the movement, he was found lacking in authority.

He withdrew into himself, and in the end, spoke only to his dead father. In his dreams, he asked him: 'How can I serve God?'

The Baal Shem climbed a high mountain and threw himself into the abyss. 'Like this,' he answered.

Another time the Baal Shem appeared to him as a mountain on fire, erupting into a thousand flaming fragments: 'And like this as well.'

— The Maggid of Mezeritch —

'Why are you crying, Mother? Because the house is burning?' – 'Yes.' – 'We shall build another, I promise you.' – 'It's not the house, son. If I cry, it is because a precious document is being destroyed before our eyes.' – 'What document?' – 'Our family tree; it is illustrious, you know.' – 'Don't cry. I'll give you another. I'll start anew, I promise you.'

At the time, Dov-Ber was five.

Born in Volhynia in 1710, ten years after the Baal Shem, the future Maggid of Mezeritch came from a poor family. He was a brilliant student, and like the Baal Shem, married young and earned a meagre living first as a teacher of children and later as a wandering preacher. He was respected throughout the region, and known to be honest, severe and demanding. Destitute, he found shelter in an abandoned hut, and that is where he and his wife lived in utter misery and also where their son, Avraham, was born.

A story is told that, exasperated by his wife's complaints, one day Dov-Ber cried out: 'So be it, I shall curse my people, since they could but will not help us.' Then he went outside, and staring at heaven, continued: 'May Your people know happiness, peace and wealth.' And after a sigh, he added: 'But its money, the money it is refusing me, may it be thrown to the stones and into the brambles.'

Though he remained poor, he never complained of it again. On the contrary, he turned his poverty into a virtue. Like most early Masters, he had at first been a fervent adversary of Hasidism. Both as a Talmudic scholar and a mystic believing in self-mortification, he did not approve of the Baal Shem's way. Dov-Ber's way was to make life harder, not easier. He himself led a sober, inward-directed existence, sometimes fasting from one Saturday to the next. He inflicted pain on his body until it became unbearable and he fell gravely ill. Physicians were consulted, but all confessed their helplessness. Then someone suggested he see the Baal Shem, the visionary-healer everyone was talking about. He went. Out of medical necessity rather than intellectual curiosity. But he went.

Expecting some relief or perhaps even a cure, but certainly not a sign powerful enough to make him deviate from his set path.

We know that their first meeting was a failure. Even though the visitor had expected little, it was worse than a disappointment; it was nothing. The Baal Shem told him a bizarre story about coachmen and horses (similar to the one he told Yaakov-Yossef of Polnoye), and that was all. The sick and anxious Maggid countered the Master's small talk with gruff silence. I didn't come from so far away to listen to stories about horses, he thought. Unable to communicate, the two men seemed to have nothing in common.

Bitter at having wasted his time, the Maggid returned to the inn and prepared himself for the journey home. The horses were harnessed, the carriage waiting, when a messenger arrived summoning him to the Baal Shem. He agreed to go back. Why? Perhaps he felt that having come this far, he might as well give the healer a second chance. It was midnight when they met again. The Baal Shem handed him the Book of Splendour, the Zohar: 'Can you read?' – 'Yes.' – 'Well then, read!' The Maggid obeyed. 'That is not the way one reads,' the Baal Shem interrupted. 'I can see that you know how to decipher the signs, but your knowledge lacks soul.'

That was the turning point. The room filled with light. The Maggid stood at Sinai again; he saw the fire and understood how much he lacked. He also understood that the Besht was the only man capable of helping him reach the heights. He became his disciple, his witness, his foremost apostle. Later, while spreading the Master's teachings, he went so far as to authenticate the most incredible stories by stating: 'I was there.'

Example: 'When the Baal Shem ate, an angel came down, seized his food and turned it into an offering of fire. I saw it, I was there.'

Did he believe his own stories? Probably. He loved to repeat them. He told stories about his Master but only rarely quoted him. Maxims, parables, key ideas of the Baal Shem, one finds in the work of others. The Maggid leaves us nothing but tales heavy with miraculous deeds. No doubt that was his way of conveying his personal concept of the Rebbe – the Master vested with almost unlimited powers – and also of accentuating the exclusive intimacy that characterized his relationship with the Baal Shem. As though he alone had been privileged to see what the Master had hidden from others.

'What did you learn in Mezeritch?' Rebbe Aharon of Karlin was asked. – 'Nothing at all.' – 'What do you mean?' – 'Yes,' he said, 'in Mezeritch, I learned that I am nothing at all.'

'And you?' Rebbe Levi-Yitzhak of Berditchev was asked. 'What did you discover at the Great Maggid's school?' – 'I discovered that God exists, that He is of this world, of all worlds.' – 'But, Rebbe, everybody knows that!' – 'No,' answered the illustrious Rebbe of Berditchev. 'They say it everywhere, but in Mezeritch they know it.'

A third Hasidic Master, Rebbe Shmelke of Nikolsburg, testified in his own way: 'A long time ago, in the blindness of my youth, I mortified my body so it would tolerate my soul. Since Mezeritch, I know that cannot be right. Body and soul must and can live in harmony.'

These three stories are characteristic. They show the quality of the pilgrims attracted by Mezeritch and also the diversity of knowledge they drew from it.

'After the death of our Master Israel Baal Shem Tov, the Shekhina herself shouldered her bundle and stick and moved from Medzebozh to Mezeritch,' legend tells us by way of several renowned disciples. Authentic or apocryphal, no matter. It illustrates a fact: it was the Maggid who took over. From that moment on he was undisputed head of the rapidly expanding movement, and its centre, therefore, shifted elsewhere. Briefly contested at first, his authority soon went unchallenged. Moral guide, teacher, experienced tactician, seasoned organizer and outstanding visionary combined in one person, Rebbe Dov-Ber of Mezeritch counted three hundred disciples, or so they say, of which thirty-nine became leaders and founders of dynasties in their own right.

With him, Hasidism underwent its first structural if not ideological mutation: from the realm of legend to that of history. Even those historians who, for reasons best known to themselves, questioned the physical existence of the Baal Shem, never denied that the Maggid of Mezeritch was his successor.

We know only what we are permitted to know about this spiritual leader who shrouded himself in mystery. While he himself put nothing down on paper, his disciples transcribed his commentaries on Torah and Talmud, his interpretation of Zohar, his words of advice and parables, and quoted them abundantly in their own works. Levi-Yitzhak of Berditchev carried his zeal to extremes; he recorded the Master's most trivial remarks. Another disciple, Rebbe

Zusia of Onipol, went further yet: he devoted his entire life to scrupulously repeating everything he had heard in Mezeritch.

Thus we know many facts about his origins, his childhood, life before and after his decisive encounter with the Baal Shem. We know, for example, that in his youth he liked to rise at dawn and walk beside the streams and lakes; he was learning the art of listening. We know that he was nearsighted. That he limped. That he was constantly afflicted by obscure pains. That he trembled before speaking in public. We also know that he ate and slept as little as possible; that under his severe exterior hid a generous man and tender father. But above all, we know his incomparable, un-equalled role in the development of Hasidism and the enrichment of the exalted universe that is its own.

In Mezeritch, new centre of learning, talented men abounded. Among them were Elimelekh of Lizensk, Zusia of Onipol, Shneur-Zalmen of Ladi, Israel of Kozhenitz, Yaakov-Yosseph of Lublin. One could even meet some of the Baal Shem's companions, such as Pinhas of Koretz or Yaakov-Yosseph of Polnoye. Together and individually, they acknowledged the Maggid as their guide. Each of his disciples received from him whatever he needed to take root and fulfil himself according to his own truth. To some the Maggid taught *Nigla*, the revealed science, to others *Nistar*, the esoteric science reserved for the select few. At the same time, and with equal conviction, he showed the simple uneducated people that merely by reciting the prayer *Sh'ma Israel*, they could be worthy of redemption. For each he found the right word, the needed gesture. In his presence, people realized how much was still to be learned. They suddenly became aware of depths within themselves never recognized before. And that to achieve total awareness, they needed his help. Those who indulged in mortification, he taught that the body is sacred as long as it is alive and that to mutilate it is an offence to God. Those too comfortably ensconced in their existence and neglecting the virtue of fear, he showed what fear could be.

Many whose lives had been transformed by the Baal Shem, and many others who wanted to change theirs, flocked to Mezeritch. The Maggid knew whom to attract and encourage and whom to turn away. His intuition was such that he gave meaning to all waiting and corrected all shortcomings. If we are to believe his admirers, he, like his Master, could accurately describe people simply by looking at an object of their making.

All testimonies concur: the Maggid had mastered the art of winning the absolute loyalty of men by upsetting their equilibrium.

His methods relied on surprise and shock. His pronouncements were as unexpected as his silences. To one visitor he made a single comment: 'The horse who knows he is a horse, is not. Man's major task is to learn that he is not a horse.' To another he said: 'Just as there is light and darkness in the world, there is light and darkness in man's mind.' On his lips, ordinary sentences took on the weight of confessions. 'When the sick Maggid told a simple story,' according to Israel of Rizhin, 'the bed he rested on would shake violently, and so would the privileged few present.' The Baal Shem made people dream, the Maggid made them tremble.

A man, a mystic, came to see him. The visitor had given up food and sleep and was seeking total renunciation. The Maggid first directed his son, Rebbe Avraham, to feed him by force. Then he ordered him to repeat after him, word by word, the ritual confession, the *Vidui: Ashamnu, bagadnu, gazalnu* – We have sinned, we have betrayed, we have stolen. The man fainted. When he came to, the Maggid sent him away, ordering him never to let it happen again: some words are as important as deeds – some words *are* deeds.

Another visitor, a Hasid and noted Talmudic scholar, came to seek his advice. He was afraid he was losing his faith. The Maggid did not engage the man in lengthy philosophical discussions, but instead asked him to repeat with him, over and over again, the very first prayer every Jewish child learns by heart. And that was all.

'One day,' Rebbe Wolfe of Zhitomir tells us, 'we were all sitting around the table in the House of Study. It was a Friday afternoon. We could hear the Maggid, in his study next door, reading the Sidra, the weekly portion of Scripture customarily read on Shabbat. Suddenly he stopped, the door opened, and there he was, standing motionless in the doorway, staring at us, or perhaps at someone beyond us. His whole being was on fire, but most of all, his face, most of all his eyes. Seized with panic, Rebbe Pinhas, Rebbe Shmelke, Rebbe Elimelekh and Rebbe Zusia ran into the street. Rebbe Levi-Yitzhak hid under the table. As for me, gripped by a strange exultation, I began to applaud with all my strength – and to this day I regret it.'

And do you know how Rebbe Avraham Kalisker came to attach himself to the Maggid's court? For years he had lived in seclusion, refusing to meet people so as not to take time away from Torah. One day he heard a Hasid quote the Maggid's interpretation of *Umala haaretz kinyanekha*, the earth is full of things that permit man to acquire a partnership with God. Rebbe Avraham Kalisker needed no more: he climbed out the nearest window and hurried to Mezeritch. Later he told the famous Gaon of Vilna: 'What *I* learned in Mezeritch? One simple truth: *vehai bahem*, Torah is given to man so he may celebrate life and everything that makes life a source of celebration.'

The Holy Seer of Lublin testifies: 'Once I heard the Maggid say *Ein Ke'elokhenu*, no God is like our God, the last prayer of the service. At that very moment the skies parted and I saw the words coming alive before my eyes: I *saw* that there is no God like our God.'

One day the Maggid invited Rebbe Wolfe of Zhitomir to say grace after the Shabbat meal. Afterwards he asked him: 'What did you feel?' – 'Two hands on my head,' said the astonished disciple. – 'That was the Prophet Elijah ordaining you a rabbi,' said the Maggid.

As for Shneur-Zalmen, the illustrious author of the *Tanya* and founder of the school of Lubavitch, he praised the Maggid's vast erudition. Not his supernatural powers. He would say: 'Miracles? In Mezeritch? Who had the time to notice them all?' As for himself, Shneur-Zalmen, he was impressed only by the prodigiously acute and prolific mind of the Maggid. Himself a noted scholar and philosopher, he stated without the slightest hesitation: 'Whatever I know is nothing compared with what he knows.'

On the other hand, we have the testimony of another great Hasidic figure, the mysterious Leib, son of Sarah, who proclaimed to anyone willing to listen: 'I came to the Maggid not to listen to discourses, not to learn from his wisdom; I came to watch him tie his shoelaces.'

In Hasidic vocabulary, the Great Maggid means the one from Mezeritch. What made him great? We shall enlarge on this later; for the moment let us say that the impact of certain Masters must be measured by evaluating the men they inspire. Those who made up the Maggid's 'court' were personalities of the first rank. That they chose him to be their leader proves that they, who were known as his peers, believed in his superiority.

For he acceded to leadership by means of a formal election. There are three versions describing the event.

Here is the first: It happened on the second day of Shavuot, also the first anniversary of the Baal Shem's death. The *Havraya Kadisha*, the entire holy assemblage made up of his disciples, was gathered around a table presided over by Rebbe Hersh, the late

Master's son. Suddenly Rebbe Hersh rose, removed his white kaftan, and wrapping it around the Maggid's shoulders, wished him *mazel tov, mazel tov*, congratulations. After a moment of surprised silence, all those present joined in approvingly: *Mazel tov, mazel tov,* may the good star accompany our new leader.

Second version: Just before he died, the Baal Shem told his disciples that the one among them who would teach them how to overcome pride would be his successor. The problem was put to each of them; the Maggid happened to be called first. His answer: Since pride is one of God's attributes, man cannot uproot it entirely, all at once; it must be fought every day and at every moment. This reply was so favourably received, no one else was questioned.

The third version is the most poetic. It excludes the direct participation of the Baal Shem and leaves the decision entirely in his disciples' hands. They are said to have agreed that the one among them who would reveal something new about the late Master's life, his work or his teaching, would become his successor. And each told all he knew. Stories and quotations followed one another. When the Maggid's turn came, he related that every Friday, before Shabbat, the Baal Shem Tov would leave his body and exchange it for a new one. 'I saw him do it with my own eyes,' said the Maggid. He was the only one to see it.

Later, of course, more legends were created emphasizing the Maggid's superiority over his companions, for he had been the Master's favourite disciple. Once the Master is believed to have told him: 'I need you. Whether a source is blessed or not depends on the person drawing from it.'

Another time the Besht was overheard saying: 'If only Dov-Ber could go to the *mikvah*, he would bring the Messiah.' But being too sick, always, he couldn't go to the ritual baths. So close was the relationship between Master and disciple – still according to Hasidic legend – that after giving him his blessing, the Baal Shem asked the Maggid to bless him in return.

Hasidism's historians tell us that the two men met around 1752, eight years before the Baal Shem's death. There are those who claim that the Maggid visited the Baal Shem only twice, the second – and longest – time for six months. How did the two men become so close so quickly? No one knows. Master and disciple both possessed the secret of *kfitzat haderekh*, of juggling time. But whether the Baal Shem really saw the Maggid as his heir has never been established.

Actually, the Baal Shem had at least two other disciples

comparable in importance to the Maggid: Pinhas of Koretz and Yaakov-Yosseph of Polnoye. The first is remembered as the sage, or 'brain', of Hasidism; the second, as its first chronicler and historian.

Rebbe Pinhas, a profoundly humble man, never aspired to the throne; Rebbe Yaakov-Yosseph did. It seems that at first Rebbe Pinhas even supported him. Against the Maggid.

Yaakov-Yosseph was well known for his loyalty to the Baal Shem. In fact, he almost never left him, content to live in his shadow. His words on Hasidism are the first of their kind. He spent thirty years compiling them, and the Baal Shem's name is mentioned in them 280 times. He considered himself the Master's favourite scribe – and favoured he was. The Master had a special liking for him, that is certain. One day he cried out, and there were witnesses: 'Master of the Universe, when I die I shall not ask to be rewarded for my good deeds, but only for having brought You my Yossele.'

Why then wasn't Yaakov-Yosseph chosen? It isn't clear. Perhaps because he was too rigid and not sociable enough. His relationships with people, especially leaders, were awkward. Jealous by nature, he probably lost his temper with anyone who approached or claimed to have come close to the Master, feeling perhaps that no one else could understand the Master. And then, of course, he was too intellectual for the majority. Their attitude was: let the makers-of-words remain with their solitary studies and refrain from involvement in community affairs, where deeds have priority over thoughts.

Yaakov-Yosseph took his defeat badly. He felt bitter, rejected by his colleagues, misunderstood, a victim of injustice. His friend Pinhas of Koretz did his best to comfort him with a parable: 'When the king retires at night, his crown rests on a nail fastened to the wall. Why on a nail, which is nothing but a common object? Why not on a minister's head? Because the minister might take himself seriously and believe he is the king. No such danger with a nail.' Yaakov-Yosseph must have been lacking in humour; he was not to be consoled. His relations with the Maggid and his followers deteriorated until he refused even to partake of their Shabbat meals. He would stay home and eat there by himself. His bitterness became unbearable when he realized that ... his books did not sell. The story goes that when on a visit to Berditchev not a single buyer appeared, he flew into a rage and threatened to curse the whole town. To appease him, Rebbe Wolfe of Zhitomir urgently dispatched an anonymous messenger to purchase one hundred copies. And the town was saved.

Fact or anecdote, it reflects the individual fate of the man and not his work. From the very beginning, his work added an indispensable foundation to the movement. Perhaps the Maggid was chosen over him because Hasidism even then preferred the spoken word to the written one, experience to knowledge and people to books. Yaakov-Yosseph taught; the Maggid inspired. Yet the Maggid's aim was not merely to inspire his disciples, but to train leaders. During the Baal Shem's lifetime Hasidism had been one man; the time had come to make it into a movement. A centralized, coherent and structured movement with objectives and rules, disciplines and prerogatives.

Both excellent strategist and administrator, the Maggid succeeded in a few short years, twelve to be exact, in establishing and firmly implanting a Hasidic network spanning all of Eastern Europe. Thanks to the Maggid, the flame kindled by the Baal Shem made its way into thousands of widely dispersed communities, small and large. He knew precisely whom to send where to carry out what mission; nothing escaped him, he left nothing to chance.

He had his own reasons for sending Aharon of Karlin to Lithuania and Elimelekh of Lizensk to Galicia. Each could succeed only in the place he was sent; they were not interchangeable.

Dividing Central Europe into more or less well-defined regions, he assigned a Rebbe to each whose task it was to lay the groundwork. What were the means at their disposal? A few tales, a few melodies and an unshakable faith in the Baal Shem's way. And everywhere they found people willing to listen, and willing to join. These Rebbes, these emissaries knew no borders. They crossed the highest mountains and the deepest valleys; nothing could stop them; they never left feeling they had sown in the wind.

Rebbe Menahem-Mendl of Vitebsk was asked what he had accomplished in Vitebsk. His answer: 'When I arrived there, I found torn clothes and whole hearts; now it is the opposite.'

Elsewhere, among the poverty-stricken tribes of Galicia, the task of the Maggid's emissaries was to bring hope and consolation to people living in despair and humiliation. To upset the established order, rock the institutions, tear down the barriers separating poor and rich, scholar and craftsman, peasant and townsman. And above all, to show that to be Jewish could be a link, a faith in new beginnings.

Conceived by the Baal Shem, the Hasidic idea owes the Maggid its adaptation, its practical application. Before him, it was impulsive, vague, fragmentary. Idealized in the extreme, it was vulnerable. Its core needed to be protected and strengthened, it needed a supporting framework and the external marks of an expanding movement. And most of all it needed to be anchored in reality.

The instrument? The Tzaddik, the Rebbe. The Master, the Just Man. Here again the Maggid turned a vague concept of the Baal Shem's into a viable doctrine. As he saw it, the Tzaddik had to combine the virtues and gifts, as well as fulfil the roles and obligations, of saint, guide and sage. Spokesman for God in His dealings with man, intercessor for man in his dealings with God. Required to be almost a superman, he was expected to accept pride without becoming proud; to incite anger without succumbing to it; to strive for goals beyond his reach, assuming full responsibility for possible consequences and contradictions. The Tzaddik had to know the art of speaking, the better to remain silent, and the art of silence, the better to speak.

By placing the emphasis on the Tzaddik, by setting almost unattainable standards for him, the Maggid, contrary to his predecessor, focused his attention on the elite, on his immediate circle, rather than on the average Hasid. His circle of intimates was exclusive. To want and seek admission meant nothing. To deserve it meant little. The Maggid chose his disciples personally, according to criteria known only to himself. A thinker like Shneur-Zalmen and a primitive soul like Leib, son of Sarah, seemingly moved in two entirely distinct words. Yet each in his own sphere had attained a kind of perfection and glory. The same could be said of all the others; each occupied a well-defined place in the Maggid's hierarchy. Legend tells us of one exception. One particularly talented follower is said to have gained admittance into the inner circle, and having tasted too many secret fruits too soon, took to drinking and later, to everyone's amazement, to raving and ranting; saying things, wild things ... Hasidic chronicles mention him only rarely and with reticence; they evidently find it embarrassing to admit that one of the Great Maggid's most brilliant students could have turned out so badly. The other disciples – all of them – did the Master honour by becoming zealous missionaries, tireless preachers, bearers of dreams and Hasidic exultation, wandering from country to country, from village to village, from congregation to congregation, creating a kingdom whose prince was the teller of tales who sang and made others sing.

This made it necessary for the Tzaddik to lead a deliberately ambiguous existence, ambiguous on two levels: he had to be an example one admired but did not emulate, and remain open to the world while retaining his link to a universe both secret and inaccessible.

The reason is clear. For the simple man to experience and survive disasters past and present, for the simple mind to absorb, however unwillingly and unwittingly, enigma and pain and contend with the daily tedium and worries of an opaque existence; for the expatriate going through life as a suspect and undesirable stranger, what was needed was a messenger familiar enough to understand, yet unfamiliar enough to suggest the unknown, mystery, escape. What was required, above all, were men who inspired confidence; there had to be hope even if one could not solve one's problem alone. And since the Tzaddik, by definition, knows the answer, it means there is an answer. Trials and misfortunes, therefore, do have a meaning and do not dissolve into nothingness; they leave their imprint in a collective memory assured of survival. That is another of the Tzaddik's roles; he must encourage the Hasid by teaching him never to consider himself useless, abandoned, negated by a universe he does not understand.

Thus, the Maggid was the answer to a need that was particularly acute in a multitude of obscure regions of Poland, the Ukraine, Rumania, Hungary, Austria and White Russia. His school provided these isolated communities with leaders. Thanks to him, the Jew had someone to turn to in his anguish: his Tzaddik. Who had to be conscious of the almost unlimited powers vested in him both in the visible and the invisible present to carry out his mission. His own soul needed to be sovereign, or else how could he presume to influence another's? And if his own destiny eluded him, how could he even try to affect another's? The Maggid interpreted the Talmudic saying *Veda ma lemala mimkha* as follows: *veda*, know, that *ma lemala*, what occurs up above, *mimkha*, derives from you as well. Whatever the event, *you* are its origin; it is through *you*, through *your* will, that God manifests Himself.

It is said that one day the Maggid decided that the time had come to bring man's exile to an end. The decision caused alarm in heaven. He was asked: 'Who do you think you are to dare tampering with the celestial order?' — 'I am the *Tzaddik hador*, this generation's Just Man,' he replied. — 'You? Prove it.' — 'Very well, my disciples will furnish you the proof.' Gathered hurriedly, they were asked point-blank: 'Am I or am I not this generation's Just Man?'

Thunder-struck, the disciples remained silent. The Maggid repeated his question; nobody said a word. He tried a third time and again was met by silence, always the same silence. It was a strange refusal, one that has remained unexplained to this day. One wonders why these blindly devoted men refused, at the critical moment, to support their Master. What is known is that, contrary to his predecessor, he never tried again. It was written that the Messiah still had to stay with the angels for a long time to come. Man would have to wait.

His former opponent, Rebbe Pinhas of Koretz, seems to have reacted to this episode when he declared: 'If I wanted, I could make the Messiah come as easily as I lift a straw, but I prefer to rely on God.'

Yet the Maggid wished his disciples to develop confidence in their own powers; failing that, they could not adequately discharge themselves of their rabbinical functions. Flagrant display of pride? Perhaps. But since man and especially Just Man is created in God's image, he may and must, under certain circumstances, assume one or another of His attributes. *Umilbashto anava,* God's cloak is humility, was interpreted in Mezeritch as meaning: humility should be like a cloak; one must know how to take it off sometimes.

And yet, to offset the danger inherent in such a concept of the Just Man, the Maggid frequently stressed the importance of humility as a cardinal virtue. Only a humble man can afford ambitious impulses approaching vanity. The line between pride and vanity is thin and the stakes are high. He said: 'You may observe every commandment of Torah, you may purify and perfect yourself by obeying every law, and yet, if at the last moment your consciousness is tainted by a single vain thought, then all has been in vain. And you can wrap all your good deeds, all your worthy intentions into a bundle and throw it into hell.'

The struggle against pride evidently was a major problem for the Maggid and his school. Everybody spoke about it so much and so often, one wonders if anything else really mattered.

A notorious Mitnagged – opponent of the movement – discussing the subject with Rebbe Wolfe of Zhitomir, voiced his astonishment. He complained: 'I have troubles with my son-in-law. Since his Mezeritch adventure, all he ever talks about is his fight against pride. I don't understand: what does he have to be so proud of? He does nothing, has nothing, knows nothing. I, on the other hand, studied with the Gaon of Vilna, know half the Talmud by heart, am generous with the needy, attend services three times a day and lead a saintly life. And yet, look at me: do I look like I must fight pride?'

Dialogue between Elimelekh of Lizensk and his brother Zusia of Onipol:

'Where and how should man begin to serve God?'

'Simple,' said Elimelekh, 'if he begins by seeing how small and insignificant he is, he will appreciate the greatness of God.'

'What!' said Zusia. 'Let man begin with himself? How arrogant! Let him instead look up at the Lord's greatness and then he cannot but realize how very small he is.'

Since neither convinced the other, they sought the Maggid's counsel. His comment: 'Actually, you are both right; both your attitudes are correct. Still, it is safer for man to start his quest aware of his limitations namely, with himself. He who lies on the ground cannot fall down.'

On another occasion the Maggid said: 'Let him who wants fervour not seek it on the mountain peaks – there he will find only storms; rather let him stoop and search among the ashes.'

He undoubtedly had common sense. His teachings include practical advice and admonitions that could be published under the title: the education of a Rebbe. He was a thorough teacher; he even taught his disciples the art of speaking in public. His advice: 'Whenever you deliver an address stop before the end, before you have said it all.' And also: 'Remember that a good speaker must become one, not with his audience, but with his words; the moment he hears himself speak, he must conclude.'

To Rebbe Zusia, he gave the following advice:

'Listen, I cannot teach you the ten cardinal rules governing the conduct of man wishing to serve his Creator. However, there are three things you can learn from a child and seven you can learn from a thief. From an infant learn how to laugh, how to cry and how to keep constantly busy. From the thief? First of all: that whatever he does, he does secretly. Two: that whatever he does not obtain today, he will try to obtain tomorrow. Three: he is loyal to his accomplices. Four: he is ready to sacrifice himself for the object of his desire, even though it may have no value to others. Five: once the desired object becomes his own, he loses interest. Six: he is not afraid of hardship. Seven: nothing on earth could make him change trades, in other words, he does not want to be anyone but himself.'

Though the Maggid had flashes of humour, they were few. Earnest to the point of solemnity, concerned with the image he projected, he did not encourage informality and certainly not distractions. In his eyes, only the essential was permissible. People came from far away to hear him utter a single word, which then sufficed to feed a lengthy meditation, or they came simply to spend Shabbat under his roof.

Among the pilgrims: Solomon Maimon, famous philosopher, friend of Kant and Mendelssohn. He came for a specific reason of his own; he wanted to see the Maggid and evaluate him. The Maggid refused to receive him, and the offended philosopher was kept waiting until the end of the week before he was admitted. He tells us: 'Came the first meal of Shabbat ... There was white everywhere ... The Maggid was dressed in white ... Even his snuffbox was white ... Around the table, the disciples were singing. The Maggid asked each of them to recite a verse of the Biblical passage to be read the following day. Then he took all the quotations and wove them into a discourse. And every one of his followers was certain that the Master was speaking to him alone.'

In Mezeritch the climate was one of tension and stress. People lived on the brink of nervous exhaustion; the very idea of diversion was sacrilegious. The Maggid was feared, and that was how he wanted it.

One Yom Kippur, legend tells us, it happened that the Maggid, who then still resided in Medzebozh, inadvertently touched a fringe of the ritual shawl covering the Baal Shem. He was seized by uncontrollable trembling. And when he leaned against the table, the table, too, began to tremble.

His disciples did not need to touch him to start trembling. It was enough for them to see him – even from afar.

No, he never laughed. But sometimes he smiled.

A very pious and very wealthy Jew wanted to impress him with a description of the austerity to which he subjected himself. 'Tell me what you eat every day,' the Maggid inquired. – 'Oh, almost nothing. Bread and salt.' – 'That's bad,' said the Maggid, 'that's very bad. I order you to eat white bread and cake, and also to drink sweet wine.' – 'But, Rebbe, why?' cried the astounded Hasid. – 'I shall tell you why. You see: if you are content with black bread and water, you will come to the conclusion that the poor can subsist on stones and spring water. If you eat cake, you will give them bread.'

Another anecdote: A famous physician, attached to the royal court of Prussia, offered him a bargain: 'I shall heal your body if you will heal my soul.' – 'Agreed,' said the Maggid, 'let's see which one of us will succeed.' If one is to believe legend, the physician became a Hasid while the Maggid remained incurably ill.

And still another story: A farmer and his wife pleaded with him to intercede on their behalf: 'We are childless; we want a son.' – 'Very well,' said the Maggid. 'That will be fifty-two rubles [fifty-two being the numerical value of *Ben*, the Hebrew word for son].' The couple bargained, offered half. To no avail. The Maggid would not budge: 'You want me to pray for you? Then you must pay the price.' Finally the peasant became angry, and turning to his wife, he said: 'Let's go home, we'll manage without him, we'll say our own prayers and God will help us without charge!' 'So be it,' the Maggid said, and smiled.

The Baal Shem's words had been: 'Sometimes God seems very removed from man – why? It is the father's duty to teach his son to walk. To accomplish this he moves forward and backward without warning, at the risk of letting the child stumble and fall.'

Dov-Ber had his own comment: 'God, in His infinite love, re-strains His powers to enlighten, so that man may receive step by step, stage by stage, the revelation of what lies beyond his limits: that is the way of a father teaching his son to walk.'

But wherein lay the greatness of the Great Maggid of Mezeritch? And why is he still referred to in that way today? He left no work of Talmudic scholarship, no ethical system, no new philosophy. Whatever we know about his towering personality – his charisma, insight and complexity – we know from his followers; we must take their word for it. Moreover, a close analysis of ideas attributed to him leads to the conclusion that primarily he tried – and suc-ceeded – to perpetuate the Baal Shem's theories; the so-called Beshtian Hasidism. His views on *Tzimtzum haelokut*, the stricture of divinity to permit the birth and growth of the world, are taken from the Baal Shem, who had taken them from the Lurianic Kab-bala. The same applies to his concept of the Shekhina's omnipre-sence, even in evil and misfortune. *Let atar panui minei*, the Baal Shem had proclaimed, God dwells in all things – even in sin, and assuredly in the sinner.

It must be said: the more he learns, the more the child in me is disconcerted by the Great Maggid. The Maggid's contribution as a theoretician does not seem fundamental. His attempts at resolving metaphysical problems – relationships between man and God, man and man, man and himself – indicate no breakthrough, no revolutionary approach. Whatever he said, the Baal Shem had said before, directly or indirectly. The victim's cry and the executioner's laughter, the injustice inherent in the weakness of the poor and the arrogance of the rich, understanding pushed to its limits by its fascination with infinity, man's solitude as opposed to God's, the link between Good and Evil, the presence between the vision of death and the vision of death's Victor. These questions had troubled the Baal Shem as they had troubled those whose heritage he claimed. Even the role the Maggid ascribes to the Master inside the community can be traced to the Baal Shem. In general, the importance of his work lies in its continuity rather than its innovations.

In fact, not only did his Master's greatness exceed the Maggid's, even his disciples often surpassed him, each in his particular domain. Shneur-Zalmen eclipsed him in matters of Halakah and speculative philosophy; Levi-Yitzhak of Berditchev, in his love for the people of Israel and its every member; Shmelke of Nikolsburg, in Talmudic scholarship; Zusia of Onipol, in humility; and Aharon of Karlin, in rhetoric. The Maggid must have been aware of it. Often he would muse aloud: 'What sin did I commit that I became a Rebbe? And a famous one at that?' Sometimes he would add: 'I wish it on the wicked.' How is one to explain his impact on peers and disciples alike? A result of his versatility? Of his infirmity? Or of the impression he created of possessing more than one key to more than one gate? Or simply because he wore the glorious crown of the first Master?

It probably had to do more with his followers than with him, and one must look to them for the signs and reasons of the Maggid's greatness. They needed a guide, a Rebbe to overcome their doubts, their solitude. Mezeritch was for them what Medzebozh had been for the Maggid: refuge, stability, presence. After Mezeritch, they knew that the road started elsewhere and ended elsewhere. The same motivations that had driven the Maggid to the Baal Shem bound his own disciples to the Maggid. The greater they were, the deeper their inner solitude and their need for someone to lean on, someone to shield them against excessive pride and exaggerated humility. They came to Mezeritch seeking human contact as much as knowledge. They needed to belong, to be a part of a spiritual fraternity. They needed to feel that others shared their thirst, even if their ways of quenching it were not always the same. And also they craved confirmation that they were partners in a beautiful, exhilarating adventure that would bring them closer together. To be in Mezeritch meant not only to be with the Maggid, but also to live with comrades, friends and allies.

They felt that self-perfection could be attained only through others, an idea that is basic to Hasidism. From the moment they realized that the road to God leads through man, and that man is God's only link to His creation and the key to its mystery, their paths had to lead through Mezeritch. The Maggid then became the symbol of their individual and collective quest. He himself remarked about his disciples: 'I found light locked in a closet; all I did was open the door.'

Was this his sole merit? His only claim to greatness? Surely not.

He was great because he *dared* succeed the Baal Shem. He must have known that inevitably comparisons would be drawn and that inevitably he would be the loser.

He was great because he understood the importance of *transmitting* teachings and new discoveries. He accepted his role as vessel of communication; of executor rather than innovator. Instead of trying to found a new movement, he used his talents to consolidate the one he had inherited.

And then, too, he was great because he foresaw the need to train spiritual leaders for the many isolated and neglected communities; perhaps he intuitively knew that European Jewry was embarking on a long and bloody journey, and that it would need all the help and support it could get.

Another thing, both rare and perhaps more revealing than any other: once his disciples became leaders in their own right, the Maggid did not begrudge them their fame and accomplishments. Not did he ever reproach them for seeking new ways; he wanted them to be different. His thirty-nine disciples did not resemble him, nor did they resemble one another. Each went on to establish his own dynasty, a school bearing his own seal, expressing his own views about man's destiny in general and the people of Israel's in particular. Rather than keeping them dependent on him, he wanted them to reign as sovereigns and in his name. He, the Maggid of Mezeritch, heir of the Baal Shem, was the bond between them.

Yet he was not like the Baal Shem, and therein lies another clue to the Maggid's greatness. Succeeding the Master, he sought neither to emulate nor to resemble him. He had his own style of living, his own kind of relationship with people. No one else would have dared deviate so completely from the Master's path. Most would probably have striven to achieve total identification with the movement's founder by following in his footsteps and by adhering as closely as possible to his established ways. Had the Maggid done this, he would have become another Baal Shem, a small, more or less successful imitation.

The Maggid rejected easy answers and chose a different road. That was his way of paying homage to the Master's work. He understood that to remain faithful to his teacher, he needed the strange mixture of courage and devotion required to stray from the Master's course. His 'deviationism' was a synthesis of continuity and innovation, yet he never became a dissident. The Maggid owed it to himself, *not* to the Baal Shem, to keep alive the Baal Shem's image, his legend and his heritage.

And so Mezeritch did not become another Medzebozh. Unlike the Baal Shem, the Great Maggid rarely left Mezeritch and avoided crowds. The Baal Shem had been constantly on the move, showing interest in men of many backgrounds, everywhere; the Maggid addressed himself to a select few. The Baal Shem had told stories; the Maggid made speeches. The Baal Shem celebrated services with the crowd, and the larger it was, the happier he was; the Maggid prayed alone, and only at the end of services were nine privileged disciples invited to join him in a *minyan*.

The Baal Shem had been accessible and always ready to be of service. Anyone could come and see him without having to go through intermediaries. Not so the Maggid. He was the first to appoint a *gabbe* or *shamash* (secretary, servant, guard) to keep intruders away.

More than his Master, the Maggid seems to have had an affinity for drama and staging. The Baal Shem had wandered around dressed alternately as a coachman or a peasant, a woodcutter or a vagabond. The Maggid had a different vision of himself. He assumed the role of high priest and habitually donned the white flowing robes of that office. He inspired respect. The Baal Shem had inspired love.

Towards the end of his life, the Maggid used crutches, which made his already impressive appearance even more awesome. His sickness became one more barrier erected between himself and the outside world.

And then a strange thing happened: the Maggid decided, unexpectedly and without explanation, to move from Mezeritch to Onipol. Why? The reasons are not clear. Not much is said about the move in Hasidic literature. Was it caused by the increasingly virulent attacks of the opposition, the Mitnagdim? Possibly. But if

that is the answer, it is not complete. For the move does not seem
to have resolved the conflict, which continued more savagely than
ever; geography had little to do with the war between the fanatic
Hasidim and their equally fanatic opponents.

(Besides, the attacks were directed more against his apostles than
against the Maggid himself. These followers of his, accomplished
missionaries though they were, did not have an easy task. Clerical
and secular leaders alike treated them as reformers if not outright
heretics. They were subjected to many humiliations, especially in
the important centres of the Ukraine and White Russia. But the
more persecuted they were, the more support they gathered.)

How then is one to explain the Maggid's precipitate departure?
Perhaps he felt his work was done; his disciples, influential Rebbes
and known Tzaddikim all, no longer needed him. Disillusioned,
desperately ill, he may have felt left out and useless.

Or perhaps he longed for privacy and solitude. Having devoted
his entire life to others, he may have wished to withdraw into
himself to better evaluate the changes that had taken place inside
him while he was engaged in changing the image so many Jews had
of their place in society.

Another possibility. Perhaps this highly intuitive man had a premonition of disillusionments to come: conceived as a movement of
opposition, Hasidism was on its way to becoming just another
establishment.

Whatever the motives, the move which occurred in 1772 seems
not to have profoundly affected the Hasidic world. True, more
dramatic events marked that particular year. Poland was dissected
and divided between Germany, Austria and Russia, bringing more
suffering for more Jews. When nations fought among themselves,
more often than not, the Jews were the ones to pay the price.

That year also saw the first Hasidic book, the *Toldot*, by Rebbe
Yaakov-Yosseph of Polnoye, published and – publicly – burned. It
was the year the Mitnagdim prevailed upon the prestigious Eliahu,
Gaon of Vilna, to excommunicate the Hasidim. Hasidic leaders
considered launching a counteroffensive, imposing a counterban.
The Maggid withheld his approval; he wished to prevent a deepen-
ing of the rift. Better to endure and wait. But the anti-Hasidic
measures multiplied and became unbearable, particularly in Lithuania. The Hasidim were persecuted as though they were outside
the law. And so, one memorable night, ten of the Maggid's followers assembled in the House of Study, and by the eerie light of
black candles, pronounced the solemn and awesome incantation

which, according to tradition, banishes foes from the living community of Israel. Suddenly, in the midst of the ceremony, the
familiar sound of crutches was heard approaching: the Maggid. He
was sad and angry: 'You have lost your head' was all he said. And
there they remained, unable to move, stricken with remorse, having
grasped the full meaning of his words uttered like a verdict; they
had lost him as their head, he was going to leave them. Forever.
Soon thereafter he consoled them: 'I promise you that whenever
Hasidim and Mitnagdim will quarrel, the Hasidim will win.'

When he died a few months later it was snowing. A storm was
blowing furiously over the village as if to sweep it away. Wrapped
in his ritual shawl, his phylacteries on his forehead and left arm, he
was surrounded by his intimates. His last words: 'Keep together,
stay united, always.'

They did not, though, not really, not for long, yet his tales
remain intact, and through them we feel close to the Maggid's
disciples, and through them, to the Maggid himself, and to the Baal
Shem. And through all of them we are linked to the most fervent
moments of Jewish imagination and Jewish soul; without them our
history would be poorer, much poorer, for it would be a dreamless
history, devoid of nostalgic legend.

'Only you, Lord, know why sometimes I rank myself ahead, and other times after, others,' Rebbe Barukh of Medzebozh exclaimed one day.

A proud man, prone to fits of anger and depression, this grandson of the Baal Shem's, brought up by the Maggid of Mezeritch and educated by Rebbe Pinhas of Koretz, claimed to be different from the other Hasidic Masters of his generation, and he was. He believed that everything was due him, for he saw himself as heir, not to his father, who went almost unnoticed, but to his grandfather. Did he truly believe that he alone was the Baal Shem's legitimate successor? Possibly. The fact is that to him every Rebbe was a potential rival and usurper. He declared himself superior to all of them.

This open arrogance could not fail to cause him trouble and provoke hostilities. His own brothers-in-law complained about his whims and frivolities and went so far as to denounce him to the Great Maggid. Whose grandson was to say later: 'Rebbe Barukh of Medzebozh tried to ascend to heaven by stepping on the heads of other Tzaddikim.'

He was forever dissatisfied, distrustful, suspicious; his grudges were universal in scope. Yet people forgave him his excessive language, his abrupt changes of mood. His visitors were blessed, even as he insulted them, even as he cursed them. To a child who had surprised him in a domestic quarrel, he said: 'You don't understand; what you have just witnessed was a discussion between God and the Shekhina.' Legend has absolved him. And more: it has granted him a place of honour. He is the only one to be called 'Rebbe Reb' Barukh.

At the time of the Baal Shem's death he was only three, yet he remained obsessed by him. He wanted to resemble him, equal him. Sensing his failure, he often gave in to bleak anxiety and gloom. Though he fought as hard as he could, he was plagued by self-doubt. How was he to know whether the Hasidim's admiration was intended for him or his grandfather? To bring some diversion and cheer into his life, he retained the services of a famous jester: Hershele Ostropoler. This Hershele, devoted but brazenly impudent, became the only person to stand up to him and tell him the truth openly.

A story: One evening Hershele lights a candle. Reb Barukh reprimands him: the room is still too dark. The next evening Hershele lights a dozen candles. And Reb Barukh scolds him again: 'Are you trying to blind me?' – 'I don't understand you,' says Hershele. 'Yesterday you were angry with darkness, today you are annoyed with light . . .' Whereupon Reb Barukh burst out laughing: 'You want to teach *me* when and how I should unleash my wrath upon the world?'

'This world,' he said, 'is filled with light for whoever knows it, and covered with darkness for whoever loses his way . . . As for myself, I live in it as a stranger. So does God. Thus our relationship is that of two strangers in a hostile land.'

Another time: 'Imagine two children playing hide-and-seek; one hides but the other does not look for him. God is hiding and man is not seeking. Imagine His distress.

'The greatest merit of the Prophet Elijah,' he said, 'is that when he fought the kings and crushed the idols, the people did not react as to a miracle but instead cried: God is our God.'

Another time: 'To attain truth, man must pass forty-nine gates, each opening on to a new question. Only to arrive finally before the last gate, the last question, beyond which he could not live without faith.'

He died at fifty-four. At his bedside, the Zohar was open at the age where there is mentioned a certain 'wrath blessed from above and from below', and whose name is: Barukh.

Menahem-Mendl of Vitebsk was the only true disciple of the Maggid of Mezeritch to have met the Baal Shem; the Maggid himself had introduced him. Menahem-Mendl was eleven years old at the time and already known as a brilliant Talmudist.

Surrounded by his faithful, the Baal Shem looked at the boy searchingly and began to tell him a story that some of those present forgot immediately and whose hidden meaning eluded the others; only he, little Menahem-Mendl, remembered the tale in all its details and understood its significance: it was his life's story, from its first to its last day. The honours, the duties, the responsibilities, the illnesses, the disappointments, the journeys to the Holy Land; it was all there.

Later, whenever his health worried his friends, he would reassure them: 'I still have one half, or one quarter, of the way to go.'

This is how he became Rebbe:

The Maggid of Mezeritch, receiving a delegation of his followers from Vitebsk, entrusted them with his belt and cane. They were to be delivered to a certain Rebbe Menahem-Mendl, who lived in their town.

When the travellers returned home, they began looking for the fortunate man in their midst. In vain. There was no Rebbe Menahem-Mendl in Vitebsk. In their zeal to find him, they questioned even the passers-by on the streets. So doing, they came across a shabbily dressed woman, who told them: 'I know one Mendl, only one, my son-in-law.' They rushed to his house and without a word handed him the Maggid's cane and belt. Menahem-Mendl accepted them, and at that very moment his visitors realized that he had become another.

'My mission on earth,' he said, 'is to recognize the void – inside and outside me – and fill it.'

Considerate, discreet, he was well liked by people of all backgrounds, and at all the courts. The Maggid publicly displayed his affection for him, appointing him to blow the shofar on Rosh Hashana. When Menahem-Mendl left for the Holy Land, the honour went to Levi-Yitzhak of Berditchev, who, overcome by emotion, clasped the shofar and fainted. 'His predecessor, Menahem-Mendl, saw further and did not succumb to fear,' the Maggid commented.

To friends expressing their admiration, he said: 'Far from me the idea of rejecting your praise. I shall need it. And the day I shall face the heavenly tribunal, I shall request your appearance as my witnesses. Each of you will then justify my life by praising me, by stating what he thinks of me just as he does now. And I shall be happy, sure of having won my case. But then, at the last moment, one member of the court will ask me: 'And you, Menahem-Mendl, what do *you* think of yourself? And I shall become humble and silent again.'

'To fear punishment is nothing,' he said. 'What we must fear is sin.'

Like all Hasidic Masters, he lived wholly in his expectation of the Messiah's coming. Mornings he would go to the window, look outside and sadly remark: 'He has not yet come, for the world is still the same.'

His most beautiful words: 'Man is the language of God.'

*

Enthusiastic, filled with ardour and exultation, Rebbe Aharon of Karlin was Hasidism's emissary to Lithuania and Russia. Tirelessly he made the rounds of towns and villages, braving and challenging adversaries, establishing networks – small but numerous – wherever he set foot. By continuously giving of himself, body and soul, this child of well-to-do parents, raised in comfort, fell prey to an obscure ailment which carried him away in three days; he was thirty-six. In Mezeritch, the Maggid mourned for him, comparing him to the High Priest Aaron, brother of Moses.

Here is Rebbe Aharon's commentary on Jacob's ladder, represented in the Bible as standing on earth, its tip touching the sky: 'Let man stand erect, his feet solidly planted on the ground, and his head will touch the sky.'

'If I were given a chance to change places with Abraham, I would refuse,' he told a Hasidic audience. 'You see, God needs men like Abraham, not fools like me.'

One day he was heard crying: 'There are two possibilities. Either God is king of the world and I am not doing enough to serve Him, or He is not, and then it is my fault.'

A friend, on his way home from Mezeritch, where he had spent a few years, knocked on Rebbe Aharon's door. It was late at night.

'Who is it?' asked Reb Aharon.

'It is I,' the visitor replied innocently, sure of being recognized.

'God alone has a right to say *I*. Earth is too small to contain two *I*'s. Haven't you learned that where you come from?'

His friend understood that he still had much to learn and returned to Mezeritch that very night.

Aharon of Karlin taught his followers not to hate life and not to renounce its wealth. Sadness turns into sin, he told them, because it dulls the mind; eventually it becomes hate, self-hate. And whoever hates himself will in the end hate others.

He also said: 'He who does not strive upwards, falls; he who does not better himself, loses ground.'

Disciple of the Maggid, Rebbe Wolfe of Zhitomir chose to remain preacher, rather than be crowned Master. Thence his concern with language.

'Thought is essentially infinite,' he said. 'What confines it is the spoken word. Then why does man try to express himself? I'll tell you why: the spoken word's function is to humanize thought.'

He said: 'I fail to understand the so-called enlightened people who demand answers, endless answers in matters of faith. For the believer, there is no question; for the non-believer, there is no answer.'

Before his death, Rebbe Wolfe told his servant: 'I can see . . . A day will come, and it fills me with fear. The world will lose its stability and man his reason . . . A day will come, and it makes me tremble. Do you hear me?'

'Yes, Rebbe. I hear you.'

'I ask of you to tell it to our people. Tell them that on that day none will be spared, not even men like me or you. We shall have to delve deep into our consciousness to find the spark. Will you tell them?'

'Yes, Rebbe. But . . . when that day comes, what must they do in order not to go under? Do you know the remedy, Rebbe?'

The sick man sighed: 'When that day comes, tell our people that I have foreseen it.'

He turned against the wall, and was gone.

— Levi-Yitzhak of Berditchev —

A story: The Rebbe notices a coachman, who to save time runs through his morning prayers while greasing his carriage. He does not scold him. Instead, he lifts his eyes to heaven and asks it to be his witness:

'Look at Your people, God of Israel, and be proud. What does this man do while working on his cart? He prays. Tell me, do You know of any other nation that has You so completely in its thoughts?'

Another: On his way to the synagogue to celebrate Shabbat services, he meets an 'enlightened' young man who pulls out his pipe in overt defiance and lights it. The Rebbe stops to remind him: 'Surely you're forgetting that today is Shabbat?'

'No, I haven't forgotten.'

'Then surely you are ignorant of the law that forbids us to smoke on Shabbat?'

'Not at all, I know all your laws,' the smoker impudently replies.

The Rebbe looks the young man over. He refuses to be provoked; instead he turns to Him for whom every being also signifies provocation: 'Did you hear? True, he violates certain of Your commandments. But You must admit one thing: nobody will coerce him into telling a lie.'

The Rebbe of these anecdotes is of course none other than Levi-Yitzhak Derbaremdiger (the Merciful), better known by the name of his town: Levi-Yitzhak of Berditchev. His stories, dialogues and litanies can be attributed to no one else. His monologues are poems, his poems are legends, and all bear witness for man. Always he appears as our spokesman.

A contemporary of the Great Maggid of Mezeritch, he occupies a very specific place in the Hasidic movement as well as in the life of every Hasid. His popularity equals the Baal Shem's. Even today, today more than ever, he commands our respect and affection. No

European Diaspora Master since the Baal Shem has left so profound a mark on the Jewish imagination.

As a child, I visualized him as a powerful, invincible defender of the weak, a dispenser of mercy ready to risk all and lose all in the pursuit of truth and justice. He was my hero then, he still is. Often, when I try to go back in time to my own sources, what I remember are his songs and his pleas. And when what is required is a buffer between victim and persecutor, between moribund and death, it is he who comes to mind. To invoke his name, says Hasidic tradition, is to formulate a wish and have it granted. 'The greatness of Levi-Yitzhak of Berditchev?' my grandfather asked. And answered: 'He was a fighter.'

Yet he was not a Rebbe in the accepted sense of the word. He sought neither to spread his own doctrine nor to surround himself with disciples, followers and admirers. Berditchever Hasidism originated and disappeared with him. He founded neither school nor dynasty. The house he built, he carried inside him.

That is perhaps the most important reason for the unanimous esteem the other great leaders of the movement manifested for him. He was no one's rival. Shmelke of Nikolsburg called him: 'My disciple in *Nigla* – oral tradition – and my Master in *Nistar* – esoteric tradition.' Shneur-Zalmen of Ladi put it this way: 'God is a Tzaddik up there and Levi-Yitzhak is one down here.' Reb Barukh of Medzebozh claimed that angels and seraphim envied him his fervour. Nahman of Bratzlav, himself an ardent rebel, covered him with praise and saw the light of Israel in his light. Another non-conformist, Menahem-Mendl of Kotzk, stated categorically that the gates to the sanctuary of love had been opened by Levi-Yitzhak. After his death, they had fallen shut again.

Though a friend to all Rebbes and Rebbe of all their disciples, he belonged to no clan. He was above rivalries and refused to become embroiled in the many quarrels that divided the movement. Protector of Israel, he pleaded for any and all Jews unjustly accused and unjustly punished. His most beautiful adventures, the most beautiful accounts and stories of his adventures, are those that show him in his role of attorney for the defence, challenging and remonstrating the Judge. As a child, I loved them and saw in them nothing but love and friendship. Today I feel their weight of despair and revolt – and love them even more. I often look at them; I owe them much. Sometimes I dip my pen into their wealth before I write.

Who was he? Only the broad outlines of his life are traced. Little, almost nothing, is known of his childhood. We know that he was born in Galicia in 1740. That his was a sharp inquisitive mind. That he became a Talmudic scholar at a very early age and that he married very young. He was twenty when the Baal Shem died. He could have met him, but didn't. He probably wasn't interested; the recently founded movement held no attraction for him. He went to Shmelke of Nikolsburg to study Talmud and its commentaries, not Hasidism. Impressed by his learning and thirst for knowledge, Rebbe Shmelke paid him very special attention. Here was a student to his liking; not a wasted move, not a wasted word. 'He has never uttered a single word in vain,' Rebbe Shmelke said later. And so he took him along to Mezeritch, where, at the Maggid's side, Levi-Yitzhak was to discover that the Jewish condition must be lived rather than studied.

Newly married, Levi-Yitzhak came to spend the High Holy Days with his father-in-law, an influential personality in the community. One Simhat Torah eve he was invited to recite the prayer opening the procession and dance. Flattered, Levi-Yitzhak went to the pulpit, draped his ritual shawl around his shoulders – and took it off. A moment later he put the shawl back on, only to remove it again. This went on for a long time, under the watchful eyes of an amazed congregation. Suddenly Levi-Yitzhak pulled off the tallith again and shouted angrily: 'Since you claim to be both Hasid and Talmudist, you can say the prayer yourself!' And he went back to his seat.

That evening, at the dinner table, his father-in-law protested: 'You embarrassed me in public, I would like to understand.'

'I'll tell you what happened,' Levi-Yitzhak said calmly. 'I was wrapping myself in my tallith, when the *yetzer-hara*, the evil one, the tempter, offered to say the prayer with me. "You?" I asked. "Are you worthy of it?" – "Are you?" he countered. – "Yes," I said. "After all I study Talmud." – "So do I." – "You study? Where?" – "With you." – "But with me it's different. I am a Hasid." – "So am I." – "Who is your Rebbe?" – "The same as yours." – "The Great Maggid of Mezeritch?" – "Himself. Every time you go to him, I accompany you." At that point,' said Levi-Yitzhak, 'I was overcome by anger. – "Since you possess so many qualities, so many virtues, you don't need me; take the tallith and say the prayer without me!"'

An anecdote which lets us glimpse his temperament, his total indifference to public opinion. However, if by acting and speaking in this manner he had hoped to convert his father-in-law to Hasidism, it must be said that he failed miserably. His father-in-law forbade him to return to his Masters. To regain his freedom, Levi-Yitzhak began to fast, and this hunger strike, the first in the annals of Hasidism, was crowned with success.

Levi-Yitzhak returned to the Maggid and acquired a reputation as a Talmudist. Several communities offered him rabbinical posts. But luck was against him: wherever he went, he ran into the opposition of Mitnagdim, who provoked and bullied him, not because they bore him a personal grudge but because it was the custom.

This was the time of the first violent clashes between the Hasidim and their opponents, who adhered to a stricter, more conservative interpretation of Judaism. The Gaon of Vilna had only recently published his first edict of excommunication; it was being read in all the congregations. The Maggid's disciples responded in kind. Fanaticism reigned on both sides. No Jew was permitted to remain aloof. For a teacher to be accepted by one side was sufficient cause to be repudiated by the other. The synagogue became a battleground, the street resounded with insults because of an omitted or added verse. Especially in the Ukraine, people went so far as to call in the authorities to force cantors to officiate in the manner of the conservatives. Worse yet, Rebbe Shneur-Zalman of Lyady was arrested and indicted for treason. 'They denounced him, they did it!' inveighed the Hasidim. The climate of irrational hostility in both camps took on intolerable proportions approaching mass hysteria

Levi-Yitzhak tried hard to stay out of the scuffle. His faith in God, in man, in what binds one to the other, was too great, too genuine, for him to sanction differences between men. His temperament and convictions being what they were, he could only deplore sectarianism in any form. Yet it was no use: wherever he went, he found himself thrust into the eye of the storm.

Named to succeed Rabbi Shmelke in Ritchvol, he was severely put to the test. Cabals, calumniations, mockery; and no one to come to his aid. Exhausted, spent, he ran away. It was the eve of Simhat Torah.

His tenure in Zolohov, where he assumed a post at the age of twenty-five, left him with equally unhappy memories. Six years later he was unemployed once more. Invited to establish himself in Minsk, he accepted. Only to encounter similar attacks, similar virulent and malicious campaigns of slander. One day, while he was visiting his Master in Mezeritch, people broke into his house, smashed everything in sight and left his home a shambles. More-over, when Levi-Yitzhak returned, he found another rabbi had taken his place.

More peregrinations followed. In the end he was stranded in Berditchev. He was forty-five and free at last to start his work in a fairly stable if not peaceful atmosphere. Here too, there were Mit-nagdim, fewer but as vocal and active as elsewhere and who made life anything but easy for the new rabbi. Yet with the years the hostility waned. Thanks to the Rebbe, Berditchev became a sanc-tuary of Hasidism. And when he passed away, twenty-five years after his arrival, the community council refused to engage a succes-sor; one does not replace a Levi-Yitzhak. The chronicles confirm the fact that after him there was no *Rav* – appointed rabbi – in Berditchev. There were rabbinical judges – *Dayanim* – yes. But there never was another *Rav*.

Gentle and considerate in his dealings with people, he seemed naïve, almost childish. Yet he did not lack humour. When challen-ged, his rejoinders were fast and witty, rarely offensive. The fol-lowing incident was exceptional.

He was invited by a rabbi to address a gathering of tailors and bakers, all hostile to Hasidism.

'It is written,' said Rebbe Levi-Yitzhak, 'that when the Messiah will come, nature will provide man with ready-made bread and clothing. I could never understand why. But now I do. So as not to need either tailors or bakers, nor even their rabbi.'

On another occasion, during a public debate in Warsaw with Avraham Katznelenbogen of Brisk, a Mitnagged and formidable opponent, he became involved in a discussion of certain customs newly introduced into Hasidic services.

'Why do you shout so loud in synagogue?' Rabbi Avraham asked. 'Do you think He is so far away? Too far away to hear you?'

'Not at all,' answered Levi-Yitzhak. 'We know that God is near and that He is listening. If we shout, it is because we want *you* to hear us.'

Still, he stayed away from a similar debate in Vilna. The Maggid of Kozhenitz had advised him to abstain: 'If they should ask you why, contrary to custom, your eyes remain open while you recite the *Amida*, how will you reply?'

'What?' said Levi-Yitzhak, surprised. 'My eyes stay open? But I see nothing when I pray!'

'That,' said the Maggid of Kozhenitz, 'I know. But they, our adversaries, do they know it?'

Levi-Yitzhak gave in.

Which did not happen often. Usually he could not be stopped in the middle of a project. Too impulsive to consider consequences or worry about ridicule, he charged headfirst, sure of himself, confident that he would find the words that would be needed.

Walking down the street one day, he received the well-aimed contents of a garbage can on his head. Inquiries revealed the culprit to be the wife of a fierce, malicious Mitnagged. Unruffled, the Rebbe continued to the House of Study, where he pronounced the incident closed:

'Don't be angry with her, Lord, it's not her fault. Poor woman, she wishes only to please her husband. Can you blame her for that?'

An episode which gives a measure of the man: His imagination, his ingenuity were never at a loss; somehow he always managed to invoke extenuating circumstances for others. He himself did not get off so easily; he was his own most severe judge. 'Why do all Talmudic tractates begin with page two? To remind us that even if we know them from one end to the other, we have not even begun.' Every night before falling asleep he reviewed his day: 'Levi-Yitzhak sinned today,' he would cry, 'but Levi-Yitzhak promises not to do it again. He made the same resolution yesterday? Yes, but tonight he really means it.'

One is tempted to believe that his humour was unconscious, almost involuntary. To get the laughers on his side was not a manoeuvre or a strategy; he had too much respect for things human – and what is more human than man's weaknesses – to make them an object of laughter. If he amused people, it was done unwittingly.

Infinitely serious, he would transpose trivial offences and quarrels into theological disputations by introducing a third – omnipresent – character: God, thus conferring a timeless dimension to otherwise childish and futile subjects. By siding with his aggressor, he naturally provoked laughter. Only it was a special laughter, the kind that is aimed not at the adversary but at the entire situation which distributed the roles so badly or so well.

One day he heard a preacher delivering a violent sermon, calling down fire and brimstone upon the community and its sins, real and imagined. Levi-Yitzhak reacted only after the peroration: 'Do not listen to him, Lord! What he said, he had to say. Don't you see? This is his trade. Preaching is how he earns his living. Surely he has a family to feed, three daughters to marry. Give him the money he needs and let him cease slandering Your children.'

As for Levi-Yitzhak, he never said a bad word about His children. On the contrary, he extolled their virtues in his own heart and to God. His motto: man must criticize himself and praise his fellow man. He pushed this line of thought to the point of holding himself responsible if mankind was in bad straits.

He told this story: 'One morning I noticed that the people of my town did not respect me any more. Troubled, I sought to understand why. At last I found that it had nothing to do with them and everything to do with me. I simply had lost all respect for myself. And why should others be more charitable than I? So I decided to work on myself. As a result, people around me began to treat me with increased consideration. First my family, then my neighbours. From family to family, from street to street, the change made itself felt, until it spread to the whole town. I was esteemed again.'

By improving himself, the Rebbe affects others; that is a major principle of mystical thought. Let one human being attain perfection and the entire species shall be saved from falsehood. Levi-Yitzhak subscribed only partially to this form of egocentricity; he preferred to help man in more direct ways. He talked to them, guided them; he offered himself to them, if only as a sounding board.

Meeting a notorious non-believer in the street, he asked him: 'Do you know that I envy you?'

'Whatever for?'

'Because, according to our sages, if you ever repent, all your sins will be counted as good deeds.'

There are two endings to this story. One is that the non-believer let himself be persuaded. The second, that he cried out: 'If you envy me now, Rebbe, wait until tonight, you'll have so much more to envy by then!'

During another encounter, he is said to have succeeded in

convincing his opponent, a noted philosopher who enjoyed provoking rabbis and theologians by using dialectical evidence to
demonstrate the non-existence of God. This man arrived in
Berditchev to find Rebbe Levi-Yitzhak in deepest meditation.
Suddenly, without preamble, the Rebbe looked up straight into his
eyes and said gently: 'And what if it were true after all? Tell me,
and what if it were true?' The philosopher later confessed that this
question had moved and troubled him more than all the affirma-
tions and arguments he had ever heard before or since.

Levi-Yitzhak knew when and with whom to share his certainties
and his quests. He knew when to become embroiled in a heated
exchange and when to fall back into the passivity of the collective
Wait. Though he had mastered the art of striking rejoinders, he
knew when to remain silent.

He had no illusions about men, yet he loved even the most sinful
and ignorant among them. When the notables of Berditchev reproached him for associating with people of inferior rank, he
replied: 'When the Messiah will come, God will arrange a feast in
his honour, and all our patriarchs and kings, our prophets and
sages will of course be invited. As for myself, I shall quietly make
my way into one of the last rows and hope not to be noticed. If I
am discovered anyway and asked what right I have to attend, I
shall say: "Please be merciful with me, for I have been merciful
too."'

The destitute, the ignorant, the misfits sought him out. His presence made them feel important; he gave them what they needed
most: dignity.

Was it within his powers to change their lives? Though one
ought not to generalize, it would appear from his legends
that his impact on people transcended language. His arguments
were less important, for instance, than the way he celebrated
services. His smiles were fraught with greater meaning than his
sermons.

At the time when he was still residing in Minsk, he sent for an
obscure teacher named Aharon, who lived in a faraway hamlet.
This teacher, young and shy, was reluctant to follow the messenger.
Finally he was convinced and was brought before Levi-Yitzhak,
who received him warmly: '*Barukh haba*, Rebbe Aharon, welcome.
Be seated, Rebbe Aharon of Karlin.' The visitor, surprised by such
honours, shook his head. That was all. The two men sat down, one
facing the other, without saying a word. Two hours went by; not a
sound. Then, obeying the same impulse, they exchanged a smile –

in silence. And that is how they parted – in silence. Neither one ever disclosed the meaning of that smile, the content of that silence. All we know is the result. The obscure visitor became a famous Tzaddik.

Like the Baal Shem, Levi-Yitzhak changed those who approached him. And like the Baal Shem, Levi-Yitzhak felt most at ease among ordinary people. He maintained contact with other Rebbes – Elimelekh of Lizensk, Shmelke of Nikolsburg, the Maggid of Kozhenitz and, naturally, the great Maggid of Mezeritch – but he came to them almost as would any Hasid. He preferred following to being followed. Genuinely humble, his love went out to the humiliated and the hungry. Drawn to and touched by their misery, he saw it as a grace. Penniless himself, he pitied the rich 'who lose more than they gain'. His salary he divided among the beggars. His despairing wife complained to the rabbinical court that her husband – who, incidentally, presided over that court – failed to comply with the terms of their marriage contract. Too busy running from village to fair, from street to synagogue, from shelter to orphanage, he neglected to meet his family's needs. Levi-Yitzhak pleaded not guilty. This contract, he explained, committed him to clothing and feeding his family with money honestly earned. Well, for a rabbi, that is not always easy.

There is a strange story told in this connection. It is rumoured that his wife signed certain promissory notes to a local squire, vowing to convert to Christianity if, within the appointed time, she did not redeem her pledges.

In truth, her husband had no notion of money nor did he understand why people seemed so eager to acquire it. Observing a man hurrying down the street, he called to him: 'Where are you running?' – 'I'm looking for work.' – 'And that is why you run? And what if the work were looking for you? If God were looking for you?' For him, money existed only for man to give or to beg. When the community council considered the creation of a unified appeal for the needy so as to discourage itinerant beggars, he declared that the idea reminded him of Sodom – where beggars were unwanted – and threatened to resign: the poor must not be tampered with. The council was forced to yield.

His was an impulsive, unpredictable nature. One never knew what to expect from him.

Once he climbed to the roof of a building facing the marketplace.

He watched the merchants buying and selling, he listened to the
screeching horse dealers, and suddenly he began to shout at the top
of his lungs: 'Good people, do not forget, do not forget that God
too is to be feared!'

Every once in a while he dispatched his servant to one or the
other of the neighbouring synagogues: 'Look neither to your right
nor to your left, walk straight to the bimah, pound your fist on the
pulpit and make the following announcement: 'Know ye, men and
women, know that God exists and that He is of this world, of this
world too!'

People resisted him but – in Berditchev – no one mocked him.
People listened to him and respected him, though he was odd and
clumsy and everything happened to him. He could not light the
Hanukkah candles without burning his fingers, nor could he take
the ethrog out of the cupboard without breaking the glass door.
Attending the Seder of the pedantic Rebbe Barukh of Medzebozh,
he tipped over the table. He went to the well and barely missed
falling in. Whether absent-minded or in a trance, he seemed to
have little sense of reality. Nor was he aware of the disorder he left
in his wake. His inner life detached him from real life. When a
gang of hoodlums beat him mercilessly, he did not interrupt his
prayers for a moment; as though he never felt his wounds. Impervi-
ous to the outside world, he was not afraid of suffering; he
ignored it. He fought pain in his own way. Accompanying his
dead son to the cemetery, he began to dance, crying: 'Lord, you
entrusted me my son with a pure soul and that is how I give
him back to You.'

No wonder that Mitnagdim, opposed to anything that smacked
of sensationalism, fought him so bitterly and with such determination, especially in the early days. They complained about his manners, his manias – what they called his taste for dramatics – in
short, his way of life. In his capacity as official rabbi, he should
have, in their opinion, devoted more time to study and less time to
services. He did the exact opposite. Like Rabbi Akiba long ago, he
worshipped with such abandon that the frightened faithful instinctively moved away. He gesticulated, howled and danced,
jumping from one corner to the other, pushing and overturning
whatever was in his way. People ceased to exist for him. When he
prayed, he himself ceased to exist. Sometimes the faithful became
tired of waiting and went home, leaving him alone in the House of
Study. This even happened on a Passover eve.

He prayed with fervour because he believed in prayer. A story he liked to tell: 'I was there when a thief was being caught. I heard him whisper: "Too bad, I'll try again, and next time I'll do better." From this thief I learned that one must always be prepared to try again.'

But he believed just as much, if not more, in fervour. His own was boundless. Whatever he did, he did without reservation, with his entire being. He often fainted in the middle of services. The slightest prayer exhausted him; it involved more than his faith, it involved his life.

But above all he believed in the coming of the Messiah. Drawing up his son's engagement contract, the scribe had specified that the marriage was to take place on a certain date in Berditchev. Levi-Yitzhak furiously tore the contract to shreds: 'Berditchev? Why Berditchev? This is what you will write: "The marriage will take place on such a date in Jerusalem, except if the Messiah has not yet come; in which case the ceremony will be performed in Berditchev."'

He was flamboyant, like so many among his peers. He, in turn, intrigued, disconcerted, fascinated and frightened many of his contemporaries. Some knew him without understanding him; others loved him without knowing him.

That he made a spectacle of himself is true enough. But that was the man's essence. It has been speculated that he considered his exhibitionism to be his best cover. That was the opinion of Elimelekh of Lizensk, who asked Aharon of Zhitomir: 'Why would you wish to stay with me? Follow your Master, Levi-Yitzhak.' – 'Him I already know, now it is you I want to know.' – 'You don't realize what your mouth is saying,' Elimelekh scolded him. 'You think you know Levi-Yitzhak. You don't even know the coat that covers him.'

Still, other Masters considered him dangerous for the non-initiated and warned against too close association with him.

A disciple of Moshe-Leib of Sassov, a certain Avraham-David, future Rebbe of Bucsacs, planned to spend Shabbat in Berditchev. The Tzaddik of Sassov asked him: 'Will you be able to resist laughter?' – 'Yes, Rebbe.' But Avraham-David had overestimated his strength. Delirium struck during the first Shabbat meal. Without apparent reason, he burst into laughter and could not stop for thirty days and thirty nights. Rebbe Moshe-Leib then wrote to his Berditchever friend: 'I sent you a whole vase and you gave it back to me shattered into a thousand pieces.'

An episode which has never been fully explored. Hasidic chronicle limits itself to providing it with a happy ending. Levi-Yitzhak,
moved by compassion, rescinded the punishment. The disciple recovered. But why had he laughed in the presence of the Master and
the entire audience? How could he have been guilty of such utter
lack of respect towards his hosts? After all, he was not just anybody;
what did he see, discover or understand in Berditchev to make him
laugh at the holiest moment of the week, in front of one of the
most exalted and exalting figures of Hasidism? We shall never
know.

*Levi-Yitzhak admired King Solomon, the wisest of our sove-
reigns. Why? Because, according to the Midrash, he mastered all
languages? Because he knew how to speak to birds? No. Because he
understood the language of madmen.*

We shall never learn the truth. The entire period is taboo; one
particular period of the Rebbe's life. Hasidic texts barely allude to
it. It would seem that he succumbed to a severe nervous depression,
deeper than any he had experienced before. We know, for example,
that one night, having strayed into what was known as Tanners'
Street, he was seized by infinite almost inhuman sadness – and
fainted. We also know that he was obsessed by the suicide of a
poor little beadle who had hanged himself from the synagogue's
main chandelier, thinking thus to 'honour' God. If he went to see
other Masters with such regularity, it was probably to escape his
own phantoms, which after being repressed for many years, overwhelmed him in the end.

He withdrew into himself, became a recluse. Suddenly he was
incapable of carrying out his official duties, and instead spent his
time 'reading, very fast, from a small book that never left him'.
Prostrate, he let his gaze wander over beings and places. He whose
passion had kindled sparks in every heart was now burned out; a
frightened, hunted man. A spring had broken. What exactly was he
suffering from? Overwork? Were all the trials and humiliations
taking their toll? Were the accumulated frustrations driving him
into despair? A number of Tzaddikim met to help him. They attributed his ailment to deeper causes. Yitzhak-Eizik of Komarno
stated: 'This is the angels' revenge; he forced their hand.' Another
thought it a punishment; it seems that Levi-Yitzhak had once
doubted both his own powers and his followers' sincerity. A third

claimed that he had fallen victim to a quest pursued too far; the secret science may not be practised with impunity. Whoever defies celestial order leaves himself open and vulnerable. Had Levi-Yitzhak discovered that the soul can become the enemy of reason? Or that fervour, pushed to its limits, opens on to the abyss? That abrupt transitions may beget insanity? Could he have understood that his pleas were not bringing forth the expected results? That God could easily decide not to receive them, not to hear them? No one knows. And more surprisingly: no one even tried to find out.

True, his was not a unique case. Many other Hasidic Masters were similarly afflicted: Barukh of Medzebozh, Nahman of Bratzlav, Elimelekh of Lizensk, the Holy Seer of Lublin and, according to some sources, the Baal Shem himself. All, to varying degrees, struggled against melancholy. Perhaps because they looked so hard and so much at suffering, they could see nothing but sorrow in the end; because they listened so hard and so often to a thousand voices of sadness, they came to wish that they were deaf and dumb. Yet Levi-Yitzhak was a case apart: his breakdown was ignored; it went unmentioned. As though the chroniclers of Hasidism were reluctant to let him be seen as a tortured and broken man. Anyone else – but not him. He had no right to be defeated, even temporarily. Anyone else could be subject to lapses; not he. Legend required him to remain equal to himself, brimming over with faith, vigour and creative rapture.

Fortunately, his crisis lasted but one year. He recovered almost overnight, and without outside help, closed the parenthesis and was himself again. During the next fifteen years he again plunged into the battle to protect his people against scores of dangers and slanders, a battle that was then reaching its climax. In a way, his fall became a point of departure. After silence and solitude, after the sting of disappointment, Levi-Yitzhak attained new heights and a power whose roots were in his quarrels with God. These quarrels one may safely situate in time between his crisis and his death. His daring, his frankness were drawn from his very despair. So was his revolt.

For the first time a Rebbe took man's defence against his Judge, and that from a position of strength, during the High Holy Days, in the presence of the entire community. And lest someone fail to understand, he expressed himself not in the sacred tongue, but in Yiddish and sometimes in Polish. He did not consider the sacred tongue suitable for battle. Not even for the battle with God.

Others before him had carried on dialogues with God. But none had ever dared take a stand against God. None had gone so far as to judge Him and threaten Him. '*Zol Ivan blozen shofar!*' Levi-Yitzhak cried out during Rosh Hashana services: 'If You prefer the enemy who suffers less than we do, then let the enemy praise Your glory!' Nor did the Rebbe hesitate to remind God that He too had to ask forgiveness for the hardships He inflicted on His people. Thence the plural of Yom Kippurim: the request for pardon is reciprocal.

One day he noticed a man in the synagogue whose eyes were filled with tears. It was before *Kol Nidre*.

'Why are you crying?' he asked.

'I can't help it. The tears keep coming. I was a pious man and well-to-do. My wife was hospitable and devout. And suddenly He intervened and turned me into a heap of rubble. I lost my wife, my home. And here I am, desperate and destitute, with six children on my arms. That isn't all. I had a prayer book that meant much to me. He burnt that too. I don't know how to pray any more; all I can do is weep.'

The Rebbe ordered that the man be given a prayer book just like the one he once had, and then he asked: 'Will you pray?'

'Yes.'

'Do you forgive Him now?'

'Yes,' said the Jew through his tears. 'Today is Yom Kippur; I must forgive.'

'Well then, it is up to You to do the same,' roared Levi-Yitzhak. 'You, too, must forgive!' And he intoned the sombre, solemn melody of *Kol Nidre*.

Another time he offered God a bargain: 'We shall give You our sins and, in return, You will grant us Your pardon. By the way, You come out ahead. Without our sins, what would You do with Your pardon?'

One Rosh Hashana he told this story: A woman arrives at the synagogue out of breath; she is late. She notices that services have not yet started. And so she addresses God: 'I wish to thank You for telling Your children to wait awhile. What could I possibly wish You? I wish You to be proud of them, as I am proud of them.'

Once he remained standing at his pulpit from morning till night without moving his lips. Earlier he had issued a warning to God: 'If

You refuse to answer our prayers, I shall refuse to go on saying them.'

Another story: It was Yom Kippur. The faithful, weak from fasting, were waiting for the Rebbe to begin the *Mussaf* prayer, but he too was waiting. An hour went by, and another. Impatience turned into anguish. This time the Rebbe was really going too far. It was late. Why was he waiting? When he finally emerged from his meditation, he explained: 'There is in our midst someone who cannot read. It is not his fault; he has been too busy providing for his family to go to school or study with a teacher. But he wishes to sing. And so he allows his heart to speak: "You are God; I am but a man. You are Almighty and know everything; I am weak and ignorant. All I can do is decipher the twenty-two letters of the sacred tongue; let me give them to You to make into prayers for me and they will be more beautiful than mine."' The Rebbe raised his voice: 'And that, brethren, is why we had to wait. God was busy writing.'

If other mystics maintained I-and-Thou relations with God, he, Levi-Yitzhak, threatened Him with breaking off these same relations. In this way, he wished to demonstrate that one may be Jewish with God, in God and even against God; but not without God.

He was not content merely to ask God questions, like Abraham and Job before him. He demanded answers, and in their absence, drew his conclusions. To accede to holiness against God, that was what he was seeing. 'If we were to accept the Rebbe of Berditchev's reasoning,' said Barukh of Medzebozh, 'there would not be a single Jew towards whom God is not guilty.'

Levi-Yitzhak's arguments were considerable: 'From the moment You concluded a covenant with Your people, You have consistently tried to break it by testing it; why? Remember: at Sinai You walked back and forth with Your Torah like a peddler unable to dispose of his rotten apples. Your Law, You offered it to every nation and each turned away contemptuously. Israel alone declared itself ready to accept it, to accept You. Where is its reward?'

Another time he made a terrifying statement: 'Know that if Your reign does not bring grace and mercy, *lo teshev al kissakha beemet*, Your throne will not be a throne of truth.'

He also said: 'When a Jew sees tefillin on the ground, he runs to pick them up and kisses them. Isn't it written that we are Your tefillin? Are You never going to lift us towards You?'

Before *Mussaf* service on Yom Kippur, he cried out: 'Today is Judgement Day. David proclaims it in his Psalms. Today all Your creatures stand before You so that You may pass sentence. But I, Levi-Yitzhak, son of Sarah of Berditchev, I say and I proclaim that it is You who shall be judged today! By Your children who suffer for You, who die for You and the sanctification of Your name and Your law and Your promise.'

And also: 'You order man to the aid of orphans. We too are orphans. Why do You refuse to help us?'

His depressions can probably be linked to the misfortunes he watched rain on his people. One Passover eve, tortured by the mystery of collective suffering and evil, he burst out, pleading: 'Tonight we celebrate our Exodus from Egypt. According to tradition, four sons question the father on the meaning of the event. No, not four, only three. The fourth does not even know the question. I am this fourth. Not that I lack questions, Lord. But I don't know how to put them. Anyhow, even if I knew, I wouldn't dare. And so I don't ask You why we are persecuted and massacred in every place and under every pretext; but I would at least like to know whether all our suffering is for You.'

Despite his public outbursts, it never occurred to anyone to accuse him of blasphemy. For two reasons. First: Levi-Yitzhak never sulked indefinitely. Once he had spoken his mind, he came back to God. His reproaches vented, his threats uttered, he resumed – freely and as a free man – the ancient, majestic litany of *Kaddish*. The questions remained questions, but he could go on. He could begin and build on the ruins. Second: Jewish tradition allows man to say anything to God, provided it be on behalf of man. Man's inner liberation is God's justification. It all depends on where the rebel chooses to stand. From inside his community, he may say everything. Let him step outside it, and he will be denied this right. The revolt of the believer is not that of the renegade; the two do not speak in the name of the same anguish.

Thus the revolt of Levi-Yitzhak of Berditchev enhanced his legend. He emerges from it more than a guide, more than a Master. One sees him as the strong and daring brother on whom one may rely.

Let us conclude this sketch with a story an anonymous Hasid told me in the kingdom of night and mist:

Before he died, Levi-Yitzhak, swore in the presence of his closest followers that once up there, he would refuse all rest until he would be allowed to put an end to man's distress. To prevent him from keeping his promise, the celestial creatures turned him into an angel of fire. And that is why the Messiah is so late in coming. And that is also why, added the Hasid, we are here, forgotten, forsaken, expelled from divine and human memory. None of these atrocities would be possible if Levi-Yitzhak, our defender, could intervene.

But the questions of the Berditchever Rebbe, and his challenges too, flung at the face of a sky in flames, have survived him. They follow us and give us the strength and courage to claim them and retell them as if they were our own.

——— *Elimelekh of Lizensk* ———

Once upon a time, somewhere in a Lithuanian village, a certain Eliezer Lipman, known for his wealth and generosity, meets a beggar on the way to the village. He stops his carriage and invites him to get in.

The beggar refuses: 'I still haven't earned anything all day.'

'How much could you possibly earn?'

'A lot. Twenty-five ducats. Maybe.'

'I'll give them to you, come along.'

'No,' says the stubborn beggar. 'I can't.'

'Why not? Since you won't lose anything!'

'True – but money isn't everything. I must think of the people who regularly, once a week, open their doors and hearts to me. If they don't see me today, they'll worry.'

'Don't let that bother you, I'll go myself – I'll go from door to door – to reassure them on your behalf. But do come along – I can't bear to see you walk so far.'

Dropping his mask, the beggar – a messenger in disguise – congratulates Eliezer on passing the test: 'As a reward, you may look into your future. The fact is, you have only one year to live. I tell this to you so that you may use the time to good advantage and put some order into your life.'

Eliezer gave up his business, and devoted himself so completely and exclusively to serving God, that he was granted a twenty-year reprieve.

And five children, including Zusia and Elimelekh.

One night while the brothers were still leading a deliberately anonymous and restless existence, they were stranded at a village inn where a wedding was being celebrated.

Excited by the wine and noise, a band of ruffians, eager for new distractions, decided to have some fun with the two uninvited guests huddled in a dark corner behind the hearth. For no particular reason, Zusia was the one they grabbed. They made him twirl and stumble and let the blows rain on him before letting him go. An hour later they started all over again. And so it went until late into the night.

'Why does it have to be you, always you?' whispered Elimelekh. 'Such is the will of God,' Zusia groaned weakly.

'I have an idea. Let us change places. They are too drunk to notice. You'll see, next time they'll take me – you'll be able to rest.'

He was wrong. For at this very moment one of the drunkards cried out: 'But there are two of them! And it's always the same one we honour with our company! That's not good, that's not right! Let's take a look at his friend . . .'

Later Zusia told his brother: 'You see? It's not up to us; we are powerless. Everything is written.'

This anecdote beautifully illustrates the lives of Zusia and Elimelekh – the great figures of Galician Hasidism towards the end of the eighteenth century.

All his life Elimelekh aspired to fulfil himself through suffering, which taunted him by eluding him. Whereas Zusia, constantly beaten by life and tormented by Him who gives life, considered himself to be the happiest of men.

Zusia: a picturesque character, rich in colour, worshipped as a saint, praised as Tzaddik and affectionately remembered as the 'Fool of God'. His younger brother: a natural leader, founder of a major new school. Without either, Hasidism would have been different. Together they gave its future a countenance. In years to come, for a Rebbe to be whole, he had to be both Rebbe Zusia – innocence and humility personified – and Rebbe Elimelekh, supreme incarnation of authority and power. Their two portraits – so distinct and yet intertwined – have remained singularly alive in Hasidic memory.

Zusia was the first to be attracted to Hasidism – by its way of life more than by its doctrine – and had to use great persuasiveness, for a long time, to draw Elimelekh along. But once he succeeded, they became inseparable.

Together they experienced the awe and rapture that characterized Mezeritch; together they were received by the Great Maggid, who accepted them as disciples; together they chose to live three years of exile and abstinence to purify their souls and thoughts; and still together, they travelled through the Polish countryside, 'raising sparks' and kindling flames everywhere they went.

One tradition has it that every place they stayed – even for just a night – became annexed to the Hasidic kingdom. And that the places they could not reach remained outside Hasidism. There is a curious legend that tells of the two brothers arriving in a small village near Cracow with the intention of staying overnight. But they were restless and felt compelled to leave. As dusk fell, they left. The name of the village: Auschwitz.

Disciples of the Maggid, they could have known his Master. Elimelekh was forty-three when the Baal Shem died. Both he and his brother had many opportunities to leave their native Lithuania and seek him out. Yet they did not. Perhaps because Lithuania, stronghold of the Mitnagdim, was closed to Hasidism more completely and for a longer time than Poland and the Ukraine.

Little is known about the years that preceded their adherence to the movement. Only that their mother, a devout though utterly uneducated widow – she couldn't read the prayer book but knew all the prayers by heart – had not only the earliest but a major influence on their development. Also that Elimelekh's passion was the Talmud, whereas Zusia was a dreamer and leaned towards pure contemplation. Perhaps he had heard a wandering preacher, a storyteller, evoke the wonders to be seen and experienced in Mezeritch, for he decided to go there. Not in search of scholarship or wisdom, but of fervour and salvation.

While Elimelekh was studying and working his way through the tangled texture of Talmudic concepts and arguments, Zusia spent his days and nights roaming the woods, singing and dancing for God. To his brother he explained: 'I am like the servant who loves his king but may see him only through a hole in the wall. You are like the prince who may stay in the presence of the king provided you learn the art of using words.'

Of all the disciples of the Great Maggid, said Israel of Rizhin, Rebbe Zusia was the only one not to pass on what he had learned. And this is why: because as soon as the Maggid began talking, Zusia would fall into ecstasy and make so much noise that he would be sent out. How could he have repeated what he hadn't heard?

Not Rebbe Elimelekh. He listened so well that he eventually became almost a copy of the Maggid. Like the Maggid, he was sombre and moody, while Zusia was the extrovert constantly astonished to discover himself alive in God's world. People remembered Elimelekh as 'a tall man, with a short overcoat and a straw belt around his waist'. Zusia wasn't even noticed. Elimelekh liked to carry a watch and concentrate his attention on it so as 'to link himself to time and the world'. Zusia was far too absent-minded to attach himself to any object. One brother was as demanding and merciless as the other was tolerant and gentle. Zusia, like Levi-Yitzhak of Berditchev, was incapable of finding fault with others; his brother wanted all men to be perfect. Elimelekh preached severity. Zusia advocated compassion. Totally dissimilar, they were united by legend. One cannot mention the one without remembering the other. Elimelekh was feared, Zusia was loved. Fear and love: the two feelings a Tzaddik must inspire.

Zusia, of course, refused to be looked upon as a Tzaddik. He was content to remain the failure, the victim of victims, the eternal child. Though a member of the Maggid's intimate circle, he was the only one not to wear a crown, not to hold court, not to have his own Hasidism. But if there were blows falling somewhere – chances were they would rather fall on him. Honours he despised, preferring to admire rather than be admired, preferring the poverty of the poor to the poverty of the rich.

To a wealthy villager who offered the two – now famous – brothers his big comfortable house, one of them – probably Zusia – gave this reply: 'This is not the first time we visit here; on previous occasions we stayed with a poor farmer who received us as if we were his brothers. Why do you invite us now? Are you impressed by our carriage and horses? Then invite the horses; we shall stay with the farmer. As we did before.'

Another pair of famous brothers, Shmelke of Nikolsburg and Pinhas of Frankfort, put the following question to the Maggid of Mezeritch: 'It is written in the Talmud that man must thank God for the bad things as well as for the good; is that not asking too much of man? Who would have the strength to praise the Lord for being punished?'

'Go and have a little chat with Zusia,' said the Maggid.

Zusia was well known in Mezeritch. And everyone there knew that he was sick and burdened with countless miseries and ailments; that he was spared nothing.

'Zusia, how can you thank the Lord? What about your suffering?'

'My suffering?' asked Zusia, amazed. 'Who is suffering? Not I. I am happy. Zusia is happy to live in the world that God, blessed be He, created. Zusia lacks nothing, needs nothing. Everything he wants, Zusia has, and his heart is filled with gratitude.'

He had not even understood the question.

On another occasion he nevertheless felt it necessary to explain the problem of good and evil, and he did it in his own inimitable way: 'True, suffering exists. Like everything else, it too comes from God. Why does it exist? I'll tell you: man is too weak to accept or absorb divine charity, which is absolute. For that reason, and that reason alone, does God cover it with the veil that is pain.'

In his extreme naïveté, he simply could not conceive of anything in creation not testifying to God's mercy. Unhappiness he dismissed as a figment of the mind. Wounds were opened only to be healed. When his own wife made his life miserable, he showed her his pillow, drenched with tears, and she repented and became good. No tear is in vain, no prayer goes unheard. If woman can be moved, would God remain inflexible? Man has no reason to complain.

He came to an inn and noticed birds in a cage. Naturally he freed them. Birds are meant to fly. And naturally the innkeeper thought otherwise – and gave him a lesson without words. No matter, here was Zusia, back on the road, his body aching but his spirits high, carefree and deliriously happy. Man is made to be happy, even when his tormented flesh cries out in pain.

His capacity for happiness was equalled only by his humility. Once he was heard groaning: 'I am unworthy of addressing my prayers to You; I am not even worthy of giving You my tears. Instead – listen – I shall whistle. That's all.'

In his own eyes, he was the worst of sinners. He was convinced that if he was alive so long, it was to suffer – and expiate – as long as possible. It is said that every day he recorded all his deeds and thoughts in a little notebook; in the evening he would reread what he had written and cry until his tears had erased all traces of his writing.

Menahem-Mendl of Kotzk said of him: 'Just as there are scientific geniuses, there is one in matters of humility, and I mean Rebbe Zusia.'

He had a secret admirer and benefactor, a merchant who occasionally dropped a few silver coins into his bag. Ever since he had begun this practice, this man's business flourished. So he thought to himself: If this poor devil can do so much for me, why not go to his Master, who can do more! And so he went to see the Maggid of Mezeritch and gave him a donation. Next day his affairs took a turn for the worse. Perplexed, he sought out Zusia. Who explained to him that when man makes no distinction in giving,

God makes no distinction either; but when man shows himself particular, God does the same.

Before Rebbe Zusia died, he said: 'When I shall face the celestial tribunal, I shall not be asked why I was not Abraham, Jacob or Moses. I shall be asked why I was not Zusia.'

His brother, imagining the same scene, lent it a more optimistic ending: 'They will ask me if I was just; I shall say no. Then they will ask me if I was charitable; I shall say no. Did I devote my life to study? No. To prayer perhaps? No again. And then the Supreme Judge will smile and say: "Elimelekh, Elimelekh, you speak the truth – and for this alone you may enter paradise."'

With the advent of Rebbe Elimelekh, Hasidism enters a new phase. The era of Tzaddikism opens.

Not that he was the first Tzaddik – or the only one. The Maggid of Mezeritch had more than one disciple, and each in his own way, in his own area, became his successor. But it was Rebbe Elimelekh who developed the concept and role of the Tzaddik and built a movement if not a doctrine around him.

The time: the last decades of the eighteenth century. On the surface, all signs are encouraging. The movement has withstood the death of its founder – in 1760 – and of its organizational architect, the Maggid of Mezeritch, twelve years later. If in the beginning there was a danger that Hasidism would become too centred on one person, one leader, that danger has now vanished. The movement proved itself strong enough to withstand the first internal dissensions and power struggles among the pretenders to the throne left vacant first by the Baal Shem, then by the Maggid. The Maggid had had to overcome considerable resistance before asserting his authority; his successors did not, for they were many. Hasidism now had several centres – and all were flourishing.

The Maggid had wanted this decentralization for his own reasons – which had to do with Jewish politics, not with international relations. Events confirmed his vision. With one centre built around one figure, Hasidism might not have survived the series of severe crises which began erupting throughout Eastern Europe in 1772 – the year of the Maggid's death.

Poland was divided among her three neighbours: Russia, Prussia and Austria. And once more the Jewish community broke up into newly created geopolitical entities, each facing a new set of problems from within and without. The fact that each region, and in many cases, each city and town, had its own guide to rely upon, surely helped Hasidism maintain its initial momentum, while continuing to spread in various directions at once. One Master could not have coped with all the different needs.

Elimelekh settled in Lizensk in 1777, and that is where he died eleven years later. During that period Lizensk became one of the capitals of Hasidism. Among Elimelekh's disciples one could find such distinguished figures as the Holy Seer of Lublin, Menahem-Mendl of Riminov, the Maggid of Kozhenitz, the Apter Rebbe . . .

After the founder – the Baal Shem – and the architect – the Great Maggid – came Elimelekh – the teacher, the practical man who translated abstract concepts into simple language for simple people.

What and who is a Tzaddik according to Lizensk? Rebbe, rabbi, guide, conscience, tutor; he is the sublimation of man's self. He is what man can be, wants to be. He is the chosen one who is refused nothing, in heaven or on earth. God is angry? He can make him smile. God is severe? He can induce him to leniency. His followers owe him blind and unconditional allegiance. *Emunat Tzaddikim*, faith in the Rebbe, is one of the basic tenets of Lizensker Hasidism. He who hesitates, who wavers, cannot be helped. To question the Rebbe is worse than sin; it is absurd, for it destroys the very relationship that binds you to him.

If his behaviour appears bizarre, it means the Hasid does not possess the required powers of understanding. So complex is Elimelekh's dialectical approach that the Tzaddik's relationship with the 'higher spheres' is never clearly defined – yet the common mortal may not question its existence or its efficiency. Whether he chooses to sing or laugh, to smile or be unpleasant, to open up or withdraw into meditation — *he* knows what he is doing; that should be enough. One must not try to understand. One must admire, that's all. Let him choose poverty while accepting donations; let him simulate joy but spend nights in lamentation; let him *boast* of his humility – nobody has the right to take exception. What he does, he does well, and for you. A superior, almost perfect being – meaning that his thirst for perfection is almost perfection – he uses his mysterious powers to redeem the sins of his generation. No matter what the Tzaddik does, he transcends his own person. His suffering confers a meaning upon all suffering; and when he eats, he cleanses the very act of nourishing the body.

'If they had left me alone, if they had left me in peace for two years,' said Rebbe Elimelekh, 'I would have made the Messiah come.'

Like the Baal Shem and the Great Maggid of Mezeritch, Elimelekh linked individual salvation to universal redemption. A Tzaddik is called upon to play the most vital role in human drama, just as the Messiah would in cosmic drama. Though the two roles are not identical, they are related. Which explains why, at one point, a Tzaddik *must* assume responsibility for the Messiah's *not* coming. Like his two immediate predecessors, Elimelekh is said to have planned a momentous journey to the Holy Land – and like them, had to abandon the project: times were not propitious as yet.

His asceticism, his self-flagellation are legendary. 'Whoever shows self-indulgence will die without repentance,' he stated flatly. Sometimes he would tell his servant to follow him into the forest: 'Let us go and punish a rebel.' Out of sight in the woods he would ask the servant to whip him, 'for I am the rebel'.

Once he remarked: 'So many people come to me with their pleas. One cries for health, another for bread, a third for a better life. Why do they come to *me*? Because in truth I am responsible for their sickness, their hunger and their misery.'

Does that mean the Hasid's own responsibilities are diminished? Surely not. Only shifted. He is responsible for what happens to the Tzaddik – for *his* cries, for *his* spiritual anguish. One needs the other. For the Tzaddik represents man's potential; he is all that every Hasid wishes to become, could become. Granted, it is given to every man to attain perfection. Granted, too, that the Tzaddik owes his position of Tzaddik only to himself. Whoever works on himself long enough, obstinately enough, will in the end break his chains. Ancestry means nothing. A descendant of the Baal Shem is no worthier than any other man. Like the Baal Shem, Elimelekh left his throne not to his sons but to his disciples, none of whom had titles other than those they had acquired themselves. Titles every Hasid can acquire, if only he tries. Failing that, he can set his sights on a secondary project: to labour for salvation by attaching himself to a Tzaddik who thus becomes his other self. If he cannot be Tzaddik, he will be Hasid. And the Tzaddik will be Tzaddik to the extent that the Hasid will be Hasid. Except that a perfect Hasid is worthier than a Tzaddik who no longer is Tzaddik.

The Hasid-Tzaddik relationship, therefore, must exist under the sign of faith, and contrary to what one may think, it reinforces the faith in God.

Faith in God was so absolute in Lizensk that Rebbe Mendl of

Riminov – so the story goes – once refused to pick up a gold coin he saw lying on the ground. If God wishes me to have it, he thought, I will get it without having to bend down.

It is because the Hasid believes in God that he believes in the Tzaddik, who, according to the terms of their tacit agreement, must bring him closer to God. The school of Lizensk illustrates this relationship with the Biblical verse: *Vayaaminu baadoshem uv-Moshe avdo*, and they had faith in God and in his servant Moses. Because they believed in the one, they could believe in the other, thus becoming worthy of the miracle of the Red Sea crossing. And enabling Moses to speak on their behalf – and sing. *Az Yashir Moshe*, and that's when Moses began singing. Singing? He? Wasn't Moses a stutterer? He could sing, Hasidim say, because his people now had faith in him. Thus, faith in one's Tzaddik makes one an active participant in the Tzaddik's work and partly responsible for his being the omnipotent, omniscient figure he is. When Rebbe Elimelekh says: 'I remember perfectly the scene of revelation at Sinai; not only do I remember myself standing there, but also the souls on my left and on my right,' the miracle is not only his memory, but also the fact that he raised other souls by linking them to his own. Because the Tzaddik does not speak for himself alone, he has great authority in heaven. The Talmudic saying *Hatzaddik gozer vehakadosh barukh hu mekayem* – the Just Man commands and the Lord obeys – is taken literally in Lizensk. Elimelekh, inadvertently or unconsciously, compares the Tzaddik to the Just Man who is obeyed by the Lord, his servant; a comparison that drew sharp criticism even from his peers. Can it be interpreted in a context other than blasphemous? Yes, since God is everywhere, they claimed in Lizensk, and every act derives from His will, it follows that this applies also to the Tzaddik's 'orders'; even when he addresses God, he is but carrying out His will.

One understands why in Lizensk, even more than in Mezeritch, the struggle against vanity played a major role: because of one spark of silly pride, the entire structure could collapse, no matter what its initial purpose.

Nothing is worse than pride; it lures man into usurping the place of the Creator, Rebbe Elimelekh taught his followers.

Rebbe Zusia asked his brother: 'It is written that Adam's soul contained all others. Which means ours too. How then do you explain that you did nothing to prevent him from committing his sin?' Rebbe Elimelekh's reply: 'If Adam hadn't sinned, he would have become vain.'

At the ritual baths, Elimelekh met a Jew who had come from Hungary to spend Shabbat at his court. 'You took the trouble to come from so far away for this idle faker, this liar, this make-believe Rebbe?' asked the Tzaddik, whom the visitor had not recognized.

'How dare you?' the Hungarian Jew replied angrily. 'How dare you slander a saint and sage of Israel?'

In the evening they met again, but this time in the Master's house, in the presence of his disciples. The visitor, petrified at first, began to sob, asking to be forgiven: 'I didn't know, holy Master . . .'

'Dry your tears,' the Rebbe reassured him. 'You told me your truth, and I told you mine.'

A somewhat similar anecdote has Zusia as its hero.

In an inn somewhere, a wealthy guest mistakes him for a beggar and treats him accordingly. Later he learns his identity and comes to cry his remorse: 'Forgive me, Rebbe, you must – for I didn't know!'

'Why do you ask Zusia to forgive you?' Rebbe Zusia said, shaking his head and smiling. 'You haven't done anything bad to him; it is not Zusia you insulted but a poor beggar, so go and ask the beggars, everywhere, to forgive you!'

Both replies sound authentic, though one seems more humble than the other. Elimelekh was complicated; his brother was all of one piece. Zusia was Zusia all the time – and wanted to be nobody else. Elimelekh wanted to be both Elimelekh and Zusia: hence he could simultaneously preach joy and practice asceticism, cling to the external marks of power and denounce power, put his hands into the fire and oppose mortification. Like many Tzaddikim after him, he led a double life. Publicly, he followed the path traced by the Baal Shem, while privately exploring labyrinths of pain and suffering.

Yet at no time did he go so far as to suggest that the average Hasid try to follow in his footsteps. At his school, the Tzaddikim of Apt, Sassov, Lublin, Ropshitz, Riminov and Kozhenitz learned that they must be available to their followers at all times and in all matters. They learned to take a part in the lives of their Hasidim, to be interested in their business affairs, to help arrange their marriages, settle their differences and organize collections to pay their debts. Elimelekh taught them the art of counselling in times of distress, of jolting the complacent and appeasing the tormented.

Lizensk meant total involvement on the part of the Master and the disciple alike. 'Solitude is no solution,' Elimelekh said. 'Rather than isolating your lives, isolate your thoughts.' Lizensk meant total concern on the part of every Hasid for his fellow man. A disciple – Rebbe Zekharia-Mendl – wrote: '. . . At Lizensk, Hasidim love each other more than husbands love their wives and fathers their children. They live in harmony. They help each other in every way. All he possesses, the Hasid shares with the others. Including his fears and hopes . . .'

Rather than teach Kabbala or theology to his Hasidim, Elimelekh gave them a *zetl koten:* a short list of little things to do every day, when rising in the morning, when praying, when engaging in business, when being alone or with others. It is a seventeen-point programme on how to be a good Jew . . . with a minimum of effort. Theology was left to the Tzaddikim; Hasidim needed simple answers to not so simple questions.

It is said that the Rebbe's involvement with his followers was such that they could be identified instantly. Anyone who saw him or was seen by him, carried him away in his eyes. Nobody passed through Lizensk unchanged.

But Rebbe Elimelekh was not to enjoy a peaceful old age. He had succeeded too well. His teaching had borne fruit sooner and in greater abundance than he had expected.

He who had wanted, like his Master the Maggid of Mezeritch, to provide the greatest number of leaders to the greatest number of communities, suddenly felt left behind, superfluous. Unlike the Maggid, he seems to have succumbed to jealousy. He who had helped his disciples to become Tzaddikim, now found their success intolerable. He who had urged his favourite disciple Yaakov-Yitzhak – the future Seer of Lublin – to free himself of his hold and start on his own course, regretted it now. Yaakov-Yitzhak, established in a small locality named Lanzhut, attracted the best elements away from Lizensk. Legend has recorded a heart-rending cry of the great old man: 'I still want to live!' He sent emissaries to Lanzhut, alternately demanding, urging, pleading for a reprieve. Let Yaakov-Yitzhak wait – a few months, a few years at most – and I'll lift him up even higher, even higher than myself. Too late. Yaakov-Yitzhak had already entered Hasidic history. Elimelekh then asked that he at least move farther away; Lanzhut was too close to Lizensk. Yaakov-Yitzhak could not bring himself to refuse. He moved to Lublin, where he became known as the Holy Seer. The break between Lizensk and Lublin was sad but absolute.

Hasidic scholars try very hard to explain and even justify this break by comparing it to the 'breaks' that long ago had occurred between the Prophet Elijah and his successor Elisha, and between Moses and Joshua. They say that the Seer understood that old Rebbe Elimelekh was too saintly for the new generation. And that for a disciple to show his measure, he must cut the ties with his Master. Moses and Joshua, Elijah and Elisha could not reign together; neither could Elimelekh of Lizensk and the Holy Seer of Lublin.

Too facile – and superfluous – an explanation. Judaism never claimed to be monolithic. Its teachings are a sum, a synthesis; they represent all currents, those of the Masters *and* those of the disciples. Though given once, Torah is received a thousand times in a thousand ways; each man contributes to its enrichment.

The reasons for Rebbe Elimelekh's resentment towards the Seer of Lublin must be sought not in theories but in human nature. For jealousy – any jealousy, even that of a Master towards his disciple – is human.

And agonizing. Hasidic tradition refers to it with embarrassment and sadness. Elimelekh appears as a changed person, unrecognizable. Bitter, ill-tempered, physically ill, he refuses all food, all contact with the outside world. He hardly speaks; after *Maariv*, the evening service, he retreats into total silence. Suspicious, he sees treason everywhere. He thinks himself surrounded by spies; he doubts even the most loyal of his admirers and calls them flatterers and hypocrites.

One Saturday night, as soon as Shabbat was over, he hurried to a certain Reb David to check whether he was at home; no, he wasn't. Later Reb David, who had spent Shabbat with the Seer, tried to justify himself: 'I thought I would climb on to his shoulders so I could reach you, Rebbe.' But Elimelekh wasn't fooled. And legend, with more than a touch of cruelty, adds that Reb David was punished for his betrayal; he died the following year.

Rebbe Elimelekh seems also to have harboured resentment towards his own children, though they cherished him and defended his throne and name to the very end. He left them nothing: 'Let them be poor, let them live off charity, and if they themselves are not deserving, they should be given nothing.'

When he died – in 1786 – he took even Lizensk with him; it left geography to enter legend.

Yet he had unquestionable greatness. Few schools can be compared to his. His disciples, founders of dynasties all, worshipped him. Even the Seer never disavowed his Master, just as his own disciple, the Jew of Pshiskhe, did not disavow him when he left Lublin to establish his own school and lead his own rebellion.

But that belongs to another story.

Disciples III

A great miracle-maker himself, it is by miracle that Rebbe Israel, Maggid of Kozhenitz, stayed alive. Emaciated, so weak he had to be carried to services for more than fifteen years, he regained his strength only when he prayed. Then he became a changed man. He would sing and dance feverishly, his body rejuvenated and well again. The rest of the time he spent in bed muffled up in heavy blankets, receiving admirers and disciples, and if need be, interceding on their behalf, frequently with success. As a wonder rabbi, he had no equal.

A healer of bodies and souls, he 'gave' children to childless couples, redistributed the wealth of the rich among the poor, appeased the dead and their mourners. For Jews and Gentiles alike, he was a last chance, an ultimate hope.

It is said that princes and generals came knocking at his door, requesting his advice before they made a decision, before they went to war.

Those who believed in him, and they were many, did nothing without his approval. They came from far away to see him, if only for one fleeting moment. Some considered him a second Israel Baal Shem Tov.

A story: When Elimelekh of Lizensk felt his hour approach, he made his last will known. To Mendl of Riminov he bequeathed his brain, to Yehoshua Heschel of Apt, his tongue; to Yaakov-Yitzhak of Lublin he left his sight, and to Israel of Kozhenitz, his heart.

That is what the Maggid of Kozhenitz became: his generation's heart.

He said: 'What is man? A speck of dust, flawed and doomed to nothingness. And yet, here he is addressing God, familiarly at that, is that not a reason to be grateful?'

And also: 'Man aspiring to heights must reach for them through others, with their help and helping them. If all of Israel's children joined hands, they would form a chain and touch the celestial throne.'

Another time: 'Every man must free himself of Egypt every day.'

A woman begged him to pray for her; she wanted a child.

'My mother was as unhappy as you are, and for the same reason,' he told her. 'Until the day she met the Baal Shem Tov. She presented him with a cape. I was born the following year.'

'Thank you,' the woman said, beaming. 'I'll do as your mother did. I'll bring you the most beautiful cape I can find.'

The Maggid of Kozhenitz smiled: 'No, that won't help you. You see, my mother didn't know this story.'

Adam, ancestor of all mankind, visited him in a dream: 'You have prayed for yourself – for your purity – and your prayer was heard. Now I would like you to pray for me.'

He said: 'The greatness of Torah lies in the way it changes every day, thus providing man with a primary satisfaction every day.'

As a young man he would stay up late into the night studying. His father suspected him of wasting his time playing and wandering through the streets. He would punish him for being idle. Israel suffered the blows in silence.

Later, when he was famous, he was asked why he had not protested his innocence to his father.

'It is not given to everyone to suffer for the Torah,' he explained.

In his relationship to God, he saw himself as a messenger: 'Send me anywhere to do anything, I am ready.'

This he was still repeating after years of confinement to bed.

His favourite prayer is mine too: 'Master of the Universe, know that the children of Israel are suffering too much; they deserve redemption, they need it. But if, for reasons unknown to me, You are not willing, not yet, then redeem all the other nations, but do it soon!'

They were called the 'Holy Brothers': Samuel, nicknamed Shmelke, the elder of the two, was a rabbi in Nikolsburg, while Pinhas served in the same capacity in Frankfort.

During Reb Pinhas's formal investiture, while notables and dignitaries were extolling his virtues, a strange expression came over his face.

'What are you thinking of?' he was asked.

'I have the odd feeling I am attending my own funeral,' he replied.

During the corresponding ceremony in Nikolsburg, Shmelke attracted people's attention by talking to himself in a low voice: 'I tell my mouth to repeat what my ears are hearing; and it all sounds absurd.'

The two brothers enjoyed extraordinary prestige even in non-Hasidic circles. The anathema cast upon the disciples of the Maggid of Mezeritch hardly affected them. Their scholarship was too well known for them to be excluded from the community; their Halakhic works set new standards.

Still, legend recalls them not as scholars but as Hasidic Masters.

A story: Once upon a time there was a beadle who would awaken the faithful and call them to prayer. Frail, sickly, he would scratch at the door or window, nothing more. Terrified, people would jump from their beds and hurry to services.

'This power,' said the beadle, 'I have from Rebbe Shmelke. Years ago I was in his service and he taught me the art of jolting people without making a sound.'

Whoever came to see Rebbe Shmelke with outstretched palms left bearing a gift. One day, when he had not a single piece of change, he gave a beggar a ring he saw lying on the table. It belonged to his wife, who, when she heard the story, complained loudly: 'How could you, didn't you know this was a valuable ring, a diamond ring?'

Whereupon Shmelke ran out of the house in pursuit of the beggar, shouting: 'Friend, listen, that ring is valuable! Don't let the jeweller cheat you! You mustn't sell it too cheap!'

He said: 'The rich need the poor more than the poor need the rich. Unfortunately, neither is conscious of it.'

Rebbe Shmelke told the following: 'Basing myself on the Talmudic saying that if all men repented, the Messiah would come, I decided to do something about it. I was convinced I would be successful. But where was I to start? The world is so vast. I shall start with the country I know best, my own. But my country is so very large. I had better start with my town. But my town, too, is large. I had best start with my street. No: my home. No: my family. Never mind, I shall start with myself.'

Accompanied by his faithful disciple Moshe-Leib of Sassov, he went to Vienna, where he was received in audience by Queen Maria-Theresa.

'Why don't you look me straight in the eyes?' Her Royal Highness inquired.

'I cannot detach my eyes from the ground, Your Majesty, I owe it more than I owe you; earth gives us man and also takes him back.'

Before he died, he told his followers not to cry. He said: 'Death is not a stranger to me. For my soul is that of the Prophet Samuel. Like him I am a Levi, like him I shall die – today – at the age of fifty-two. Only they call him Samuel, whereas I shall remain Shmelke. Is that a reason for you to cry?'

And he drew his last breath.

Rebbe Yaakov-Yitzhak was almost blind, but in Lublin he was called the Seer; between fits of depression, he preached joy. He presided over a royal court, but he personally served its paupers. His disciples – according to tradition they numbered four hundred – were held to a rigorous discipline permitting no deviation, though he himself had dared to be a rebel during his years of apprentice-ship.

He was a disquieting, awesome figure. From all accounts, he frightened people. His strange eyes, one different from the other – the right very large, the left almost invisible – reputedly could see 'from one end of the world to the other', and had the power to scan the stifling depths of the soul. One glance at a person would tell him whether he was a descendant of Cain or Abel. This gift of vision he considered a burden; that is what he stated in public. He did not wish to see what the world had to show him; he did not like his eyes.

It is said that in his youth he deliberately chose to live seven years with his eyes closed.

And also that he took walks through the forests and sat on anthills.

And also that having climbed to the peak of a very high mountain one day, he attempted to throw himself into the abyss.

'But why, Grandfather?'

'Don't try to understand. One either likes or dislikes the Seer. But one mustn't try to understand why.'

'Who saved him?'

'A friend. He grabbed him by his belt.'

After a pause, my grandfather added: 'The Seer never forgave him.'

Desperately, he fought the anxiety that undermined him. He even tried to 'outlaw' it by proclaiming it the worst of sins. But it came back, day after day, choking him and squeezing him as in a vice. He startled his followers by forming a friendship with a non-believer, a well-known rake. 'I like him,' he said, 'because he's cheerful.'

His first Master, Rebbe Shmelke, had understood and sent him to Rebbe Zusia. With a note of recommendation: 'Try to teach him joy.'

'Not easy,' my grandfather said to me, his eyes shining with mischief. 'Joy can be learned only from Hasidim, not from Masters.'

Yet, despite his depressions, the Seer was constantly growing in stature in the eyes of his followers; his sphere of influence widened from one Shabbat to the next. People came to Lublin to study, to meditate, to do penance and rearrange their inner life. Some came to stay, others came and went.

He said: 'How strange, all these people who came from far away, they are sad when they arrive, but by the time they leave, they are gay and confident, whereas I . . .'

A long pause: 'I am sombre, and so I remain; mine is a black fire, one that gives no light.'

But that, his followers did not see or refused to see.

Perhaps they found it easier that way. They were content simply to watch his fire burn.

The disciples he guided on the path to perfection were bound to him by an intense admiration that bordered on worship. One of them was asked: 'Since you were so many and so powerful, and had a Master of such outstanding talent, why could you not make the Messiah come?' And the disciple replied, unsmiling: 'The question is a valid one. But you see, in Lublin we lived in such ecstasy, we hardly felt the hardship of exile.'

The Seer's powers of suggestion were exceptional; they transcended the individual. His battles he fought alone; his victories he shared with all his disciples and followers.

Thence the prestige and esteem he enjoyed with the other Masters. The Maggid of Kozhenitz and Menahem-Mendl of Riminov were his allies; Ber of Radoshitz and Naftali of Ropshitz, his devoted admirers. Even Barukh of Medzebozh showed him affection. Welcoming him to his home one Shabbat, he questioned him: 'They say you are a Seer; where are we?'

And the Tzaddik of Lublin's answer: 'I see us in the Holy Land; we are entering Jerusalem, soon we shall cross the sanctuary's threshold.'

And the same landscape appeared before the two men's eyes.

In his moments of despair, he was known to say: 'Woe to the generations whose leader I am.'

Also: 'People come to me because I do not understand why they come.'

And also: 'The wicked man who knows he is wicked, well, I prefer him to the Just Man who knows he is just.'

Demanding of man that he assume his condition and not till his neighbour's field, he said: 'There are many paths leading to perfection; it is given to each of us to choose our own, and by following it with great dedication, we can make it become truth, our only truth.'

The Seer's best disciple, the Jew of Pshiskhe, took him at his word. And left him to teach new, revolutionary ways. And so the circle closed; like his Master, Elimelekh of Lizensk, the Seer in his turn thought himself betrayed, abandoned, robbed.

But unlike Elimelekh, he continued the struggle. Instead of foundering in his personal tragedy, he went back to work with renewed vigour. Better still, there was a new dimension to his purpose, a universal dimension. He wanted nothing less than to put an end to all conflicts, to all wars; he wanted to end exile.

With his two friends and allies, Mendl of Riminov and the Maggid of Kozhenitz, he devised a detailed strategy, combining their powers to bring about final redemption. The tasks were divided – the roles distributed – the secret well kept. Unfortunately, the mystical plot failed. Punished by God, all three conspirators died during that same year (1814–15).

Six months before his death, the Seer, who had been meditating in the privacy of his room, fell out of the window; a mysterious fall, referred to as a divine malediction.

'It was Satan's doing,' my grandfather assured me, 'it was Satan's vengeance.'

As far as my grandfather was concerned, the Seer, whose personality he loved, had come too close to his goal. Satan could not help but wish his downfall.

A valid hypothesis. Except that it fails to take into account the future Seer's earlier suicide attempt. And his illness. And also the timing: his fall occurred on the eve of Simhat Torah.

'The Seer's life belonged to the crowds who worshipped him,' said my grandfather. 'His death belonged to him alone. One must respect it and approach it with great care.'

So be it. May legend have the upper hand. Once more. Satan: the obvious culprit, he explains everything but settles nothing. And so, after all, he was the one who pushed the Seer and provoked his fall. No wonder: solitary men attract him.

... Outside, in Lublin, there was dancing and singing. The throngs were rejoicing in the Law, becoming drunk on memories and hope. Defeated, the Seer lay on the ground, his body writhing in pain. The celebration was at its height.

Israel of Rizhin

When Israel Baal Shem Tov felt his hour approaching, he promised the disciples gathered at his bedside that as soon as he would arrive in heaven, he would use all his influence to hasten the coming of the Messiah.

When his soul reached heaven, he expressed the wish to meet the Redeemer. His wish was granted; one refuses nothing to a Baal Shem. But the encounter provoked in him such exultation, such ecstasy, and lifted his soul to such heights, that he forgot his promise.

His successor, the Great Maggid of Mezeritch, knew of this mishap and was determined not to fall into the same trap. 'I shall know how to immunize myself against ecstasy,' he vowed before he left this world. 'I shall not ask to see the Messiah. I shall see everyone but him; and so he will go down to earth.'

But to disarm him, he was made into an angel, and he too forgot what he owed the people below.

'I shall not let it happen to me,' promised Levi-Yitzhak of Berditchev. 'I shall not succumb to temptation or submit to any order. I shall refuse to enter paradise, I shall refuse to leave human history. I shall annoy and go on annoying the Judge of all judges, the Father of all living things. I shall tell Him what His duties are towards His children, who are less stubborn than He. I shall speak, I shall shout . . .'

He did stir up much noise, and did oppose resistance. To their astonishment, the angels had to use force to push him into paradise.

'Do not worry,' said Israel of Rizhin, who told this tale, 'do not be afraid, I tell you. I shall resist better and longer. I shall not forget.'

I confess my prejudice in favour of this last Rebbe. As a Wizsnitzer Hasid, my grandfather felt close to Rizhin. And so do I. Wizsnitz is but a branch of Rizhin, and Rizhin is . . .
'What is Rizhin, Grandfather?'

'Rizhin is the House of Rizhin, full of daily wonders and splendour. Rizhin is the Hasidic kingdom in constant state of celebration, it is Jerusalem away from Jerusalem.'

And after a while: 'And the Rizhiner . . .'

He smiled nostalgically. My grandfather always smiled when talking about the first Rebbe of Rizhin, usually referred to as 'the Rizhiner'. And my childish heart was pounding while listening to him.

'The poorest land has its king; and this king has the Rizhiner's face. I am sorry I didn't know him. I was born too late. Ten years or so after his death . . . It seems that our Rebbe looks like him . . . so they say . . . Well, the same sap nourishes the tree and the branch; still, the branch is not the tree.'

Grandfather stopped talking but went on dreaming. He smiled at someone and I tried vainly to guess at whom. But in my memory his smile remains associated with the Rizhiner.

To evoke his image is to tell his story, a disturbing story, both beautiful and deceptively simple. A story which marks the beginning of an era and the end of another. After him the Hasidic movement was no longer the same. After him came the inevitable process of decline. The source recedes into the distance and we find that we are no longer thirsty.

It happens whenever and wherever man, moved by compassion, attempts to change the existing order and accepts responsibility for a world he has not created. He takes a step forward, he stretches out his hand to a friend, a companion, a stranger perhaps. Refusing merely to speak of love, friendship and truth, he decides to live them. He rejects mediocrity and evil, vulgarity, falsehood and easy solutions. He considers himself a revolutionary, determined to discover new paths, willing to fight the universe and its ruler. If he fails, no great harm is done; he'll start again tomorrow.

But woe unto him who succeeds. Nothing corrupts revolutionary movements more – and more radically – than success. For the first generation, the pioneering one, is followed by that of opportunists. The third continues the first out of habit; the fourth, out of inertia. Eventually the movement turns its battle inward, splitting into factions, groups, sects, one against the other, one against all. Substance gives way to superficiality. Personalities replace ideas; slogans replace ideals. The lofty goals are lost; the message is forgotten. Now the struggle revolves around titles and positions. The process is predictable, ineluctable. No surprise is eternal, no passion immortal. At dawn, night will have lost its prophets and their promises. No school ever succeeded in keeping alive the vision and aspirations of its founders. Nothing is harder than to maintain the dream after it has moulded reality. Nothing is as dangerous for victory, be it spiritual, than victory itself. If Moses led the Hebrews through the desert for forty years, it was perhaps to preserve the authenticity of their first victory over the Pharaoh and themselves. One does not win battles without paying a price, and it is usually one's innocence. Whatever the triumph, sooner or later it begets conditions which call it into question.

All this has been illustrated by most movements. And in a way, on a reduced and infinitely less harmful scale, it has also been illustrated by the non-violent though revolutionary movement of Hasidism. The story of Israel of Rizhin could therefore serve as both example and warning.

Born in 1797, Israel of Rizhin was Hasidism's favourite child and last undisputed leader. Was it because he was the great-grandson of the Maggid of Mezeritch that he enjoyed a special privileged status? Be that as it may, he had no known enemies or even opponents. People loved him, asked nothing more than to love him. They forgave him everything: his predilection for solitude, his lack of erudition, his pride, and in a more general way, the new path he was taking, so different from the one the Baal Shem had opened a century earlier in the Carpathian Mountains.

From the very beginning, he behaved like a spoiled child, a prince entitled to all honours. 'I was seven,' he said, 'when I visited Vienna. There I was received with such pomp that nothing impresses me any more.' Nothing but the best was good enough for him. Whatever he wanted, he was given. His every whim was satisfied. His elegant suits were made to measure. He was both handsome and rich, and from the beginning he craved wealth and loved beauty. During the latter part of his reign he owned a palace with servants, musicians and stables. His synagogue in Sadigor accommodated three thousand worshippers. He never went anywhere without a suite of a hundred or so aides, cooks, coachmen, musicians and intimates. On Passover his guests were served on golden dishes. Rizhin was a temple and the Rebbe its royal presence. Every Shabbat brought another attempt to re-create the lost splendours of Jerusalem. The singing was reminiscent of the Levites; the repasts evoked memories of sacrificial ceremonies.

Hasidim, by the thousands, converged upon Rizhin and, later,

Sadigor, simply to be in Rizhin and Sadigor, simply to see the prince in his palace, the prince on his throne, the prince and his wealth – and strange as it may sound, nobody was shocked, nobody called it scandalous; the Rebbe was above reproach, beyond judgement.

There were great Masters among those who came to see him: Hersh Riminover, Yitzhak-Meir of Ger, Yitzhak of Worke, Haim of Tzanz – and even a rabbi as far removed from Hasidism as Shamshon-Raphael Hirsch of Frankfort. None lifted an eyebrow. All returned to their homes impressed if perhaps not conquered by the Rizhiner's personality.

True, they realized how different his concept of Hasidism was from theirs, from the one they had received from their Masters. Once upon a time, in Medzebozh and Mezeritch, in Tchernobil and Berditchev, the Hasid had tried to overcome poverty by means other than money, to defeat sadness by means other than ostentation. Hasidism in those days mocked appearances and denigrated comfort. The Baal Shem had lived in misery and so had his disciples. They had advocated joy within misery, hope despite misfortune, despite injustice. They had believed in generosity towards others and severity towards themselves. They had lived for each other, for their fellow man; they had helped one another attain knowledge, and above all, self-knowledge. They had lived and survived, fully realizing their needs and desires.

Once upon a time Hasidism had meant emphasis on inner truth and fervour; a return to nature, to genuine beauty, to identification. A Hasid would see a tree and become that tree; he would hear the song of a shepherd and become that song and that shepherd – that was his way of coming closer to the essence of man. He had no need for castles and servants in order to feel at home in God's creation. To possess meant nothing, to be meant everything. Thus, it is no coincidence that the heroes of the Baal Shem's legends were mostly beggars. His way of telling us that it is more important to possess oneself than to possess; more important to be than to appear.

But in Rizhin it was the aristocracy that set the law. In Rizhin, greatness had to be displayed to be recognized. What counted was the mask, not the face; the reflection, not the source.

The question naturally arises; why? What did Israel of Rizhin want to prove, discover or refute? Whom was he challenging? What game was he playing and – most importantly – why was he permitted to play?

The fact is he could have been criticized, castigated for his style of living, for the economic and social gap he was creating between himself and his followers; but he wasn't. He could have been opposed and challenged on the grounds that within Hasidic terms of reference, his extravagance was bordering on heresy. But he wasn't. He was free to do and say whatever he wanted, in any way he chose. As a founder of a dynasty, he was protected, untouchable.

It is said that when Avraham Yehoshua Heschel of Apt proclaimed a day of fasting and prayer out of solidarity with a certain Jewish community in distress, on that same day the Rizhiner Rebbe summoned his musicians to play for him. Yet the Apter Rebbe did not take it as an affront. His only comment: 'No one can understand the ways of the Rizhiner.' Other Rebbes adopted the same attitude. Out of respect rather than complacency. He was a Rebbe unlike others, a special case, a destiny apart.

But why such favouritism? Why such privileges? What made him so special? The fact that he was the direct descendant of the Mezeritcher Maggid? Or because he represented, almost from the beginning, a real force within the movement, a force with which other leaders had to reckon? Was there something else, and if so, what was it?

Whatever the reason, the fact remains that his popularity kept growing; his fanatic followers saw to it. His legend exerted a magic appeal on the masses, it captivated their imagination, starved for things sublime. His biography – embellished by popular storytellers – became that of a saint, prophet and prince in Israel. It was said that his soul was among the four Moses brought back with him when he returned to earth at Sinai. The other three being those of Shimon Bar-Yohai, Yitzhak Lurie and Israel Baal Shem Tov.

The Rizhiner himself claimed that he had been on earth three times. First as a young prince in the Kingdom of Judea, then as a young priest in the Temple; this was the third time.

Once, when he was five – or ten, opinions vary – his ritual belt slipped and fell to the ground in the presence of his powerful protector, the old Rebbe of Apt. The old Tzaddik bent down, picked it up and girded the youngster's waist, explaining: 'This is how one performs the commandment of *Glila*, of girding the scrolls of the Torah.' On another occasion he said: 'The Rizhiner has forgotten nothing of what the angels taught him before he was born.'

Perhaps that explains why, as a child, he refused to study. His tutor reportedly complained that his illustrious pupil was not the most promising of students. Could young Israel's refusal to read the required books, to prepare his homework be ascribed to lack of interest or ambition? That seems unlikely. More probably, it was excessive ambition and a desire to do everything better and faster by taking shortcuts. And also to show he had received the Torah 'directly from God'. Soon he became so sure of himself that he professed having no need to study. Whatever he said became interesting and important because he said it. To Moshe of Savran, who came to visit, he showed his stable and spoke with pride of his magnificent stallions. All the pious and saintly visitor found to say afterwards, in the way of commentary, was: 'All this talk of horses was allegorical. Actually, the Rizhiner was referring to the celestial chariots, symbols of the mystical relationship the Creator maintains with creation.'

His more formal discourses, though rare, were not particularly scholarly. A few commentaries on Torah, several ingenious findings on Midrash and Zohar. What people remembered mainly were his sayings. For instance: 'How is one to distinguish the silent sage from the silent fool? The sage doesn't mind being silent.' Also: 'Look around you. Works of art everywhere are cherished, honoured and protected, while man – God's masterpiece – lies in the dust.' But even his most ardent admirers admit that his personality was his strength; his impact was due to the quality of his presence, not to his scholarship.

A certain Yaakov-Yosseph of Koretz told him of his plans to move to a remote village to be a schoolteacher. 'What?' exclaimed the Rizhiner. 'Another schoolteacher? No! I want you to become rich!' And so great was the Hasid's faith in his Rebbe that he went into business and in a few short years amassed an immense fortune.

Was that the Rizhiner's secret? His ability to push his followers to the limits of their potential? And beyond? Perhaps. But then why did he need such pageantry? The Baal Shem in his wooden hut had caused incomparably deeper changes in his faithful. In fact, the Rizhiner's ostentatious wealth should have repelled and offended many a visitor. It didn't. On the contrary. As his fortunes multiplied, more and more poor people flocked to his court. What attracted them? Curiosity? A possibility of sublimation? Escapism? The fact that they liked him, worshipped him, proves that they needed someone like him to admire and idolize. Perhaps they needed to see that it was possible for a Jew to live like a prince; for them he was a reflection of past grandeur, a continuation of ancient and glorious times. He reminded them of what they had once been. There was so much poverty lurking behind every door, so much fear to be contained in every heart, that the sight of a Jew crowned and gratified was enough for them. He was their illusion, their holiday.

Still, it became necessary to invent a plausible explanation that would justify his eccentricities. So they said: 'Poor Rebbe. Beneath his princely robes he is dressed in straw. We honour him, but his heart is in mourning.' And they would shake their heads: 'Poor, poor Rebbe. His shiny leather shoes are without soles; he walks on snow, his body is bruised. He suffers even while he appears happy.' The proof? He never ate in public, slept three hours a night, spoke little, sought solitude and eschewed noise. In constant meditation, he moved in other worlds. But what about his properties? His valuables? His riches? He had to accept them. In order to fool Satan. For where would Satan set his traps for the Just? In synagogues, in Houses of Study, in the poorhouse, but surely not in a princely palace, under the golden robes of someone whose demeanour was that of a nobleman, not that of a Tzaddik. Satan covets only the humble; the conceited, the already corrupted leave him indifferent. That is why, they maintained in Rizhin, the Rebbe had to cover himself with gold and show himself proud.

And proud he was. Just like his father, Rebbe Shalom-Shakhne, the Maggid of Mezeritch's grandson.

The Kotzker Rebbe had said: 'God is where He is allowed to enter.' For Shalom-Shakhne, it was: 'God is where I am.' To Barukh of Medzebozh, who offered to join forces with him and rule the world, Shalom-Shakhne is said to have replied: 'Thank you, but I can manage perfectly well alone.'

Thus the Rizhiner followed a pattern. Authoritarian, arrogant, he brooked contradiction from nobody. To annoy him was a risky affair. He warned people that 'he who speaks evil of me is guilty of blasphemy and will be blackened in this world and the other'. By offending him, one exposed oneself to losing one's sanity, one's livelihood, one's life.

Once he urged a merchant to increase his donation to a certain charity.

'Rebbe,' the man objected, 'I don't mix in your business, please don't mix in mine.'

'Nu-nu,' answered the Rizhiner. 'We shall see.'

The man went bankrupt.

Another version of the same story:

'If you don't mend your ways,' the Rizhiner warned, 'you won't stay rich.'

'Then you won't stay Rebbe,' came the reply.

'*Nu-nu*,' said the Rizhiner. 'We shall see.'

And the poor rich man discovered the price of disrespect and the meaning of poverty.

To his admirers who were indulging in Hasidic 'elbow-pushing' around him, he said: 'Why must all of you be near me? Isn't it enough to be in one room with me, under one roof, sharing one sky?'

When the Seraph Uri of Strelisk died, his followers came to the Rizhiner and asked him to be their Rebbe.

'If you want to stay,' he told them, 'stay. But on one condition: learn to say your prayers silently, respectfully.'

To a child crying with disappointment because the Rebbe did not have six wings – like the angels in Talmudic descriptions – he murmured softly: 'But yes, I do have them; I have six sons.'

Yet despite his fame and munificence, his life unfolded under the sign of tragedy. The son who went astray. The twenty-two months spent in prison. The escapes, the tribulations, the years of uncertainty and waiting, the burden of responsibilities. Like his father and grandfather before him, he died young. Of his grandfather he said: 'He came down, did what he had to do and went back. What's the use of lingering down here?' He, too, owed it to himself to live as fast and as intensely as possible – and not linger.

He was engaged at seven, married at thirteen, and at sixteen he ascended the rabbinic throne. At forty he was arrested and jailed in the fortress at Kiev, summarily charged with treason and complicity in murder. He was linked with a vaguely formulated plot aiming to crown him 'King of the Jews', and the assassination of two informers. Eighty other Jewish dignitaries were taken into custody at the same time.

The Rizhiner's imprisonment sent shudders through the Jewish community. His faithful moved heaven and earth to free him. Clergymen were asked to intercede. Ministers were petitioned, governors bribed. The Czar himself was approached. Intrigued by the story of a 'Jewish king', the ruler of all Russians ordered him brought before him. The story goes that just as the Czar was about to set him free, their eyes met, and the Czar decided he had 'the eyes of a revolutionary' and sent him back to solitary confinement.

Chronicles relate that the august prisoner cried often, 'but never in the presence of strangers'.

After his release on bail he fled to Austria, where he changed his name and nationality. Austria and Turkey offered him citizenship, but to the astonishment of officialdom, he requested to have his documents show him to be a citizen of . . . Jerusalem.

Nor were his troubles over. He continued to be a hunted man. The Russian authorities wanted him back. His case became a complicated international affair involving governments on the highest level. Metternich studied his case, the British ambassador was instructed by his government to follow developments closely and report back. St Petersburg requested, demanded, threatened and spared no effort to secure his extradition – and failed. The Rizhiner, settled in his new estate at Patik near Sadigor, now had influential Austrian protectors. Thanks to his presence and his activities, the area prospered and bloomed. The economic situation of the people in and around Sadigor had never been so good. The region had become a new centre of attraction. Thus, even the Gentiles had good reason to pray for the Rizhiner's safety and freedom.

Among Jews, his fame reached unprecedented heights. With the added aura of martyrdom his position now was even more secure and unchallenged. The most puritan Hasid could no longer object to his royal privileges: he had paid for them. Even the Rebbe of Kotzk, the fierce and savage seeker of truth, the uncompromising enemy of vanity, paid him homage. Only a man chosen by God becomes target and victim of the Czar. Any man who suffers unjustly becomes God's instrument. If punishments bear the divine seal, the same is true for rewards. After spending almost two years in prison – for nothing – a man acquires certain rights, including the right to assert that life in a palace is but a new, unexplored dimension of his trials. To deny him this right is to repudiate the cause of the one who suffers and of suffering as well.

Thus, people flocked to him in ever larger numbers. To see, to touch the one who had come from far away bearing such memories. Add to that the striking beauty of his person. Whoever saw him could not forget him. He inspired such awe as one might expect to feel in the presence of a king risen from the depths. Everything about him was regal, even his melancholy air, his reassuring gestures, his reserve. His painful past became a bond. It is easier to confide in someone who has suffered greatly. And then, he knew what words were needed to inspire confidence, to reassure. His good sense and logic were proverbial; many famous Gentiles came to seek his advice. A frequent visitor was Marshal Wittgenstein (in 1828), who liked to discuss world events with him. Rich and poor, pious and enlightened, peasants and intellectuals, to all of them Sadigor meant warmth and reassurance, if only for one encounter, one Shabbat.

Was the Rizhiner considered a miracle-maker? Not really. Rather a sage. He was known for his wisdom, not for his mystical powers. He was too modern, too liberal a man to indulge in meddling with the supernatural. When told that gangs of hoodlums were attacking defenceless Jews in his own town, he was not content just to pray for their safety: he ordered the younger men to organize groups of self-defence. He wanted his Hasidim to be healthy and normal, free of complexes. To set an example, he himself rode horses, exercised, and cut his own wood every morning.

He possessed yet another quality that made him even more appealing to his people: a sense of humour.

A man once said to him: 'Rebbe, I so wish to repent, but I don't know what to do.'

'And to sin, you knew what to do?'

'Yes, but that was easy. First I sinned, then I knew.'

'Exactly. Now do the same the other way around. Start by repenting; you'll know later.'

Rebbe Meir of Premishlan once sent him a letter with an urgent question: 'Custom requires one to eat kreplach on Shavuot. How many should one eat? There is no book to tell us. Yet one would be too little, three too many, and two is an even number, and we know that even numbers come from unholy spheres. What is one to do?' The Rizhiner – unruffled – provided this solution: 'Eat one – but make sure it is as large as two.'

A pragmatist, he urged his Hasidim not to waste the possible for the impossible, immediate gains for remote or abstract rewards. He advised them to help one another instead of aspiring to redeem generations yet unborn, to raise themselves one step above the ground instead of walking on clouds. He urged them to keep their means as pure as their purpose, if not more. Often he illustrated his ideas with tales and parables. One theme came back again and again: A traveller loses his way in the forest; it is dark and he is afraid. Danger lurks behind every tree. A storm shatters the silence. The fool looks at the lightning, the wise man at the road that lies – illuminated – before him. The first task of the traveller is to find his way back to man's world; then he may think of ways to change its face.

'Rebbe,' a Hasid asked, 'how is one to worship God without lying to oneself?'

'I'll tell you how. Make believe that you're an acrobat walking a tightrope high above a precipice. What can you do to keep your balance? Whenever your body pulls you to one side, you must pull to the other.'

And also: 'In your daily occupations, remember this: don't do anything that is forbidden, and even that which is permitted, do without undue haste.'

Eloquent and pithy, he knew how to laugh at himself.

'The Talmud,' he said, 'compares Satan to an old, foolish king. I understand why he may be a king; he rules over man's passions. Why old? Because he is older than man himself. But why a fool? This I finally understood when I was in jail. He was with me, even there. I said to him: "Fool that you are! Why are you here? I have no choice – but you?"'

He disliked Maimonides. First, because Maimonides was a philosopher, and philosophy was not the Rizhiner's strongest subject, and second . . .

'I'll tell you why. Theoretically I should like him, for he refutes Aristotle's theories, so dangerous for the faith. But imagine Jews like you and me reading Aristotle's theories in Maimonides' work and falling asleep *before* he refutes them?'

Like all Hasidic Masters, he saw God's presence in every man, in everything: 'Man,' he said, 'cannot *not* do God's will. Even the wicked obey Him. If their negation has any strength, it is His. Fortunately for them, they are not aware of it. If they were, they would die of spite.'

Yet despite his agile mind and sharp tongue, he lost three verbal duels.

The first to a ferryman, the man who helped him flee Tsarist Russia by carrying him on his shoulders. They were wading through the river at night when the man suddenly stopped and said: 'Rebbe, if you want me to continue to the other side, you had better promise me a place in paradise right now.'

The Rizhiner conceded: this was not the place or the time to argue.

The second defeat came on the occasion of the engagement ceremony of his son to Hersh Riminover's daughter. In the presence of dozens of noted guests and hundreds of their admirers, the Rizhiner addressed them as follows:

'It is the custom on such occasions, before the signing of the contracts, for the parents of the future couple to recall who they are and who their ancestors were. Well, know that my grandfather was Rebbe Avraham Malakh, a saint, an angel among men. His father was the celebrated Maggid of Mezeritch, who was himself a direct descendant of Yehuda Hanassi, Yohanan the Shoemaker and King David. And you, Riminover Rebbe, what is your lineage?'

'Oh, I am neither son nor grandson of rabbis,' Hersh of Riminov answered. 'My father was a simple tailor, poor but honest. He taught me neither the timeless truths of Torah nor the splendours of the Zohar. Still, he did teach me something about his trade. Yes, he taught me never to spoil what is new, and always to mend what is old.'

The Rizhiner smiled and kept silent.

The third episode opposed him to his friend Meir of Premishlan. They met on the road. Rebbe Meir travelled in a modest cart drawn by a pitifully skinny horse, while Israel of Rizhin was seated in a sumptuous carriage with four exuberant horses in harness. The Rizhiner, ill-at-ease, felt the need to explain, apologize: 'The roads are bad, there has been so much rain. One horse alone would not be enough to pull me out of the mud . . . just in case.'

'I understand,' said the Rebbe of Premishlan, who liked to speak of himself in the third person. 'Yes, Meir understands. Mud is a danger and horses can be of help. But, you see, Meir has only one horse and so he must be careful, very careful indeed, not to sink into the mud.'

Again the Rizhiner smiled and said nothing.

But usually the last word was his. And not only when talking with friends or admirers. There are those who insinuate that what he really wanted was to be the last man to pronounce the last word in history and the first thereafter; in other words, that he dreamed of incarnating the Messiah.

Did he actually believe himself qualified for the role? Some of his remarks indicate that he did. For instance, he said: 'All the Tzaddikim speak of the day of redemption, but I remain silent. It reminds me of a wedding. The parents and relatives are agitated. And noisy. Only the bridegroom stands aside, sombre and impassive. And remains silent!'

This theory would in a way explain his affinity for silence, his whims, his taste for pomp, by linking them to the expectation that the Messiah will be more than Saviour; he will be King, the king of times to come.

And here I must confess that I, grandson of Dodye Feig, Hasid of Wizsnitz, am unable to accept this theory. The Rizhiner was too clever, too lucid a man to play a game whose perils he well knew. He knew the end that lies in store for false Messiahs. The true Messiah does not behave like a Messiah. He does not covet honours or gold. Nor does he reveal what must remain hidden. The Rizhiner knew all this, he had to know.

How then is one to interpret his parable about the wedding? Could he have seen himself not as the bridegroom, but as a guest, a special guest close to the bridegroom, and closer than anyone to the Messiah? Was that why he spoke of him so often? More than any of the other Hasidic Masters? Hasidism, as conceived and elaborated in Rizhin, was more Messiah-oriented than any other.

He may have sensed that only the Messiah could save future generations of Jews from the fate that was awaiting them. The last of the great early Masters, he saw himself as heir to the Maggid of Mezeritch and the Baal Shem. Like them, he strove to mark the future. His failings and failures do him honour; they are those of a man determined to force God's hand. Such a man must lose.

Obsessed, literally, by the messianic promise, the Rizhiner understood that man will never be strong enough to bring about universal change. Like the Grandfather of Shpole and Levi-Yitzhak of Berditchev, he turned to God and took part in His quarrels with man, and like his predecessors, pleaded the cause of man.

He said: 'It is written that *it is because of our sins that we were chased from our land*; and I say that is false. Exile preceded our sins. Just bring us back and You shall see that not one Jew will feel like sinning.'

Another time: 'You must put an end to exile because exile itself is a sin; the most dangerous of all.'

And also: 'Be our Father and we shall be Your servants; we shall be Your servants only if You are our Father.'

He addressed God in terms reminiscent of Levi-Yitzhak of Berditchev, but with less humility: 'I am not a slave come to ask favours of the king. I come as a counsellor to discuss matters of state.'

One day he cried out: 'Master of the Universe, how many years do we know each other? How many decades? So please permit me to wonder: is this any way to rule Your world? The time has come for You to have mercy on Your people! And if You refuse to listen to me, then tell me: what am I doing here on this earth of Yours?'

Another time he shouted angrily: 'Why is the Messiah so late in coming? Does he think the next generation will be better? More deserving? I tell him here and now that he is wrong! They will be worse, much worse!'

His exceptional intuition helped him decipher the future. He foresaw what was to come. The world was doomed, mankind rushing to its fall. In a dehumanized, arid universe, robbed of desire and salvation, disorder would be on a cosmic scale and so would guilt. With the dawning of the end of time, good and evil would go hand in hand, would become one. Light would become indistinguishable from darkness, daybreak from dusk, silence from words, words from truth, truth from fear and fear from death.

Yes, he was a tragic figure, for he sensed the futility of his endeavours. 'A day will come,' he said, 'when ignorance will reign. Mediocre men will feel at ease on earth and above, while men of spirit and conscience will be alienated. The most pious Jew will be incapable of reciting a verse from the Psalms. I tell you this so you will know: that is how it will have to be, that is how it will be.'

Another prediction: 'A day will come when all nations will begin hating Jews; they will hate them so much, with such passion and violence, that the Jews will have no choice but to go to the land of their ancestors, to the Holy Land. And then, woe unto us and woe unto them, for it will be the beginning of redemption.'

Once he explained why he liked to marry people but refused to intercede in heaven for them to have children: 'I foresee that from the next century on, people will have souls so ugly, so repulsive, that one will not be able to stand their sight. Well, we must accept what we are given – but pray to obtain it? No.'

The most striking of his visions: 'A day will come when man will stop hating others and hate himself; a day will come when all things will lose their coherence, when there will be no relation between man and his face, desire and its object, question and its answer.'

And then, this story he loved to tell:

A young Hasid of the great Maggid of Mezeritch married the daughter of a fierce Mitnagged, who forced him to choose between his family and his Rebbe. The son-in-law swore that he would not return to Mezeritch. But after a few months, or perhaps years, he could not resist the impulse to join his companions and their

Master. When he returned home his angry father-in-law marched him to the local rabbi for a judgement. The rabbi consulted the *Shulkhan Arukh* and issued this verdict: since he had broken his promise, the young man was to give his wife a divorce at once. Overnight the young man found himself on the street. He had no means of his own, no relations. Inconsolable, refusing all nourishment, the young Hasid fell sick. With no one to care for him, he died shortly after.

'Well,' continued the Rizhiner, 'when the Messiah will come, the young Hasid will file a complaint against his father-in-law and the local rabbi, both guilty of his premature death. The first will say: "I obeyed the rabbi." The rabbi will say: "I obeyed the *Shulkhan Arukh*." And the Messiah will say: "The father-in-law is right, the rabbi is right and the Law is right." Then he will kiss the young plaintiff and say: "But I, what do I have to do with them? I have come for those who are not right." '

The messianic idea and dream were so deeply rooted in the Rizhiner that he – or his son David-Moshe of Chortkov, opinions vary on this – prepared a special room in his apartments called the 'Messiah's chamber'. All his most valuable and valued belongings were stored there and no one was allowed inside.

Still, as time went on, the Rizhiner must have felt that he would die without having welcomed the 'Bridegroom'. He had long struggled with sadness. Towards the end of his life, he yielded to sorrow.

The prison experience had marked him, and made him withdraw further into solitude. He now received his disciples only on Fridays. Like his great-grandfather, the Maggid of Mezeritch, he would retire to his room for prayers, while in an adjoining room, the faithful prayed, relying on a disciple posted at the door to signal the beginning or end of various passages in the service.

Little is known about his last moments. Not as much as about his son Nahum's, who, several hours before he died, washed from head to toes, put on his Shabbat clothes, lay down on his bed and bade his friends sing; and sang with them until they sang no more.

The Rizhiner was given more time to prepare. On the eve of his last Yom Kippur, he paused on the synagogue's threshold, put his hand on the mezuzah and murmured: 'May I become sacrifice and expiate for the entire household of Israel.'

He died one month later. He was fifty-four.

*

One hundred and twenty years later, the Rizhiner is more enigmatic than ever.

His habits, his talents, his tastes and his charisma; his tendency toward exhibitionism and theatrics remain a mystery for the student or Hasid who, like myself, believes in his greatness.

It is difficult to accept the idea that he loved riches for the sake of riches. True, he was neither philosopher nor teacher, but he was a remarkable figure, an influential leader; all testimonies agree on that point. Such a Rebbe is not drawn to wealth for the usual reasons. I choose to think that his ambitions were not materialistic. I would like to believe that he was trying to prove something, defy someone; we shall never know what or whom. And perhaps that is the way he wanted it. It may be part of the mystery he wished to create around himself. Just as we do not understand the extreme asceticism of the solitary Rebbe of Kotzk, we find it difficult to understand the extreme taste for luxury of the Rizhiner. Who knows, perhaps the two attitudes were meant to conceal one and the same secret.

That he did not amass the gold and silver for himself is certain. An austere Master such as Haim of Tzanz said: 'The Rebbe of Rizhin is ready at every moment to sacrifice himself for the people of Israel.'

For the student assessing the totality of his deeds and words, there can be no doubt: the Rizhiner, his gaze reaching far into the distance, thought and acted always in collective terms; his plans transcended the limits of possession. He was concerned with what was in store for man and his soul; nothing else.

The pomp and pageantry of his court? Perhaps this was his way of consoling and comforting his poor Hasidim by showing them that the dream was there; that they could see it if they tried, and that the reality of exile does not preclude the royal vision of redemption. Perhaps this was his way of reminding them that *malkhut* – royalty – is also an attribute to God, and that the God of Israel is also King of Israel, a king whose often destroyed and dispersed kingdom nevertheless remains indestructible. Perhaps he wanted to add emphasis to Reb Aharon Karliner's warning: 'We are all princes; to forget that, is the gravest sin of all.'

Could he have had still greater ambitions and justifications? Perhaps. Renunciation contains a certain joy, a certain kind of ecstasy no possession can provide. Could the Rizhiner Rebbe have chosen flagrant dramatics and wealth out of despair, or rather: to attain despair? Could he have tried to go to the end of his satiated desires in order to reach his own naked being? Is it conceivable that having come to the realization that he would never resemble his ancestors, the Maggid and the Baal Shem, he wished to show them that despite his wealth and marks of distinction, despite appearances, he was following in their footsteps? And that appearances have their own secrets? Is that why he so frequently referred to the Messiah? To bring an end, once and for all, to appearances?

Of course, these are so many hypotheses. For me, Israel of Rizhin remains a mystery; he resists analysis. As much as I like the character, something about him troubles me. I feel it is too pat an explanation to point out the ease of attaining purity inside misery, and that true merit consists in living alone in a crowd; in remaining humble at the peak of fame and poor in the midst of wealth. Instinctively, I am suspicious of material gains accompanied by spiritual justifications. The scenery may well influence both the action and the cast on stage. The means *can* influence the end. And every game runs the risk of ultimately defining itself by its own rules.

We are back to the question: who is Israel of Rizhin? I see him as a poet, a tragic visionary condemned to agonizing lucidity. He may have known he was the last of his dynasty. He may have known that after him Hasidism would not be the same. That future disciples would have the Masters they would deserve and that all would live and perish in a world that did not deserve them.

One thing he must have known: that it is not enough to call the Messiah to make him come.

Disciples IV

Before Hersh Ziditchoiv's soul was sent down to earth, Satan appeared before the celestial court to lodge a complaint: 'This soul must not be given to men; it will make saints of them. And signify my end. With Hersh of Ziditchoiv as my adversary, I am beaten in advance. I protest, I demand justice . . .'

The court deliberated and decided: 'Your argument is valid, but we cannot turn back. Our decisions are irrevocable. This soul that frightens you will inhabit Rebbe Hersh. But, to reassure you, another soul will be sent down for another man who will have all the signs, qualities and virtues of a Rebbe; the crowds will admire and praise him. And with the exception of this court and yourself, nobody will know that this man owes allegiance not to our sacred and divine authority but to you alone.'

How is one to know? How does one recognize purity in a man? And how can one be sure? I remember putting this question to my grandfather. He chuckled and his eyes twinkled when he answered: 'But one is never sure; nor should one be. Actually, it all depends on the Hasid; it is he who, in the final analysis, must justify the Rebbe.'

David Zlates, disciple of the Seer of Lublin, refused to become a rabbi. He persisted in wanting to remain disciple. After the Seer's death, he joined Hersh of Ziditchoiv's followers, then Meir of Premishlan's and, finally, Israel of Rizhin's

It is said that one Shabbat, the Seer invited him to recite the blessing customary at the end of a meal. Rebbe David demurred. 'I order you to obey,' shouted the Seer. 'Whoever accedes to the higher spheres may not retreat from them!' David did as he was told. But thereafter, whenever his followers came to seek his advice or help, they found his room empty. David the Hasid was with another Master. As a simple Hasid.

'You'll grow up, you'll see,' my grandfather had said. 'You'll see that it is more difficult, more rare to find a Hasid than a Rebbe. To induce others to believe is easier than to believe. To give, easier

than receive. And,' added grandfather, 'a Hasid is more to be envied than his Master.'

Menahem-Mendl of Riminov said: 'To pronounce useless words is to commit murder.'

Moshe of Ujhely waited his whole life for the Messiah; he never went to bed at night without reminding his sons: 'If he comes, wake me right away!'

Near the end of his life, this is how he spoke to God: 'Master of the Universe, my strength is gone; I am exhausted. You must send us the Messiah. You have no choice. Don't think I'm asking this for my own salvation. If you wish, I am ready to deny myself even a single ray of light and joy. Believe me, I am ready to sacrifice my life and my soul and undergo the terrors of eternal night if that be the price of Israel's redemption. I know, Master of the Universe, that I am the last of the last, but I love truth and I say: if I had known that my hair would turn white without my eyes ever beholding the Saviour, I could not have gone on living. You held me, you kept me going with hope, with faith. You procrastinated, day after day, hour after hour. You fooled me. Is it really so clever, so charitable, to mock an old man like me? I ask You!'

I remember grandfather blessing me: 'May you see the Messiah put an end to exile and the reign of evil.' A blessing that almost came true. It was night. I found myself transported into a strange and distant kingdom. In the shadow of the flames, the exiled were gathered. They came from everywhere, they spoke every language and all told the same story. Seeing them together under the fiery sky, the child in me had thought: This is it; this is the end of time, the end of everything. Any moment the Messiah will appear out of the night, the Messiah of fear, the Messiah of death. I thought of my grandfather and I trembled for him, for myself. And for his blessing.

Said Hune of Kolochitz: 'Nothing and nobody down here frightens me; not even an angel, not even the angel of fear. But the moaning of a beggar makes me shudder.'

And Moshe-Leib of Sassov to his friend Uri of Strelisk: 'You cross the country from one end to the other, collecting money to free this man from prison, marry this orphan girl, help that widow. I know, I know all that. But I have no money; never had any. I would like to help you and I don't know how. I would like to do something for you, but I don't know what — Wait! I've got it! I know what to do; I know how to help you: Uri, my friend, Rebbe of Strelisk, I shall dance for you!.

And I try to imagine my grandfather in the train that carried him away. They tell that some danced, others sang and still others prayed — fervently, joyously, as though they anticipated a celebration, a reunion. And he? I try to see him, but I cannot. And so I shall never know whether my grandfather, Dodye Feig, the Wiznitzer Hasid, went to his death singing or dancing for a man, for a child, or for a tale he will never tell.

When the great Israel Baal Shem Tov saw misfortune threatening the Jews, it was his custom to go into a certain part of the forest to meditate. There he would light a fire, say a special prayer, and the miracle would be accomplished and the misfortune averted.

Later, when his disciple, the celebrated Maggid of Mezeritch, had occasion, for the same reason, to intercede with heaven, he would go to the same place in the forest and say: 'Master of the Universe, listen! I do not know how to light the fire, but I am still able to say the prayer.' And again the miracle would be accomplished.

Still later, Moshe-Leib of Sassov, in order to save his people once more, would go into the forest and say: 'I do not know the prayer, but I know the place and this must be sufficient.' It was sufficient and the miracle was accomplished.

Then it fell to Israel of Rizhin to overcome misfortune. Sitting in his armchair, his head in his hands, he spoke to God: 'I am unable to light the fire and I do not know the prayer; I cannot even find the place in the forest. All I can do is tell the story, and this must be sufficient.' And it was sufficient.

It no longer is. The proof is that the threat has not been averted. Perhaps we are no longer able to tell the story. Could all of us be guilty? Even the survivors? Especially the survivors?

One day the king summoned his counsellor and told him of his anguish: 'I have read in the stars that all those who will eat of the next harvest will be struck with madness. What shall we do, my friend?'

'Nothing could be more simple, Sire,' replied the counsellor, 'we shall not touch it. Last year's harvest is not yet exhausted. You have but to requisition it; it will be ample for you. And me.'

'And the others?' scolded the king. 'All the subjects of my kingdom? The faithful servants of the crown? The men, the women, the madmen and the beggars, are you forgetting them? Are you forgetting the children, the children too?'

'I am forgetting nobody, Sire. But as your adviser, I must be realistic and take all possibilities into account. We don't have enough reserves, not enough to protect and satisfy everyone. There will be just enough for you. And me.'

Thereupon the king's brow darkened, and he said: 'Your solution does not please me. Is there no other? Never mind. But I refuse to separate myself from my people and I don't care to remain lucid in the midst of a people gone mad. Therefore we shall all enter madness together. You and I like the others, with the others. When the world is gripped by delirium, it is senseless to watch from the outside: the mad will think that we are mad too. And yet, I should like to safeguard some reflection of our present glory and of our anguish too; I should like to keep alive the memory of this determination, this decision. I should like that when the time comes, you and I shall remain aware of our predicament.'

'Whatever for, Sire?'

'It will help us, you'll see. And thus we shall be able to help our friends. Who knows, perhaps thanks to us, men will find the strength to resist later, even if it is too late.'

And putting his arm around his friend's shoulders, the king went on: 'You and I shall therefore mark each other's foreheads with the seal of madness. And every time we shall look at one another, we shall know, you and I, that we are mad.'

In a distant land, a prince lost his mind and imagined himself a rooster. He sought refuge under the table and lived there, naked, refusing to partake of the royal delicacies served in golden dishes – all he wanted and accepted was the grain reserved for the roosters. The king was desperate. He sent for the best physicians, the most famous specialists; all admitted their incompetence. So did the magicians. And the monks, the ascetics, the miracle-makers; all their interventions proved fruitless.

One day an unknown sage presented himself at court. 'I think that I could heal the prince,' he said shyly. 'Will you allow me to try?'

The king consented, and to the surprise of all present, the sage removed his clothes, and joining the prince under the table, began to crow like a rooster.

Suspicious, the prince interrogated him: 'Who are you and what are you doing here?' – 'And you,' replied the sage, 'who are you and what are you doing here?' – 'Can't you see? I am a rooster!' – 'Hmm,' said the sage, 'how very strange to meet you here!' – 'Why strange?' – 'You mean, you don't see? Really not? You don't see that I'm a rooster just like you?'

The two men became friends and swore never to leave each other.

And then the sage undertook to cure the prince by using himself as an example. He started by putting on a shirt. The prince couldn't believe his eyes. – 'Are you crazy? Are you forgetting who you are? You really want to be a man?' – 'You know,' said the sage in a gentle voice, 'you mustn't ever believe that a rooster who dresses like a man ceases to be a rooster.' The prince had to agree. The next day both dressed in a normal way. The sage sent for some dishes from the palace kitchen. 'Wretch! What are you doing?' protested the prince, frightened in the extreme. 'Are you going to *eat* like them now?' His friend allayed his fears: 'Don't ever think that by eating like man, with man, at his table, a rooster ceases to be what he is; you mustn't ever believe that it is enough for a rooster to behave like a man to become human; you can do anything with man, in his world and even for him, and yet remain the rooster you are.'

And the prince was convinced; he resumed his life as a prince.

The author of these tales is Nahman of Bratzlav, whose stories are among the most spellbinding in Hasidic literature. They constitute a universe of their own in which dreamers go beyond their dreams, beyond their desires, swept away by their quest for imagination and salvation and an infinite craving for innocence and wonder.

(He reminds one of Franz Kafka, whom he preceded and – according to some – inspired. A tempting and even plausible hypothesis. Separated by more than a century – Rebbe Nahman was born in 1772 – the two men seem to have shared the themes and obsessions that lend their work its realistic yet dreamlike quality. Their heroes live their lives by imagining them, and their deaths by telling them.

There are more striking similarities: the Tzaddik from the Ukraine and the novelist from Prague both died young; the Rebbe at thirty-eight, the writer at forty-one. Cut down by the same ailment: tuberculosis. Both demanded that their writings be burned. And each had a faithful friend, a devoted interpreter, an apostle to whom we owe their work's survival. What Max Brod was for Kafka, Reb Nathan had been for Rebbe Nahman.

But while Rebbe Nahman wished his writings destroyed, he wanted to preserve their essence: 'Make my tales into prayers,' he told his followers. Prayers and not relics.

Before he died, he gave orders to throw his notes into the fire: 'To send them back up there.' Nathan believed it to be his duty to obey – and did. He lacked the combination of vision and audacity of a Max Brod. The tellers of tales resembled each other more than their two fervent apostles.)

Another story: that of the royal messenger unable to accomplish his mission.

The king had sent a letter to a wise but sceptical man, who, in his faraway province, refused to accept it. He was one of those men who think too much, who complicate their lives by complicating small things. He couldn't understand, not in the slightest, what the king might want of him: 'Why would the sovereign, so powerful and so rich, address himself to me, who am less than nothing? Because he takes me for a philosopher? There are more important ones. Could there be another reason? If so, what reason?'

Unable to answer these questions, he preferred to believe the letter a misunderstanding. Worse: a fraud. Worse yet: a practical joke. 'Your king,' he said to the messenger, 'does not exist.' But the messenger insisted: 'I am here, and here is the letter; isn't that proof enough?' – 'The letter proves nothing at all; besides, I haven't read it. And by the way, who gave it to you? The king in person?' – 'No,' confessed the messenger. 'It was given to me by a royal page. In his name.' – 'Are you sure of that? And how can you be sure that it comes from the reigning sovereign? Have you ever seen him?' – 'Never. My rank does not permit or warrant it.' – 'Then how do you know that the king is king? You see? You don't know any more than I.'

And without unsealing the letter, the sage and the messenger decided to learn the truth once and for all. They would go to the end of the world, they would question the very last of mortals, but they would know.

At the marketplace, they accosted a soldier: 'Who are you and what do you do?' – 'I am a soldier by trade and I am in the king's service.' – 'What king?' – 'The one to whom we swore allegiance; this land is his. We are all here to serve him.' – 'Do you know what he looks like?' – 'No.' – 'Then you have never seen him?' – 'Never.'

The two companions burst into laughter: 'Look at him! This man in uniform insists upon serving someone he has never seen and will never see!'

Further on, they met an officer: yes, he would willingly die for the king; no, he had never had the honour of seeing him, neither from close by nor from afar.

A general: same questions, same answers, clear and precise. He, too, thinks of nothing but to serve the king, he lives only for him and by him; and yet, even though he is a general, he cannot boast of ever having set his eyes upon the king.

'You see?' says the sceptical sage to the messenger. 'People are naïve and credulous, and rather foolish; they live a lie and are afraid of the truth.'

And they laugh. They laugh with such despair that in the end, they will understand that there must be a link between the voice and the call, between man and his road; in the end they will understand that their feeling of despair is not absurd, for it may well be the link that binds them to the king.

The king, in Rebbe Nahman's terms, is not the enemy of the sage, nor is the sage the enemy of the prince. All aspire to a particular metamorphosis in order to escape their condition. But whereas the hero of the Jewish novelist from Prague moves in a sordid universe, a universe dominated by dark violence and implacable ugliness, the Rebbe's hero wins the favour of the king.

All of Nahman's characters find themselves before obstacles to be overcome, walls to be climbed, strangers to be conciliated; only they succeed, their adventures end happily, in harmony rather than in renunciation. Once arrived at the end of their tribulations, they understand their meaning. Cast into the secret that awaits them and no other, they know that it is not evil; on the contrary, it spells liberation and salvation. Nothing in the romantic universe of Rebbe Nahman is truly evil; in the end, all things become man's allies.

Rebbe Nahman – or Hasidic imagination, the celebration of the word, the glorification of legend, inspired and bewitching. Rebbe Nahman – or flight directed inward.

A figure so complex as to either make you dream or make you lose the very desire to dream. His life, rich in exploits, seems to lie under the sign of paradox and fever, on mountain peaks and precipices, in outright hallucination and never, never in security.

A great-grandson of the Besht, he quarrels with almost every great personality that claims his heritage. As a Master, founder of a school, he transmits his vision of the world by telling tales, masterworks of their kind, rather than by enunciating theories. As a Kabbalist he is accessible, as a Rebbe he is not. Ascetic, an enemy of doubt, he frequents the so-called emancipated intellectual circles whose vocation and pastime it is to doubt and oppose asceticism. An intolerant believer, he plays chess with free-thinkers; their faith in nothingness intrigues him. Sick, he hates doctors; poor, he despises the rich. He forbids his disciples to read philosophical works, Maimonides included; yet he has read them all. Arrogant with some, humble with others, and always with the wrong person, he is never the same though he never changes, as though there were two of him. And sometimes the saint behaves like a comedian.

All this we know, thanks to Reb Nathan, his biographer turned hagiographer. His confidant too. The Master told, and went on telling, him his intimate thoughts fired up by delirium. His tormented childhood, his adolescence and his crises, his paroxysms of anxiety followed by surges of ecstasy. Detailed episodes, startling images often clumsily sketched: the facts and how they are told bear the mark of authenticity.

Thus we know that Nahman was a turbulent child, secretive and stubborn. A poor pupil, he cried easily and complained to God about God. He was a troubled, anxiety-ridden adolescent who sometimes would run away from home, visit the Baal Shem's grave and come back exhausted, his eyes aflame.

When he discovered his body, he had to muster all his strength to fight its desires, an excruciating fight described at great length in the notes taken down by Reb Nathan. But he emerged victorious. 'For me,' he said, 'men and women are all the same; I react to both in the same way.' And another time: 'From now on I shall fear woman no more than I fear the angel.'

His was an intense life, filled with 'falls and staggering ascensions', punctuated with fasting and sleeplessness. He suffered silently, 'his teeth clenched until they could have cracked a piece of wood' – and sometimes he would 'scream and howl quietly'. It was a life of disorder, streaked with lightning and painful, exalting sensations. 'He had ups and downs by the thousands, by the tens of thousands,' Reb Nathan said later. 'After much work, he would succeed in rising high – only to fall, over and over again, innumerable times in the course of a single day.'

Before Reb Nathan's advent, he had acquired a close friend in the person of a certain Reb Shimon; they studied together. One day Rebbe Nahman abruptly invited him to leave with him for Hungary and live there in anonymity and poverty. 'Here, too many people know me,' he said. 'They respect me for my lineage. In Hungary they won't think twice about making me suffer.' The journey never took place. 'No need to leave,' he announced to his companion. 'I shall be persecuted here, too.'

He was right. When he was married at thirteen, he was already more famous than many spiritual leaders of his time. He couldn't help but arouse their hostility sooner or later. 'Only a bundle of straw does not provoke opposition,' he remarked later. His temperament was so unstable, his sensitivity so acute, his intelligence so lively and precocious, that he experienced and received life like a wound. That, too, we know, thanks to Reb Nathan.

A strange fellow, this Nathan, referred to as 'from Nemerov'. To view him as a simple witness, or as a scribe by appointment to the court of Bratzlav, would be to underestimate his worth. He was no less original a disciple than his Master was a Rebbe. Each in his way attained fulfilment. If the interpreter lived solely for the Rebbe, the Master in turn expressed himself solely through his biographer. Who said of the Rebbe's work: 'In it you will find the mind of the Master, only the voice is mine.'

That Reb Nathan was more than an instrument became evident at the death of Rebbe Nahman. His favourite collaborator, first among his peers, was accepted almost as an independent Rebbe.

People sought his advice, solicited his blessing and attended his services. They described his prayer as a commentary on the Prayer. But he himself, faithful and unassuming to the end, refused all roles other than that of disciple; it was the only one to his liking. He said: 'The whole world is mad and so am I; except that I had the good fortune of seeing one lucid being.' He also said: 'Blessed is he whose eyes have met the eyes of Rebbe Nahman; blessed is he whose eyes have met mine that have looked into the eyes of Rebbe Nahman.'

What had driven him to the Tzaddik of Bratzlav? A dream, he said. 'In my dream, I went to the bakery to buy rolls. On the way, I halted, deeply troubled: could this be my life's purpose? To take little rolls from one man in order to give them to another? Nothing else, nothing more? At that moment, a man appeared before me and said: 'If you would like me to help you, hold on to me.' It was Rebbe Nahman.'

Rebbe Nahman gave him a warm welcome: 'We know each other a long time, but this is the first time we see each other.' The visitor was moved and won over. From that moment on he was another man.

For him, it was love at first sight. He gave up his travels, neglected his affairs and even his home. He changed his own life to better integrate himself into his Master's. 'If the earth were covered with daggers,' he said, 'I would willingly walk it from one end to the other for one glimpse of the Rebbe's holy face.'

His task: to collect the Rebbe's teachings, his table conversations, scraps of thoughts and sentences uttered here and there; his dreams, his moods, his anecdotes; absorb them all, then write them down, giving them continuity and form. A grateful Nahman praised him. 'Every one of you has his share in my tales,' he told his intimate disciples, 'but you, Nathan, have the biggest share of all.'

A compliment? No. A statement of fact. Thanks to Nathan's talent, his foresight and vigilance, the thoughts and legends of the Master have been preserved for us. Scrupulous, exacting to the point of fanaticism, he submitted his notes to the author for corrections and comments. Thus we sometimes may read a certain story on two levels, from two points of view: as told and as listened to by the teller himself. Nathan went even further; with future readers in mind, he did not content himself with transcribing a particular piece, but added his own explanatory observations, sometimes even describing the circumstances surrounding its creation. Thanks to him, Rebbe Nahman's readers are privileged to be present at the birth of several of his fables.

It is Nathan who tells us exactly when and why Nahman decided to become a storyteller. In 1806 when he declared: 'I can see that my ideas have no effect on you, therefore I shall tell you stories; and I shall tell them in Yiddish so as not to give you the excuse of having misunderstood.' He also said: 'If one is to believe what people say, stories are written to put them to sleep; I tell mine to wake them up.' Another time: 'I tell you my dreams also because a dream is but the story of a dream; yet the story of a dream is more than a dream.'

Five years after the Master's death, Reb Nathan turned editor and printer to further his cause. Prohibited in Russia – where they were considered too sad and depressing – Rebbe Nahman's tales were published in Poland. In his foreword, Reb Nathan wrote:

> Pause and marvel at these wonders. If you are a man, if you have a soul, you cannot help but bite your lips and take your life into your hands; your hair will stand up on your head, for stunned, you will read words that will entrance the most hardened of hearts. Every word here conceals a deep intention, every character is linked to an ancient and timeless truth.

Rebbe Nahman himself considered his tales sacred; he thought of them as being inspired, perhaps even revealed. And to this day, his followers repeat them – after saying a special prayer – to probe them for secrets accessible only to the initiated. They repeat them to one another like incantations, to purify themselves by purifying the word that names beings and voices in time and space.

I remember reading these stories as a child and, spellbound, thinking that I had understood them. Now I re-read them, and though I am still under their spell, I no longer understand them. Some seem too simple, others too complicated; sometimes both at the same time. Frequently their form is what misleads me; sometimes it is their inner structure. The more I read, the more I get the feeling of being left behind, of being incapable of continuing to the end. And then I fear that there will always remain a zone of silence, a zone of darkness which I shall never pierce. Never will I retrace the steps leading back to the teller; I shall see neither what he saw nor what he refused to see. I shall not live his adventures, though I may sometimes claim those of his heroes and their victims as my own.

His tales? Each contains many others. Imagine a series of concentric circles whose fixed centres are buried in man's innermost being: the I inside the I, conscience become silence and peace, memory inside memory. And all are inhabited by princes and sages. By haunted creatures seeking one another, one in another. By survivors of calamities, refugees, fugitives, messengers and innocent children, orphans and beggars endlessly roaming the world only to meet again in a cave or in a palace, reunited and fulfilled in ways that go beyond the experience they have gone through or been subjected to, perhaps unwittingly. Following them, we plunge into the supernatural, and yet the word miracle is never pronounced. For in the Bratzlaver's universe everything is miraculous, even the most common event. On his lips, the most deprived, most primitive of men are endowed with powers; his objects have the gift of song, just as his forest, his trees, his animals and his morning breezes all have the gift of laughter.

More daring than the most daring of the surrealists, trusting only his intuition, Nahman creates freely, impulsively; he rejects all logic, inductive or deductive; he obeys no law, acknowledges no influence. 'Time does not exist,' he asserts, meaning his tales as well as the world; he goes so far as to exclude it from primary creation. According to him, God gave man everything – except time.

Thus, the notion of time never enters Rebbe Nahman's work. Neither does the notion of place. Continuity? He prefers unbridled, irresistible and sovereign fantasy disdainful of frontiers, all frontiers; those of the mind as well as those of lands inhabited though cursed. His characters are forever leaving one another: sometimes to hide behind others for no reason. Impossible to know who is playing what role and for how long. The episodes arbitrarily fit into one another, follow one another, becoming inextricably tangled. And then, just as arbitrarily, they reach an abrupt ending, as though the teller had exhausted his patience and wanted to finish quickly in order to start anew. The tone is epic, the pace fast and erratic. Every fable contains ten fables, every scene is a mosaic whose every fragment is a tale, a scene in itself. One easily loses the thread. There are too many *maassioth betokh maassioth*, too many tales inside the tales Rebbe Nahman tells us. One ends up forgetting the main, subterranean plot. Like Nahman's heroes, the reader-listener no longer has any notion where he is or what might be awaiting him at the next step; he is helpless, lost in a strange land.

At first glance, this may seem surprising, for Rebbe Nahman could impose a discipline on himself when he wanted to or deemed it necessary. He was too skilled a craftsman to botch a tale. If he sustains our attention to the end in spite of the dispersion of his characters, it is only because he is a master of his craft. But then, how could he who in the secondary, not to say minor, episodes attached such importance to the smallest intricate patter, to every detail – the colour of a cloud, of twilight; an old man's expression of wonder, a passer-by's sneer – how could he neglect the framework and underestimate the importance of the work's very structure? Why did he leave so many gaps? Threads leading in too many directions at once; action ten times suspended – and seven times resumed? Have they a purpose? The answer is contained in the question. The same failings – or apparent failings – may be found in all his tales, in everything he created; therefore they must be deliberate, translating his concept of creation, of the art of transmitting legends and also of their author.

It is as though he wanted people to understand that it is more important for man to halt and consider the mystery of his own life than that of the world's origins. Danger and evil are not in the walk towards death, but in the digression. Man advances towards more than one goal, lives on more than one level, loves and despairs in more than one way for more than one reason. Yet he does not even know whether his deeds fall into a main or secondary pattern or if his awareness is blessing or curse. The human condition gains in impact at the very moment it breaks apart. Every fragment contains the whole, every fissure bears witness that man is at once the most fragile and the most tenacious of creatures.

Rebbe Nahman is more concerned with man than with mankind. Because he reacts more directly to the individual. His relationship to earth and heaven is filled with as many secrets as are contained by heaven and earth. Rebbe Nahman tightens the episodic events and lets the canvas flutter because he prefers the moment to years, the infinitely small to the infinitely large, the jolts of a life to a lifetime without surprises.

Here is the most beautiful of his tales, the most obscure too, entitled: 'The Story of the Seven Beggars'. It was his favourite. We know this because, once before telling it in public, he confided to

Reb Nathan: 'I am now going to tell a story which, since the creation of the world, has been heard only one time: before the destruction of the Temple. Even the Prophets don't know it. Only one man knew it – the one who put it into words.' And he added: 'We should go into town, as far as Brodi, enter the main synagogue, ascend the bimah and invite the public to come in throngs and listen . . .'

Once upon a time there was a king who abdicated in favour of his son. The coronation took place amid merriment and exuberance. There was singing in the streets and drinking in the squares. Comedians and musicians, troubadours and jugglers amused the people of the court; others entertained the crowds from morning till night and into the early hours. At the height of the festivities, the king turned to his son and said: 'I see in the stars that one day you shall lose your throne. Promise me you will not let it sadden you; promise me that you will continue to be of good cheer. Then I will be too, though my gaiety will be of a special kind.'

The new king was kind and charitable. He was a patron of the arts and encouraged the free exchange of ideas. He wanted his subjects to be happy. If someone wanted money, he made him rich. If someone aspired to honours, he helped him attain them. Thus the kingdom gained in wisdom and love what it lost in military power; the warriors forgot their trade and their desire to reap glory by killing or defying death. And then the king was overcome with sadness and began endlessly questioning himself: what am I doing in this world and what is my place in it? He had changed.

Well, in another country a great panic broke out and its inhabitants fled. While crossing a forest, two very small children – a boy and a girl – became lost. They cried and cried, for they were hungry. Along came a beggar, a bundle on his back, his eyes empty, expressionless. The children appealed to him and he gave them some bread. 'Where do you come from?' he asked. – 'We don't know,' answered the children. When he wanted to leave they begged him to take them along. He refused. Only then did they realize that he was blind. He left them with a wish: 'Be like me.'

The next morning, famished, they began to cry again. And a second beggar came to their aid; he was deaf. Like the first, he refused to take them along, but also formulated the wish that they be like him. The third day it was a stutterer's turn to offer them some bread and his blessing: 'Be like me.' The fourth beggar had a twisted neck, the fifth was a hunchback, the sixth had no arms and the seventh, no legs. And each wished them to be like him.

Then the children left the night and the forest, and becoming full-time beggars, they visited towns and fairs. Wherever they went they aroused compassion. And so, they made a career. And became famous. Whereupon it was decided that they should marry. The engagement was celebrated on a market day. As for the wedding, it was to take place on the king's birthday, in a huge cave decorated with leaves and large stones in place of tables. They would be given what was left from the royal banquet, and all would eat to their hearts' content. And all would sing with joy.

But the newly-weds remembered their early years in the forest and regretted the absence of their first benefactors, the seven beggars with big hearts and curious benedictions. More than anything, they wanted to see them again, just once. And lo and behold there appeared at the entrance of the cave, their very first friend, the blind beggar. 'I have come to take part in your celebration and bring you my present . . .' And he began to tell them a fable: 'It is not I who am blind; it is the world. Moreover, I am neither old nor young; I have not started to be. The great eagle has confirmed it to me . . .'

The next day, the second day of festivities, the second beggar made his appearance before the newly-weds, who silently had evoked his memory. This is what he told them: 'I am not deaf, but my ears perceive only the absence in the world. Some mourn the absence of happiness, others rejoice in the absence of misfortune. It is to this absence I am deaf. Therein lies my strength. The population of the great city of abundance has confirmed it to me . . .'

The third day saw the arrival of the third beggar, the stutterer, who said: 'I do not stutter at all. On the contrary, I am an orator by profession and avocation. But I like to express nothing but perfection. Furthermore, I am a singer, and my song contains the wisdom of wisdom. The man of true grace has confirmed it to me . . .' And he, too, began to tell them a story:

In the centre of the world there is a mountain and on this mountain there is a rock and out of this rock there spouts a spring. Well, everything has a heart. Even the world has a heart, a heart that is a complete being with a face, hands, legs, eyes and ears. And this heart is full of fire and anxious to go back to the spring, at the other end of the world, at the other side of the abyss. This heart is doubly unfortunate; the sun pursues and dries it. To survive, it contemplates the spring. But the longer it contemplates the spring, the greater its desire. Yet, as soon as it comes closer to the mountain, the peak disappears, and with it, the spring. And then its soul leaves, for it lives only in the love it feels for the spring. And if it were to stop, the whole world would be reduced to nothingness. Thus it must remain far away, on the other side, protected by a bird, its wings spread wide, condemned to look at the spring, knowing that they can never meet.

And so it went. The young couple had the joy of a reunion with the fourth beggar and the fifth and the sixth. And every day they listened to another tale. But when Rebbe Nahman reached the sixth day of the wedding week, he stopped. Later he confided to Reb Nathan that the story of the seventh beggar would be told only after the coming of the Messiah.

As for the beginning of the tale, it had been forgotten long before. As a matter of fact, what happened to the king who was crowned in his father's lifetime? Did he lose his throne? Did he succumb to sorrow, or did he succeed in safeguarding the 'special gaiety' of his father?

No matter. What is important for Rebbe Nahman is the fable inside the story, the legend begotten by the fable, the dream buried inside the dream. The king matters less than the beggars, less than the possessed creatures with extraordinary gifts who reign over horses, sounds and eyes. Creatures that are kind, disinterested, understanding, ready to fly to the aid of princes lost in the forest, of princesses abducted from their castles or of old men deprived of their childhood. They all know where to look, where to go. And they tell us. As soon as they come onstage, they make us the richer for having heard their tale, for having felt their talent. There is one who knows how to listen to noise. Another who knows where day and night meet. And a third who hears the moon complaining to the sun.

A bewitched magic world, dominated and magnified by the word. 'Words can silence rifles,' says Rebbe Nahman. And also: 'One may give life to words with words.' Words can tear down the most solid of walls. The word is the most exciting of all discoveries, the most terrifying too.

'It is written,' Rebbe Nahman says, 'that the Just Men obey the word of God. This should be read differently: Just Men make the word of God.' A literal translation, which on the Master's lips means: Just Men compose the language with which God creates

His universes. Prophets transmit the word of God, Just Men conceived it. Often in the form of tales.

Every word is a tale, they said in Bratzlav. Example: Torah. Or Talmud. Or Zohar. The tale of the Law is as important as the Law. And it is more profound than its commentaries.

Should one attribute an intention, a mystical content, to Rebbe' Nahman's legends? The school of Bratzlav says yes. The king is said to be God; the unhappy prince, the people of Israel; the princess, the Shekhina, the Torah or the Messiah. The fable is said to be nothing but a showcase. The characters and their obsessions are said to come from an ancient source, sacred and perennial. Their ephemeral and invented relationships are said to conceal a superior and timeless meaning.

Example: Once upon a time there was a prince who was forced to leave his father's palace. Months went by. Even years. He became homesick and restless. Exile was weighing heavily on him, he was losing ground, changing, closing himself to hope. Then one day a messenger brought him a letter from his father. Which only made his pain more acute, for it reminded him of his home and of what he had lost. He would have given anything to see his father again, to embrace him or touch a fringe of his royal robes. He was crying soundlessly when suddenly he pulled himself together; the thought had come to him that he need not be sad and sorry for himself — didn't he have a precious, unique letter in his hand? For the handwriting of the king reflects the will of the king and therefore *is* the king ... Smiling, he began to kiss the letter. It was a link to his royal past and proof that his father was alive. That this letter was written and sent, meant that the king was king and that the prince, though in exile, still was prince.

The parable is clear enough: to bear exile, Israel must console itself by and in the Torah. It must retain a strong hold on the letter and the will of God.

For, said Rebbe Nahman on another occasion, every man is called upon in his own way and at his own level. God summons one man with a shout, another with a song, and a third with a whisper. As with the shepherd and the sheep: so long as the sheep do not stray too far, they can hear the shepherd's flute, who in turn can hear their bells. But as soon as they stray too far, they will no longer hear — or be heard.

Who is the shepherd if not God? Who are the sheep if not Israel?

And the bell is the Torah which reminds both of the dangers of distance and separation.

Several of the Hasidic Masters of the period evidently did not greatly appreciate the symbolism of these tales. That a Rebbe should waste his time and that of his faithful inventing fables, well, one could accept that. But that his tales should speak not of saints or miracle Rebbes but of princes and shepherds, of anonymous beggars and horsemen, of sages and messengers – and not even Jewish ones at that – could only dismay them. If only he had spared their feelings by inserting a few more conventional Hasidic legends here and there, praising the powers of the Tzaddik and the faith of the followers, the rest would have aroused less resentment. But Rebbe Nahman was stubborn: he cared about his beggars and his princes.

Nor was criticism restricted to his literature. His general conduct also gave cause for disapproval. The 'bad company' he was keeping, his fierce individualism, irked many. So did his pronounced taste for mystery and ambiguity, his disdain of public opinion. He was castigated for his contacts with the clandestine Frankists, who, perpetuating the thoughts and practices of their late leader, believed in redemption through evil.

Of course, in Bratzlav people knew how to explain and justify the Master's behaviour. To put a man out of the mud, the Just Man must set foot into that mud. To bring back lost souls, he must leave the comfort of his home and seek them wherever they might be. 'In every man, there is something of the Messiah.' In every man, in every place. The Kabbala says it, the mystics repeat it. To free mankind one must gather the sparks, all the sparks, and integrate them into the sacred flame. A Messiah who would seek to save only the Just, would not be the Messiah. The others must be considered too – they must be prepared. Miscreants need redemption more than saints. And that is the reason – we are told – why Rebbe Nahman braved so many dangers in so many inhospitable territories – alone.

An explanation that failed to placate his opponents. They had other reasons to be vexed with him. The Grandfather of Shpole, who liked him in the beginning, turned against him the day Rebbe Nahman came to settle in his town; he felt that Nahman was taunting him. Others were appalled and angered by the way he lived, which was different from their way. Though as famous as they, he refused to resemble them. He rejected what they paraded;

he disparaged what they praised. Stability and honours meant nothing to him. He surrounded himself with young people and brushed aside the old and the rich, for the same reasons. The first he dismissed as 'loaded with sadness' and the second as 'loaded with debts'. Yet everywhere else, old men were respected for their wisdom and rich men for their generosity.

Furthermore, he prescribed solitary and silent meditation to his followers; he even advocated retreats far from the community, which seemed contrary to Hasidic tradition in which collective living and praying are indispensable to salvation. Traditional Hasidism had enounced: the self finds fulfilment by losing itself in the collective self. Rebbe Nahman said that it is better to first concentrate on the individual self by isolating it from the rest. Thus, every Bratzlaver Hasid devoted an hour a day to solitary meditation. Removed from the world and even from the Rebbe. Here it must be remembered that since the Baal Shem's time, the links between Rebbe and Hasid were presumed to be indestructible and necessary, necessary for the Rebbe to be Rebbe and the Hasid, Hasid. What right had Rebbe Nahman, great-grandson of the Baal Shem, to extol the virtues of isolation and silent song? Was he denying the importance of these links?

Sometimes he would go away for weeks, leaving his disciples confused and his family penniless. He abhorred customs and possessions, considering that they impede freedom. He moved from place to place, from discovery to discovery; he loved to travel and to live anonymously. One knows that he played with the idea of breaking away: 'I shall take my wife and go far away, and from the sidelines I shall observe people and laugh about the things they do.' He feared boredom more than illness, repetition more than sin. 'The angels never repeat their litanies,' he said, quoting the Talmud. And he went on to explain: 'The angels praising the Lord are never the same; the Lord changes them every day.' Rebbe Nahman's conclusion: 'Whoever repeats himself displeases God and moves away from him.'

Precepts and demands of such severity inevitably provoked crisis upon crisis. Living in a constant state of anxiety, Rebbe Nahman frightened those around him with his sudden, unpredictable changes of mood. Perfectly illustrating his own comparison of human thought and self-awareness with the perpetual movement of a pendulum, he alternated between highly communicative ecstasy and the blackest of depressions, toppling from *gadlut hamokhin* – exuberant frenzy – into stifling depths, *katnut hamokhin*. Gay, his gaiety knew no bounds; the story of the seven beggars is a story he told to 'show you how one rejoices'. Sad, he dragged the whole world into his despair.

From his window facing the marketplace, he saw one of his followers, a certain Haikel, hurrying down the street. He called to him and invited him up. 'Haikel,' he said, 'have you seen the sky this morning?' – 'No, Rebbe.' – 'And the street, Haikel, have you seen the street this morning?' – 'Yes, Rebbe.' – 'And now, do you see it still?' – 'Yes, Rebbe, I see it.' – 'Tell me what you see.' – 'People. Horses. Carts. Gesticulating merchants, excited peasants, men and women coming and going, that is what I see.' – 'Haikel, Haikel,' said Rebbe Nahman, shaking his head. 'In fifty years, in two times fifty years, there will be – on this very spot – a street like this one and another market similar to this one. Other carriages will bring other merchants to buy and sell other horses. But I shall no longer be here and neither shall you. So I ask you, Haikel, what's the good of running if you don't even have time to look at the sky?'

One of his disciples left us this prayer: 'Master of the Universe, You know the extent of my ignorance since I don't even know if I shall die one day. Help me. Make me know, make me aware. Make me conscious of death awaiting me without any chance of escape. And that I shall be alone to confront it. Alone. Without friends, without anyone. Alone and abandoned by memories, desires and passions. Make this image penetrate me. The yellowed image of a sullen corpse.'

And of man's destiny, Rebbe Nahman leaves us this description: 'A man condemned to death, seated in a cart drawn by two horses who know the way, the way to the gallows. The two horses are called Day and Night, and how they run, how they gallop!'

No Rebbe before him had ever spoken of life and death in these terms. None had ever imposed such a nightmarish vision upon his disciples.

A Rebbe owed it to himself to appear strong and stable, sure of himself and his powers. A Master owed it to himself to be a solid support, readily accessible to any follower in distress.

And so, Rebbe Nahman's peers had little use for him. Some set upon him with a savagery without precedent in Jewish tradition. The Grandfather of Shpole said: 'To anyone tormenting Rebbe Nahman, I promise a place in paradise.' There were those who went so far as to ban him and his faithful. The text of the excommunication edict includes a series of astonishing prohibitions: 'It is forbidden to marry their offspring, to share their meals, to negotiate with them. Also forbidden: to attend their services, to speak to them, to answer their questions. Also: to pity them or feel for them even a semblance of compassion . . .'

It must be noted that this kind of proclamation must not be taken too seriously – it wasn't then. Intramural quarrels were relatively frequent in those days, in those circles, and there was an excessive use made of bans and counterbans on all sides; nobody followed them to the letter. Still, there was a difference in this case; most of the in-fighting took place among disciples – with the Rebbes staying outside and above the scuffle. In Nahman's case, even the Rebbes were implicated. At first the conflict was ideological. The Grandfather of Shpole said: 'He came three generations too early!' To which Rebbe Nahman is said to have replied proudly: 'No. I came three generations too late!' Fuelled by rumours and gossip peddled from court to court, the philosophical disputation degenerated into personal feud. Being in the minority, Nahman and his disciples were subjected to many humiliations, which sometimes took on the proportions of a veritable campaign of persecution.

Rebbe Nahman expressed satisfaction. The more he was attacked, the more content he claimed to be. He said: 'My opponents think they do me harm; in fact, they help me enormously. My every success I owe to them.'

He also said: 'I need people to take issue with me. It allows me to raise myself moment by moment – at every moment I change being. If I thought that I am now where I was before, I wouldn't want to live in this world.'

Nor did he remain passive. He returned every blow. And elegantly at that, never debasing himself to designating his persecutors by name. Rather than answering anyone in particular, he settled his accounts with all of them at once. For him, all his adversaries were alike – he called them 'the stars' or 'the celebrities'. He put them in their place with a few well-chosen sentences that cracked like a whip. 'These people who don't know how to behave, here they are calling themselves leaders of men!' Also: 'Since Satan is overworked and cannot take care of the whole world by himself, he relies on the services of the celebrities.' And again: 'Incapable of fulfilling his mission, which is to kill mankind, the Angel of Death has enlisted the aid of the physicians – who demolish the body – and of the "celebrities" – who destroy the mind.' In the presence of

his daughter, he ridiculed a famous Tzaddik who for nine years
had prayed with fervour thinking that his Hasidim were listening in
the anteroom; he thought he could hear their whispers. At the
end of nine years he opened the door. A cat was scratching the
floor.

He recognized but one authentic Rebbe: himself.

Pride? Yes. Egocentricity? Yes. Disconcerting traits in a Rebbe?
Yes again. Ordinarily the Hasidim are the ones to sing their Master's
praise. In Bratzlav, the Rebbe outdid, in this respect as in many
others, his own admirers. To the latter he said: 'Every one of you is
a non-inhabited, non-inhabitable desert, that is why the Shekhina
avoids you ... and that is why I walk day and night. I cross the
desert to make it habitable.'

Another time: 'If I were to reveal my wisdom, mankind could
subsist without food or drink.' And also: 'The roads languish with
desire to feel themselves trodden by men who go to see the Tzaddik.
Whenever a man interrupts his journey, the roads go into mourning.'

And to his faithful he said: 'There are three things I have already
done for you. One: I broke your vanity, even in your prayers. Two:
thanks to my influence on you, your sins will be lame sins. Three:
from now on, you will be able to unmask impostors, for you have
tasted wine of quality.'

And still another time: 'The Messiah will be the one to comment
on my work.'

His peers were enraged by such arrogance. Nobody else
mattered, nobody else deserved to be heard and admired. Once he
started, nobody was spared, not even the Baal Shem: 'I have no use
for his secret writings; and if my grandfather wishes to see me, he
knows where to find me.' He considered himself an equal of the Ari
Hakodesh and Rabbi Shimon Bar-Yohai. 'In the world of eternal
truth,' he said, 'they will all need me and all will want to hear what
I have to say on the fleeting moment.'

How is one to reconcile such pride with one's image of a Rebbe
whose virtues, by definition, should include humility?

Rebbe Nahman would answer that a Tzaddik is comparable to
the Creator and not to His creature. He is beyond our comprehen-
sion; we are incapable of understanding and incompetent to judge
him. His standards, his criteria are not ours. He is above pride and
humility. 'He alone is humble who says he is and remains so,' he
said.

And also: 'Those who admire and praise me don't know me any more than those who hate and denigrate me.'

Also: 'There are two erroneous concepts going around the world. The first: that a Just Man cannot make a mistake; and the second: that he cannot remain great even if he has made a mistake.' The Tzaddik has the right not only to err, but even to boast of it. He has the right not only to appear vain, but even to be vain. 'Actually,' he remarked one day, not altogether seriously, 'I possess all the attributes, all the qualities of the Messiah. Except that he will come – I won't.'

Let us stop here. Rebbe Nahman had a sense of humour. The key to his enigma? His ability to laugh. To better understand its full import, we must study attentively an event that marked his life: his journey to the Holy Land.

The journey of a visionary, a pilgrimage worthy of the teller and of his tales. Abounding in unpredictable, incredible adventures that succeed one another at dazzling speed, it is a race towards the unknown, toward nothingness.

The Egypt campaign is at its height; Napoleon wants Jerusalem. Once again war is pounding at the gates of the Holy Land. That is the time Rebbe Nahman, accompanied by an anonymous disciple, chooses for his visit. In vain do people try to reason with him, to dissuade him; he seems drawn by an irresistible force. Communications with Palestine are infrequent, dangerous? Never mind. He cannot stay still, his impatience turns into suffering. And yet, a while later, hardly has his foot touched holy ground than he has had enough; he wants to retrace his steps and return home without losing another minute . . .

As reconstituted by Reb Nathan, this true epic is among the strangest and most beautiful the Bratzlaver Rebbe ever told.

Both journeys, going and coming, are strewn with mishaps lying in wait for him. All the obstacles in the world seem to accumulate in his path. He attracts danger, he flirts with disaster. No trial is spared him. No sooner does he take to the sea, than a storm breaks out; no sooner does he decide to rest in a certain town, than the plague makes its entrance. Everything frightens him, everything happens to him. In the Holy Land a young Turk spends hours staring at him silently before challenging him to a duel. Elsewhere he is suspected of being a spy in Napoleon's service. He escapes the epidemic that ravages Tiberias only to find himself in beleaguered Akko. He climbs the walls of a fortress only to awake on board a warship where sailors try to teach him the use of guns. The sea is his enemy, but so is land. Hunted, persecuted, he moves from town to town, from prison to prison. Trial follows trial as he appears everywhere at the most inopportune moment and attracts the attention of the most merciless men. He even succeeds in falling into the hands of pirates. In the words of Reb Nathan: '. . . our Master and his companion fell prey to many mishaps in every town and every village, but the Holy One, may He be blessed, came to their aid and protected them from plague and sword, from hunger and thirst and captivity, and they returned home in peace.'

But let us go back for a moment. During his first passage through Istanbul, Nahman – if one is to believe his biographer – behaved in a more than strange manner: 'Like a good-for-nothing, he wandered around barefoot, without belt or hat, his clothes turned inside out showing their lining, and indulging in all kinds of childish pranks. He went through the marketplace like those urchins who run and gesticulate and snicker among the merchants; he threw himself into make-believe fights, just like a boy playing war against the Frenchman, using real war tactics.'

Moreover: Rebbe Zeev, a venerated Tzaddik then living in Istanbul, had welcomed him with respect and honours. In return, Rebbe Nahman mocked him openly: 'On Shabbat, while Rebbe Zeev was praying on the bimah as behooves a saintly man, Rebbe Nahman was serenely partaking of his meal. Just as he pretended to be asleep when Rebbe Zeev, surrounded by his followers, sat down at the table singing.'

And also: to the many people who assailed him with questions, Nahman refused to disclose who he was and where he came from. One day he claimed to be Cohen; the next, he chose to be Levi or Israel. As though he deliberately wished to cover his tracks and arouse anger. He flew into a rage over nothing and humiliated all who approached him, provoking people into beating and insulting him. In the end they doubted his reason and thus fulfilled his profound wish.

Yes, he did want people to look at him askance. That is why he changed his identity every day, and his disguise as well. He wanted to be *another*. Comedian, impostor, clown. Anything but Rebbe. Anything but Tzaddik. Hence his disconcerting behaviour of simpleton, of escaped lunatic. He wanted people to see him as a poor vagrant forsaken by God and forgotten by man, adrift, coming from nowhere and going nowhere.

Why this game? To what end? To acquire what knowledge of

what subject? These grotesque movements, these borrowed masks, what could they mean? Why was the Rebbe posing as a madman in Istanbul's public square?

From Bratzlav comes the following explanation: it was only a ruse. To deceive Rebbe Zeev? Not at all. To fool Satan, who was endeavouring to thwart Nahman's project, the way he had done with the Baal Shem. By disguising himself, by playing the carefree, careless madman, Nahman succeeded in outwitting the enemy and pursuing his journey.

As for me, I would rather not apply to Rebbe Nahman the Hasidic standards implied by this hypothesis. I lean towards an explanation that places the accent on his laughter.

Laughter occupies an astonishingly important place in his work. Here and there, one meets a man who laughs and does nothing else. Also a landscape that laughs. And a man who hears time, and everything he touches, roar with laughter – and hears nothing else.

Laughter that springs from lucid and desperate awareness, a mirthless laughter, laughter of protest against the absurdities of existence, a laughter of revolt against a universe where man, whatever he may do, is condemned in advance. A laughter of compassion for man who cannot escape the ambiguity of his condition and of his faith. To blindly submit to God, without questioning the meaning of this submission, would be to diminish Him. To want to understand Him would be to reduce His intentions, His vision to the level of ours. How then can man take himself seriously? Revolt is not a solution, neither is submission. Remains laughter, metaphysical laughter. 'Hell exists,' said Rebbe Nahman, 'not in the other world, but here. Only no one dares to admit it.' Also: 'God, I pity You, yes, I pity You! You should not have invented the world, created man. They cause You nothing but trouble.' And also: 'When the Messiah will come, nothing will change, except that people will be ashamed of their foolishness.'

Rebbe Nahman knew how to laugh, wanted to laugh. Mostly about himself. He played with the urchins to mock the Rebbe inside him. He played war to show the absurdity of wars. He posed as a madman to deride reason and appearances, and as a penniless nomad to underline the grotesque aspect of possessions. He played the clown to rid himself of the last vestiges of pride that persisted inside him. All this he could not do where he was known. That is why, at home, he went to the other extreme: he disarmed his pride by pushing it to its limits, by exaggerating his own importance in all areas, in all spheres. By conferring upon himself unlikely dimensions, he deliberately made himself into a caricature. To provoke laughter. And certainly also to exasperate his adversaries. These adversaries he used as a pretext, as a front. He aimed higher. Pride, his falsest and most successful mask, allowed him to laugh louder yet.

In one of his tales we read: 'Once upon a time there was a country that encompassed all the countries of the world. And in that country, there was a town that incorporated all the towns in the country; and in that town there was a street in which were gathered all the streets of the town; and on that street there was a house that sheltered all the houses of the street; and in that house there was a room, and in that room there was a man, and that man personified all men of all countries, and that man laughed and laughed – no one had ever laughed like that before.'

Who is that man? The Creator laughing at His creation? Man sending Him back His laughter as an echo, or perhaps as a challenge? Will we ever know?

Describing Rebbe Nahman on his deathbed, Reb Nathan speaks of 'a kind of smile on his face' while he whispered: 'And here there approaches an immense and terrible mountain. And I am not sure whether we are walking towards it or whether it is coming towards us.' Taking notice of his sobbing faithful, he threw them this sentence: 'My flame will glow till the end of time. Don't cry, I shall not forsake you.' His Hasidim took his words as a promise and gave them a literal interpretation. As a result, they decided that he would have no successor. For them, the Tzaddik of Bratzlav remains alive. When they speak of him, they use the present tense. That is why they are surnamed 'the dead Hasidim', or, 'the Hasidim of the Dead'.

In my town, there were none. I met some of them later in Jerusalem, where their *shtibl* is the centre of attraction for those who like stories and songs of a particular quality, marked with nostalgia.

If you should ever go there, you will see Rebbe Nahman's armchair. Dismantled by his Hasidim before they left the Soviet Union, this armchair crossed many borders, piece by piece, before landing in Jerusalem. Not one part is missing. Not one Hasid of this strange brotherhood died on the way. The old watchman of the Rebbe's tomb, a Russian convert to Judaism and Bratzlaver Hasidism, benefited from the same miraculous protection: eluding a thousand dangers, he arrived unscathed in Israel.

Many are the followers of Nahman who to this day travel as far as Oman to commemorate the date of his death by meditating at his grave and reciting psalms.

But my first Hasid of Bratzlav, I met *over there,* in the kingdom of night. He repeated to anyone willing to listen the words of his Rebbe, the only Rebbe to survive himself: 'For the love of heaven, Jews, do not despair!' He prayed and told stories. I have forgotten his name. But not his voice. I can hear it still: 'Do you know when Rebbe Nahman was really alone? When he was not alone. That is what he said. He could scream silently in the midst of a crowd and his cry was heard in the far corners of the earth . . . Like us here. We are never alone. And yet, we have never been so alone. Nor so silent. Only our cry has not been heard.'

He also liked to quote another of Rebbe Nahman's thoughts: 'Two men separated by space and time can nevertheless take part in an exchange. One asks a question and the other, elsewhere and later, asks another, unaware that his question is an answer to the first.'

One night someone asked him: 'What would your Rebbe Nahman say to the thousands of men, women and children who live and die here in one place, in one night? Who could answer their question?' There was silence, and then a whispered sigh escaped his painfully twisted mouth: 'Who says that we are question? And what if our death were answer?'

To conclude, let us retell one of Rebbe Nahman's tales, a tale which, like all those he left behind, is both of this moment and timeless:

'Once upon a time there was a king who knew that the next harvest would be cursed. Whosoever would eat from it would go mad. And so he ordered an enormous granary built and stored there all that remained from the last crop. He entrusted the key to his friend and this is what he told him: "When my subjects and their king will have been struck with madness, you alone will have the right to enter the storehouse and eat uncontaminated food. Thus you will escape the malediction. But in exchange, your mission will be to cover the earth, going from country to country, from town to town, from one street to the other, from one man to the other, telling tales, ours — and you will shout, you will shout with all your might: Good people, do not forget! What is at stake is your life, your survival! Do not forget, do not forget!" '

And the friend in question could not help but obey. He entered the legend with fiery shadows. And this legend encompasses all other legends. It is haunted by a creature that reigns over all others, and this creature is laughing, laughing and crying, laughing and singing, laughing and dreaming, laughing so as not to forget that he is alone and that the king is his friend, his friend gone mad – but the king, is he laughing too? That is the question that contains all the others and gives life to its own tale, always the same tale, the tale of a king and of his friend separated by madness and united by laughter, fire and night.

—— *The School of Pshiskhe* ——

Once upon a time, a time when there were still Jews in Cracow, Jews who were not afraid to dream at night, there lived in that city a man named Eizik, son of Yekel.

Devout, poor and naïve to boot, he found life more than he could handle; night and day he worried: there was rent to be paid, and the butcher and the tutor; there were daughters to clothe and marry. And time was getting shorter and shorter.

Eizik, poor Eizik, what was he to do? What was there to do except worry? He prayed. Day after day, at every service and even between services, in the synagogue and in the street and at home, he begged the Lord to remember His debt-ridden and tormented servant who could go on no longer. To no avail. God seemed not to listen. Nevertheless, our Eizik continued to send Him his requests; it made him neither less pious nor less poor.

And then, one night, he had a strange dream: he saw himself swept away into a distant kingdom, inside its capital, under a bridge, in the shadow of an immense palace. And a voice told him: 'This is Prague, this is the Vltava and over there, the palace of the kings. Now look and look well, for under this bridge, at the spot where you are standing, there is a treasure; it is waiting for you, it is yours. Your problems are resolved.'

In the morning Eizik mocked himself: dreams are very pleasant, they don't cost anything, but they don't serve any purpose either. He dismissed the entire matter from his thoughts. But that night, as soon as he closed his eyes, the same vision took hold of his mind: the capital, the palace, the bridge. And the same voice asking: 'Do you want to be rich, or would you rather keep your worries?'

What nonsense, Eizik thought. Go to Prague? What an idea! He had no desire to go there; he didn't know anyone there. And furthermore, it was far. And expensive. And he had no money. If he did, he would know what to do with it. The rent, the butcher, the tutor. Well, between dreams and prayers, Eizik would choose the prayers; in fact, there's even one to exorcise dreams.

Of course, the tale does not end there. Next evening, for the third time, Eizik heard the voice: 'What? You haven't left yet?'

Annoyed more than intrigued, he decided to put an end to all this foolishness; he decided to obey. Or at least go through the motions. And so he started the journey, on foot. A few weeks later he arrived in Prague, famished and exhausted. He recognized the river, the bridge, the palace; it was starting all over again: he was dreaming again! But no, it was not a dream. This really is strange, he thought. There was a certain spot under the bridge that looked oddly familiar. What if I tried? What do I have to lose? I should dig a hole, take a look. But careful, not so fast. The bridge is guarded, the soldiers must not become suspicious. Eizik prowled the area indecisively, trying to summon his courage, until he was noticed and arrested. The captain of the guards accused him of spying. Too frightened to invent a story, he told the truth. The dreams, the worries, the long walk begun in Cracow, the memory and the voice of that memory. He was convinced, Eizik, that the officer would call him a liar and order him shot. And so, he thought he was dreaming again when the dangerous captain burst out laughing. He laughed so hard that tears ran down his cheeks: 'No, is that really why you came from so far away? You Jews are even more stupid than I thought! Now look at me, such as you see me here, if I were as stupid as you, if I too listened to voices, do you know where I would be at this very minute? In Cracow! Yes, you heard me correctly. Imagine that for weeks and weeks, there was that voice at night telling me: "There is a treasure waiting for you at the house of a Cracow Jew named Eizik, son of Yekel! Yes, under the stove!" Naturally, half the Jews there are called Eizik and the other half Yekel! And they all have stoves! Can you see me going from house to house, tearing down all the stoves, searching for a nonexistent treasure?'

Of course Eizik was not punished. Of course he hurried back home, moved the stove and, of course, he found the promised treasure. He paid his debts, married his daughters, and as a token of his gratitude, built a synagogue that bears his name: Eizik, son of Yekel, a poor and pious Jew who remained pious even when he was no longer poor.

Like most Hasidic tales and parables, this one has more than one author. It has at least two: Nahman of Bratzlav and Simha-Bunam of Pshiskhe. Rebbe Nahman replaced Prague with Vienna, and said: 'The treasure is at home but the knowledge of it is in Vienna.'

Rebbe Bunam liked to repeat it every time he accepted a new disciple: 'Remember Eizik, son of Yekel; the treasure, the one that is yours, is to be found only in yourself and nowhere else, not even in your Tzaddik.'

An intelligent and unintimidated student could have asked the Master an embarrassing question: Did the treasure in fact belong to Eizik, to Eizik alone? What about the captain of the Royal Guard? What about his share? But then Rebbe Bunam could have answered – as some of his followers do – that this tale illustrates the importance of dreams and not treasures. And also that two people may have the same dream, and that one man's dream may become another's reality.

However, on Rebbe Bunam's lips – and in the tradition of Pshiskhe – the parable had a more precise meaning, more directly linked to the problems and preoccupations of his times: man may attain perfection without a Tzaddik – and knowledge of the absolute may be acquired only from within, never from the outside. He who thinks he must go somewhere – anywhere – to find someone – anyone – to help him discover truth, had better stay home. Alone. That is the message of Pshiskhe . . .

Pshiskhe: a small *shtetl* in Poland, where the Baal Shem's Hasidism, born of fervour and contemplation, experienced a renaissance under the sign of anger and anxiety.

We are at the beginning of the nineteenth century, right in the middle of the Napoleonic wars. Churning in blood and fury, Europe is turning itself upside down. Frontiers, thrones, loyalties, and systems change overnight. The earth trembles. Nations discover new passions, liberating but deadly. History moves and bursts into flames. And the blood flows. Priests change their styles, kings their thrones. Patriotism, romanticism, nationalism – so many words newly come to life – prove themselves powerful enough to drive men to breaking their visible and invisible chains.

In the rabbinical courts, these events are endowed with a messianic dimension. One speaks of Gog and Magog, of their gigantic, apocalyptic war. The Hasidim are more and more convinced that the real battles are being waged not by emperors and generals but by Tzaddikim, who, unfortunately, are to be found on both sides. If only they could mobilize their powers in support of the same emperor, the same army, the war would come to an end and redemption would be near.

To hasten that event, three great Masters combined their efforts:

the Seer of Lublin, the Maggid of Kozhenitz and Rebbe Mendl of
Riminov. They drew up a plan of action. Which failed. And the
three conspirators, punished by God, died before the year's end.

An undeserved punishment. The three Masters had meant well.
The Jews needed the Messiah, perhaps more than ever. Society as a
whole was moving forward in all areas, and as usual, left the Jews
excluded from the family of nations.

In Eastern Europe especially the Jewish people needed redemption. Persecuted by the Poles, fanatic anti-Semites, the Jews felt just
as threatened by Austrian liberals. A young Talmudist had a choice
of military service on the one side and emancipation – that is,
secular education, free-thinking morality; in short: atheism – on
the other. Add to this the various economic measures that made
the Jews' life miserable everywhere and especially in the more
isolated townships, where they were forced to live like outlaws,
dependent on the good graces of the curate and the whims of the
landowner. They were hard hit with taxes, ransoms and laws
enacted for the sole purpose of keeping them in a state of perpetual
humiliation. Drained by the pogroms and false messianic hopes,
they had reached the end of their endurance; they were on the
brink of despair. Without Hasidism, they would have resigned
themselves to perdition.

Let us recall: What was Hasidism in the beginning? One man –
and then many – who knew how to restore to the individual a
sense of sacredness and confidence in his ties with the community.

To the isolated Jew, living as an outcast, the Rebbe said: 'Your
experience is not meaningless, it is part of an entity that takes it
into account. Know that eternity is present in every moment; that
every table may become altar and every man high priest. Know
that there is more than one path leading to God, but that the surest
goes through joy and not through tears. Know that God does not
like suffering and sadness and least of all those that you deliberately
inflict upon yourself. God is not that complicated; He is not jealous
of your happiness nor of the kindness you show to others. On the
contrary: the road to God goes through man. The sleeping child,
the mother caressing him, the old man listening to the rustling of
the leaves: God is close to each of them, in each of them God is
present.'

At that moment in Jewish history, it was a powerful, irresistible
message. By putting the accent on friendship and love, on impulse
rather than on asceticism, erudition and the strict observance of

THE SCHOOL OF PSHISKHE

the Law, Hasidism brought back to the fold large numbers of Jews who, faltering under the weight of their burden, came close to conceding defeat.

That is why, in less than fifty years, the movement swept over these parts of Europe. The Baal Shem's companions and the disciples of the Maggid had succeeded beyond their hopes: the spark kindled between Kossov and Kitev, here it was, illuminating the sky of the night, the faces of the night, over there, beyond the horizon. Not one community that did not bear its mark. There were three major centres of Hasidism: in Ukraine, in White Russia and in Poland. And the movement was proud of its philosophers such as Shneur-Zalmen of Ladi, of its defenders such as Levi-Yitzhak of Berditchev, of its preachers, storytellers, heroes and saints. Their opponents tried to stem their rapid-fire progress. In vain. Hasidism triumphed because it made itself the advocate of a new Judaism, a smiling Judaism as it were, reconciling man with the idea of happiness. It was, in fact, a resounding call to joy.

Hasidism succeeded also because it created Rebbes who symbolized it. The Rebbe: confessor, master, guide and above all: father. He does not invoke lightning; he is gentle, kind. As the shepherd of an ill-starred flock, he defends it against the iniquities of man and heaven. Thanks to him, those who have been tried may catch their breath and no longer feel forsaken by the God of Israel and the people of Israel.

As a result, it was suddenly easy to be a Hasid, to be a Jew. One knew where to go, what to do and say, what blessing to request and how to obtain it. The Rebbe had all the answers. By taking upon himself the suffering of his followers and of the entire Jewish people, he alleviated that suffering. Did he really accomplish miracles? Yes or no, yes and no; it didn't matter. What was miraculous was that the Jew suddenly discovered within himself the desire and strength to sing and celebrate life at a time when the sky was darkening with crimson clouds and the threat was becoming closer and more defined. Thanks to the Rebbe, the Hasid could persevere and gradually regain self-confidence; he could claim his place in time and in hope. Within the confines of exile, he built his temple and his kingdom and lived in them. Yes, the Baal Shem had won his battle. The Jew, in his oppression, had freed himself from the inside; he was going to remain Jewish. The Maggid of Mezeritch, too, had reached his mark; he had opened the way, the others had but to follow. Every Rebbe now had his disciples; every Tzaddik, his faithful.

The most striking triumph of all was in Poland, where the opposition lacked men of the Gaon of Vilna's stature. They had no one strong enough to challenge the early Masters. They tried here and there, in Cracow, in Brodi, in Lemberg, to organize campaigns; some fanatics even excommunicated 'the new sect'. To no avail. People shrugged their shoulders and followed the call, the song of Hasidism.

Which was fine, but had its disadvantages. The victories were too swift. Without resistance, a new movement risks weakening from within. Intellectually and socially. And sometimes even morally.

In Lithuania, where recruiters and followers had to fight for every position, every new member, Hasidism benefited. Opposition stimulates and enriches; it adds depth to thought and mind. To challenge an Avraham Katznelenbogen or a Gaon of Vilna was no trifling matter. Forced into a defensive position by the attacks and accusations of the most prestigious rabbis, and into accepting confrontations on a level that precluded subterfuge, the leaders of Hasidism had to remain in a constant state of alert and fight every abatement in intensity, every tendency toward vulgarization.

In White Russia and, to a certain extent, in the Ukraine, the movement also succeeded, often for the same reasons, in forming a considerable intellectual elite.

In Poland it developed the other way; Hasidism was in control and became, very quickly, very popular, in the best and the worst sense of the word. It was an establishment, respected, respectable, with it own set of laws and customs, celebrations and prohibitions. And here the Mitnagdim were the ones to be harassed, for they were in the minority; the privileges went to the Hasidim. Who, on the strictly Jewish level, felt secure.

Thus, it was easy success, rather than adversity, that loomed as the obstacle. Hasidism's objectives changed even though its essence remained the same. The role of the Rebbe evolved. From trusted friend and adviser, the Master turned into miracle-maker and creator of effects, easy effects. Unlike the Baal Shem, who brought man closer to God and His creation, the new Tzaddikim presumed to mediate between individual and destiny. Result: Jews neglected their studies and craved glitter and luxury. After all, the rest was up to the Tzaddik; let him accomplish miracles, since that was his vocation. Result: the movement lost in quality what it gained in numbers; form replaced content, fame replaced purity.

This was particularly true in small communities, centred around

Tzaddikim of secondary rank. So much so that, in Riminov, Rebbe Mendl protested against a growing influx of miracle-makers: 'Gather a thousand worshippers around a piece of wood, tell them to shout that there is a miracle, and the piece of wood will start to produce them, your miracles!'

Another danger: some of the Masters were beginning to found dynasties, a practice totally alien to early Hasidism. The Baal Shem had said that every man is a potential Baal Shem, spiritual values not being hereditary. Thus he had been succeeded by the Maggid of Mezeritch rather than by his son Rebbe Tzvi-Hersh. And so it had been with the Maggid; he was succeeded by his disciples. The seat of Pinhas of Koretz remained empty. And at the death of Mendl of Riminov, his friend and servant was called to replace him. But traditions had changed: in Lublin the son of the Seer was treated as a crown prince. Elsewhere the Hasidim were deep in quarrels over prerogatives and influence.

What had happened to the adventure started in the Carpathian Mountains one generation earlier, an adventure that had required those who participated to reject ornaments and external symbols of distinction? In the beginning, Hasidism had represented a promise, a commitment, a vow of authenticity that every man renewed every day; it had all been simple then, and filled with grace. And now? On one side there was the Rebbe and on the other his admirers, different and therefore separated from him. The Baal Shem's message, the Baal Shem's song, could this be what they were, all they were? Having swept away rigid institutions with a gust of fresh air, was Hasidism in turn becoming just another institution? With its guides and guided, its princes and servants? With a Rebbe who was important and a Hasid who was not? Was this Hasidism as conceived and lived by the Baal Shem?

It is against this background that one must enter Pshiskhe, if one wishes to understand what took place in Pshiskhe and why and at whose behest.

Three rebels. Yaakov-Yitzhak, called the 'Jew', Simha-Bunam, and Menahem-Mendl: the school of Pshiskhe.

All three had spent time with the Seer, in Lublin. The youngest, Menahem-Mendl, had been the first to leave; the oldest, Yaakov-Yitzhak, the last and most reluctant.

A rabbi's son, Yaakov-Yitzhak had an ordinary and studious childhood. Even as an adolescent he stood out among his comrades because of his erudition, and also because of his reserve, his shyness, his melancholy ways. He married young. His wife, a baker's daughter, did not bring him happiness; in fact, she made him rather unhappy. (He once told the story of an angel who was punished for being too harsh with man; he was condemned to live on earth and marry.) Was that why he never laughed? He was obsessed by the idea of death, particularly in his youth. Rumour has it that he wanted to die. Fortunately, he met Moshe-Leib of Sassov and Avraham Yehoshua Heschel of Apt, who took a liking to him and won him over to the movement. Shortly afterwards he left for Lublin on their advice, and there became the favourite disciple of the Seer, who for many years accorded him special consideration. His knowledge, his memory and analytical gifts were legendary. In Lublin, anyone who was not content with the scraps of wisdom the Seer distributed to the crowd, came to study with Yaakov-Yitzhak. Eventually, the Seer ordered him to preside at his own table, his own court. But the disciple succeeded too well, mostly with the younger intellectuals. Confronted with the intrigues and calumniations resulting from his success in the Seer's circle, he left Lublin and went to settle in Pshiskhe, determined but with a heart heavy with remorse.

Remember: what the Rebbe of Pshiskhe did to the Seer, the Seer had done to his Master, Elimelekh of Lizensk. The two Masters and the two disciples had many traits in common; even their relationship had evolved in the same manner. In Hasidism, history repeats itself. The Seer had never blamed Reb Elimelekh; the Rebbe of Pshiskhe never showed any resentment towards the Seer and considered himself his disciple to the end. Nor did Yaakov-Yitzhak of Pshiskhe ever concede that there had been a break between him and the Seer. And yet, as we shall see, it was indeed a break; the disciple had veered from the Master's course, until in the end they frequently opposed one another.

The names they acquired are revealing. The Seer – the visionary, the prophet – saw himself as an exceptional, superior being, whereas his disciple, choosing anonymity, rejected his very name and identity.

Why was the latter called the 'Jew'? The texts of Pshiskhe offer many explanations. Since his name – Yaakov-Yitzhak – was the same as the Seer's, he did not want to use it, out of respect for his Master. Another: he had of the Jew – Jewish man – so noble an image, that all his life he aspired to be worthy of it. Still another: out of modesty, he never gave himself credit for his scholarly innovations, but instead attributed them to an anonymous 'Jew', which, after all, he was. Also this one: going from fair to fair, following the Baal Shem's example, he came upon the Prophet Elijah disguised as a peasant. And he stared at Elijah so intently that he moved the prophet to anger. 'Jew,' he burst out, 'since you know, why do you talk?' Actually, the 'Jew' hadn't done any talking at all, but he kept the name so as not to refute the prophet.

However, there is another, more plausible hypothesis which sees in the nickname a choice, a conscious or subconscious act of protest; there were already too many Tzaddikim, too many Masters. Therefore, he preferred to define himself simply as Jew, a man like any other. All his sayings and fables reflect his aversion to the excesses of the crowned elite. Just like the Baal Shem Tov, he placed man – and not his title-bedecked leader – at the centre of creation; like the Baal Shem Tov, he distrusted the establishment.

The 'Jew' saw himself as the Baal Shem's disciple. His taking up residence in Pshiskhe was meant as a return to Medzebozh. Like the movement's founder, he had begun his vocation by tutoring small children; like him, he dressed as did the village men and, like him, roamed from place to place, in search of experiences and encounters. If the Baal Shem was the Master of the Name, he became the Master of the Surname.

His departure from Lublin provoked an outcry. His enemies spread rumours that there had been a personal feud between Master and disciple. It was not true. He regularly went back to Lublin from Pshiskhe; he did everything possible to avoid secession. He remained faithful to the person of his Master – though not to his views – even after the Seer rejected him in the end, asking him never to return.

Ideologically, the break was interpreted as a warning signal. Beware! anyone indulging in excessive comfort runs the risk of succumbing to illusion! His key word was *teshuva* – which means both repentance and return. Return to God and to the sources. It was time to rethink values and concepts, to take stock and start anew.

It was the first conflict, the first revolution, inside Hasidism. Never before had young purists dared question what was established, and put their elders, their parents and the entire movement on trial. These rebels, guided by the Masters who formed the school of Pshiskhe, acted out of idealism; therefore no official sanctions were ever taken against them.

Which is surprising, since the 'Jew' and his two successors had rather unkind things to say about the Hasidic establishment. Of the Seer, the 'Jew' said that he was a great teacher *in spite of* his miraculous powers. Miracles, he would say, are not difficult to perform; it is more difficult to be a Jew. He also said: 'I think that I could make the Messiah come, but these so-called Tzaddikim, with their lack of humility, are hindering me.' To his friend Bunam, he complained: 'I am sad. When I think of the history of our people, I despair. Though there are many dark spots in our history, God has always given us leaders, guides to help us pull through. We have had Moses. Then Joshua. The judges, the kings, the prophets. Then the Tanaim, the Amoraim, the Gaonim, the Kabbalists. Lately we have had the Baal Shem, the Maggid. And they have helped us. Now I realize that with the passing years, the light is waning; darkness is closing in on us. What will happen to our people?'

His disciple, Menahem-Mendl of Kotzk, echoed his words in a still more alarming way: 'We are going farther and farther away from the light at Sinai, yet we do not come any closer to the light of the Messiah!'

'When the Messiah will come,' said the Pshiskher Jew, 'all the Rebbes and their followers will run to welcome him. But he, the Messiah, will turn away, saying: "Take your leaders, take them out of my sight!" Then the Hasidim will come back – alone.'

Characteristic, too, his praise of an unknown blacksmith: 'Whatever I know, whatever I possess, I owe to him. He was my neighbour when as a newly-wed I lived in my father-in-law's house. The blacksmith would rise before me and wake me each day when he started pounding his anvil. One morning I said to myself: "If he works so hard and gets up so early just for money, can I do less to enrich my soul?" The next day I was up before him. The blacksmith took it badly; he thought: "If this greenhorn, who does nothing and needs nothing, sacrifices his sleep for nonsense, how can I, who have a family to feed, stay in bed?" Next day he rose even earlier. This tacit competition was a boon to me; every day I studied a little more, and thanks to it, thanks to the blacksmith, I acquired everything I possess.'

Yet, to the question 'What did you learn in Lublin?' he replied cryptically: 'To fall asleep without difficulty.'

Clearly: in Pshiskhe one preferred blacksmiths who plied their trade to Tzaddikim who plied theirs; namely, who exaggerated.

But then, why did the 'Jew' accept the title, the crown of Rebbe?

Because he was compelled to? Possibly. For it was customary among the Hasidim of the period to elect a leader among themselves. And once elected, whether he liked it or not, he had to accept their decision. This happened in the case of Rebbe Bunam, Rebbe Mendl and, much earlier, the Great Maggid of Mezeritch. The Jew of Pshiskhe was in no position to refuse. In his case, the Seer himself had made the decision. But the real reason was more subtle: the 'Jew' accepted because he was convinced that he would not be a Rebbe like the others. And he was right.

He refused honours, privileges, rejected flatterers and overly servile admirers. He did not claim to impose his will upon heaven. In contrast to his peers, he did not discuss their day-to-day problems with his callers; he had no desire to solve them in their stead. His primary goal was to restore a climate of spirituality to the movement. The practical problems and worries of the individual were not his concern; he left those for God to handle. His task was to save the movement, which was losing ground, relying more and more on artifice. Fervour and prayer were given precedence over study and knowledge. The external signs of Hasidism were assuming too much importance; what was needed was a return to inner life. Masters and disciples were too pleased with each other and themselves; what they needed was a jolt.

His faithful disciple and companion, Rebbe Peretz, accompanied him to the forest one day. Listening to the birds' chirping, Peretz said: 'I would like to understand what they are saying.' – 'And what you, yourself, are saying, you already understand?' was the Master's retort.

Another time: 'One talks and talks of paradise; one does this and that to earn one's share of it. As for me, I would gladly give up mine to anyone who will offer me a drink!'

One Shabbat, after the third meal, he averted his face, and in a voice echoing his distress, addressed his guests: 'Tomorrow you will be going back to work – and you work hard, I know. If I asked you why you work so hard, you would tell me that it is not for your sake, but for the sake of your children; that you wish them to grow up to be good Jews, loving man and fearing God. Yes, that is what you would tell me. That is what, for thousands of years, man has been saying in every language. Man works and works, never for himself but always for his child, who in turn will work for his ... As for me, I am waiting ...' He paused, before continuing even more sadly: 'I am waiting for the true child.'

Whom did he mean? The Messiah? Perhaps. But it is also possible he simply meant the father who would admit in all honesty that he was working for himself. For the 'Jew' despised nothing as much as insincerity, as feigned sincerity.

To tear down his disciples' defences, to jolt them out of their patterns of behaviour, he would resort to shock tactics. The student who had chosen silence to purify language, he ordered to attain his goal by speaking. An emancipated Jew came to discuss theology with him. Without a word the 'Jew' took off his hat and placed it on the man's head. The visitor began to stammer and found nothing further to discuss.

To him, what mattered was the effort spent rather than the result obtained. He said: 'The Just Man loses at night what he has won during the day; to earn it again the next day, he must work just as hard as the day before.' Nothing is given and everything remains to be taken, it was thought in Pshiskhe. Better to raise the profane to the level of the sacred, than to lower, to debase, the sacred to the level of the profane. Better to bring man to the Messiah, than to bring the Messiah to man. Not easy? Never mind. What was important was to know. To know that the goal was not yet reached. To believe that by saying the truth one has told the truth is a delusion. To believe that one can lie to man without lying to God is another. 'The seal of God is truth,' said the Jew of Pshiskhe, 'for it precludes any possibility of forgery; a counterfeited truth is no longer the truth.' A truth that is broken or divided is not truth. In Pshiskhe, nothing was lower than hypocrisy. 'I think,' said Reb Bunam, 'that I could reform any sinner – except a liar.' And the worst liar, according to Pshiskhe, is the one who lies to himself.

Pshiskhe's militancy understandably antagonized many of the more traditional Hasidic strongholds. There were those Rebbes who felt themselves personally attacked, and therefore started their own offensive. They tried to move the debate from the ideological to the personal level.

Pshiskhe became the subject of gossip and defamation within the Hasidic universe. People said anything they could think of to discredit the 'Jew' and those who rallied around him. They went so far as to call a meeting of noted Tzaddikim – including Naftali-Hersh of Ropshitz – to put the new school on trial. The 'Jew' was accused of lacking respect for the Seer, of wanting to take over his throne, of introducing dangerous ideas and reforms into the movement, of shifting services (in Pshiskhe, there were no set hours for prayers), of inciting the young against their fathers and against the Masters they followed.

In vain did the 'Jew' implore the great figures of Hasidism, the Maggid of Kozhenitz, Mendl of Riminov, to use their authority to make peace between Pshiskhe and Lublin; the conflict continued.

Even more so since Pshiskhe had its own uncompromising fanatics who were opposed to any compromise or reconciliation. They believed in *azut dikdusha*, the virtue of saintly arrogance; and they used it. In-fights are always the most bitter, and this one was no exception. Each side accused the other of deviating; worse: betraying the vision and doctrine of the Baal Shem. Pshiskhe claimed that the others had renounced their Hasidic ties. Lublin returned the compliment.

Still, as long as the 'Jew' was alive, the quarrels were somehow kept under control. Faithful to the Seer to the very end, he did not want to cause him pain, he did not want his image to be marred. Though he was slandered and dishonoured by the intrigues of the Lublin court, the 'Jew' refused to turn against his old Master. Had he lived longer, he might have averted the final break. But he died young, at the height of his powers. What contributed to this premature death? The disappointment of being repudiated by the Master he loved? The death-urge of his youth? He who was so strong physically – he could 'crack five nuts with one hand' – suddenly took ill. Nothing is known of the specific nature of his ailment or the circumstances surrounding his death; his final days are shrouded in mystery. All one knows is that he died at forty-eight, in 1818. Precisely one hundred years before the end of the First World War. His second successor, Menahem-Mendl of Kotzk, went into seclusion in 1839, a century before the second conflagration involving entire peoples and continents.

Between the two, there was Rebbe Bunam, who in his own way was no less interesting than they. Interesting because he resembled neither. He was wise – profoundly wise – whereas they were extremists. They looked their part; not he. He didn't even look like a Rebbe. He dressed differently; in the manner of the 'Germans', meaning: according to what was fashionable in the cities. Everything about him was elegant: his dress, his walk, his ways. Despite his Talmudic training and erudition, he earned his livelihood first as a wood merchant and later as a pharmacist. He is the 'Merchant of Danzig' and the 'Pharmacist of Pshiskhe' referred to in Hasidic literature. Names he himself invented – and kept to the end.

He was known as a traveller and lover of the picturesque, the bizarre. On his journeys through big cities, on business, he would visit strange places and meet . . . even stranger people. He played chess and cards; he debated with the emancipated and the atheists, the so-called enlightened; he played the guitar. Nor did he mind going to theatres and taverns – he enjoyed their atmosphere. Worse, he was even known to go to cabarets occasionally, for the purpose, of course, of bringing sinners back into the fold and onto the road towards salvation.

And yet, at the death of the 'Jew', the orphaned disciples did not turn to one of his sons, but to the Merchant of Danzig. Why to him? Because he was more qualified than the others? Or because he had been the 'Jew's' faithful companion? And his friend as well? Because he had followed him from Lublin? Or because in Pshiskhe the way was already being cleared for Menahem-Mendl of Kotzk? Could Rebbe Bunam have been nothing more, nothing else but a transition, a human bridge between two volcanoes? Or was this but another way for Pshiskhe to defy the establishment by saying: 'Look! Our Rebbe is a pharmacist and not the son of a famous Tzaddik! He doesn't even look like a Rebbe! See how appearances can be misleading!'

There could be truth in each of these hypotheses. The fact remains that Rebbe Bunam himself was surprised by his election: he neither sought nor wanted it; he was . . . drafted. Even after he was nominated, he refused to 'receive' Hasidim and behave like a Rebbe. Yet, in retrospect, he seems to have been the best candidate possible, and certainly the most qualified. He may have been less inspired than the other two, but he was their equal in inspiring others. And that, after all, is the secret and strength of the true Rebbe: to know how to inspire.

One of his disciples explained Rebbe Bunam's greatness: 'Remember what happened to Elisha? Elisha was a simple shepherd who spoke to his cattle, not to humans. Then one day he met the Prophet Elijah and from then on he was another person: his soul had caught fire. Rebbe Bunam? You want to know about Rebbe Bunam? Simple. No matter how hardened, how icy your soul may be, at his touch it will burst into flames.'

No wonder that countless young Hasidim came running to Pshiskhe. Just as they were to do later in Kotzk, newly-weds abandoned their wives, sons forsook their parents. Drawn by the call of a renewed Hasidism, they came with nothing but their thirst for fervour, truth and revolt. Pshiskhe became the magnet that attracted the intellectuals and the idealists, just as Kotzk did a few years

later. Pshiskhe symbolized the courage to question, to try the experiment again by stripping away its blemishes and burdens.
Hasidism in Pshiskhe was young and daring again, its enthusiasm
was vital enough to overcome all obstacles and expose all taboos.

So strong was Pshiskhe's appeal to the young that the conservative leaders of the movement, determined to stem the current,
decided to react publicly. The wedding in Ostila, famous in Hasidic
literature, provided the opportunity. In the presence of some two
hundred Tzaddikim, headed by the venerable Rebbe of Apt,
Pshiskhe was put on trial. Much has been written about the wedding and the verbal joust that became more important than the
wedding. Accusers and defenders outdid each other in eloquence,
erudition and comparative Hasidic ideology. After hearing the
arguments for and against, Avraham Yehoshua Heschel of Apt
refused to condemn Pshiskhe. A wise decision: because of it,
Hasidism can take its place among the rare movements that
permit deviation and rebellion within. Pshiskhe, though opposed
to traditional Hasidism, remained inside the movement.

What was the key message or idea of Pshiskhe? That the greatness
and tragedy of man's condition lie in the very ambiguity of that
condition. Man must believe that the entire universe was created
for him alone, but also, that he is less than dust. Man is at the same
time the corpse he will be and the carrier of life that he is, sym-
bolizing, as long as he breathes, his own immortality. Man is vulnerable and weak – too weak to know the truth – yet he is also
omnipotent, for his quest is its own ultimate justification.

Naturally, there are nuances; the 'Jew' meant man when he
spoke of the Jew; Rebbe Bunam meant the Jew when he spoke of
man. Both men, and their successor in Kotzk even more, wanted
man to believe that it is within his means to draw strength from the
despair that is his lot. Since man is alone, he helps his fellow man
and thereby breaks his own solitude.

Each of the three expressed himself in his own way: the 'Jew'
preferred sayings; Rebbe Bunam liked parables; and Menahem-
Mendl of Kotzk chose silence.

Also: The 'Jew' died young. The Kotzker Rebbe died alone,
terribly alone. Rebbe Bunam died blind. Hearing his wife's sobbing,
Rebbe Bunam said to her: 'Why do you cry? Are you afraid? I am
not. All my life I have done nothing but learn how to die.'

Rebbe Bunam was a magnificent storyteller. Every one of his
tales is a mixture of humour, melancholy and wisdom.

A funny story: 'One day I felt like telling a story, or rather, I felt a story in me that wanted to be told. Except that I was afraid; it was what you would call a daring story. I felt that if I told it, my most ardent followers would stop calling me Rebbe. As for my enemies, they would know why they hated me. Yet I could not repress the story; it wanted to be told. So I told it. And to my great surprise, even my enemies began to admire me.'

An image: 'Sometimes it seems to me that every man is a solitary tree in the midst of the desert; and God has no one else in the whole world just as man has no one but God in the whole world.'

A parable: A prince bought a pure-bred stallion, and to protect him from thieves, locked him into a stable built of stone. Its gate was bolted and guarded by an armed watchman. One night when he could not fall asleep, the prince went for a walk. He passed in front of the stable and thought that the watchman was looking perplexed. 'Hey,' he called to him, 'what's on your mind?' – 'There is this question that is bothering me: when you sink a nail into the wall, where does the mortar go?' – 'An important question,' said the prince. 'You do well to think about it.' And he went home and back to bed. An hour later he still could not fall asleep. So he went down again, out to the yard and the watchman, who sat there with his head propped in his hands meditating. 'What now,' said the prince, 'what are you thinking about now?' – 'Well, you see, it's like this: when you eat a bagel, what happens to the hole?' – 'A profound question,' said the prince. 'You do well to concern yourself with it.' And he went back to his quarters. He came down a third time, and for the third time the watchman seemed in a quandary. 'Another question?' asked the prince. 'Yes – and this is it: I tell myself that the stable is here, the walls are here and I am here – but the stallion, where in the world is he?'

A saying: 'If God offered me the possibility of changing places with Abraham, I would refuse. God needs someone like Abraham, not a blind old fool like Bunam.'

Usually, Rebbe Bunam explained his parables while making it clear that their true and deeper meaning defied explanation. 'The secret of the secret cannot be divulged,' he said.

A story: Once upon a time, there was a prince cleverer than most. One evening he stumbled upon a drunkard in the street and decided to teach him a lesson he would not forget. He had his men take him to the castle and put him to bed. On a chair next to his bed he had them lay out the robes of a bishop. And nothing else. Next morning, when the drunkard awoke, he couldn't remember where or who he was. The servants helped him put on his priestly robes and addressed him with the respect due to a bishop. Which was fine, except that he didn't remember ever having been a bishop. Still, after a while, the first doubt crossed his mind: I may think that I am a drunken peasant who is dressed like a bishop, but what if it's the opposite? What if I am a bishop who thinks he is a drunken peasant? He decided to wait and see. For the moment he had nothing to lose. Only when the servants brought him a gold-encrusted prayer book, did he get frightened: now he would know the truth! If I can read, I am the bishop, he thought. If I can't, I am the drunkard. He opened the book and – couldn't read. Panic-stricken, he was on the verge of confessing everything, when a new doubt entered his mind: perhaps he was a bishop after all! The fact that he could not read was no real proof. After all, what guarantee was there that other bishops could?

The moral of the story? Man must not trust appearances. That is one of the dominant themes in the haunted universe of Pshiskhe. Another recurrent theme: that of the missed opportunity, the frustrated impulse. Man could – but does not – want. Or he wants only when it is too late. Then, and that is the worst of all maledictions, he forgets that he can.

Another tale, the saddest of all: Wanting to punish his son, the king sends him into distant exile. Suffering from hunger and cold, the prince waits to be recalled. The years go by; he has lost the very strength to wait for the royal pardon. Then, one day, the king sends him an emissary with full powers to grant the prince's every desire and wish. His message delivered, the emissary waits for the prince's instructions. Who asks him for a piece of bread and a warm coat, nothing else. He has forgotten that he is prince and that he could return to his father's palace.

In Pshiskhe, where there was no limit on the demands made upon oneself, man immunized man against oblivion.

'Oblivion is at the root of exile the way memory is at the root of redemption,' the Baal Shem had said. But in Pshiskhe, ultimate redemption was of only marginal interest. One thought about the coming of the Messiah but one did nothing to bring about its advent prematurely. One worked on oneself rather than on God. The individual's goal was not to make the Messiah come but to go towards him, to make earth and the heart of man livable for man. The wait was going to be long? Never mind. There were enough things to be done in Pshiskhe; there was no hurry. Besides, the idea of messianic times was an alarming one. Reb Bunam gives this description of them: 'In those days, the summer will be without heat, the winter without frost, the wise will have forgotten their wisdom and the Hasidim their fervour.'

His successor went further. Menahem-Mendl of Kotzk understood that all these signs, all these evils could occur without necessarily heralding redemption. Thence his anguish: Could it be that there is no link between creation and Creator, between the eyes and what they see, between the dread of flight and that of reunion? Could it be that man is incapable of speaking of his suffering even to Him who inflicts it?

That is what Pshiskhe represents to the storyteller of today: gates opening upon the past and throwing an oppressive light upon the present, the eternal present, the treasure that makes us run from Cracow to Prague and from there to Rizhin and Sighet, when in fact it is nowhere to be found. For one among us – a Hasid of Pshiskhe? a child in Wizsnitz? – has already found and lost it. But he has not forgotten it, not yet.

— *Menahem-Mendl of Kotzk* —

Somewhere in Central Europe, beyond the horizon, between Warsaw and Lublin, there was once upon a time a small village whose name made people dream and shiver: Kotzk.

The year is 1839.

It is winter. And snowing. Nestling close to one another, huts and cabins slowly vanish into the soundless night. The sky hangs low over deserted streets. The village is holding its breath; seen from the outside, it is a ghost village.

And yet, in a rustic wooden lodge, the most passionate, the most demanding disciples of Hasidism are readying themselves, on this Friday night, for the first of the Shabbat meals.

In the House of Study, seated around the rectangular table covered with the traditional white tablecloth, the Hasidim do not feel the biting cold. Their eyes are upon a tense, forbidding man: the Rebbe. They wait, as is their custom, for him to sanctify the wine and the bread. But the Rebbe's thoughts are elsewhere; he is in no hurry. Where is he? What is he doing? What could be on his mind on this peaceful evening that is like any other? He is struggling with his breath like a sick man; his eyes, staring at the candles before him, reflect an ancient though nameless anguish. The assembled guests are silent, oppressed; something about him makes them uneasy, frightens them. They sense an oncoming event: who knows what walls of what fortresses the Rebbe is about to overturn to clear the way for what storms? The silence is heavy with foreboding. No one dares move. Or even glance at his neighbour for reassurance. They wait for time to be torn open, for thoughts to be unveiled. And then the Rebbe – in his fifties but older-looking – his face fierce and terrifying, throws back his head and . . .

This is where the tale ends. Something happened; nobody knows what. One hundred and thirty years after the event, the mystery remains. Rather than testify for history, or at least chronicle, the witnesses seem to have vowed never to speak of anything related to the incident. None broke what seems to have been a conspiracy of silence to keep a secret whose meaning likely escaped them.

All we know is that secret there was. Something out of the ordinary happened in Kotzk that night; something incomprehensible, unspeakable. Hasidim refer to it still today, but only in carefully shrouded terms and only among themselves. Some speak of it as of an eclipse, others as of an ailment of obscure origins. Some suggest that on that evening the Rebbe chose, for reasons known to him alone, to surprise heaven and earth by refusing to serve as their link and justification.

Among the more or less fantastic versions circulating among Hasidim and their opponents, let us mention a few, if only to throw some light on the stage, the setting and, most of all, the central character.

After an interminable silence, says a Jewish Polish novelist, the Rebbe violated the Shabbat laws by reaching out to extinguish the Shabbat candles.

A second image: emerging from his meditation, the Rebbe is said to have suddenly cried out against the scandal of the adversities seemingly inherent in Jewish history. He is said to have shouted: 'Am I to conclude that *let Din velet Dayan*, that it is a history without judge and without justice?'

The third version is even more realistic: having learned of the new pogroms that were laying waste the Jewish communities of Poland and Russia, the Rebbe reportedly flew into a rage and pounded the table with his fist, roaring: 'I demand that justice be done, I demand that the Supreme Legislator obey his own Laws!' As it happened, the passage in Scriptures to be read on that particular Shabbat related Esau's bartering away his rights as firstborn to Jacob. And so he continued: 'It is written in the Talmud that Esau later shed three tears, so much did he regret the bargain. And it is for these three tears that we continue to pay with our blood throughout our long exile. Well, how long are we to go on paying? Will it never end?' When he noticed the expressions of horror in the audience, he burst out with redoubled anger: 'Why are you staring at me like that? Are you afraid? Of what? Of whom? I find this fear of yours repulsive, disgusting! You are nothing but liars, flatterers, cowards! Go away and leave me, do you hear me, I wish to be alone!'

Which one of these three versions – there are others – corresponds to truth? Again, nobody knows. However, one does know that all have the same ending: the Rebbe fainted and had to be carried to his quarters. Where he remained twenty years. Until his death.

After the incident, weeks and months went by during which he admitted no visitors, and showed no interest in what was happening outside. He followed services by peering through two holes drilled in his door for the purpose. When called to the Torah, he appeared muffled in his ritual shawl, dishevelled and glassy-eyed, sowing panic as he passed. He hardly ate or slept, and refused to let himself be touched by doctors or comforted by friends. He no longer taught, not did he participate in any work. He cared neither to give nor to receive. He showed no interest in any of the disciples who continued to flock to him from everywhere, drawn by the troubling mask he showed them. Sometimes, at night, one could see him hunched over the table, staring into space, a shadow among the sickly, timorous shadows cast by the yellowish flame of a flickering candle.

The Rebbe: Menahem-Mendl of Kotzk. Or, more simply: Mendl of Kotzk. The Master-against-his-will, the angry saint, the divine rebel. Among the thousands of Hasidic leaders, great and small, from the Baal Shem's time to the Holocaust, he is undeniably the most disconcerting, mysterious figure of all. Also the most tragic.

As with the others, there is a disparity between the man and his legend. But in his case, it is the personality that stands out, that marks. In his case, reality surpasses imagination. If there is in Hasidism a Master greater than the image he projects, an image undoubtedly rearranged and embellished, it is he.

The stories one tells about him, and they are many, barely situate him and throw but a feeble light on his personality; they do no more than hint. Every fragment contains him, but he is more than the sum of all fragments. He is the flame that draws the sparks, a free and powerful flame that rises and carries the world along. The more one talks about him, the deeper his mystery looms. Alive, people dared not look him in the face; dead, but strong in his legend, here he is still, judging us as if he were our contemporary.

He left no portrait, no personal possessions. It is as though he never existed. Whatever we know about him – his habits, his boundless projects, his sudden fits of anger, his calls and his silences – we learn from the rare companions and disciples whose presence he tolerated. It is said that he set his meditations to paper but that he destroyed the pages as quickly as he covered them; he burned at night what he wrote during the day.

One says of him what one said of his two predecessors: that he wished to condense all there is to say but cannot be said about man, his destiny and his passage on earth . . . into a single page. This page, by itself, was to constitute a work entitled: 'The Book of Man'. He wrote it every day only to tear it up as night fell.

'Do you know why I don't publish anything?' he asked a visitor. 'I'll tell you why. Who would read me? Not the scientists, not the scholars; they know more than I do. To wish to read me, a man would have to feel that he knows less than I. Who might that be? A poor villager who works hard all week. When would he have the time to open a book? On Shabbat. When, at what time? Not on Friday night; he would be too tired. Saturday morning? Reserved for services. Following which, he comes home at midday, enjoys his meal, rushes through the customary songs and goes to lie down on his sofa, at peace with himself. Finally, he has a chance to glance at a book. He takes mine; he opens it. But he has eaten too much; he feels heavy. He gets drowsier by the minute; he falls asleep, and here is my volume falling from his hands. And is it for him – for that – that I should publish a book?'

On his deathbed he was still obsessed by the fear that his writings might survive him. Anxiously he questioned his old friend Yitzhak-Meir of Ger: 'Have you searched everywhere? In all the hiding places? Are you sure that everything is burned? That everything is ashes?'

There remains only his oral teaching. And his legend.

A legend of fear and trembling, lacking the joy that is a characteristic of Hasidism. One listens to it and feels bitten, scorched by a black and living fire shielded by a night without dawn.

Unlike other Hasidic tales, those of Kotzk, about Kotzk, rarely make one smile. They do not amuse, they do not appease, they trouble the teller as much as the listener; both come away with the same uneasiness, almost a remorse at being alive, at feeling – or not feeling – trapped in a universe doomed to falsehood and decay. 'It is written,' he said, 'that God looked over His work and found that it was good. Not I. I am more particular, more demanding than He. The world such as it is, I have no use for, except to blow my nose into it.' To a disciple who complained about the imperfections and gaps in creation, he replied: 'Could you do better? If so, what are you waiting for? Start working!' But he himself felt it was hardly worth the effort. 'The world,' he said, 'deserves not even a groan.' To him, it was inconceivable that man could see himself other than as a stranger – to his time, to his surroundings, a stranger to his fate. He said: 'I don't belong here; this is not my place.'

The tales, the sayings of the Kotzker Rebbe are easy to identify; impossible to mistake them for another's. They bear his mark, his scar. While those attributed to other Masters often seem interchangeable, his belong only to him. Indeed, they spring from a world which is a world all his own and in which one senses contained violence, dark and brutal powers, and the obsessions and conflicts of a man struggling with what negates yet attracts him, with what exalts yet mows him down: death, faith and the absolute. It is a world where man, despairing of his condition, deliberately, lucidly, chooses to probe deeply into his despair to seek, to hunt down a possibility of victory, however imprecise, however obscured by night.

Mendl of Kotzk wants man to be thirsty for truth, for the absolute, and never mind if he never reaches his goal and never mind if truth blinds and kills whoever discovers it, if the absolute takes revenge on whoever glimpses it. Faith? Faith is not all. There is the faith of the weak man who deceives himself. For Mendl of Kotzk, 'Thou shalt not steal' meant: 'Thou shalt not steal from thyself; not deceive thyself.'

He notices a young student lost in thought, and asks him: 'Do you remember the Talmud's advice: "Whoever meets a wicked man needs only to lead him to the House of Study." Ha! Did you actually think that by bringing him here, your task would be done? It isn't so. Every place has its wicked; the market and the House of Study each has its tempter. He is not that easily disposed of.'

Faith then is not an absolute refuge. Even truth, the world of truth, is vulnerable to corruption. But then, where lies the solution? In total rejection of compromise. It may not be within man's power to find truth, but it is up to him to reject lies, hypocrisy and cheating. And to uproot the thief he clandestinely carries inside him. As far as Mendl of Kotzk is concerned, all the sins of the world weigh less than the conceit born of self-deception. Man does not lower himself by his failures but by the alibis he invokes. Rather perish than mutilate the truth; that is Kotzk. It is the merciless challenge of man looking squarely at himself. Who does not believe he is making a great gift to God when he performs a good deed. And who observes the Law for its own sake rather than to please anyone, not even God. Result: whereas elsewhere one learns to serve God publicly and betray him in private, in Kotzk it was, if one may say so, the opposite. People claimed that it was easier to catch any other Hasid in flagrant sin than to catch a Hasid of Kotzk in flagrant obedience to the Torah.

A disciple tells him his woes: 'I come from Rizhin. There, every-thing is simple, everything is clear. I prayed and I knew I was praying; I studied and I knew I was studying. Here in Kotzk every-thing is mixed up, confused; I suffer from it, Rebbe. Terribly. I am lost. Please help me so I can pray and study as before. Please help me to stop suffering.' The Rebbe peers at his disciple in tears and asks: 'And who ever told you that God is interested in your studies and your prayers? And what if He preferred your tears and your suffering?'

At this level, man is forced to choose between two extremes: reaching out to the stars or escaping towards death; savage truth or destructive illusion; ultimate reward or irrevocable malediction. It is one or the other; there can be no middle ground. Said the Rebbe of Kotzk: 'The middle of the road is for horses.' For man, the road to God is not a royal way but a solitary path situated very high or very low: 'I stand with one foot in seventh heaven and with the other in the depths of the abyss.' Compromise is for the weak; concession for the cowards. 'What I ask of you?' he told his disciples before going into seclusion. 'Be strong! If that implies resisting fate, then you shall have to resist fate. If, in your search for truth, you must stand up to God, well, so be it.'

One Simhat Torah eve, the Rebbe watched his faithful dance holding the scrolls of the Law. 'That's not the way to dance!' he commented, looking angry. To please him, they started over again, this time with more fire. 'No,' he said, annoyed, 'that's not how one dances.' After several more failures, the Hasidim froze into an attitude of waiting. And the Rebbe exploded: 'Imagine yourselves on a mountain peak, on a razor's edge, and now: dance, dance, I tell you!'

Difficult? No matter! Who says that to be a man means to keep one's balance? Who says that to be a Jew is to accept oneself and submit? 'Let the heart fly into pieces,' he roared, 'let the shoulders come unhinged, let heaven and earth collapse, but man must not stray from his path!' Obstacles are unimportant. On the contrary, the more of them, the greater the merits of trying. Little does it matter if, going from discovery to discovery, one comes up against an unknown God, a God who does not compromise; one must continue one's quest, and nothing else counts. Thus it is not really surprising that Mendl of Kotzk should have praised the unsuspected qualities of a Pharaoh; he knew, that one, how to defy even God! 'What a fellow,' the Rebbe marvelled, 'he didn't cringe as soon as the blows started falling; he persevered!' What is important is to accept the challenge, to fight the battle; what is important is to choose an opponent more powerful than oneself.

Jacob did it. He fought the angel all night. Victorious, he sent him away at dawn. That was a mistake. He should have guessed the angel would come back more than once, in more than one disguise, perhaps even disguised as Jacob. Except that Jacob, in the meantime, had become Israel, who one night dared confront God and associate his mystery and name to His.

All his life Mendl of Kotzk continued this struggle with the angel and night. Alone. Alone against man, alone against heaven, against generations of dead ancestors and ancestral traditions that weigh on every memory.

That is why, in all the tales relating to him, what is stressed is the question rather than the answer, the thirst rather than what quenches it, the quest rather than the goal. What counts is the action, and never mind if it is desperate. What counts is what is missing, and never mind if it is never found. For the Rebbe of Kotzk, man is the lonely fighter who, beyond a certain point, expects nothing further from anybody: 'The Messiah will come and there will be nobody left to redeem.'

Surely, the exemplary wrath of Kotzk, born in Pshiskhe, went against the course charted by the Baal Shem and his companions. The song of the Baal Shem was stifled in Kotzk, transformed into a call of warning and despair.

Like the 'Jew', like Rebbe Bunam, Mendl of Kotzk is a Rebbe unlike other Rebbes, opposed to other Rebbes. The goal he sets for himself and the means he uses turn him into a magnet and his school into a hotbed of agitation.

He rebels against anything that is established and revered, he strikes out at all the taboos of the movement. In his opinion, one speaks too much of love and perfection; one uses words that are too big too often. The most pure, the most beautiful concepts, for being repeated too frequently and too smugly, lose their meaning, their vigour, their weight of silence. He, Mendl of Kotzk, decides to save Hasidism by redefining its objectives.

Ambitious, arrogant, he wishes to go beyond his limits; he considers himself the Baal Shem's equal. 'The Baal Shem never said there would never be greater than he!' Nor is he content merely to spread his teachings. He has nothing but contempt for those who take the beaten paths, for those who yield to habit; to imitate another or oneself is equally debasing. His ambition? To open unexplored roads, become a forerunner, a pioneer himself, throw over customs, social conventions, unmask the cheaters, review the progress already made and expose its traps and its illusions. Failing this, the movement would flounder and lose its substance.

He turns impudence into a virtue. Blind faith irritates him as much as mediocrity. 'In hell,' he says, 'one prays better than in paradise.' For the worshippers crowding the Tzaddikim's ante-rooms, he has nothing but contempt. 'Ten Just Men,' he says, 'were able to save Sodom, the city of sin. But ten sages would not enlighten an assembly of fools. Worse: a thousand fools would turn a sage into just another fool.' Appeals to caution have no effect on him; there is no recalling him to order; he is not to be intimidated. Pressure incites him only to further action. The more he is attacked, the less vulnerable he considers himself. Awe-inspiring, contemptuous of love, he pushes ahead, no risk too great for him. And too bad for those who fail to understand him.

And so, with him, the sanctuary is set ablaze. Flames that perhaps are heralding other conflagrations on two continents. A Europe fragmented by the lightning of wars wonders about its future and rejects its past. Nations change their faces, their destinies. Revolution in France, revolution in America. Napoleon reshapes the universe, kings fall, others extend their powers. History stirs and makes men shudder; it even makes them think. Thus Kotzk is neither coincidence nor anomaly. The Rebbe's groping search, filled with existential anguish, progresses in a solitude culminating in delirium. For him, anxiety and solitude recover their rights in Hasidism.

Who is Menahem-Mendl of Kotzk? Born in Goray in 1787, this glazier's son marries at fourteen, receiving a dowry of one thousand ducats. A year later, unhappy with his orderly, predictable life, he breaks with his father – an ardent and notorious adversary of Hasidism – and joins the Seer of Lublin, whom he eventually leaves to follow the Jew of Pshiskhe.

'In my town, long ago, there was an old man who told stories; I loved to listen to him. He would tell what he liked and what he knew, and I would remember what I needed. That is how I became a Hasid,' Rebbe Mendl reminisced.

At the death of the 'Jew', he remains with the 'Jew's' spiritual heir, Rebbe Bunam, and eventually succeeds him. He is then forty years old. At first, he resides in Tomashov and then in Kotzk, where at the age of seventy-two, almost blind, he departs as though disgusted with life.

A life lived under the sign of revolt against his father, then against his first Master and, in the end, against his own admirers. With the passing years, his rebellion gains in audacity and intensity; he aims it at all of creation and sometimes even beyond.

Already in Lublin and in Pshiskhe he is conspicuous among the other disciples, constantly swimming against the current. He is nicknamed 'Mendl the Dark', so sombre, withdrawn and gruff is he. He never takes part in the collective activities of the court. He speaks little, prefers not to be spoken to. His knowledge and prestige as a Talmudic scholar are such that he is left to do as he pleases. He is free to live in seclusion. He is considered strange, but the opinions of others leave him indifferent. Cloistered within himself, his contacts with the outer world are rare. Compliments bore him, social amenities exasperate him. Pious tears and noisy lamentations arouse in him a disdain he is not loath to display. The Seer, who keeps an eye on his favourite students, finds it necessary to have a word with him. He starts by commending him for his work, for his dedication, for the progress made in all areas, then he enjoins him to be more sociable: 'Be careful, Mendl, your path leads to melancholy; it is dangerous, it is unhealthy!' Mendl is outraged. That the Seer should give him a lecture, all right. But that he should compliment him or speak of risks is unacceptable. Does he think Mendl can be impressed or frightened? Mendl has no use for a Master who protects his disciples instead of lacerating their souls! He moves on to Pshiskhe without taking his leave from the Seer.

In Pshiskhe, where he has come to find himself a Master, he also meets companions: Rebbe Bunam, Rebbe Henokh, Rebbe Hersh, and Rebbe Yitzhak-Meir, future Rebbe of Ger.

This is how the latter came to take a liking to him: it was on New Year. During *Minha* services. The whole assembly was praying with fervour. Only Mendl, standing motionless in a corner by himself, prayed without moving his lips. This reticence, this implicit refusal, attracted Yitzhak-Meir's attention. He became, and remained, Mendl's friend.

Mendl, a frantic non-conformist, has his own way of saying his prayers. His way is to remain silent. He is the only one to refuse when asked to recite psalms for the dying Seer. 'The cry one holds back is more powerful,' he said later. Also: 'Certain experiences may be transmitted by language, others – more profound – by silence; and then there are those that cannot be transmitted, not even by

silence.' Never mind. Who says that experiences are made to be
shared? They must be lived. That's all. And who says that truth is
made to be revealed? It must be sought. That's all. Assuming it is
concealed in melancholy, is that any reason to seek elsewhere?

Here we are back at the key word of Kotzk: truth. The best-kept
secret in creation, it counts for more than life and for as much as
faith, and perhaps more than faith. In Kotzk, truth becomes obsession. It takes precedence over everything, shifts everything around.
Even prayer, even study. And certainly joy, ecstasy and peace of
mind. Man was created not to know happiness but truth. To discover it, one must start anew; everything must be reviewed. Man,
chosen by God, must choose Him in turn. All ready-made answers,
all seemingly unalterable certainties serve only to provide a good
conscience to those who like to sleep and live peaceably. To avoid
spending a lifetime tracking down truth, one pretends to have
found it. But, so one says in Kotzk, revelation itself, once it has
become a habit and a front, becomes suspect. The Rebbe would
trade all the riches of the world for one grain of truth. Riches?
What riches? The word makes him sick. So does the sight of money.
Everything that shines nauseates him. Honours? He despises them
for others and even more for himself. Thus it is not surprising that
the very functions of rabbi provoke in him a fierce resistance; he is
too much of an individualist to accept the notion that a man,
whatever his title, could resolve the problems of his fellow man.
You cannot live, you cannot fulfil yourself by proxy; no one can
seek in your place. The thief in you is underhanded, he hides inside
you, he *is* you; you must dig deep to root him out. No one will dig
in your place. No one will lay claim to truth in your stead, in your
name. No one will be your intermediary, just as you cannot be
another's. Your relationship with truth is your affair and no one
else's. And so, Mendl the Dark refuses the position of rabbi. He
sees himself rather in the role of anti-rabbi. But even his resistance
has limits; in spite of his protests, Mendl finally gives in to his
companions' wishes; after Rebbe Bunam's death he ascends the
throne.

More precisely: his friend Yitzhak-Meir gives up the crown in
his favour. The Hasidim would have preferred Yitzhak-Meir, who
is closer to them, more accessible. They respect Mendl the Dark
but he confuses them. They do not understand him nor do they
understand the uneasiness they feel in his presence.

The two friends spent a whole night in a tavern, discussing,
trying to convince one another to take charge of Pshiskhe's souls

and thus assure the school's continuity. No part of their conversation has come down to us; chronicle has recorded none of their arguments. All that is known is the outcome.

Named to succeed Rebbe Bunam, the young Menahem-Mendl settled down in Tomashov for two years, undoubtedly the two most beautiful years of his life; everything still seemed possible to him.

Bursting with enthusiasm, energy and boundless imagination, he turned his court into a laboratory for new ideas, into an experimental centre for a renascent Hasidism. People said: 'The spark kindled in Pshiskhe is now ablaze in Tomashov.' The flowery speakers, the miracle-makers, were to be found elsewhere. Tomashov was dominated by a far more exalted need; that of knowledge, of truth. The Rebbe did not deal in the supernatural, nor did he promise paradise and pardon; his faithful did not lapse into beatitude in his presence. Together, in one common impulse, they explored, they sought; Hasidism had become an adventure once more.

Young people were flocking to Tomashov from every corner of the land; it was becoming the capital of youth. At times one could witness odd scenes: mothers, abandoned wives, besieging the Rebbe's house, begging him to return their sons or husbands to them. To no avail. Every being, said the Rebbe, owes his life to three authors: father, mother and God. And God's share in man has priority. Besides, even if he had relented, his students would have refused to leave him. One does not leave a place, a community where every moment is an experience; one does not leave a man who lets you share in something unique: a liberation of the universe in terms of the individual.

In the battle of the generations, the Rebbe came out the winner. The young followed him. Enchanted, they asked nothing more than that he let them link their destiny to his. The parents wept and stormed in vain; the sons remained in Tomashov. With the Rebbe who, like an older brother, almost like a comrade, instilled in them his ideas and thirst for renewal. They danced, they sang, they studied together; they shared joys and discoveries, failures and longings; they lived in a kind of kibbutz. Joint assets, communal kitchen. Equality extended even to the House of Study; nobody enjoyed special rights or privileges. Often the Rebbe would walk the fields and forests with them, and there, in direct contact with nature, he would speak to them of his projects, his ambitions. And, following the Baal Shem's example, he would share his dreams with them.

Dreams to make one's head spin; romantic perhaps, but surely poignant. Captivating, unreal dreams, turning around an obsession: if he were to succeed in recruiting a spiritual elite, he could change the world.

It was in Tomashov that these theories began to take shape. Let them bring him ten courageous men, strong and pure – free of all lies – and they would tame, they would master fate. 'If I had a few companions [three hundred?] ready to climb the roof of the universe with me, coiffed with sauerkraut and girded with straw, to shout that God is God, victory would be certain!'

A striking image, more fiery than poetic, which shows his peculiar concept of his relations with the absolute and with his allies. From the latter he demanded total allegiance. *Emuna*, on his lips, meant not faith but loyalty. Whoever wished to join him had to forget all terrestrial concerns and bonds. One cannot at the same time covet the pleasures of the senses and carve oneself a place in the beyond; one cannot at the same time crave the essence and the accessory, the being and the superfluous. The absolute tolerates no fragmentation, no rival.

Tomashov took the place of Pshiskhe, Mezeritch and Medzebozh. Whoever entered, stayed. Stimulated to the limits of his capacity, the Hasid felt himself to be privileged. 'Know this,' wrote Yitzhak-Meir to Henokh of Alexander, 'just as there was lightning and thunder at Sinai, there now is lightning in Tomashov.' And Rebbe Mendl, without false modesty, made this remark to his intimates: 'I shall tell you who I am. There was the Great Maggid of Mezeritch, there was Shmelke of Nikolsburg, there was Elimelekh of Lizensk, there was the Seer of Lublin, there was the holy 'Jew' of Pshiskhe and there was Rebbe Bunam. I am the seventh, the sum, the substance; I am Shabbat.'

But the prelude of Tomashov came to an abrupt end. The local rabbi had his misgivings about the feverish activities of the Hasidim; they eluded his authority. The relationship soon became poisoned. Rebbe Mendl decided it would be best to move. To Kotzk, a small town – population: 1652 Jews, 1270 Christians. In no time at all it became famous.

Why Kotzk? Because there the Rebbe had a devoted admirer in the person of the local rabbi – which simplified matters greatly. Legend, however, provides a more picturesque explanation: the Rebbe and his faithful were wandering from village to village, nowhere finding a hospitable place to settle down. In Kotzk they were welcomed by flying stones. 'Well now, this is a good omen,' the Rebbe is said to have commented, 'here at least the people are not indifferent.'

During the next ten years the Rebbe worked on himself and his disciples as though they were metaphysical raw material, elaborating his concept of man projected into the universe between God and death.

He said: 'God sends souls down to earth and then brings them back by making them climb ladders. Thence men's preoccupation: souls upon souls, all in pursuit of ladders. Some give up; they throw themselves towards heaven, and fall. Never mind. They will try again.'

Falls did not discourage him. He seemed drawn to, hypnotized by, the abyss. The idea that he might find an answer, that he might glimpse a certainty at the end of his voyage, only increased his anguish.

To his friend Yitzhak-Meir, he said: 'When he cursed the serpent, God condemned him to slither on the ground and feed on dust. What a strange malediction! The serpent will never be hungry, is that a malediction? Yes, it is, and a dreadful one at that!'

A need that could be satisfied, a thirst that could be quenched were of no interest to him. A God whose intentions he would understand could not suit him. To Rebbe Yaakov of Radzimin, who told him that the purpose of man was to work for the perfection of his soul, he replied disdainfully: 'No, no, it wouldn't be worth it. The purpose of man is to raise the sky.' To raise it until it becomes unattainable. Rather look at a sky way up high, lost in the clouds, than see it in the mud, at your feet.

Easier said than done. Stated the Kotzker: 'It is easier to extract Israel from exile than exile from Israel.' The problem is that men want to live in this world as much as in the other. 'Since God is God, let Him come down from His throne. Let him visit the huts, the hearts in distress. There are children to be fed, to be clothed, there is the wife to take care of, the creditor to placate; there is the head that is bursting.'

Confronted with worshippers who saw in him a rabbi like all the others, here to help them carry their burdens, the Rebbe cried out: 'What do they want from me? Why do they harass me? How am I to make them understand that it is not my task to fill their stomachs and appease their sleep?'

A man began to sob: 'I am a widower and poor; I have seven hungry children at home.' – The Rebbe shook his head: 'What do you want me to do? Comfort you? I won't do it. It's too much for me. Ask God: let Him comfort you.'

'Pray for me,' a Hasid begged him. 'Things are going badly, I need help; intercede on my behalf.' – And the Rebbe answered him harshly: 'Are you too sick to say your own prayers?' – 'I don't know how.' – 'What? You don't know? *That* is your true problem!' And he dismissed him.

One night he awakened his friend Hersh Tomashover. There he stood, a candle in his hand, saying: 'Look, here in my heart there is such pain, such terrible pain, and they, out there, think of nothing else but haunting me with their foolishness and foibles.'

The old intimacy and comradery between Master and disciples that had existed in Tomashov is gone. Disillusioned and bitter, the Rebbe detaches himself more and more from his followers. The extraordinary Rebbe is burdened with disciples who are ordinary Hasidim. They irritate him and he shows it. He becomes impatient, intolerant, more unrelenting than ever. These people, riveted to their bodies, annoy him; he thinks they do it on purpose. Their timorous servility makes him nasty. He sees everything as being petty, derisive: 'Whoever believes in miracles is an imbecile, whoever does not is an atheist,' he says.

Impossible to do the right thing. He states something and promptly denies it. Not content to revel in paradox, he drives it to paroxysm. He demands erudition but does not hesitate to mock it; he stresses the importance of preparations for services, but services themselves are dispatched almost absent-mindedly. The external signs of joy repel him, but he does not appreciate those who think to 'buy' God with tears. He aspires to wrest man from his all too human condition, yet at the same time he declares that sanctity itself must be human. Man who addresses God in a familiar way incurs His displeasure as much as man who treats Him as a stranger.

Of course, the more strangely he behaves, the more his prestige grows. This displeases him. In the other Hasidic courts he is criticized denounced; he rejoices. He finds his disciples' praise much mbarrassing. He feels stifled, he would like to be free, break s, but his faithful are in his way. He is convinced of it; lding him back. He would give anything to see them go. , let them turn against him. But they do not. On the contrary, their numbers increase. This living knot, tense with contradictions, clearly is in touch with invisible forces. They admire him, they would lift him to the clouds. Fortunately, he is on his guard. He gives free rein to his rage: 'Long ago, in my youth, when I could still see inside myself, all these people did not dare approach this closely!' The more he screams, the more they crowd his doorstep. He wins men by the fear he inspires.

From now on, in Kotzk, one lives in awe and fear. And in misery as well. (Letter from the Rebbe to his friend Yitzhak-Meir: 'If you have had no news from us, it is because we lack the money for stamps.')

In Kotzk one does not speak; one roars or one keeps quiet. One spends one's time fighting, cheating desire; one does the opposite of what one feels like doing. One eats when one is not hungry, one does without water when one is thirsty. One prays either later or earlier than is customary. The Rebbe says: 'When one feels like shouting and doesn't, this is when one truly shouts.' A convalescing Rebbe David is questioned by his father: 'You thought you were going to die?' – Yes, that was what he had thought. – 'And what did you feel?' – 'The need to recite the *Sh'ma Israel* to proclaim my faith in God.' – 'And did you do it?' – No, the son had checked himself. – 'Very good,' cries the Rebbe of Kotzk, 'you're a true Hasid!'

Silence in Kotzk is so heavy, so dense that it tears the nights. One doesn't dream, one is delirious. One doesn't walk, one runs. One walks a tightrope, and it is he, the Rebbe, who holds both ends. He is present in all eyes, in all thoughts; he paralyzes. One runs after him, but he flees. Sometimes he awakens a faithful and tells him: 'Go away, I am the Master here.' And the other bursts into sobs. It is enough for him to look into someone's eyes for the other to faint. 'Why do you address God by calling him Father?' he scolds a young man. 'Who told you He is your father? Did He? If you want Him to be, you must force Him!' Another time he stops a disciple: 'Do you know where God resides?' And as the other gapes in astonishment, the Rebbe continues: 'I'll tell you: He resides where He is allowed to enter.'

With his questions, his unpredictable outbursts of anger, he terrorizes people; as soon as he appears, they feel guilty. Guilty of weakness, of cowardice. 'Faces, faces, you all have faces,' he cries one night, 'but is there one, just one, that could compare itself to God's?' Created in God's image, man owes it to himself to resemble Him, to be whole like Him. Says he: 'I prefer a total miscreant to a

Jew who is only half Jewish.' And his also these harsh, harrowing words: 'If I am and You are because I am myself and You are Yourself, then I am I and You are You; but if I am because You are, then I am not I and You are not You.'

His words are repeated over and over; they are endowed with special meanings. One hesitates between the desire to understand and the fear of violating an interdiction. In the end, even his friends are at a loss. Without explanation, he will praise someone he publicly insulted the day before. His wife is sick; he does not leave her bedside for weeks. His son gets married: it takes a great deal of persuasion to make him attend the wedding.

Another contradiction: he who has but contempt for earthly matters becomes interested in politics. He offers his support to the Polish national revolution against the Russian occupant. He signs proclamations and appeals, lends his name to collect funds. The Poles are subdued, crushed. And the Rebbe, threatened with arrest by the Russians, changes his name: Halperin becomes Morgenstern.

A change which in no way affects his fate. He remains the rebel he was. He only goes deeper into the shadows that crowd his universe. Some of his disciples, among them Mordhai-Yosseph of Izhbitze, begin to balk: 'He is going too far; we need a human being, not a seraph, to lead the way.' The Rebbe senses the growing opposition, but does not condescend to take offence. And that is when the mysterious incident, mentioned earlier, takes place. The break occurs. 'Broken are the tablets of the Law,' exclaims Mordhai-Yosseph, the dissidents' leader. And like his Master had done earlier, he leaves, taking along a large number of disciples. Wounded in his pride, the Rebbe does not hide his resentment. He who had hoped to found an elite was losing his best men, and for what petty reasons! Because he did not show enough concern for their daily bread! His disappointment is doubly bitter.

A few faithful remain, men of distinction all: Yitzhak-Meir, Yehiel-Meir of Gostinin, the Gaon of Sokhatchov and Yitzhak of Worke. But the Rebbe is inconsolable. Perhaps he loved those who left him in spite of what they had done. They resembled him, they dared defy him, even him.

A   in a little while, some of the dissidents return; he chases
    ay: 'Why did you come back? To see me? Am I a chimney
    t you should stare at me like that?'

    vn, cantankerous, his eyes reddened from lack of sleep,
    empt, speaking in abrupt sentences, the Rebbe aspires

to nothing but silence and solitude. 'There is nobody I want to see,' he tells his faithful friend Hersh Tomashover. 'Tell them to leave me alone; use a cane if you must.' Another time: 'I shall throw myself on these beggars like a wounded bear separated from his brood.'

From this period there remain, recorded helter-skelter by chronicle, a cry of anguish, a story, a parable. The same shudder runs through them all.

A parable: The Midrash tells the episode of the traveller who loses his way in the forest. He sees a castle in flames. It's an empty castle, thinks the traveller. Suddenly he hears a voice crying: 'Help, help me, I am the owner of the castle!' And the Rebbe repeats: 'The castle is ablaze, the forest is burning, and the owner cries for help; what does it mean? That the castle is not empty and that there is an owner!'

And the Rebbe began to tremble and all those present trembled with him.

An offering: Yitzhak of Worke, one of the rare disciples that the Rebbe of Kotzk continued to receive after he went into seclusion, greeted him on that certain day the way he always did: 'Peace upon you, Rebbe.' – 'Don't say that! You hear me? Don't call me Rebbe, I am something else. You want to know who I am? A goat, yes, a goat! You don't believe me? Well, then listen to the story of the holy goat, which is the story of an offering.

'Once upon time there was a Jew who lost his snuffbox. He searched everywhere, for it meant a lot to him. And then he was too poor to buy himself a new one. When he could not find it anywhere, he began to cry. While walking and searching, he cried and cried. Until he suddenly realized he was in the middle of a forest. And in this forest he came upon the strangest creature, and the most generous as well: a goat. A holy goat, who roamed the roads of time and of the universe waiting for midnight. And every midnight he touched the heavens with his immense horns, awakening the stars and inspiring them to sing the glory of that which is eternal. "Why are you so sad?" the goat asked. And the Jew told him the truth; that he had lost his snuffbox. – "Is that all?" the goat asked. "Nothing could be simpler, it is foolish to cry; I'll help you. Do you have a knife? Yes? Good; take it out. And now, cut yourself a piece of horn and make yourself a snuffbox."

'The Jew didn't have to be told twice. When he came back to the village the people marvelled; his tobacco had the smell of paradise.

He was harried with questions until he admitted that it was not the tobacco but the snuffbox. In the end, he had to tell them the whole story. No sooner had he finished, than the entire village population ran for their knives and into the forest, where they did indeed find the most amiable and saintly goat in the world. And they began to cut his horns, which became smaller and smaller by the minute until they disappeared altogether. And so, that same night, the goat was no longer able to touch the sky to wake up the stars and make them sing; he could only look at them from far away, with longing and a little remorse. . . That is why I forbid you to call me Rebbe, do you hear me?'

A visit: One night the Rebbe walked up to Feivel the Watchman, who was asleep: '*He* was here, did you hear him?' Taken aback, afraid to vex the Master, Feivel stammered: 'Yes, I heard him.' He didn't know whom the Rebbe meant, but he could not keep himself from trembling. And the Rebbe went on musing: 'He came, he said what he had to say, he left again. My ears can still perceive the sound of his steps but his voice no longer reaches me.'

'Some of the things he said I understood only forty years later,' said the Gaon Avraham of Sokhatchov. Forty years? Three times forty.

A stranger to his own generation, Mendl of Kotzk seems to belong to ours; he could be our contemporary. His anger is our anger, our revolts reflect his.

Yet the figure remains obscure, unexplained. It cannot be helped. Kotzk cannot be explained; with some luck, it can be told. For Kotzk, within the Hasidic movement, is an experience transmitted from being to being, lips closed and eyes meeting eyes. A question that continues, unreconciled with either time or life, Kotzk is neither philosophy nor social system; Kotzk is a narrow and solitary road whose beginning touches its end; a road where silence enters the word and tears it apart the way the eye tears apart what it sees. Kotzk means throwing off despair through despair. Kotzk means prison become sanctuary.

Let us come back to our starting point, that fateful and harrowing Shabbat when the Rebbe, pushed to the limit of his endurance, chose to protest against the scandal of history.

Why did he withdraw from man? What did he want to say, and to ⟨wh⟩om, in his solitude and silence? What enemy was he hiding ⟨from?⟩ And which one was he pursuing?

⟨The⟩ texts suggest that his seclusion, from a certain point on, ⟨was forc⟩ed upon him. Sequestration? Possibly. It was necessary ⟨for⟩ both the Rebbe and his Hasidim; he was spreading panic. Who can measure the effect on a disciple of seeing his Master in the throes of depression? Better to limit their contacts.

But scholars seem to agree that in the beginning, the Rebbe's isolation was of his own choosing. He fled crowds for fear that they would absorb him, that his being would be swallowed by theirs. And then he clung fiercely, jealously, to his secret. He even said it: 'Once revealed, every secret is diminished.' In order to receive the Law, Moses had to climb the mountain alone.

Did Mendl of Kotzk blaspheme? It hardly matters. The fact is that noted religious personalities – the Rebbe of Ger, the Gaon of Sokhatchov, the Rebbe of Worke – remained loyal to him to the end. They had undoubtedly accepted the fact that while he could speak to God in ways different from their own, he nevertheless asserted their common faith.

Perhaps his break with society corresponded to a disillusionment on another level. Could he have become aware of the change that had occurred in him? Earlier he had been afraid never to discover truth; now he was afraid that he had already discovered it. Therefore, there was no solution; whether man turns to one side or the other, he still encounters fear. The link between man and God, between man and his fellow man? Fear. God wants to be feared rather than loved. And Mendl of Kotzk protests: 'If that is life, I don't want it; I'll go through it as a stranger. If that is man, what is the good of saving him?'

Another hypothesis: Could he have foreseen that one hundred years after his retreat another fire would set the continent ablaze, and that its first victims would be Jewish men and women abandoned by God and by all mankind? Could it be that from that moment on he planned to fight fire with fire – attempting to prepare us, demanding that we be strong, intransigent, capable of resisting evil no matter what form it takes, the comfort of faith included; capable of resisting even God and the hope in God?

Be that as it may, since Menahem-Mendl of Kotzk, we know that man can become drunk on God, that man can offer Him his soul and his reason as well. That man can become mad of God, on God.

His last words were: 'At last I shall see Him face to face.'

We don't know – nor will we ever know – whether these words expressed an ancient fear or a renewed defiance. In the final analysis, Mendl of Kotzk will have had a dialogue with one single Being. And the story of Kotzk is the story of that dialogue – a story that burns as burns the castle, as burns the forest. But thanks to Kotzk, we hear a voice and we know that the castle is not empty, that history is not deserted; somebody is there and he is calling us.

Afterword

. . . Having reached the end of his first pilgrimage to the sources of Hasidic experience, the narrator feels a need to explain himself briefly; if only to define the meaning and motivation of his undertaking.

Obviously, his purpose was not to create a scholarly work of critical analysis. Nor does he claim the role of either historian or philosopher; the only role that suits him is the one, less presumptuous though more limited, of storyteller who transmits what was given to him, as faithfully as possible, yet lending it his own voice and intonation and sometimes his wonder or simply: his fervour.

Here then is a volume that could have been composed or structured in a different way; this Master rather than that, one more legend added to so many others.

For the teller of these tales has chosen his subjects following fancy rather than reason, in the course of various lectures given here and there in France and the United States. He might have chosen to outline the theories or sociological and theological implications of Hasidism. Instead, he was seduced by the idea of bringing back to life some of the characters that peopled his universe, the universe of his childhood. They fascinate and haunt him still, ever more. For the Hasidic movement that preached brotherhood and reconciliation became the altar upon which an entire people was immolated. Sometimes the child in me tells me that the world did not deserve this Law, this love, this spirit and this song that accompany man on his lonely road. The world did not deserve the fables the Hasidim told them; that is why they were the first to be caught and swept away in the turmoil.

These Hasidim, whose fate my grandfather shared in life as in death, were part of my world. I responded to their simplicity, their love of beauty. They knew how to worship. And trust. They had mastered the art of giving and receiving. Of sharing and taking part. In their communities, no beggar ever went hungry on Shabbat. In spite of their poverty, their misery, they asked nothing of others.

And were endlessly surprised by and grateful for the smallest expression of warmth, of generosity. Therefore, they could not survive in a society ruled by cold cruelty, a cruelty both impersonal and absurd.

Why is there a renewal of interest in them today? Is it that man feels guilty? Does their death weigh on his conscience? Perhaps. But there is something else: he is moved and troubled by their message, its loss irrevocably linked to his own inability to believe and persevere. 'God is prayer,' said Rebbe Pinhas of Koretz. And never has modern man been more closed to prayer.

It must be pointed out that all the conditions that existed in the eighteenth century, when Hasidism came into being, prevail again today. Physical and emotional insecurity, fallen idols, the scourge of violence. Where can one go, where can one hide? 'Hell exists and it is of this world,' said Rebbe Nahman, 'but none dares speak of it.' Wrong. Today everyone dares. Never before has mankind known such anguish. Such ugliness. Man walks the moon but his soul remains rivetted to earth. Once upon a time it was the opposite. Despairing of the present, man seeks beauty in legends. Like the Hasid long ago.

In his universe, beggars are princes; the mute are sages. Endowed with special powers, vagabonds roam the earth and change it. Such is the nature of Hasidism: the accent is placed on presence and also on transformation. In Hasidism, everything is possible, everything becomes possible by the mere presence of someone who knows how to listen, to love and give of himself. The essence of a Hasidic legend? An attempt to humanize fate.

And so the story that I have tried to tell here has been told more than once, by more than one person. It is always the same, and I, in turn, do nothing but transmit.

A needless repetition? No. Repetition, in Judaism, can assume a creative role. Of Eliezer Ben-Hyrkenos it was said that he never pronounced a word he had not heard from his Master. Strange compliment. Could Rabbi Eliezer have invented nothing, composed nothing? On the contrary: he did much. Still, it was by repeating the teachings that linked him to Moses and through him to God, that he contributed to Jewish thought and destiny. To transmit is more important than to innovate. Every question a disciple will ask his Master, and that until the end of time, Moses already knew. Yet, we must ask the questions and make them ours by repeating them. In Hebrew, the word *massora*, tradition, comes from the verb *limsor*, to transmit. In our history, this need to communicate, to share, comes close to being an obsession.

Of course, all experiences cannot be transmitted by the word. There are those that must be transmitted from being to being, by a whisper or a glance, or – and why not – through laughter. Rebbe Henokh of Alexander knew that when his Master, Rebbe Mendl of Kotzk, told him funny stories, he was actually lamenting the destruction of the Temple in Jerusalem. And when, at the conclusion of Shabbat, I listened to the old men speak of their respective Rebbes, I closed my eyes to see what they were seeing.

The Baal Shem, the Maggid, Levi-Yitzhak, Israel of Rizhin; now it is my turn to show them the way I saw them as a child, as I see them still. They are subjective, incomplete, these portraits, with their share of unavoidable repetitions, errors and gaps. They may well say more about the narrator than about his characters. Perhaps he only told the tales of Nahman of Bratzlav or Mendl of Kotzk to show how they influenced his own attitude towards language and what it conceals, towards man, his truth and his solitude.

Perhaps he spoke of Levi-Yitzhak of Berditchev only to claim his heritage. And of Zusia of Onipol only to acknowledge what he owes him, what he owes all these Rebbes of another era who have remained his Masters. The omission of certain illustrious figures is due only to chance, nothing else. Shneur-Zalmen of Ladi, Haim of Tzanz, Yitzhak-Meir of Ger, Meir of Premishlan, Naftali-Hersh of Ropshitz, Mendl of Kossov, Moshe of Ujhely; each one of them founded a school, each is a source of enrichment. The teller of tales hopes to show this later; this is but the beginning of his pilgrimage. If the priorities seem arbitrary, it is because they are dictated by his childhood. In his town, for instance, one spoke more of Rizhin than of Ger, one felt closer to the Baal Shem than to his commentators. Thus his choice stems from criteria no one else is obliged to accept. He takes what he needs and leaves the rest for another time. If he favours a particular legend over another, it does not mean that it is any truer but only that he heard this one and not the other. If a certain tale is attributed to two, three or five different Masters, it becomes his gift to the one he loves most. Nor will he be the first to do this; every Hasid does it, and has done it since the Baal Shem. Why, then, shouldn't he?

All the more since – in his role of storyteller, and that is the essential point – he has but one motivation: to tell of himself while telling of others. He wishes neither to teach nor to convince, but to close gaps and create new bonds. Nor does he try to explain what was or even what is; he only tries to wrest from death certain prayers, certain faces, by appealing to the imagination and the nostalgia that make men listen when his story is told.

Somewhere a Master

Contents

Pinhas of Koretz

One day, a young Hasid came to see Rebbe Pinhas of Koretz, known for his wisdom and compassion.

'Help me, Master,' he said. 'I need your advice, I need your support. My distress is unbearable; make it disappear. The world around me, the world inside me, are filled with turmoil and sadness. Men are not human, life is not sacred. Words are empty – empty of truth, empty of faith. So strong are my doubts that I no longer know who I am – nor do I care to know. What am I to do, Rebbe? Tell me, what am I to do?'

'Go and study,' said Rebbe Pinhas of Koretz. 'It's the only remedy I know. Torah contains all the answers. Torah *is* the answer.'

'Woe unto me,' said the disciple. 'I am unable even to study. So shaky are my foundations, so all-pervasive my uncertainties, that my mind finds no anchor, no safety. It wanders and wanders, and leaves me behind. I open the Talmud and contemplate it endlessly, aimlessly. For weeks and weeks I remain riveted to the same page, to the same problem. I cannot go farther, not even by a step, not even by a line. What must I do, Rebbe, what can I do to go on?'

When a Jew can provide no answer, he at least has a tale to tell. And so Rebbe Pinhas of Koretz invited the young man to come closer, and then said with a smile, 'You must know, my friend, that what is happening to you also happened to me. When I was your age I stumbled over the same obstacles. I, too, was filled with questions and doubts. About man and his fate, creation and its meaning. I was struggling with so many dark forces that I could not advance; I was wallowing in doubt, locked in despair. I tried study, prayer, meditation. In vain. Penitence, silence, solitude. My doubts remained doubts. Worse: they became threats. Impossible to proceed, to project myself into the future. I simply could not go on. Then one day I learned that Rebbe Israel Baal Shem Tov would be coming to our town. Curiosity led me to the *shtibl*, where he was receiving his followers. I entered just as he was finishing the *Amida* prayer. He turned around and saw me, and I was convinced that he was seeing me, me and no one else. The intensity of his gaze overwhelmed me, and I felt less alone. And strangely, I was able to go home, open the Talmud, and plunge into my studies once more. You see,' said Rebbe Pinhas of Koretz, 'the questions remained questions. But I was able to go on . . .'

What did Pinhas of Koretz try to teach his young visitor? One: Not to give up. Even if some questions are without answers, go on asking them. Two: Doubts are not necessarily destructive – provided they bring one to a Rebbe. Three: One must not think that one is alone and that one's tragedy is exclusively one's own; others have gone through the same sorrow and endured the same anguish. Four: One must know where to look, and to whom. Five: God is everywhere, even in pain, even in the search for faith. Six: A good story in Hasidism is not about miracles, but about friendship and hope – the greatest miracles of all.

A variation of the same story: Fearing that his faith would be weakened by doubts, Rebbe Pinhas decided to go to Medzibozh to see Rebbe Israel Baal Shem Tov, the founder of the Hasidic movement. By coincidence, that day the Besht,* as he was known, happened to be visiting Koretz. Rebbe Pinhas quickly returned to Koretz and ran to the inn where the Baal Shem was staying. There he heard the Master explaining to his followers the passage in Scripture describing how Moses stood with his arms raised in prayer, giving his people the strength to do battle against the Amalekites.

'It happens,' said the Master, 'that a person can feel troubled; it happens that a person's faith can waver. What does one do then? One turns to God in prayer and implores God to help one recapture one's true faith.'

And Rebbe Pinhas understood that the Besht had meant him too.

Though he was one of the Besht's closest companions, Rebbe Pinhas never formally joined the Hasidic movement. He chose to remain on the sidelines, watching with interest and amusement what was happening onstage.

After the death of the Founder, his peers wanted Rebbe Pinhas to at least assume the role of mediator in the power struggle between the two factions representing the two contenders for the succession: Rebbe Dov-Ber of Mezeritch and Rebbe Yaakov-Yosseph of Polnoye. But Rebbe Pinhas refused.

Actually, he himself would have made an excellent candidate to succeed the Besht. He was respected and celebrated by scholars and disciples alike. The Besht's affection for him was well known.

* From the Hebrew acronym of his name.

Once the Besht was asked to give his opinion of his friends, and he did. When he came to Rebbe Pinhas he stopped: and said nothing. Rebbe Pinhas was a case apart. The famous 'Grandfather of Shpole' admired him; so did the legendary Reb Leib, son of Sarah, who called him 'the brain of the world'. Hasidic tradition has it that the Besht left his knowledge to the Maggid of Mezeritch, his saintliness to Reb Mikhel of Zlotchov and his wisdom to Rebbe Pinhas of Koretz. In Hasidic literature, Rebbe Pinhas is called 'the Sage'.

Withdrawn, reserved, modest, an individualist, he refused to be crowned Rebbe. He held no court, proposed no doctrine, promised no miracles, established no dynasty, declined honours and privileges. He had five sons but only one disciple: Rebbe Raphael of Barshad, a former beadle and gravedigger whom he had pulled out of anonymity. When Rebbe Pinhas died on his way to the Holy Land, he was succeeded by this disciple. That day at the Wall in Jerusalem, a Tzaddik saw the Shekhina – Divine Presence – in mourning.

Rebbe Pinhas: the most human, the most gracious and beautiful character among the Elders of Hasidism.

Who was he?

As is the case with most of his illustrious contemporaries, not much is known of Rebbe Pinhas' childhood and formative years. Born in 1728 in Shklov into a poor rabbinic family, of ancestors who had died as martyrs of the faith, he studied Talmud and Kabbala; he also showed an unusual interest in the exact sciences and philosophy.

He rarely spoke of his father. Instead, he frequently referred to his grandfather – also Rebbe Pinhas – who had made it his lifework to roam around Eastern Europe seeking out Jewish converts to Christianity to bring them back to the fold.

Rebbe Pinhas married young and led an austere life. For a while he taught small children and was nicknamed 'the dark teacher', perhaps because of his dark complexion, perhaps because of his taste for solitude and meditation.

Unlike the Besht, he quickly gained a wide reputation as a rabbinic and mystical scholar. His teachings contain commentaries on the Bible, the Zohar, the Talmud and even on the Code of Ethics, the *Shulkhan Arukh*.

Also unlike the Besht, it had been his wish to be able to stay in one place and do his work there – but he could not. He fled Shklov to avoid harassment and took refuge in Miropol in Volhynia. From there he moved to Koretz, then to Ostraha, where he settled. He remained there until he decided to leave for the Holy Land in 1791. On his way, he stopped in Shipitovke, unaware that death was waiting for him there.

He was kind and generous. He once overheard his wife shouting at their servant and promptly admonished her, 'Please – please never raise your voice at any human being; a human being is precious, so precious.' He himself spoke softly, patiently. A devoted husband, a good father, he rarely lost his temper. 'I don't think I succeeded in defeating vanity,' he once remarked. 'But I did succeed in controlling my anger. I simply put it into my pocket and I pull it out only when I absolutely need to.'

Contemplative by nature, he would gaze at his visitors and say nothing – thereby causing his visitors to look at him and say nothing. He prayed quietly, meditatively, shunning all visible demonstrations of ecstasy.

At the death of the Besht in 1760, Rebbe Pinhas was barely thirty-two, so he must have been quite young when they first met. The Besht treated him as an equal and went out of his way to win him over, although, unlike the Besht's other companions – such as Reb Gershon of Kitev, Reb Nahman of Kossov, and Reb Mikhel of Zlotchov – Rebbe Pinhas did not belong to any existing esoteric group. He represented no potential ally, no influential clan whose adherence was important to the new movement. No, the Besht wanted Rebbe Pinhas for what he was and not for what he possessed: he wanted him for himself and not for the movement. Perhaps he needed him more as a friend than as a follower.

'Man is not alone,' the Besht told him when they first met. 'God makes us remember the past so as to break our solitude. Our forefathers stand behind us, some of them tested or chosen by God. Whatever they did, they did for us. Whatever we do, we do for them. Long ago, in Egypt, every one of us strove for the preservation of the holy tongue, the names of our ancestors and their descendants, and the memory of the Covenant. Every one of us sat at the Prophets' feet to receive their teachings. Every one of us marched through the desert, to Sinai and from Sinai. Every one of us watched the splendour and the desolation of Jerusalem. Every one of us followed Reb Yohanan Ben-Zakkai into exile; and every one of us shared his anguish and pride. And that is why we must stay together.'

There was something delicate, reticent and yet warm, in their relationship. Their mutual respect and affection went so far as to prevent the one from trying to change the other.

Legend has it that Rebbe Pinhas visited the Besht twice – and that the Besht visited him twice. Another Hasidic tradition claims that Rebbe Pinhas learned three things from the Besht. We do not know what they were. But we do know that, in exchange, Rebbe Pinhas taught the Besht three things. Could they have been the same things?

The two friends were together on the last Shavuot they were to spend together, when the Besht was lying on his deathbed. Most of the disciples had obeyed the Master's wish and returned home. Rebbe Pinhas had stayed. At one point he began to pray, quietly but fervently, interceding with heaven on behalf of the old Master. 'Too late,' the Besht whispered, 'too late, Pinhas. What is done is done; what is done will not be undone.'

In the dispute over who was to be the Besht's successor, Rebbe Pinhas, characteristically, felt closer to the losers – in particular to the dead Master's son, Reb Tzvi-Hersh, whose name is frequently mentioned in his sayings. Rebbe Pinhas was Reb Tzvi-Hersh's ever-present and affectionate confidant and protector.

He also maintained cordial relations with another loser, Reb Yaakov-Yosseph of Polnoye, who had aspired to succeed the Besht after serving him faithfully. Feeling rejected and bitter, Reb Yaakov-Yosseph often chose to celebrate Shabbat alone. Only Rebbe Pinhas sometimes came to keep him company.

Once Rebbe Pinhas tried to console his unhappy friend with the following parable: 'When the king retires at night, his crown rests on a nail fastened to the wall. Why on a nail, a common object used by common people for common purposes, and not on the head of a minister especially selected for such a distinct honour? I shall tell you why: After a while, with the crown resting on his head, the minister might take himself seriously. No such danger with a nail . . .'

From this we may conclude that there probably was some tension in his relations with the winner, Rebbe Dov-Ber, the great Maggid of Mezeritch. Not that Rebbe Pinhas had objected to the Maggid's election, or that he lacked consideration for his virtues and talents. No. He had high regard for the new leader of the movement. But in his own gentle way, Pinhas distrusted all leaders. That is why he refused to become one himself. For a long time he wore no rabbinic garment, accepted no crown and discouraged all manifestations of admiration. He would wear shabby clothes and sit with beggars and strangers near the stove, far from the limelight. Was it that he felt unworthy or unable to guide others towards truth? Perhaps he worried too much about the perils of vanity inherent in leadership – perhaps he was afraid of fame.

The Grandfather of Shpole told the following story: 'For years and years I lived the life of a wanderer. In the company of beggars, I went from town to town, from village to village. Once we happened to arrive in Koretz on Shabbat eve. So we went to attend services conducted by Rebbe Pinhas. When the services were over, he greeted every one of us. When my turn came to shake his hand, he looked at me – and embraced me; he knew who I was. Years later, when I was no longer anonymous, I came to visit him again. Again it was Shabbat eve. Again Rebbe Pinhas greeted all the strangers. Then came my turn. He looked at me and said, "Who are *you*? Where do *you* come from?"'

How typical of Rebbe Pinhas. When *nobody* knew the Grandfather of Shpole, he recognized him. Now that *everybody* knew him, he did not.

As for the Grandfather of Shpole, he concluded the story by saying, 'It is not good to be famous, no, it is not good, I am telling you.'

Among Rebbe Pinhas' numerous aphorisms, all reflecting common sense and wisdom, many relate to the pitfalls of vanity – how to unmask it, how to fight it and vanquish it.

'If someone finds it necessary to honour me,' he said, 'that means he is more humble than I. Which means he is better and saintlier than I. Which means that I should honour him. But then, why is he honouring me?'

His disciple, Rebbe Raphael of Barshad, said: 'When I shall appear before the heavenly tribunal, its members will question me on my various sins, and I, naturally, shall do my best to invent all kinds of excuses. Why didn't I study enough? I had neither the talent nor the time. Why didn't I pray with greater concentration? I was too busy making a living. And fasting, did I do some fasting? No, no, I was too weak. What about charity? No, no, I was too poor. But then they will ask me, "If *this* is how it was – if you didn't study and didn't pray, if you lacked both compassion and charity, if you were too busy with yourself – how did it come about that you exuded such vanity?" And to this I shall have no answer, no excuse.'

Rebbe Pinhas said: 'Every sin is linked to a reason, good or bad –
with the sole exception of vanity, which needs no reason to grow
and grow. One can easily lie in rags on the ground and be hungry;
one could lack all virtues and all knowledge, and still think endlessly, I am great, I am learned, I am just.'

He also said: 'Everything I know I learned earlier, when I sat in
the last row, out of sight. Now I am here, occupying a place of
honour, and I don't understand . . .'

Of course, all Masters were aware of the spiritual threat inherent
in their position. It is difficult to claim to possess powers and not
fall into the trap of believing that one deserves them. From the
Maggid on, most Hasidic leaders stressed the absolute and constant
need to fight pride and complacency. Except that he, Rebbe Pinhas,
refused even to be tempted.

What, then, attracted him to Hasidism? Only the Besht and his
friendship? No. He stayed attached to the movement some thirty
years after the death of its founder. His motives were not only
personal; they were linked to the conditions inside the Jewish communities in Eastern Europe.

Hasidism was then the most revolutionary movement in Judaism.
It excited the young, stimulated the dreamers, the poor, the desperate, the defeated. The elite came to join; this can be seen by the
quality of the Besht's early companions. They were all great,
renowned scholars. They, too, had felt that Hasidism was accom-
plishing something vital and necessary for Jewish continuity: it was
offering hope to the hopeless and a sense of belonging to those who
needed it. The uprooted, isolated, impoverished and uneducated
villagers who, due to conditions not of their making, lived on the
edge of history, and even outside its boundaries, suddenly felt
linked to the people and the destiny of Israel. The force of the
movement lay not in ideology but in life: the Besht literally changed
the climate and the quality of Jewish life in hundreds and hundreds
of towns and villages; his victories meant survival for their dispersed
communities.

For those were cruel times for Eastern European Jewry. While
Washington and his generals fought for American independence
and the French revolutionaries proclaimed the reign of reason and
liberty, Jews in Russia and Poland were isolated and miserable.
Polish Jews were still accused – regularly – of ritual murder. A
Polish author wrote: 'Just as freedom cannot be conceived without

the right to protest, Jewish matzoth for Passover cannot be made without Christian blood . . .'

In Britain, Parliament rejected proposals granting civil rights to Jews. In Rome, Pope Pius VI condemned seven thousand Jews of his own city to public disgrace. In Russia, Jews were persecuted and massacred. Voltaire and Rousseau, Kant and Goethe, Mozart and Goya, Danton and Robespierre – all were contemporaries of the Besht and the Maggid of Mezeritch and Rebbe Pinhas of Koretz, and it was as though they lived in different worlds. Jewish history seems to have unfolded in the margin of history. In the so-called Age of Enlightenment, Jews were still relegated to subhuman status, not only by Christian fanatics but by enlightened secularists as well.

Thus the Jews had good reason to doubt society's wisdom and justice. They had good reason to doubt the absolute power of rationalism. Therefore they turned inward and became mystical. They turned to the Rebbe, for only he knew how to comfort them, how to impart to them a sense of sacredness. Suddenly, and for the first time in centuries, they realized that they were not useless creatures. In the Rebbe's eyes, every one of their gestures, every one of their prayers, no matter how awkward, counted and made a difference. The shepherd who played his pipe on Yom Kippur performed an action that had its reverberations in the highest spheres. The beggar's blessing compelled God to offer His own.

God is everywhere, said the Besht. In pain too? Yes, in pain too – especially in pain. God *is*, and that means that He dwells in every human being. In the unlearned too? Yes, in the unlearned too. In the sinner too. In the humble, in the humble most of all. He can be found. And He can be perceived by everyone. As he sits on His throne, said Rebbe Pinhas, He can be approached both through the tears of the penitent and the fervour of the worshipper. God *is*, God is *one*; and that means He is the same to people who turn to Him in different ways.

This offer of consolation was, at the same time, an appeal for unity. Within the Hasidic framework, Jews were told that they could fulfil themselves – as Jews – in more ways than one: the learned through their learning, the poor through their piety. God is not indifferent and man is not His enemy – this was the substance of the Hasidic message. It was a message against despair, against resignation; it sensitized the individual Jew to his own problems and made him aware of his ability to solve them. It taught him that hope must be derived from his own history, and joy from within his own condition.

Hasidism's concern for the wretched, for the victimized and forgotten Jew, induced many distinguished scholars to change their milieu, their way of life, and join the movement, and after the passing of the Maggid of Mezeritch in 1772, they became its leaders. They responded to a need, hence their inevitable success.

Rebbe Pinhas, too, became popular, much to his chagrin. Too many people visited him for too many reasons, taking too much of his time away from study and meditation. One Yom Kippur he addressed this plea to God:

'Master of the Universe, forgive my audacity. I know I should thank You for the gifts You have bestowed upon me, thank You for making me so liked by Your children. But do understand, please, that I have no time left for You. Do something, anything. Make people like me less . . .'

His wish was granted. People stopped visiting him at home, no longer greeted him on the street. And he was happy. But then came the Succoth holiday. As was the custom, he recited the *Ushpizin* prayer with true fervour, inviting the shepherds of our people to enter his tent and be his guests. The first one to appear was Abraham; he stood at the entrance but refused to step inside, explaining: 'If nobody comes to you, I must stay away too. A Jew must live with his people, not only for his people . . .' Next day Rebbe Pinhas addressed another plea to God. And people sought him out once more.

This, too, is part of the Hasidic message: There is a solution to loneliness – and loneliness is no solution. What is the significance of *Tikkun* – mystical reparation? Rebbe Pinhas would ask. It is to be concerned not only with yourself but with everything that goes on around you; help others and you will help yourself. You want to serve God? Start with serving His children. Knowledge is to be shared, as is faith, and everything else.

People brought him money, which he promptly distributed among the poor. Once he remarked: 'I only desire what I already possess.' How simple and how wise – better to desire what one has than to have what one desires.

Often students would turn to him for help in matters of faith. To one he said, 'True, God may be hiding, but you know it. That ought to be sufficient.' Did the student suffer less? No, but he suffered differently.

Having been told that atheists were demanding proof of God's existence, he rushed to the House of Study, opened the Holy Ark, seized the sacred scrolls and shouted, 'I swear, I swear that God exists; isn't that proof enough?'

A student suffered from such anguish that he did not dare speak about it. Rebbe Pinhas looked at him and smiled. 'I know, I know how you feel . . . but tell me, if *I* know, don't you think that *He* also knows?'

Speaking on grave and urgent topics, he would display a subtle sense of humour.

'All that is important is rare,' he once remarked. 'Millions and millions of people inhabit the earth, but only a few are Jewish. Among the Jews, only a few are learned. Among the learned, only a few are pious. And even fewer are those who know how to pray properly.'

Another time: 'God created Eve to serve as Adam's *ezer kenegdo*, according to Scripture: to help him – against him. What does that mean? Well, imagine you visit a rich man, asking for charity. He welcomes you warmly and says: "Oh, I wish I could, I so wish I could give as much as you need, as much as you deserve, but you see, I cannot; my wife is against it."'

A student asked him, 'What am I to do? I am pursued by evil temptations.' And he answered, 'Are you sure? Are you sure it is not the other way around?'

Perceptive and sharp-minded, Rebbe Pinhas was nevertheless also naïve. He was convinced, for instance, that all sickness originates in lies: a person who does not lie shall not be ill. Also: When a Jew answers a question, he defeats the enemy of Israel; if his answer is correct, all his enemies are defeated. Also: When telling lies shall be considered as grave a transgression as adultery, the Messiah will appear.

On Judgement Day, he would say, even the lectern will be judged, and sentenced.

Also: After his death a Tzaddik ascends from one level to another, higher and higher, until he becomes first a sacred letter, then a sacred thought, and finally a sacred name.

And this advice he loved to repeat in the name of the Besht: If you feel the urge to praise, praise God; if you feel the urge to blame, blame yourself.

Rebbe Pinhas' posthumously published book – *Midrash Pinhas*

– contains aphorisms, parables and insights, combining the written tradition with the oral one, sealed secrets with revealed intentions. He loved the Book of Splendour; he 'sought refuge' in the Zohar.

Redemption occupied his thoughts and dreams. What Hasid does not wait for the Messiah? What Rebbe does not try to hasten his coming? To be Jewish is to link one's fate to that of the Messiah – to that of all those who are waiting for the Messiah. How is one to accelerate events? Never mind the Kabbalistic methods. They are too complicated and inaccessible; and then, they have not proved too successful in the past. No, better try simpler ways. Better appeal to simpler people. Every human being may change the course of history; it is in the power of every individual to shorten exile.

Therein lies Rebbe Pinhas' originality. In his teachings, he assigns no important role to the Tzaddik, and certainly not as mediator between heaven and earth, as the instrument chosen by God to make His will known and implemented. Instead he stresses the importance of each individual, no matter how saintly or how ignorant. Every one of us can open the gates and thus enable the Redeemer to appear in our midst.

'If I so desired,' said Rebbe Pinhas, 'I could bring the Messiah as easily as I can lift a straw; but I prefer to rely on the Almighty. And He relies on man. If all Jews would give charity, redemption would occur.'

On another occasion he said: 'If all men would speak the truth, there would be no further need to bring the Messiah; he would be here already. Just as the Messiah brings truth, truth brings the Messiah.' Truth: Rebbe Pinhas' total obsession and all-consuming passion.

'I broke all my bones while working on myself to attain truth,' he said. 'This lasted twenty-one years: seven years to discover what truth is; another seven years to expel falsehood from my being; and the last seven years to receive truth and live it.'

Respect for truth was so profound among his friends and followers that they dared not repeat his comments for fear of misquoting him.

His heir, Rebbe Raphael of Barshad, was once stopped in the street by a man who asked him, 'Aren't you Reb Raphael of Barshad?' 'Yes . . . I think so,' replied the Rebbe.

Summoned to testify on behalf of a man whose innocence he doubted, the same Rebbe Raphael spent all night weeping: he could not bring himself to tell a possible lie. He cried and cried. And died at dawn.

Once, during *Maariv* services, Rebbe Pinhas let out a cry so full of pain that his followers were anguished. The countess who owned much of Koretz happened to pass by his window just then. 'I have never heard a cry filled with such truth,' she told her retinue. When Rebbe Pinhas was informed of her comment, he smiled; he liked it. 'Everybody can find truth,' he remarked, 'even Gentiles.' On another occasion he emphasized: 'We must love even the wicked among the Gentiles and pray for them; only then will redemption materialize.'

But, of course, his main concern was for his own community – his own people – on whose behalf he pleaded with God Himself. 'If only I knew how to sing,' he once whispered, 'I would force Him to come down and be with His children, witness their suffering, and save them.' Another time he exclaimed: 'Why do You leave Your people in exile? Why must it last so long? Only because we did not – and do not – observe Your laws? But tell me, tell me, who compelled You to give them to us? Did we ask for them, did we want them? It was You who made us receive them. Furthermore, Master of the Universe, tell me: Didn't You know even then that we would not comply with all Your laws? Still You chose us – then why are You angry?'

Like his celebrated contemporary Rebbe Levi-Yitzhak of Berditchev, he would speak to God on Yom Kippur – in Yiddish – and plead the cause of Israel with such strength and conviction that whoever heard him trembled with emotion.

Another passion that dominated Rebbe Pinhas' life was friendship.

He was a friend both to his peers and to his pupils; his role was forever that of a friend. He understood that Hasidism, in order to justify its ideals in human terms, would have to grow into a centre radiating friendship – which it did. *Dibuk-haverim* – closeness among friends – was among Hasidism's cardinal precepts. People came to Mezeritch, and later to Lizensk, Rizhin and Lublin, not only to see the Master but also to make friends, to share joys and sorrows, and help one another be it with a gesture, a word, a smile, a song or a tale.

Said Rebbe Raphael of Barshad, 'Our Master and teacher Rebbe Pinhas of Koretz invited me once to join him in his coach. Unfortunately there was not enough room. "Do not worry," our

Master said reassuringly. "Do not worry; let us be close friends
and there will be room."'

Rebbe Raphael also recalled, 'Rebbe Pinhas loved to speak of
friendship; often he referred to God, blessed be He and blessed be
His Name, as a friend, a true friend. And as he spoke about this at
length his face would be shining with love.'

This tale alone would be sufficient to make us love and admire
Rebbe Pinhas of Koretz. We have known God to be a father, a
judge, a king; we never saw Him in the role of friend to man, a role
eagerly attributed to Him by Rebbe Pinhas.

Yet Rebbe Pinhas, who sought friendship in every person, everywhere, even in heaven, spent his last months on earth in sadness.
Like most great Masters of that period, he somehow sank into
melancholy – just what he had desperately sought to avoid.

No definite facts about his change of mood and outlook are
available. We must rely on allusions, many based on intuition
rather than facts. But intuition in Hasidic literature is as important
as facts.

An unexpected event took place in the year 1791 – the last year
of Rebbe Pinhas' life. Suddenly he left Ostraha, where he had
served as Rebbe, and went to Shipitovke to bid farewell to his
father-in-law. His plan: to go and settle in the Holy Land. This was
not the first time he had felt the urge to go there. Years before, he
had been tempted by the dream and had been about to set out on
his journey when he fell sick. 'You do not want me to go,' he said
to God. 'Good, I shall stay.'

He stayed, but kept on dreaming. His love for Jerusalem was
such that he tried to imagine the city, but without success; it transcended his imagination. All he could manage to do was to imagine
someone who had been in Jerusalem.

Now he was ready for the journey. He was determined to break
with his familiar surroundings in Eastern Europe – and turn his
back on the suffering in the Diaspora.

The last years of his life were clouded by anxiety. He often
spoke of unfulfilled wishes: 'If only I could sing . . .' Or: 'If only I
could write down what my mouth is saying . . .' And also: 'I am so
afraid of being more wise than pious, but,' he added cryptically, 'I
am too ill.'

Often, too often, he was overwhelmed by gloom. 'I study
Zohar,' he confided to Rebbe Raphael; 'I explore its depths and
sometimes I feel frightened. I sit there staring at the Book of

Splendour in front of me. I look and look and I keep silent –
and that is all I do.'

Once he revealed certain secrets to his companions – only to
forbid them later to disclose those secrets to others. Still later, he
expressed regret at having revealed them in the first place.

Rebbe Pinhas began to say strange things. As he reminisced
about his visit to Zaslav twenty-two years earlier, he said it was 'to
drive a certain great power' out of Poland – with his prayers. He
wrote a mysterious letter to a mysterious Reb Yeshayahu who 'had
difficulties in *kabalat ol malkhut shamayim* – accepting the yoke of
heaven'.

He had become a changed man; perhaps he had been struck by
some secret tragedy, some personal ordeal. What could it have
been? What could have made him, the consoler, become so inconsolable?

His illness? His despair? The state of affairs in the world and at
home? Violent battles were raging between the Hasidim and their
opponents, the Mitnagdim. Excommunications and denunciations
followed one another. Numerically the movement was blooming –
in some thirty years it had prevailed in most of the deprived communities in Eastern Europe – yet the possible spiritual decline represented a real danger. Suddenly there were too many schools, too
many courts, too many Rebbes – and some of their followers had
begun fighting among themselves. Clans were formed; sectarian
loyalties were encouraged. These were still heroic times, with great
Masters such as Rebbe Elimelekh of Lizensk, the Berditchever and
the Bratzlaver kindling flames everywhere. But the impetus and
purity of the beginning were gone, or at least forgotten, in many
quarters.

Rebbe Pinhas of Koretz must have been aware of all this: the
attacks on Rebbe Nahman of Bratzlav; the dissension between
Lizensk and Lublin. He must have agonized over the realization
that Jews too – and even Hasidim – were capable of rejecting
friendship; that Jews too – and even Hasidim – could, on occasion,
lack compassion. And he must have remembered the early days,
the vision of the Besht, the sobriety of the Maggid, the intensity of
their disciples. He had witnessed three generations of leaders and
followers. Did he foresee the decline of the movement? Was that
the reason for his sadness? Or was it that, like the other Masters,
he had heard too many tales of sorrow and pain? People were
forever coming to him with their doubts and regrets, sharing with
him their anguish and misery. Was it that at one point he could

take no more? Or did he have a premonition of what would be the end of Koretz?

Was it Reb Pinhas' tragic intuition, or tragic imagination, that prompted him to set the example and move away – away from Gentile hate and Jewish laxity, away from quarrelling factions and their leaders, away from unfulfilled dreams? Or did he simply want to leave everything behind and go – go to the land of promise and prophecy, go to weep in Jerusalem over Jerusalem and for Jerusalem – and weep as one weeps only in Jerusalem?

But it was written that, like his good friend the Besht, he would never reach the Holy City. It was written that he would die on the way.

In Shipitovke, shortly before he was to leave, he began to tremble with fever. He was in pain, terrible pain, and his mind was on fire. He spoke of death with great anguish. He did not want to die – not then, not there. He was afraid to die alone, without any friends. He asked that his disciple Reb Raphael be called. When Reb Raphael arrived, he felt better. They talked and talked – and when they stopped talking, Rebbe Pinhas refused to address anyone else in the room. For two days he lay motionless and mute. Then he began calling for his old friend Reb Haim of Krasna, who was not there. On the following Shabbat his condition worsened; the end was near. Rebbe Pinhas was heard whispering, 'Haim, Haim, my friend, my brother – come stay with me . . . I am afraid . . . Save me from the Angel of Death, Haim . . . If you stay with me, my friend, I won't die.'

A rabbinical council, convened urgently by Rebbe Shimshon of Shipitovke, authorized the dispatch of a special messenger to summon Reb Haim of Krasna, who was spending Shabbat at a nearby village. The messenger carried a letter dated *Hayom Shabbat kodesh* – on this day of Shabbat. It was a race against time, a race against death.

Time won. Death won. Hasidism lost. When Reb Haim of Krasna arrived, it was too late. His friend already belonged to another world.

His mystery remains intact. We don't know what happened to him at the end of his life – we never will. He who was always lucid, calm and serene – why was he possessed by such fear at the end? What had he glimpsed? What visions did he have – and about whom? What were the questions? Were there any answers? Did he suddenly fully understand that the Jews had no friends – anywhere?

Did it become clear to him that the Messiah would be late in coming – much later than he had anticipated, much later than he had feared?

He died – and Koretz died with him. And now he has become a sacred letter, a mysterious tale, an evocative name: a key to wisdom and compassion.

His quest is our quest, his questions remain our questions . . . and we must go on.

Aharon of Karlin

Little is known about his life and less about his death; but much is known – and remembered – about his personality. In Hasidic literature he is, to this day, referred to as the great Rebbe Aharon of Karlin.

We are told that he was a handsome man of great vitality, endowed with an irresistible power of persuasion. His energy and enthusiasm were such that he could never stay in one place for long. And so he travelled through towns big and small, spreading the Hasidic message, igniting sparks and setting crowds of listeners aflame. He and Rebbe Mendel of Vitebsk jointly confronted the Mitnagdim at the first public disputation – which took place in Shklov – between Hasidim and their vocal opponents. Practically alone, he stormed the traditional rabbinic fortress in Lithuania, shaking its very foundations. Faithful in friendship, loyal to his teachers and disciples, fearless in his undertakings, he was the spearhead of the new movement.

All this is known. What is not known is how and why he died – and at such an early age.

Here is a word of advice which he was fond of repeating: When Hasidim meet, he said, they would do well to study the Zohar, the Book of Splendour, in which creation's primary secrets are waiting to be uncovered. If that should prove too difficult, let them open the Talmud and study together – be it only one page, one problem. Thus they would go back in time to the sages, the scribes, the Prophets, and finally to Moses. If the Talmud, too, should prove inaccessible to them, let them open the Bible and read the portion of the week and its commentaries, and thus be in touch with eternal truth. If that also should be too difficult, let them simply tell one another Hasidic tales about great Masters and their saintly ways; and if, heaven forbid, they don't even know or remember any such stories, then let them sing a Hasidic *Niggun* which, as everyone knows, is the key to higher spheres and sanctuaries. But what if, woe unto us, they don't know a *Niggun?* Well, in that case, let them . . . love one another.

This advice – more than any saying uttered by any Master – summarizes the attitude of the Hasidic movement: Ask the utmost of man, but accept him as he is.

Surely it is better to know the Zohar and to master the Talmud; but if you were neither fortunate enough nor gifted enough to spend years on study – if all you possess is the *desire* to pray – then that too will be enough.

In other words, prayer and study are important, but no one ought ever to despair of being unable to do either. Every person has his own path to follow, his own rhythm; every sorrow has its own remedy. True, God does demand much, sometimes even the impossible – but He leaves it up to man to choose the means by which to attain perfection.

What is a true Hasid? Beneath a torn overcoat, inside a hovel, a heart broken but yearning for perfection. And that yearning in itself is enough.

Man's goal is to be worthy of God – but God accepts him even when he is not, provided he truly wants to be; provided, too, that he love his friend and neighbour. There is no tragedy or sin in not knowing how to decipher an obscure passage of Zohar, provided the Hasid is aware of his limitations and is dedicated to seeking truth. Not everybody is capable of *Ahavat-Hashem*, love of God; or of *Ahavat-Torah*, love of Torah; but everyone must be capable of *Ahavat-Israel*, love for one's fellow man.

No wonder that Hasidism was so successful with economically impoverished and spiritually neglected Jews – and that it met such determined opposition among those for whom study was an absolute priority. For poor and uneducated Jews, many of whom lived in remote villages, it was vitally important to be told that not only were they worthy of being loved but that they were expected to give love to others. And that their love, too, carried weight both on earth and above. So simplistic a philosophy, however, could only arouse antagonism among the scholars.

And since the Jews of Lithuania and White Russia were dominated by their scholars, it was to be expected that among those Jews the opposition to Hasidism would be more violent than elsewhere. And that was precisely why Rebbe Aharon was sent by the great Maggid of Mezeritch to establish a Lithuanian centre. And indeed, he overcame the hostility of the local leadership and succeeded in building a first bridgehead – so much so that for a time the Mitnagdim called all Hasidim 'Karliner'.

Thus, when we evoke Karlin we do so in an astonishing context, for we must turn our attention, at the same time, to its fierce and pitiless opponents, headed by the great and unique Rebbe Eliyahu, the Gaon of Vilna.

Today, in retrospect, their quarrels – so violent and so intolerant – seem somewhat absurd and surely exaggerated. Their fanaticism strikes us as extreme: Really – what was the wisdom, where was the need to fight with words, and sometimes even with fists, over which prayers were to be said or omitted, what gestures were to be made or avoided, what tales were to be repeated or condemned? How is one to explain *today* the hate that existed on both sides? The ancient sages Shammai and Hillel differed in most areas of Jewish life and yet they maintained relations of mutual esteem and affection. Why was it that no authoritative voice was heard, eighteen centuries after Shammai and Hillel, to proclaim that the words of *both* the Besht and the Gaon of Vilna reflected God's living truth? Actually, the Besht and his disciples did say it – but the Gaon and his followers did not – to Rebbe Aharon's great regret, as we shall see.

Born in 1736 – the year the Besht revealed himself to his followers – Rebbe Aharon died thirty-six years later, shortly before the emergence of the great Maggid Reb Dov-Ber of Mezeritch.

Aharon's father, Reb Yaakov, was a beadle in a House of Study in Yanovo, near Pinsk. Little is known of his childhood except that he was – he must have been – a good student and that, at a certain time in his life, he appreciated the pleasures of wealth – until, according to legend, one day, as he rode in his beautiful carriage, he suddenly understood the futility of an existence devoid of eternal values. And he realized that he had reached a turning point.

A strange legend, and one that leaves us wondering: Where did he get such a carriage? How could he afford such luxury? His father was poor – was his father-in-law richer? We do not know. We don't even know how he discovered Hasidism. As in the case of most Masters, his adolescence is shrouded in mystery. Judging from his posthumous work, *Bet Aharon*, his studies covered both Talmud and Kabbala, which is not surprising: in Lithuania, every self-respecting young Jew devoted himself to study.

His first exposure to Hasidism probably came through a chance encounter with one of the movement's itinerant messengers and preachers whom the Maggid had, since 1760, been dispatching to the most distant provinces, thus extending his sphere of influence.

The philosopher Solomon Maimon writes in his autobiography that after listening to one of these emissaries, his imagination had been so fired that he had felt himself irresistibly drawn to the great Maggid. He went to seek out the Master in Mezeritch. The same must have happened to Rebbe Aharon. He left Pinsk and went to find the Maggid. The encounter changed his life. He returned to Lithuania only to fulfil a mission: to draw the recalcitrant communities into the Beshtian kingdom.

The Besht himself had made two such attempts. We know that he visited Slutsk and other cities, and that he left, having failed. Worse, that he left under duress, barraged with insults. Such is the claim of the Mitnagdim.

Another version is that local Rabbis decided to put him through an examination to determine whether or not he knew Talmud. They asked him a simple, almost simplistic, question: If one has forgotten to include the *Ya'aleh ve-yavo*, the special prayer for the first of the month, in the Silent *Amida*, must one start all over again, from the very beginning? The Besht refused to answer. The Mitnagdim say, Because he didn't know the answer. The Hasidim say, Because he found the procedure undignified. It seems that the Besht got around the questions with a keen sense of humour: Why do you want me to tell you? he asked. *I* will not forget to include the special prayer the first time – and *you* will forget it the second time as well as the first.

The fact remains that, of all the provinces in Eastern Europe, Lithuania was the most stubborn in its refusal to join the new movement, which aspired to offer a spiritual renaissance to countless dispersed and despairing Jewish communities. One easily understands why.

In contrast to the Jews of Galicia and Podolia, Lithuanian Jewry could proudly point to its scholars and students. Even the average Jew had some measure of learning, for Jews lived mostly in large cities, not in isolated hamlets. Everyone had to study Torah and belong to the community. Under the reign of the Gaon of Vilna, everyone was taught how to live and fulfil himself as a Jew. Hasidism had no great attraction for Lithuanian Jews because it answered no great need.

And yet, in spite of that – or was it because of that? – the movement's leaders were strangely fascinated by Lithuania. Rather than give up in the face of difficulty and concentrate on other areas, they kept seeking confrontation. They kept on coming back to Lithuania. Levi-Yitzhak of Berditchev was, for a while, Rebbe in Pinsk. After the Besht died, even his own son – Reb Tzvi-Hersh – left another Hasidic stronghold and settled in Pinsk, remaining there, living with his father-in-law, Reb Shmuel Hasid, until his death in 1810. The Besht's son – in Pinsk! How did he manage to survive in the midst of the endless polemics and holy wars that the Hasidim and their opponents waged with blind fanaticism? Reb Tzvi-Hersh would have been welcomed anywhere and treated with respect and affection. Yet he chose Pinsk. Why? Was it an act of defiance? To show his opponents that he was not afraid of them? Or to show the Maggid's followers that *he* would succeed where they had failed? Or else to show his fellow Hasidim that their concept of Hasidism had become too simplistic, too comfortable? That, unlike them, he continued to see in Hasidism an act of total devotion, of *Mesirat-nefesh*? And that to be a Hasid in Lithuania required more courage and faith than to be one in Podolia or Galicia? If that was the reason, then he was right: it was anything but easy to be a Hasid in Lithuania. And Rebbe Aharon and his followers knew something about it; their lot was not an enviable one.

The first campaign, the first slander, the first measures against the new movement were conceived and implemented in Lithuania. People there still remembered the sad fate of Sabatean and Frankist followers who had also pledged to redeem the Jewish people by relaxing its laws and turning its need for joy into a sacred duty. Hence every new attempt, every new experiment not in strict accordance with Halakha, was considered suspect, if not heretic.

The Gaon of Vilna, who since his Bar Mitzvah had lived in seclusion surrounded by books and manuscripts, reaffirmed the ancient belief that a Jew is Jewish only if and when he obeys all Jewish commandments. He respected Maimonides as a codifier but resented his philosophical research. The Gaon believed that laws had to be obeyed and preferably, but not necessarily, understood. And here came a movement which demanded to be allowed to change the Jewish code of behaviour; here was a movement whose leaders dared change the prayer book, abolish fixed times for services, and discredit the Talmud by claiming that to recite psalms is as important as to study Torah.

From anti-Hasidic sources and various documents we get the impression that, in some instances, the Lithuanian rationalists were surprised and distressed by the Karliner's public behaviour.

Another area of disagreement – the Mitnagdim did not particularly appreciate the fervour, the exhibitionism of the Hasidim at services. The Hasidim shouted, sang, jumped up and down, danced and often even rolled on the ground to attain ecstasy. Moreover, they organized reunions in private homes – *shtiblech* – where, from the Mitnagdim's point of view, they wasted precious hours telling stories or singing popular tunes instead of studying Torah and its commentaries. Worse: they liked to drink a little bit – or much – or a little bit too much. For the Lithuanian Jews, scholars and others, that was blasphemy. Worse: there soon appeared cracks in their unity; to their amazement and chagrin there were, among their own people, some so weak as to be taken in by the new sect – that meant the threat was becoming more and more serious. Something had to be done – the wave had to be stopped – by any means!

It must be stressed also that the Maggid of Mezeritch, a brilliant organizer, understood that the emissaries he sent to Lithuania had to be the very best, if he hoped to achieve any measure of success.

Rebbe Shneur-Zalman of Lyady, the founder of Habad, was such a man, as was his friend Rebbe Mendel of Vitebsk: between them they covered White Russia but their impact was felt in Lithuania as well. Unequalled as a Talmudist, an astonishingly perceptive Kabbalist, Rebbe Shneur-Zalman had a great deal to offer to the proud young scholars in Lithuania: Hasidism's worst enemies could not accuse *him* of ignorance.

Another factor exacerbated the tensions. During that particular period, an epidemic of diphtheria ravaged the city of Vilna and hundreds of children perished. As is usual, certain people saw in the calamity a celestial punishment. And punishment implies sin. So sinners had to be found. Easy. The Hasidim. Once the culprits were named, all other sins were attributed to them as well. They were accused of lacking respect for the Gaon. Hence for his knowledge. Hence for the Torah itself. Obviously, they had to be reprimanded, chastised; and so they were. Some were publicly beaten, others merely thrown out of the city. The Hasidic *shtiblech* were emptied, their congregants humiliated. Finally, a decision came down to excommunicate them – all of them. Letters to that effect were drawn up and circulated and even dispatched to other cities, other countries. One letter was co-signed by the Rabbis of Amsterdam, The Hague, Metz and Prague. Ceremonies of excommunication, with the ancient ritual of the blowing of the Shofar and the lighting of black candles, took place. Jews were forbidden to marry Hasidim, to eat their meat or share their meals, or even to do business with them. Copies of the edicts were posted at public fairs. Hasidic books and writings were burned. It was open war. And Rebbe Aharon Karliner was among the first targets; he was on the front line.

Let us come back to Rebbe Aharon. The Maggid of Mezeritch loved him – and so do I. The Maggid called him 'our best offensive weapon'. And rightly so. Rebbe Aharon had the special talent of being able to recognize the best young students, the most sensitive ones, and draw them closer to Hasidism. But he did not keep the newcomers with him; he immediately sent them to Mezeritch, to the great Maggid.

Hasidic legend tells us how he went about convincing Reb Chaim-Haykel of Amdur, known for his saintliness and piety, to hurry to Mezeritch.

Reb Chaim-Haykel lived in the forest as a hermit, in total seclusion, seeking perfection through mortification and fasting.

When Rebbe Aharon came to Amdur, he did not go to visit the solitary saint in the forest, but preached in the synagogue. He was an impressive speaker and the entire town talked only of his sermons. Rumours finally reached even Reb Chaim-Haykel. He became intrigued and chose not to resist his curiosity, since, after all, it involved study. Next day he arrived in town and went to the synagogue, which was packed. The audience expected another display of oratory, another session of rhetorical fireworks; everyone was convinced that, like the day before and the one before that, the preacher would again use his powers to sear the soul and elevate it to the heights of Torah where man's word and God's word fuse and become one. But the speaker was aware of Reb Chaim-Haykel's presence – the man for whom he had come. And so he surprised his audience by delivering the shortest sermon, the briefest lecture of his career – one sentence, only one. He said: 'He who does not improve, gets worse.' Having uttered these few words, he left the podium. The people couldn't believe their ears: What had happened to him? Was that his sermon, his lecture? Was he making fun of them? They were on the verge of shouting their protest, their anger, when suddenly they froze, for they saw the revered and saintly Reb Chaim-Haykel get up and push his way towards the preacher. He seemed shaken. 'Help me, please,' he said. 'Your words are now inside me, they tear me apart.' And the two men left together. 'I would like to follow you,' said Reb Chaim-Haykel of Amdur. 'So be it,' said Rebbe Aharon. 'Go to Mezeritch.'

Rebbe Aharon gave Reb Chaim-Haykel a letter of recommendation which the great Maggid read aloud, in his presence: 'The bearer of this letter has lived a life of falsehood; he sought saintliness but removed himself from it; there is no sacred spark in him to be found.' Hearing this, Reb Chaim-Haykel burst into tears. The Maggid let him weep and then said, 'Stay, I shall guide you.'

And he did. The Maggid took care of him for a whole year and made him into one of his most illustrious disciples. And Reb Chaim-Haykel became one of Rebbe Aharon's closest friends – his companion and ally against the Mitnagdim of Lithuania.

As were all his companions, Rebbe Aharon was totally attached to his Master, the Maggid of Mezeritch, and craved to spend as much time as possible in his presence.

On Friday afternoons, as is the custom, he would recite the Song of Songs in honour of the Queen of Shabbat. He had a beautiful voice, and when he sang, he never failed to attain ecstasy. Once he was interrupted by the Maggid's servant: 'Please, Reb Aharon, the Master wants you to not sing so loudly. You disturb him, and that is serious enough; but what is more serious is that when you sing, the angels in heaven fall silent; they listen to you – and this you must not allow to happen. You are not to interfere with their praise of the Almighty.'

One morning, as he began the service with the prayer *Adon Olam*, affirming God's rule over creation, he began to cry. 'There are only two possibilities,' he whispered. 'Either it is true or it isn't – and in both cases I am at fault: Either God is the King of the Universe and I am not doing enough to serve Him, or He isn't. And whose fault is it? His? No. Mine, mine alone.'

In the early days, when the two sides were still on speaking terms in Lithuania, certain Mitnagdim tried to pin him down:

'You preach Mezeritch, you dream Mezeritch, you wish to send the entire world to Mezeritch – but, for heaven's sake, what have you learned in Mezeritch, you yourself?'

'Me? Nothing,' said Rebbe Aharon.

'Nothing? Then why have you been going there so often? Why have you returned so often? What's the use of going to Mezeritch if it's to learn nothing?'

'I told you. I have learned nothing in Mezeritch. Or to be more precise: I have learned the meaning of the word "nothing" – the mystery which envelops all words. For instance, when I went to Mezeritch, I learned that I – Aharon, son of Jacob – am nothing. And yet – I exist, I am alive, I wait, I pray, I question and pray again, isn't it strange? I am nothing and yet I am *in* this world created by God, a man among men – isn't it strange to be nothing and at the same time to listen to you, talk to you, and – talk to God? . . . Well, that's what I learned in Mezeritch. As I told you: "Nothing." '

One of his friends, also a disciple of the great Maggid, once passed through Karlin on his way home. It was night and he knew nobody in the town. All the houses were dark. All the inns were silent. The stranger grew worried. Where was he going to spend the night? Why not go to Rebbe Aharon, whom he intended to visit the next day? Why not go right away? It was late – but Rebbe Aharon slept little. The question was, How to find his home? Just then he saw a solitary walker in the street. He stopped him: Would he be kind enough to point out the Rebbe's home? 'Nothing could be simpler,' said the passer-by. 'Keep on walking, and when you see a house with light in it, you'll know that is it. Anticipating a happy reunion, the man hurried on to find the house. He found it. He knocked on the window: 'Reb Aharon, Reb Aharon, open!' 'Who is it?' Reb Aharon asked. 'It is me,' said the stranger. 'Who is it?' asked Rebbe Aharon the second time. 'It's *me*,' said the stranger. 'Don't you recognize me? Have you forgotten the days we spent together in Mezeritch?' 'Only God and God alone may say "I" or "Me",' answered Rebbe Aharon. 'And if you have not as yet learned that, then you were wrong in leaving our Master. Better that you return to Mezeritch.'

Rebbe Shneur-Zalman of Lyady frequently referred to Rebbe Aharon's virtue of *Yirat-Shamayim*, of his fear of God: 'Rebbe Aharon of Karlin,' he said, 'lived in constant fear of God, yet he loved Him with his whole being. His fear was comparable to the one that seizes a man who, sentenced to death, looks at the guns aimed at his heart, ready to be fired at any moment. He is afraid to look and yet he looks – so as to increase his fear. Sometimes Rebbe Aharon's fear was such that neither images nor words could describe it.'

And yet, this terrible fear, this total awe he experienced did not stifle or diminish his love of God. He was a Hasid after all, and

Hasidism was meant to combat fear – and solitude. Hasidism defined itself, and its relationship to its members, in terms of love – exclusively.

We must also remember that the Besht, the Maggid, and other early Masters were not interested in bringing forth a new religion but wished to create a new humanity, to humanize ancient words and offer them to those Jews who had forgotten their meaning. What was the new element? To teach man the secret power of love in his relationship to God and His people. The Besht maintained that true love can envelop one's *entire* being: he who loves God loves His creation, loves His law, loves His people. And conversely: he who loves His people – meaning he who loves people – loves God; or he who loves, loves God.

Until the Besht came along, the approved ways leading to God were few. One had to choose – between asceticism and a normal life, between esoteric knowledge and oral tradition, between love of God and fear of God. One had to side with God against man, or with man against God. The Besht and his disciples attempted to reach a synthesis: It is given to man to live on more than one level, to nourish more than one dream, to attain truth and fulfilment by following more than one path – for God is present to all people – or more precisely, God is presence. Forever. *To* all His creatures – *in* all His creatures.

When a simple shepherd is overwhelmed by a feeling of wonder at the sight of a sunset, when a child wants to say something but cannot, and so repeats one word over and over again until he is understood – well, that is a sign that God's gaze is upon them. And that is the secret of all secrets: the Master of the Universe, who has created three hundred and ten worlds and reigns over the infinite, has chosen to dwell in man's heart. 'And you shall build for Me a sanctuary so that I may dwell among you' had a very personal, direct interpretation in Karlin: Every one of you will build inside himself a sanctuary for Me to live in. Why should the evil spirit be punished at the end of time? Didn't he accomplish the will of heaven by testing and tempting man? He will be punished, the school of Karlin answers, but for something else: for having tried to convince man that he is not a prince. God is the king and man is His prince, His priest and servant. Every man is a sanctuary and it is up to him to invite God inside. As Rebbe Mendel of Kotzk formulated it: God is where He is allowed to come in. God's favourite dwelling is neither a palace of gold nor an edifice of marble but man's heart – the weakest, most vulnerable organ of the body, this heart that aches because it loves – or doesn't – that is capable of shouting and being silent at the same time, of hoping and losing hope, of recognizing in God the source of both justice *and* compassion. To fear God without loving Him would mean staying aloof; to love Him without fear would lead to familiarity: thus one must do both. One must not live with fear *of* God but with fear *in* God.

It all depends on where you place the accent. In the school of Pshishke, for instance, the accent was on *Ahavat-Torah*, the love of Torah; in Medzibozh, and Rizhin, and Wizsnitz, on *Ahavat-Israel*, the love for the people; in Karlin – on *Ahavat-Hashem*, the love for God which was expressed by *Yirat-Hashem*, the fear of God, or rather, the fear *for* God – the fear not to offend, not to hurt Him. And the one did not exclude or deny the other: on the contrary, the one completed and enriched the other.

And so it appears that between a Hasid of Karlin and Hasidim of other Masters, there was no substantial difference: a Karliner did everything other Hasidim did, but he did it with more enthusiasm. With greater fervour.

That is what characterized Karlin: *hitlahavut* – fervour, enthusiasm. In Karlin one lived on the summits of mountains all the time. In Karlin the Hasid was constantly singed by sacred fire; and as he burned he shouted for more – such was his yearning to become flame and thus reach the divine source. And to forget who he was on this earth, to forget everything on this earth; to become an offering.

Rebbe Uri of Strelisk, the Seraphin of Hasidism, was an offspring of this school. Legend has it that, through his prayers, he had acquired such powers that he could obtain for his people anything they desired; therefore, each morning before services, he would make mental notes of the requests he was to present in heaven. However, as soon as he began to pray, his soul caught fire, and in his ecstasy he forgot what it was he had planned to ask.

In Karlin one tried to attain inner fulfilment by negation of the self. One hoped to create silence through words and a melody, a *Niggun*, inside silence. And prayer inside the *Niggun*. In Karlin, the *Niggun* dominated everything else.

Naturally, the opponents – the Mitnagdim – were annoyed. They found all this singing and dancing undignified, if not outright vulgar. To them, a Jew had to control his emotions and impulses; a Jew had but to follow in the footsteps of his ancestors – what was good enough for them should be good enough for him – and his ancestors certainly did not take part in spectacles.

And yet, it would be misleading to state that the dispute within Eastern European Jewry turned solely upon questions of incompatibility of customs or personalities. For, in truth, the differences between the Mitnagdim and the Hasidim are as old and as genuine as the ones that opposed the school of Shammai to that of Hillel.

The main difference rests on a basic question: What is man's aim in life? For the traditional Talmudist it was, and is, to obey God's commandments as given to Moses at Sinai; for the Kabbalist, it was to redeem the 'holy sparks' from their exile, reuniting them with the original flame. For the emancipated Jew, it was, and is, to free himself from others and himself; for the Hasid, it was, and is, to insert, to integrate his life and thoughts into God's, to seek refuge in God and offer Him love and joy – so that He, in turn, could give them back infinitely multiplied.

The Hasid insists so much on the importance of gaiety, joy and celebration, not only to surmount his sadness and despair, but also to influence God and move Him to compassion and grace. Remember the saying of the Maggid of Mezeritch: *Veda ma lemala mimkha, veda*, and know that – *ma lemala* – whatever happens up above, is – *mimkha*, conditioned by you: if you are charitable, God will be, too; if you sing, God will sing, too; your joy is bound to reflect God's.

What is the difference between the Mitnagged and the Hasid? The Mitnagged loves the Torah, whereas the Hasid loves the person who loves the Torah. The Hasid puts the accent on man, who is bound to change, while the Mitnagged places it on the Torah, which is above change. The Mitnagged finds his happiness in books, the Hasid in people; the Mitnagged seeks knowledge, the Hasid experience.

It is characteristic that though he was revered by multitudes the same way the Besht was by his followers, the Gaon of Vilna lived alone and isolated, while the Besht was forever with people, among people.

And yet they had a common enemy: emancipation. Remember: this was the era of Moses Mendelssohn, Kant and Voltaire. Religion everywhere was on the retreat; the French Revolution had even proclaimed its death and had replaced it with the new cult of reason. The effects were felt among Jews too. Young students left their families and traditional milieux and went to Berlin,

Vienna or Heidelberg. New laws would soon force Jews to give up traditional dress and customs and send their children to secular schools.

Logically, Hasidim and Mitnagdim should have joined forces against what was to become the assimilationist movement. The opposite occurred. Hasidim had to fight on both fronts. And the harder battle was waged against the Mitnagdim, particularly in Lithuania. The Gaon was merciless; his orders were precise: he wanted the Hasidim uprooted – and they nearly were.

The persecutions which had begun during Rebbe Aharon's lifetime grew more intense afterwards. When he died, his son, Rebbe Asher, was still very young, and so Rebbe Aharon's place was taken by his disciple and friend Rebbe Shlomo – a great leader in his own right.

He would say, 'I wish I could love the best of the just as deeply as God loves the worst of the wicked.'

Rebbe Shlomo was humble; he felt unworthy of leadership. He said, 'Once upon a time, it was easier; people had a sense of decency – not any more.' Another time he remarked, 'Nowadays people come up to me to tell me of their good deeds while they hide the others; once upon a time, it was just the opposite.' So humble was he that he was convinced he would go straight to hell. Legend has it that when his soul ascended into heaven and was welcomed by exulting angels, he began to shout, 'No, no, it's a mockery – my place is in hell, not in paradise'; and the Shekhina itself had to escort him to his rightful place.

But he did endure hell – in his lifetime. The Mitnagdim banned him from society, chased him from Karlin. He came to Ludomir, where he died a martyr's death one Shavuot eve when the town was invaded by Cossacks who had been given two hours to pilfer and murder. One of them burst into the House of Study where Rebbe Shlomo was praying. Legend has it that the Cossack spoke to him. But Rebbe Shlomo, in the true Karliner tradition, was totally absorbed in prayer and did not hear him; when one addresses God, one does not listen to killers. He died praying.

At Rebbe Shlomo's death, Rebbe Asher, Rabbi Aharon's son, was crowned Rebbe. He wanted to return to Karlin but could not: the Mitnagdim were still too strong. So he went to Stolin instead and there laid the foundation for another branch of the Karlin school. His son, the second Rebbe Aharon, eventually returned to Karlin.

With him, the Hasidic centre in Karlin developed and became more dynamic. Gifted scholars and students came from all over to stay at the Master's court. As charismatic a figure as his grandfather, Rebbe Aharon knew how to attract good disciples, how to play on their fantasy, how to strengthen the structure of his movement.

Like his grandfather, Rebbe Aharon stressed the virtues of love of God, fear of God, of friendship and fervour. But he also aspired to be an innovator, and he was. Conceptually he drew closer to Rizhin. Now one could also find in Karlin symbols meant to evoke dreams of past grandeur and royalty. Like Israel Rizhiner,* he placed considerable value on external symbols; they too are reminders of God's greatness. And also like Israel Rizhiner, he fought melancholy and sadness with all the means at his disposal. There were two orchestras at his court, and they would play during the after-Shabbat meal and also on Khol-Hamoed. Of course the Mitnagdim used such 'excesses', as they called them, to persecute him even more. In fact, by then the Hasidic movement everywhere was under attack.

By then the anti-Hasidic campaign had spread throughout Eastern Europe, from the Dnieper to the Carpathian Mountains. From Brody to Vilna, from Minsk to Metz, Mitnagdim publicly urged Jewish communities to expel 'the new sect'. In Lithuania, they stressed the heresy of the Hasidim in matters of Torah, in Galicia they denounced their outrageous customs. In Minsk the following measures were adopted: the Hasidic community was to be dissolved, its House of Study closed; its members were forbidden to use the Lurianic prayer book; their freedom of movement was limited so as to prevent them from leaving town to go to visit the Rebbe. Whoever wished to travel had to get a special permit. That wasn't all. Informers were hired to spy on them. In Brody, the Hasidim were warned that whoever would dress in white on Shabbat – as was the Hasidic custom – would be undressed in the street.

But don't think for a moment that the Hasidim were solely on the receiving end. No. They fought back. They hired their own spies. They issued their own excommunications. And their language was neither less brutal nor less direct. In some instances they were even craftier than the Mitnagdim. For example, they hired a man to travel through Galicia and Podolia, posing as the son of the Gaon of Vilna. And wherever he went, he told audiences that his father had ordered him to leave and be a wanderer so as to expiate

* See *Souls on Fire*.

the sins committed against the Hasidim. One can imagine the re-action of the Mitnagdim to that particular caper.

Today all these disputes seem senseless. Why should any Jew fight or hate another Jew, when the enemy does it so much better? But – don't look for logic where religious passions are involved. Both sides fought out of conviction, out of deep commitment, out of an irresistible desire to affirm the validity of their ideas and beliefs. Compared to them, today's Jew is weak, lukewarm, pallid – and nothing is worse than indifference and lack of involvement.

The great Rebbe Aharon could have left the battlefield and gone to Mezeritch or elsewhere; he could have worked among people who admired him. But he refused to choose the easy path. Obstacles did not deter him. God alone inspired fear in him – God, whom he loved. Men did not frighten him: he confronted them bravely. In Karlin, one learned that man must not fear others; in Karlin, one lived in fear only of God, meaning, in fear of giving God a love not sufficiently pure and not sufficiently whole. In Karlin, more than anywhere else, the synthesis between *Ahavat-Hashem* and *Yirat-Shamayin* was attained.

Now – let us return to the question which has been with us from the beginning: Of what did the great Rebbe Aharon die – and why so young?

Hasidic legend offers many answers, one more mysterious than the next.

Let us listen: It happened during the month of Nissan 1772. In Mezeritch everybody was busy preparing for Passover. Homes were thoroughly cleaned, books dusted. The matzo bakery was full of people. Pesach was in the air – the festival of freedom, the celebration of history.

The Maggid's closest disciples did not go home to their families; who would forgo an occasion to hear the great Maggid tell the eternal story of Exodus? Only Rebbe Aharon planned to go home to his wife, to his family, friends, disciples. He came to the Maggid to receive his blessings for the journey – and did. But no sooner had he left his Master's study than the Maggid called in his disciples and told them, 'Don't let him leave – under any circumstances!' They ran after him and when they found him in his lodgings they told him, 'Our Master wants you to stay.' Puzzled, Rebbe Aharon returned to the Maggid and tried to explain why he had to go home – he was needed there. The Maggid looked at him silently, disapprovingly, for a long moment; then he said, 'If you insist, so

be it. I cannot hold you back.' Rebbe Aharon was reassured. But –
no sooner had he returned to his lodgings than the door opened
again and his friends rushed in with the disconcerting news: 'Our
Master has asked us, for the second time, to tell you not to go.'
'But I have seen him,' said Rebbe Aharon. 'Twice. And he gave me
his blessings. Twice.' And he could not be persuaded to postpone
his journey. He returned to Karlin, celebrated the Seder with his
family and friends. And died two days later.

When the Maggid heard the news, he wept. 'With him gone,
what are we going to do in this world?' he asked.

His disciples wanted to know: 'Since you knew, why didn't you
use your authority to keep him here?' And his answer was: 'There
are times when we are given certain powers but are forbidden to
use them.'

Does this mean that had he stayed in Mezeritch he would have
lived longer? Is there an implication that his death could have been
postponed? That it was not yet irrevocable, not yet necessary, and
thus, perhaps, not natural?

I confess I don't know. I love Rebbe Aharon of Karlin, and his
premature death not only saddens but troubles me. Especially since
there is something mysterious about it, something that has never
been explained satisfactorily.

Said Rebbe Pinhas of Koretz: It was foolish of Rebbe Aharon to
die; he should have lived longer.

In Mezeritch people commented: It was his fear of God that
burned him. Or: He was too powerful for his generation; he would
meet men and so influence them that he deprived them of their
inner freedom. That was why the angels became jealous and prevailed upon God to recall him before his time.

Rebbe Shlomo Karliner said, 'Like Hanoch, he ascended into
heaven in a state of grace, in the midst of prayer; he ascended into
heaven *like* a prayer.'

All this is very beautiful, very touching, but I would still like to
know of what he died. Had he been sick? No mention is to be
found of any illness. There is a legend that tells us he was tired in
Mezeritch, so tired that he once slept through one day and one
night; and the Maggid forbade his disciples to wake him. Why was
he so tired? What was the nature of his fatigue?

His followers tell of an evening when he arrived in the House of
Study and found his disciples in tears. There were those who prayed
without fervour, others who did not pray at all. There were those
who studied without concentration, others who did not study at

all. He looked at them silently, and then began to talk, emphasizing every word, every syllable: 'My children, my children, I want you to know that joy will lift you up to dizzying heights; I also want you to know that sadness will pull you down into the abyss.'

In his writings we find frequent allusions to his search for ways of fighting melancholy, to his determination to celebrate joy and give it wings. Are we to understand that like so many of his friends and companions he too was prone to melancholy, to depressions? Had the constant tensions created by anti-Hasidic persecutions ultimately affected his health, had they played a role in his sudden illness – and death?

He thought about death often. He wanted to be prepared for it. In his *Hanhagot Yesharot*, a kind of guide to moral precepts, he often speaks about solitude: he urges every Hasid to isolate himself one hour every day so as to rethink his actions and thoughts. Also, he would like every Hasid to spend one hour a day with a friend – and confide in him.

And then there is his testament: he wanted no eulogies – and no immediate neighbours in the cemetery. His testament was written in the year of his death.

What is left of Karlin today? Most descendants of the great Rebbe Aharon perished in the Holocaust. Only those survived who managed to reach America and Palestine before the war. Reb Arele perished in Warsaw, Reb Moshe in Stolin, Reb Elimelekh in Karlin.

In the memorial book for Stolin, quoted by Zeev Rabinowits – the best authority on Karlin – we read about the death of Reb Moshe, on the 29th of Ellul 1942:

The last time I saw the Rebbe and his family was before the great deportation. The ghetto was dark; we all felt that the end was approaching. We went to the Rebbe's house. It was after midnight. There too all was dark. The Rebbetzin and her daughter-in-law were crying. In his room, the Rebbe and some of his Hasidim sat at a table, wrapped in their prayer shawls. The Rebbe had his eldest son, Nahum-Shlomo, next to him. Suddenly he rose and went to the Holy Ark, opened it, began reciting the *Viddui* . . . and broke down in the middle: Our father, our king, have mercy upon us and upon our children . . . The next day marked the end of Stolin. All the Jews were deported, but the Rebbe and his family were not among them. They remained in their room. Together. Then a fire broke out. And all were burnt alive.

Another descendant, Reb Shlomo, lived in Baranovitch. Just

before Passover, 1941, he wrote a letter to his followers in Palestine:

'My dearly beloved friends – with God's help . . . though there is nothing for us to say, and the wise man will keep silent – I tell you that those who call upon the Almighty ought not be silent. Be not silent and let *Him* not be silent.'

Most Karliner and Stoliner Rebbes and their followers were swallowed up in the kingdom of night and fire, as were other Hasidim and other Rebbes. Most of the victims who ascended the burning altar were Hasidim: the killers and they could not coexist under the same sky.

And yet, and yet. There are still Karliner in Jerusalem and in New York. And they represent living proof that the killers were denied their final victory. Go to Jerusalem, go to Brooklyn, and you will see for yourself. You will hear the Karliner sing in ecstasy; on Shabbat you will hear them sing the song composed by the great Rebbe Aharon in praise of Shabbat – a song of longing and tenderness. What was he longing for? Shabbat. God . . . love . . . redemption . . . Is it possible that he died of love? Of longing? I wish I knew. I wish even more that I were possessed by his intense longing, for the same things – whatever they may have been.

Wolfe of Zbarazh

Why did he decide to leave Europe and go settle in the Holy Land? What made him break with his familiar surroundings? The call of Jerusalem? Have not other Masters felt the same attraction for the eternal city? Why did he alone choose to make Aliyah?

Did he ever exist at all? Was he really a human being, a man made of flesh and blood? A man among other men, exposed, as they were, to both wonder and danger? Did he live among people? Did he truly see them? Did they actually see him?

If being a hero means having one's virtues exaggerated and one's powers idolized, then this Master was just the opposite. Rebbe Wolfe of Zbarazh was so unassuming, so hidden in his own shadow that he went unnoticed more often than not. As one seeks clues to him, to his life, one becomes utterly frustrated, so elusive is he – as a person, as a Hasidic Rebbe.

Not that he was the only one who was modest, austere and humble; others were too. But they were *famous* for their humility, whereas Rebbe Wolfe was not famous at all.

Other Masters sought solitude – not he. He did not consider himself important enough to disdain honours and avoid followers; he quite simply failed to notice them. When he did notice, he thought they were someone else's.

Could such a person have lived? Could the stories about him be true? Do the many legends really reflect his life?

A story: One day, Rebbe Wolfe of Zbarazh was invited to a circumcision. Naturally he accepted. One does not refuse such an invitation because, according to tradition, it is always issued in the name of Abraham himself. It was cold outside. An icy wind struck his face. As the sleigh moved slowly forward, he felt sorry for the coachman and his horse. If only he could walk . . . But it was far, too far to walk. Rebbe Wolfe began to feel more and more guilty. When he finally arrived at his destination, the inn was crowded with guests. Now that he was there, the ceremony could start. The father recited the solemn blessing, the *mohel* performed the ancient rite, and then parents and guests sat down to celebrate with food and wine the immortal people of Israel, which had just gained a new son. They sang and they danced with exuberance, and they did not notice their special guest, Rebbe Wolfe of Zbarazh, leaving the room. He had gone to look for his coachman in the courtyard. When he found him he asked him to go inside: 'You are cold and hungry; you need food and a drink.' 'But the horse?' asked the coachman. 'Rebbe, who will keep an eye on the horse?' 'I will,' said Rebbe Wolfe of Zbarazh. 'You?' exclaimed the coachman. 'I cannot allow you to do that. It would be unworthy of you.' 'Why?' said Rebbe Wolfe. 'Why unworthy? If the Master of the Universe keeps an eye on the horse, why shouldn't I? Do you think I am more distinguished than He?'

Unable to counter such a forceful argument, the coachman joined the crowd, gulped down a drink, and then another one. No one missed the Rebbe. When the meal was over and grace had been recited, the guests left the inn, and in the courtyard, near the stable, they saw a man, half frozen, who was making strange movements with his arms and legs to keep warm. When they recognized him they began shouting, 'Rebbe, is that you? *You* took care of our horses?' They were shocked, and he didn't understand why: 'What is so wrong in taking care of poor people's tired horses?'

This anecdote is significant for three reasons. One: Rebbe Wolfe of Zbarazh was convinced that, as Jew and human being, he could, and indeed should, change places with the coachman. Two: the coachman must have thought so too, for, in spite of his initial protests, he did accept the exchange. Three: once the exchange occurred, neither the host nor the guests noticed it.

Let us hasten to say that the last fact is more significant than the first: one easily understands that a great Master should be humble, but not that he be so humbled by his so-called admirers! Didn't they invite him? Didn't he come from far away? Wasn't he considered – after Abraham and Elijah, who go to *all* such ceremonies – the guest of honour? And yet, after he had had one drink, nobody even bothered to look for him. Nobody paid any attention to him, and so allowed him to go outside and freeze among the horses. Thus they demonstrated to him and themselves that he wasn't really needed. They found it natural for him *not* to be at the centre of their celebration, *not* to follow him, *not* to listen to his words, *not* to sing with him and for him . . .

Rebbe Wolfe of Zbarazh: a Master unlike any other. Granted, we have said the same thing about all the others, and justifiably so – but he is not only special: he is unique. Others are modest – or want to be but cannot; their function and their followers compel them to discard modesty in the name of and for the sake of heaven. Many Masters shunned honours in order to combat their vanity – but Rebbe Wolfe did not even feel he deserved honours. In his case, the struggle against vanity is meaningless, a waste of time. Rebbe Wolfe could not even conceive of being vain.

Rather than guide and Master, Rebbe Wolfe was a brother, an older brother for his followers. A brother who never demanded anything, never asked for anything, never promised anything – who gave by giving of himself, who listened more than he spoke, who withdrew discreetly when you no longer needed him – or before.

Let us not yet touch upon his studies, his knowledge, his hidden powers. For the moment let us simply stress his candour, his innocence. He was immune to falsehood: whatever he did, he remained authentic.

Zbarazh: a Jewish town like many others – somewhere in eastern Galicia. Which means that it endured the occupations, the harassments of various armies. Jews had lived there since the early sixteenth century and some had survived the siege of Khmelnicky, the invasion of the Turks, the raids of the Haidamacks. By 1941 there were some five thousand Jews left, and most of those were massacred that year by the Einsatz Kommandos. A town like many others, a story like many others . . .

Where and when was Rebbe Wolfe born? Somewhere in the Ukraine, in the middle of the eighteenth century. That is all we know. Why such imprecision, so many omissions? Was there an effort by the Hasidic chroniclers to stress the aura of legend in his life? Even the most common data are oddly obscured. We know, for instance, that he had children, but most historians fail to mention their names or how many they were.

His birth itself is linked to a legend:

On that night, during the High Holidays, his father, the fierce and feared Maggid of Zlotchov, had a dream: the *hazzan*, the cantor, who had died shortly before, returned from heaven. 'What are you doing down here?' the Maggid wondered. 'Tonight

souls are being reborn and sent back to earth,' said the
hazzan. 'Mine too. Why? I'll tell you why. After I left your
world, and as I prepared myself to appear before the celestial
tribunal, I searched my memory: What had I done right and
what had I done wrong? I conducted a thorough examination of
my life and came to the conclusion that I had not done too
badly: almost no serious sins, no major mistakes; in fact, it
seemed to me that I was ready to enter paradise and take my
rightful seat in its garden. Then I was led before the heavenly
tribunal and the Judge scrutinized my record. Shaking his head, he
said: You forgot one point. You forgot vanity. But because it was
my only sin, my most recent one, it was decided to send me back
into your world so as to enable me to remedy the situation ...'
Legend has it that his soul entered the body of the Maggid's son,
who later became known as Rebbe Wolfe of Zbarazh, a symbol of
humility.

It seems that in his youth Rebbe Wolfe was anything but a
Tzaddik. His behaviour left much to be desired. He wasted
days and nights with unsuitable friends doing unsuitable things.
Lazy, unwilling to study, he enjoyed the more earthly pleasures.
Was he aware of the anguish he inflicted on his poor father? The
Maggid tried to discipline him – to no avail. By the time Wolfe
turned twelve, his father was desperate. According to custom, the
father had the scribe write phylacteries for his son's Bar Mitzvah.
Came the day of Wolfe's Bar Mitzvah. Before handing the phylacteries to his son, he inspected them with great care. He read
the two parchments and replaced them in their square boxes.
And suddenly he began to weep. Tears began rolling down his
cheeks into the boxes with the *tefillin*. That was the turning point
for Wolfe. From that moment on, the young Wolfe changed his
ways. His father's tears had succeeded where his sermons had
failed.

The father – Rebbe Yehiel-Mikhel of Zlotchov – deserves closer
study. An intimate of both the Besht and the great Maggid of
Mezeritch, the Rebbe of Zlotchov was a fascinating personality.
Intensely involved with the entire community of Israel, he aspired
to be lifted up by those who were above him, and to lift up
those who were below him. In other words: No person is the first
nor is he – or she – the last. No one is absolutely just nor entirely
unjust. An individual may be both sinner and saint – at different
times or even at the same time. Whoever goes too far in one
direction may easily find himself or herself going in the other.

Excessive humility easily becomes false humility, which is dangerously close to vanity, excessive humility may numb both mind and soul. Too much modesty can prevent you from speaking up when necessary, from offering help when needed. From shouting the truth.

One morning, Rebbe Yehiel-Mikhel arrived late for services. The congregation waited and waited for him to begin, but he took his time. No one dared utter a sound – with the exception of one man, a leader of the community, who stepped forward and addressed the Rebbe: 'Excuse me,' he said, 'but . . .' 'But what?' 'You came late,' said the man. 'All right, you must have been busy. But now that you are here, why do you make us wait longer?' The Rebbe lifted his head and looked at him: 'There are many congregants here,' he said. 'Yet you alone chose to speak up. Why? Why you? Is it because you are more learned than the others?' 'No, Rebbe.' 'More pious perhaps?' 'No, Rebbe.' 'But you are richer than they, aren't you? You are worth fifty thousand rubles, right? And that is why you have the audacity to question my behaviour. Do you really expect me to be answerable to fifty thousand rubles?'

The Maggid of Zlotchov dared to speak that way because he knew his own value – not only as a leader but as a human being. He knew that to possess means little; what matters is substance. A person deserves respect for what he or she is, and not for any fortune they might have accumulated or inherited.

Of Rebbe Yehiel-Mikhel it was said that in his entire life he had never gone close to a stove for warmth, not even on the coldest winter nights. Also, that he never lowered his head towards the food on his plate, not even after days of fasting. And finally, that he never met with a man without telling him the truth.

Man is nothing but dust? True – but he can look at the sky. He is but ashes? True – but he can feel the fire. He is stronger than fire, stronger than hunger – even stronger than the forces that consume him. Contradictory? No: ambivalent. Ambivalence is characteristic of Hasidism in general, and Rebbe Wolfe's family in particular.

Let us explore this theme as it inevitably leads to dramatic dialectical situations.

Let us listen to some more tales.

One day Rebbe Wolfe heard unpleasant sounds coming from the

kitchen. Putting aside the book he was studying, he went to find out what was happening there. He should have guessed it: his wife was having another fight with the maid. 'She broke an expensive dish,' the indignant Rebbetzin explained to him. 'It was an accident,' cried the maid. 'It was an accident.' 'No, she did it on purpose,' said the Rebbetzin. 'She did it to annoy me and I am going to deduct its price from her wages.' 'Then I shall go to the rabbinic court,' said the maid. 'Go ahead. Sue me. Go right now; what are you waiting for?' The maid interrupted her work and said, 'All right, I am going to the rabbinic court.' 'Me, too,' said the Rebbetzin. 'And me too,' said her husband. 'You? Why are you coming? I don't need you there.' 'She does,' said Rebbe Wolfe of Zbarazh. 'You are the wife of a Rebbe; she is only a poor maid. She needs me to defend her.'

The tale is typical of the man: always ready and eager to defend the poor, the victim. Even when it meant opposing his own wife; even when it meant interrupting study and prayer. A person in distress came before meditation and concentration. Rebbe Wolfe was fully aware of the fact that the world was far from being just and charitable, that the oppressed were even more miserable than they appeared to be, and that many judges tended to favour the rich and the powerful. A Rebbe's wife had a better chance to be heard than her maid. He knew the facts of life, did Rebbe Wolfe of Zbarazh; he knew man's nature and he had no illusions about society's justice and mercy.

Still, how can one be simultaneously Rebbe and child, leader and follower? How can one reconcile giving and receiving, need and comfort, the duties of the Master and an awareness of not being one? Again, I can only tell you that Rebbe Wolfe of Zbarazh could. He was a Master who did not look like one. In fact, he looked like a big child lost in creation, a child who, without knowing it, illuminated the Hasidic universe. I told you before – he was different from other Masters. They performed miracles? He *was* a miracle.

One day Rebbe Wolfe was travelling from, or to, Zbarazh, to pay a sick call or perhaps to try to arrange some orphan's wedding. When he returned home he fell into a deep meditation. What about? His followers knew that his powers of concentration were total and unique. When he meditated, nothing disturbed him. And everyone respected his privacy, his occasional need for isolation. Only this time someone broke the rules. A student approached him and asked for help. He was destitute, hungry, desperate. Rebbe Wolfe listened to his woes, put his hand in his pocket, pulled out a silver coin and was about to give it to the student ... but changed his mind. He put the silver coin back into his pocket and handed the young man a copper coin instead. Understandably, the student was not too happy. 'What's the matter?' Rebbe Wolfe wanted to know. 'I do not understand,' said the student. 'What don't you understand?' 'Why the Rebbe changed his mind,' said the student. 'I will tell you why,' said Rebbe Wolfe. 'I wanted to teach you a lesson. A boy your age must never be ashamed to ask: there is no shame in receiving. What others give you isn't theirs anyway. But that is not all. I also wanted to teach you that a boy your age must not rely too much on miracles.' The student blushed, bowed his head and withdrew, but Rebbe Wolfe called him back: 'What are you thinking now?' 'I am thinking, Rebbe, that the Rebbe has just shown me a new way leading to the Almighty; man must neither feel shame nor rely too much on miracles.' 'Right,' said Rebbe Wolfe. 'That is the way that leads to God.' The young student later became one of the Rebbe's closest disciples.

And what do *we* learn from this story? First – that, surprisingly, Rebbe Wolfe of Zbarazh did have money in his pockets – sometimes. Second – that he was practical – sometimes. And third – that he was a perceptive educator with methods all his own. His many disciples not only admired and believed in him; they saw in him a Tzaddik, an exceptional human being endowed with secret powers. And all this in spite of his genuine humility – or was it *because* of it?

The question is relevant: There is danger in regarding humility as a virtue, especially in oneself; if I tell you I am humble, it means that I am not. How are we to know where true humility begins? Furthermore, how are we to reconcile man's vulnerability and his power? The Tzaddik and the Hasid? The Tzaddik and himself? On one hand, the Master – by definition – is endowed with powers; he can dictate his will on creation; he can cancel evil decrees and defeat wicked enemies. It is given to him to alter the rhythm of existence and modify the laws of nature. All he has to do is to utter one word, invoke one name, say one prayer – and the sterile mother will bear children, the broken heart will open itself to joy. The Tzaddik knows it – and *that* is his problem. He knows that whatever he desires he can obtain. How can one live with such knowledge and remain a Tzaddik?

A Tzaddik, more than anyone, must attain the extreme limits of humility, which means he must extirpate from himself the last vestiges of pride or self-righteousness. He must think of himself as unworthy and powerless – only then is he worthy of assuming power. He must subordinate his wishes, his thoughts, his aspirations, his hopes, his very heartbeat to the will of heaven; he must bend his being, his life. Let him become overly conscious of his importance and he will lose his powers instantly. Nowhere is the abyss as close to heaven as in the soul of the Tzaddik.

The Tzaddik inevitably leads a double life, thus living in constant contradiction with himself. In order to be what he is, he must think that he is not. To be a hero, he must think of himself as anything but a hero.

In his relations with his followers, the Rebbe must be *aware* of, but undaunted by, his limitations. Thus we deal with nuances of perception. A saint who knows that he is a saint – isn't. Or more precisely, no longer is. A conscience that is too clear is suspect. To ever be clear, conscience must have overcome doubt. As Rebbe Nahman of Bratzlav put it: No heart is as whole as one that has been broken. The great Maggid of Mezeritch, before him, said it differently: What do you do when you lose the key to the lock? You break the lock. So – break your heart and God will be allowed to enter. But in order to earn the right to say this to his followers, the Rebbe must lead the way and serve as a personal example. That is why the Tzaddik is often sad, whereas the ordinary Hasid is not. The Rebbe preaches ecstasy yet he himself remains melancholy, proving that he is able to reconcile sadness with happiness. Though he himself must aspire to perfection, he must be tolerant with his followers, knowing that they can only try to follow as best they may.

This complexity – one might say, this taste for paradox – is apparent also on the level of ideas. The Rebbe is expected to evolve in a mysterious universe; the Hasid must cling to reality. The Rebbe may be obsessed with eternity; the Hasid must deal with the present. The Rebbe immerses himself in the Book of Splendour, the Zohar; the Hasid studies the Bible. The Rebbe comments on the Talmud; the Hasid is satisfied with a simple prayer, a melody, a smile.

Of course, there were exceptions. Rebbe Menahem-Mendel of Kotzk was monolithic: for him, there were no half-measures, no compromises, no concessions, no consoling forgiveness. For him, it was all or nothing. Truth or damnation. Knowledge or stupidity.

But the typical Rebbe was tolerant and compassionate, always ready to reassure his followers, to comfort and console them and, above all, to stay with them. The typical Rebbe did not judge his followers; on the contrary, he tried to understand and defend them, and to make them smile.

In that tormented and torn century when the Jews suffered more than their neighbours – Jews were victims not only of the aggressors but of their fellow victims as well – in that era of upheavals, what did the simple Jewish villager need most? Peace and hope – and a sense of belonging. And in those days, who was better qualified to fill those needs than the Rebbe? He never chastised – he consoled. He was never a preacher but a friend. The Jews, poor and persecuted, were waiting for someone to tell them that while creation needs its creator, the creator too needs his creation. You miss God? He misses you too – yes, you. You may not be learned, you may not be pious – God needs you nevertheless. For there is something in you that is yours alone; there is something in every human being that can be found in no one else. You too are unique . . .

This is precisely what the Jew, at the brink of despair, wanted to hear to help him forget despair. He needed to know that he belonged to a people, a community; that he was part of history. He needed to know that someone – the Rebbe, for instance – loved him enough to take an interest in his problems and share his joys. And also that there were other men and women who needed *him* enough to invite him to participate in their sorrows and celebrations. Thus the individual was no longer alone or mute: suddenly he was swept away by the *Niggun*, the music, the poetry of the Hasidic movement; for what is Hasidism if not a powerful and irresistible appeal to poetry?

In those times – in the lifetime of the Besht, the Maggid of Mezeritch or Wolfe of Zbarazh – the Hasid could not live in silence; he needed human words, brotherly voices that would help him, against all odds, to discover the world and its beauty, nature and its promise, man and his awesome fate. In those times of great misery, the Hasid needed someone to help him see, feel, hope and remember.

It was that quality of human warmth, of genuine generosity that attracted to the Hasidic movement, for a while at least, men such as Solomon Maimon and Bernard Lazare. Listen to Lazare's narration of his discovery of Hasidism:

'People spend time in their *shtibl* at any hour of the day, any day
of the week, especially on Fridays and Saturdays. They pray, they
sing, they sleep there when they have nowhere to go ... On Saturday evening, after studying the Law, they live it and teach it. The
shtibl is the Hasid's universe: there he forgets his misery. And it is
there that, through mystical sensuality, he escapes reality ...
Strange people, the Hasidim: they sing joyous songs – and tomorrow they will have nothing to eat.'

Tomorrow the Hasidim will lose every reason to hope, or even
to go on living, but today, rooted in the present, they are carried by
a powerful song of solidarity, by an overwhelming yearning: with
their Master, surrounding him, they lift themselves up higher and
higher in order to gather up there, in seventh heaven, where they
will be given a taste of the ecstasy of eternity.

That is what the Rebbe offers his followers: something that he
himself does not possess – a refuge, a haven, a source of joy and
serenity.

But then the Rebbe, by virtue of the strength he incarnates and
the majesty he evokes, cannot but represent to his followers the
father figure par excellence, meaning someone good yet strict,
charitable yet severe, tolerant with others but inflexible with himself; in other words, a singular human being in whom all attributes
converge and in whom all contradictions are resolved. Let the
Master show weakness and hesitation, and his followers will turn
away from him.

Does that mean that Rebbe Wolfe of Zbarazh was not a Master
at all? Is it possible that we were all taken in by his legend? No:
there can be no doubt that Rebbe Wolfe occupies an illustrious
place in Hasidic literature – a place comparable to that of Reb
Nahum of Chernobyl or Reb Zusia of Onipol, whose contemporary
he was. Important witnesses left us testimonies of his influence.
Thus we are told that he was kind, docile, generous, humble –
infinitely humble – and ready and willing to suffer and die for the
sake of another human being; we know that he was straight-
forward, open-minded, warm and sensitive. What was the secret of
so much kindness in a man who lived surrounded by cruelty? Who
remained human in an inhuman society? Who responded with
generosity and serenity in an era that lacked both? What was it in
Rebbe Wolfe's personality that seemingly made him immune to
anger, hate and self-pity? Had he always been that way? Had he
changed, and if so, when? And why? Not enough of his life has
been recorded in Hasidic annals to venture an answer. Not enough

to trace the evolution of his personality. By the time we meet him, he is a mature man, a leader, a Master at peace with himself and the world.

His father, the Maggid Rebbe Yehiel-Mikhel of Zlotchov, was as known for his severity as his son was famous for his lack of severity. The father's sermons made his listeners tremble; his son's words appeased them. Whenever the father spoke, the town took on the atmosphere of Yom Kippur, the entire community turning to penitence. His rigour was so great that, according to Hasidic tradition, the Besht found it necessary to reprimand him: God and God alone may judge His creation with harshness; and even then, it is up to man to try to mollify Him. So unbending was the father that, if one is to believe Hasidic legend, he continued to fulfil the same duties after his death, chastising men and women for their sins in the world of eternity and truth . . . In the afterlife, we are told, he presides over a tribunal which judges souls without any clemency. Was this why his son chose to rebel and take on his people's defence?

Rebbe Wolfe could not bear the sight of tears. He knew that when he saw his father weep the day of his Bar Mitzvah, an occasion that should be watershed and awakening for every Jewish boy. He then went on to deepen his sense of compassion. Did he acquire secret powers? Perhaps. If so, he used them only to mitigate man's suffering. Throughout his life, he opted to suffer rather than cause suffering. To weep rather than make others weep. To yield to others rather than use force to make them yield. Such was the substance of his teaching, the essence of his existence.

A story: a peasant came to spend Shabbat under the Rebbe's roof. As was the custom in Zbarazh, he was invited to partake of all meals at Rebbe Wolfe's table, together with the Rebbe's disciples and honoured guests. The First Meal was a celebration; so was the second. During the Third Meal a regrettable incident occurred: the peasant became too hungry to wait for the meal to be served. Didn't he know that the Third Meal was the most solemn and mysterious of all? He didn't care. He was hungry and there was no food on the table. Luckily there was food in his pockets. In fact, he always carried some titbit in his pockets – just in case . . . And so he pulled out a piece of challah and some radishes and began to eat. And since he was eating, he wanted everybody to know what he was eating. So he made so much noise that the Master and his disciples found it hard to concentrate. But they tried. They sang the traditional melodies imploring the Queen of Shabbat not to leave them – not yet, not yet ... The disciples were humming nostalgic tunes and the peasant went on eating. The Rebbe spoke of his dreams of Safed and Jerusalem, and the peasant went on eating. Finally, one of the young disciples could remain silent no longer. He turned to the disrespectful peasant and whispered, 'Hey, brother, how dare you?' Others chimed in. 'What arrogance ... what ignorance ... get him out of here ...'

But then, just as the whispers of protest and indignation ran to a climax, the Rebbe raised his voice: 'Do you know what I would like right now?' His disciples held their breath. What would the Master like? Every one of them would have given his life to please Rebbe Wolfe – but what would please him right now? What would give him pleasure? They leaned forward tensely, eager to hear better. 'I would like a radish,' said Rebbe Wolfe. 'Yes, friends. What I really want now is a radish. That is all I want. Does anyone have a piece of radish for me?' And suddenly the mood shifted. The peasant was no longer the object of anger. Only of envy.

Another story: Rebbe Wolfe was journeying to a ceremony. He was late. The coachman knew it and began using his whip on his horse. The Rebbe stopped him: 'Why do you hit the poor animal? Horses are living creatures. Why do you inflict pain on living creatures?' 'But we are late, Rebbe, we are late.' 'So what? Is it the horse's fault? If we are late, why do you blame the horse?' The coachman knew the Rebbe well enough not to argue. He put the whip back in its place and began shouting instead. 'Why are you shouting at the poor horse? Horses are living creatures. Why are you shouting at living creatures?' 'But, Rebbe, what do you want me to do?' 'Speak,' said the Rebbe. 'Speak to the horse.'

To speak and not punish. To speak and not condemn. To speak in order to educate and enrich, not to repudiate and humiliate. To speak to cure, not to hurt and wound: Rebbe Wolfe of Zbarazh believed in using language exclusively on behalf of man, never as a weapon against him.

One day a number of Rebbes gathered in Lvov with the purpose of devising fierce measures against assimilation. Most of them considered the situation close to an emergency. Jewish youth was falling victim to alienation. Jewish boys and girls were imitating Gentile boys and girls. They dressed the same way, spoke the same way, visited the same places. Boys were shaving their earlocks, girls went to secular schools. Parents sent their children not to Yeshivot but to workshops. There was too much ignorance and laxity. If things were allowed to continue like that, the end of European Jewry was at hand. That is why the Rabbis had gathered in Lvov. To sound the alarm. To erect walls. To adopt new laws. To proclaim that emancipation meant treason; that modernization would inevitably lead to excommunication. The consensus was that there could be no leniency. But before the measures were put to a vote, they were submitted to Rebbe Wolfe of Zbarazh, who evidently had the power to veto them. And he did. 'What are you up to?' he exclaimed. 'You wish to excommunicate Jews? Why? Just because they misbehave I am to love them less than I love you?' The measures were discarded.

How did the Besht put it? A small Tzaddik loves small sinners; it takes a great Tzaddik to love great sinners. That is the basic principle of Hasidic teaching: our love for our fellow man must resemble God's; it must aspire to be infinite.

One day Rebbe Wolfe received complaints that certain Jews in Zbarazh spent their nights – may God forgive them – playing cards. The Master was urged to punish them or at least chastise them in public. He refused. 'They play cards?' he said. 'Let them. They won't play to the end of their lives, will they? One day they will stop. By then, they will have learned to overcome sleep and fatigue, and one day they will use their knowledge for study and prayer in the service of God. So why should I try to stop them, why should I condemn them?'

Was that his way of jesting? Did he have a sense of humour? Perhaps.

A poor Hasid came to see him, to talk to him about his poverty, hoping to obtain a blessing which would make him rich, or at least richer. He had hardly begun to speak when he was interrupted by Rebbe Wolfe, who indicated to him that another Hasid was waiting outside.

'But, Rebbe,' protested the poor Hasid, 'I just came . . . one minute ago. The man before me stayed a whole hour. Why do you discriminate? Is it because he is rich and I am not?' 'No, no, my friend,' said Rebbe Wolfe. 'Let me explain it to you: the rich man who preceded you had to talk for a whole hour until I understood that he was poor, whereas with you, one minute was enough . . .'

Still, I do not think it was meant as humour. He believed in what he said. He was convinced that the rich were also poor, that the wicked were also good, and that everybody was better than he. In this respect he went even further than the Besht. The Besht yearned to bring back sinners; Rebbe Wolfe did not look at them as sinners to begin with. Who was he to judge them – or anyone else for that matter? The Besht believed that every man was *capable* of goodness. Rebbe Wolfe believed that every person *was* good.

But then, how could he be so blind? Didn't he see evil around him? Didn't he realize that creation had been diminished by man? What did he think? That the Messiah had arrived, that Satan had been vanquished for good? How are we to explain such a degree of naïveté in a man who, after all, was duty-bound to act as leader, thus as guide, as teacher in things both spiritual and practical? How could he lead others in their everyday activities while remaining so totally out of touch with reality? How could he be both hero and anti-hero?

In truth, Hasidism in its early stages placed greater emphasis on the Hasid's role than on the Rebbe's. The Hasid was more important than the Rebbe. The Rebbe's function and *raison d'être* were to serve the Hasid, and not the other way around. Created by the Rebbe, the movement existed for the Hasid – the anonymous Jew who, as he encountered the Rebbe, ceased to be anonymous.

In those times, the Hasid came from the lowest ranks of Jewish society. And so did the Rebbe. The Besht recruited his followers among the poor, the neglected, the wretched, the forgotten, the oppressed – and was opposed by the rich, the dignitaries, the establishment's financial and intellectual elite. Who clung to the Besht? Those men and women who, prisoners of their solitude and misery, had cried and endured and despaired in silence. The nameless, faceless human beings whose entire existence seemed one endless, hopeless search for meaning and destiny came to the Besht for help.

On a different level, that was true also of the other Rebbes, the other Masters: they were far from being heroic figures. The cult of the Tzaddik as a forceful leader of men on earth and as intermediary and intercessor in heaven developed much later, three generations after the Besht. Until then the Rebbe was neither powerful nor glorious. The Besht was not a prince of Jewish thought, nor was he the son of illustrious parents; he wasn't even a Rabbi. He had appeared seemingly out of nowhere and had plunged into history and set it aflame. His origins were obscure, though it is known that they were humble. Innkeeper, lime-digger, beadle, tutor: those had been his occupations. The Besht, a hero? Until he revealed himself, people had hardly noticed him.

Most of his disciples were from modest backgrounds. Rebbe

Aharon of Karlin's father was a beadle, Rebbe Moshe Kobriner's a baker, the Kozhenitzer Maggid's a bookbinder . . . Both Reb Uri of Strelisk and Reb Mendel of Riminov were sons of tailors.

Many Hasidic Masters tried to relive the Besht's experiences. In other words, before serving as teachers, they wanted to work to improve themselves. Before they accepted the crown, they endured anonymity, changing homes and disguises, living nomadic lives, wandering from town to town, from house to house: where they ate, they did not sleep; where they slept, they did not eat. They dressed as beggars and lived as beggars. They slept on the ground and endured insults and injuries without a tear or a protest. Everybody had rights over them, while they had none. To find themselves they first had to lose themselves. To deserve to be visible they first had to become invisible. Before revealing themselves they had to be totally unknown.

Countless legends describe the preparatory stages of a Tzaddik. We see him among wandering minstrels and fugitives from justice. We find him disguised as shoemaker, coachman, milkman; occasionally he does not even look like a Jew. In those legends the Tzaddik does everything imaginable – and unimaginable – to hide his shining face in darkness.

The most moving of legends concerning the Tzaddik's pre-revelation exile tells of the two great Masters, Rebbe Elimelekh of Lizensk and his brother Reb Zusia of Onipol. It is said of them that wherever they spent the night, the Hasidic kingdom took root. They walked and walked and thus extended the boundaries of the Besht's movement. One day they arrived in a little town as dusk was falling. Noticing an inn, they went inside, hoping to spend the night there. Exhausted, they lay down behind the stove, which was the customary place for wandering beggars. Soon the place fell silent. And dark. All of a sudden, they woke in a panic, overcome by an inexplicable fear. So violent was their fear that they left the inn and the village in the middle of the night. The name of the place: Oushpitsin – better known to our generation as Oswiecim, or: Auschwitz.

As for Rebbe Wolfe of Zbarazh, his progression was different from that of his peers or predecessors. They began by being anonymous and ended up being celebrated; he remained withdrawn and unassuming all his life. When the time came to end his exile, he seems to have taken it with him. Throughout his entire adult life he felt inadequate and unworthy of leadership, of influencing others, of helping others. He never believed that he possessed keys to hidden treasures nor did he ever claim to be closer to truth than his fellow men. How could people ask him to intercede on their behalf? he wondered. How could he do for them what he failed to do for himself? More than anyone he needed help.

True, he became Rebbe; he had no choice. Like the holy Seer of Lublin and the Rebbe of Kotzk, he refused to wear the rabbinic crown; and like them, he had to yield to Hasidic pressure and ascend the throne. Being the son of the famous Maggid of Zlotchov conferred certain duties. His four brothers became Rebbes: he had to say yes as they did, lest he be accused of desertion.

Like his brothers, like most other Masters, he attracted students and their parents. To spend Shabbat in his home was a precious event. People came from afar to celebrate holidays with him and his friends. Hasidim came to ask for his advice in all matters. They drank in his words, they respected and admired and loved him, as only they could: he was their Rebbe, after all . . . He alone remained unaware of the impact he was having. He never did anything to broaden his little province; quite the contrary, he did everything to keep it small. He refused to be treated as sage or Wonder Rebbe. He performed no miracles. He did not transform dust into gold, or foretell the future or impose his will on heaven. In fact, he did nothing that seemed out of the ordinary or spectacular. In spite of his prestige, he chose to lead a life of simplicity and anonymity. A Jew among Jews, a man among men: that is what he wanted to be. He had no charismatic powers, he only fulfilled his duties towards his fellow men, speaking to and hearing the mute, holding out his hand to anyone who needed it. That is all he aspired to accomplish and that is all he did. Never pretending to be more intelligent than others or more pious, he managed to be more generous and more humble than most. What was said of Rebbe Zusia – that he was a 'genius' in humility just as others were geniuses in the sciences or in Torah – was true of Rebbe Wolfe as well. Loath to attract attention, he chose to pay attention to those who lived unnoticed. Therein lay his singular greatness.

If the stories by him or about him are so profoundly moving, it is because they emphasize his concern for the underprivileged, the outcasts, the misfits; even thieves benefited from his compassion.

One night his wife woke him up in a panic. 'Wolfe,' she whispered, 'Wolfe, I hear noises! I hear thieves downstairs. Do something!' 'All right,' he said. 'I will.' He went to the door and began shouting, 'Whatever I own, I gladly let you have! Do not worry, my dear thieves. You shall not be violating the law.'

His loyal disciples bought him a watch, and one of his less loyal visitors stole it. But he refused to admit the theft: 'All Jews are Tzaddikim,' he said. 'And Tzaddikim do not steal. If this Jew took the watch, he must have had a good reason.'

Another time, other thieves – or perhaps the same ones – entered his house at night. Again his wife woke him up. Again he went to the door. In the meantime, the thieves had fled. So Rebbe Wolfe opened the door and began shouting, 'Listen, my good thieves, listen to me: by mistake you have taken some jars with dangerous medication. Do not touch them! Do not touch them, remember, they are dangerous.'

So much self-sacrifice and kindness after a while becomes annoying. How can one live with someone who never thinks of his own welfare? How can one love someone who loves everyone? How can one empathize with a man who protects the thieves who steal from him?

Well, I find him extraordinary. To live the way he did in a world that denied everything he stood for was not easy – and yet, he behaved as though it was. He actually failed to perceive the discrepancy between the world and his outlook on the world. Like Rebbe Zusia, he suffered and didn't even know it.

So – between the world and Rebbe Wolfe, I choose Rebbe Wolfe. With cynicism all around us, I look upon Rebbe Wolfe as a teacher who can help us fight cynicism and falsehood.

Granted, unlike many great Masters, he had no messianic projects and was not involved in eschatological conspiracies; but he did something else. He brought redemption, on a small scale, to the individuals around him. He brought redemption without speaking of redemption. He performed miracles without calling them miracles.

At this point, we ought to raise again the question that has been troubling us all along: Who was he? A Rebbe in the classical sense or an anti-Rebbe in the modern sense?

The more one studies the sources, the more one gets the impression that they are deliberately vague about him: like Rebbe Hanina ben Dosa, he 'carried heavy stones in his heart'. What we do know is that at the end of his life he stopped all activities, broke all ties with his surroundings, and made Aliyah: Why? To be alone at last? Why did he seek total solitude? What did he hope to achieve? I don't know. Did he know?

As one reads and rereads all the sources about his life and work, one senses a mystery. Something must have happened to him, and we do not know what. Something must have happened, for he pulled up his roots, left Zbarazh, and went to the Holy Land. True, the Master of Medzibozh, Rebbe Barukh, sent him there. But were the two Rebbes really that close? And why did Rebbe Barukh choose him? And why did Rebbe Wolfe obey? If Rebbe Barukh needed an emissary, could he not have found a more suitable representative? In fact, anyone would have been more suitable than Rebbe Wolfe. The Tzaddik of Medzibozh and Rebbe Wolfe were at opposite poles: Rebbe Barukh personified anger, whereas Rebbe Wolfe believed in serenity; Rebbe Barukh exemplified ancient royalty, whereas Rebbe Wolfe exemplified present poverty. The one was the living example of a hero, whereas the other evoked the image of a perfect anti-hero. What was their common link, if indeed there was one? What motivated Rebbe Barukh to choose him, and what motivated Rebbe Wolfe to accept? The episode of Rebbe Wolfe's move to Palestine remains shrouded in mystery.

The years he spent there are missing in his biography: we know nothing of what he did there. Hasidic chronicles of that period record only one story – not about him but about his wife, who had to take in strangers' laundry for a living. One imagines Rebbe Wolfe's misery – even darker than in Zbarazh. One imagines him in Safed or in Jerusalem. After that, he somehow vanishes from the Hasidic landscape. Why did he go to the Holy Land? What did he do there? Whom or what did he wish to elude or confront? What happened to the disciples he left behind in Zbarazh? When did he die? Of what? In what circumstances? We have no answers. All we know is that he died sometime between 1800 and 1820. Nothing is mentioned of the events preceding his death. Something must have happened, but the chroniclers, usually so full of stories, say nothing. There is only silence – disquieting, perplexing silence – surrounding his stay in Palestine. What does it all mean?

One possible explanation: Rebbe Wolfe wanted to leave Zbarazh, and European Hasidism, and Europe itself, in order to attain a higher degree of anonymity; he wanted to flee his admirers, his disciples, and the temptations they represented to him. Perhaps in Palestine he finally managed to live off stage – without anyone considering him a hero, or watching him, or questioning him, or following him. Perhaps at last his greatest wish had been fulfilled: the Rebbe of Zbarazh had become just another citizen of Safed or Jerusalem; the Tzaddik had become a simple Jew whom no one knew or wished to know. Perhaps at last he was left to his nostalgic silence and solitude.

And it came to pass that one of the celebrated Rebbe Barukh's disciples was caught in Satan's net. The poor man was following a dangerous path leading to darkness: he read forbidden books, played with perilous thoughts, and looked into hidden areas which only the chosen may approach with their gaze. He dwelled on the edge of the abyss, tempted by damnation.

When his Master, Reb Barukh of Medzibozh, learned about this, he felt sad, but told himself, Well, the boy is young and gullible. Next time he comes, I will talk to him; I will reprimand him and bring him back to God. But the disciple kept him waiting. And in the meantime, other rumours, increasingly disquieting, reached the Master. The disciple, he was told, had stopped praying; he had stopped studying; he had stopped meeting members of the Hasidic community. In fact, he no longer lived among Jews.

Though more and more distressed, the Master told himself, He will come to see me, he'll have to; and I shall be more severe than ever, more rigorous than ever, and he will be compelled to return to the fold. But the disciple continued to stay away.

Finally the Rebbe felt he had no choice. He decided to go and see him. And one morning, without telling anyone, he left his house and journeyed to a faraway town, there to confront his disciple. And before the young man could collect his thoughts and utter a word, the Rebbe spoke to him:

'You are surprised to see me here, in your room? You shouldn't be. I can read your thoughts, I know your innermost secrets. You are alone and you are trying to go deeper into your loneliness. You have already passed through, one after the other, all but the last of the fifty gates of knowledge and doubt – and I know how you did it.

'You began with one question; you explored it in depth to discover the first answer, which then allowed you to open the first gate. You crossed that gate and found yourself confronted by a new question. You worked on its solution and found the second gate. And the third. And the fourth and the tenth – one leads to the other, one is a key to the other. And now you stand before the fiftieth gate.

'Look: it is open. And you are frightened, aren't you? The open gate fills you with fear, because if you pass through it you will face a question to which there is no answer – no human answer. And if you try, you will fall. Into the abyss. And you will be lost. Forever. You didn't know that. Only I did. But now you also know.'

'What am I to do?' cried the disciple, terrified. 'What can I do? Go back? To the beginning? Back to the first gate?'

'Impossible,' said the Master. 'Man can never go back; it is too late. What is done cannot be undone.'

There was a long silence. Suddenly the young disciple began to tremble violently. 'Please, Rebbe,' he cried, 'help me. Protect me. What is there left for me to do? Where can I go from here?'

'Look,' said Rebbe Barukh. 'Look in front of you. Look beyond that gate. What keeps man from running, dashing over its threshold? What keeps man from falling? Faith. Yes, son: beyond the fiftieth gate there is not only the abyss but also faith – and they are one next to the other . . .'

And the Rebbe brought his disciple back to his people – and to himself.

This story is not characteristic of Rebbe Barukh; normally he would have found it undignified to pursue a recalcitrant pupil. He was used to people coming to visit him at his court to pay him homage. Why, then, did he make an exception? In matters of *pikku'ah nefesh* – when a soul is in danger and in need of rescue – all rules must be discarded. Still, the way Rebbe Barukh dealt with his disciple is perplexing: he discussed faith with someone whose problem was precisely that he had no faith. A strange man, Rebbe Barukh of Medzibozh – one of the angriest among the Hasidic Masters of his time.

Like his grandfather, the Besht, whom he was eager to resemble, Rebbe Barukh did not fare well with historians. Heinrich Graetz ridiculed the Besht and Simon Dubnow underestimated Rebbe Barukh. Both judgements are unsubstantiated and unfair.

Like the Besht, Rebbe Barukh aroused passion in friends and opponents alike. Simple people were totally loyal to him; as for the Masters, their admiration for him was qualified.

Rebbe Israel of Rizhin declared: 'In his presence a pious man became more pious, a wise man grew wiser, and an imbecile more stupid.'

Rebbe Zvi-Hersh of Zhidachov so yearned to hear Rebbe Barukh sing the Song of Songs that he hid in his study. Later he confided to friends, 'The Master was in ecstasy, his entire being aflame, evolving in another world; and when he came to the verse *Ani ledodi* – "I belong to my beloved as my beloved belongs to me" – he repeated each word with such fervour that I, too, found myself thrust into another world.'

Yet how is one to explain his taste for power, his thirst for authority? The Besht did not wish to impress anyone and impressed everyone; his grandson also impressed his followers – but he *wished* to impress them. Their personalities were different and so were their life styles. The Besht was constantly travelling; his grandson held court in his palace. The Besht was poor; his grandson was not. The Besht spent himself in efforts to spread joy; his grandson struggled with melancholy. The Besht spoke softly; his grandson shouted.

No wonder Rebbe Barukh was criticized, not only by opponents of the movement but also by some of its leaders. Some disagreed with his precepts, others with his methods. Too sensitive and self-centred, he resented the slightest sign of deviation or dissension. He considered himself the only ruler – the keeper of the Hasidic flame.

There were those who objected, but rarely in public. Celebrated Masters such as Rebbe Levi-Yitzhak of Berditchev, Yaakov-Yitzhak, the Seer of Lublin, Israel of Rizhin, Rebbe Shneur-Zalman of Lyady often came to spend Shabbat under his roof. Thanks to him, Medzibozh became a capital once again, attracting Hasidim from all the provinces. Medzibozh, the small village in Podolia, became a centre for pilgrimage, a glorious symbol of a glorious kingdom.

Appropriately, Rebbe Barukh's story is linked to a legend – a legend about his mother, who has a special place in Hasidic literature.

The Besht had two children: Reb Tzvi-Hersh and his sister Udil. They were totally different in character and temperament. Reb Tzvi-Hersh was shy, unassuming, withdrawn – unable and unwilling to assure his father's succession at the head of the rapidly expanding movement.

His sister, on the other hand, was an extrovert. No woman was as romanticized, as admired in Hasidism, as she was. She brought to the movement an added dimension of youth and charm.

Udil – the name probably derives from Adele, Adella – was honoured by Hasidim as though she were a Rebbe herself. And, in a way, she was. People were used to seeing her at her father's side. Full of life, ideas, projects, she was frequently involved in important events. She generated excitement, enthusiasm; she seemed to be forever in the middle of a story. Her advice was often sought. Hasidim believed that the Shekhina rested on her face.

Married to Reb Yehiel Ashkenazy, she managed to take care of him, of their grocery store, of their two sons, and of her father. When the Besht was sick, she was at his bedside. There existed a special friendship, a singular complicity between the two. One has the feeling that he was closer to her than to his own wife – her mother.

She often accompanied the Besht in his travels, something her brother and her mother rarely did. Udil seemed to be everywhere – never disturbing, never embarrassing; on the contrary, she made herself welcome, she made people feel good. She participated in the extraordinary adventure which her father had begun; and her father lovingly encouraged her to participate more and more, taking her along even when he and his disciples went on their frequent retreats. When they prayed, when they conducted their mystical gatherings, when they celebrated, she was nearby. Udil: the feminine example of the grace, wit and beauty of the Hasidic movement.

One evening she was present at a celebration. Her father's disciples sang and danced for hours on end, seeking to achieve communion with God, aspiring to let their souls enter His. They chanted with fervour, they danced with exuberance, until they left behind all links with things earthly. Eyes closed, shoulder against shoulder, hand in hand, they danced in a circle around their Master, around God and His people. Udil found the spectacle so beautiful that it took her breath away. Suddenly she noticed that one young student was losing his balance. His shoes had so many holes they had fallen off his feet. He had to break the circle and leave his friends. He looked sad and lonely.

'Poor young man,' Udil said to her father.

The Besht smiled. 'Promise him a pair of new shoes, if he promises you to intercede in heaven to let you have another son.'

Both promised. And thus, in return for a pair of shoes, Udil was blessed with another son, Barukh. Tradition has it that she wanted him – and only him. She had given birth to one son already, the future Rebbe Ephraim, author and scholar – but Udil wanted a real Rebbe, not a writer. And she had Barukh.

What do we know about him? Much – but not enough. As we consult Hasidic sources, we detect a certain reticence towards him. Few books are devoted to him; and his place in other Masters' legends is surprisingly modest. One could say that in those he is known mostly by the hostility he aroused. The Masters found him quarrelsome, arrogant, moody, and would have preferred not to deal with him. But how could they avoid it? He was the Besht's grandson, and his impact on Hasidism could not be denied.

A few essential facts: born in 1757, he was three or four when his grandfather died. He grew up in the house of the Maggid of Meze-ritch, studied with Rebbe Pinhas of Koretz and married into a wealthy family. At first, he lived in Tulchin. Later he moved to Medzibozh, where he died at the age of sixty-eight.

He was a precocious child, and the Besht loved him. From an early age, he displayed a remarkable self-confidence and even a certain arrogance.

A legend: A disciple presented the Besht the following problem: Scripture tells us that 'Abraham lifted his eyes and saw three men before him'. The comment on this in the Zohar is that the three men were our patriarchs: Abraham, Isaac and Jacob. How was it possible? wondered the disciple. How could Abraham have seen . . . Abraham?

The question was pertinent, and the Besht was about to answer it when his grandson, little Barukh, boldly intervened: 'What a foolish question! The Zohar does not speak about people but about symbols – and our three patriarchs symbolize God's attributes: grace, power and magnificence.'

True or not, we don't know – but the story does reflect Reb Barukh's personality. Frank, almost brutally so, he continued in the footsteps of the child who spoke his mind, who treated someone else's disciple as though he were his own, and who, undaunted by the presence of the Besht, dared speak of the Zohar at the age of three.

Little Barukh loved his grandfather, and spoke of him more than of his own father or mother. Tradition has it that when Rebbe

Pinhas of Koretz saw the small boy weeping over the death of the Besht, that moved him more than the tragic event itself.

Barukh studied with Rebbe Pinhas, but failed to learn that Rebbe's concept of wealth. Rebbe Pinhas used to say, 'What shall I leave my children when I die? All the monies that my Hasidim *wanted* to give me – and that I refused to accept.' As for Rebbe Barukh, he accepted. Unlike Rebbe Pinhas, unlike his own elder brother, Reb Ephraim, he seems to have had some attachment to earthly possessions.

Once he felt the need to explain why he accepted money from his followers: 'Imagine you must go to see the king. But the king is in one place and you are in another. The king is in his palace, inaccessible, surrounded by walls and fences, with guards standing at the gates. What do you do? You bribe the guards. You begin with those standing watch outside, then you make your way inside. Naturally, the closer you come to the king, the more important the guards – and the higher the bribes. Well,' he said, with a smile, 'Tzaddikim are but keepers of the gate; they too can be bribed.'

Having married a rich woman, he could afford to study – but did not. His two brothers-in-law, both pious and learned men, were irritated by his behaviour: whenever they studied, he slept; whenever they slept, he played games. So annoyed were they that they complained to his father-in-law, who decided to take all three to Mezeritch. In the coach, Reb Barukh was humiliated by his companions: they made him sit next to the coachman. However, on the way back he had the best seat. For the Maggid of Mezeritch had told his angry visitors, 'Leave Barukh alone; he knows what he is doing, and so do I. His games are serious – *if* you know how to read them. I know and so does he. And so does God.'

With the Maggid as protector and the Besht as grandfather, Reb Barukh could not fail. He was treated as a prince by Hasidic Masters and followers alike. They were taken with his youth, his exuberance – and his memories of the Besht.

When he became Rebbe, he went to Tulchin. Why Tulchin? Perhaps because of the memories connected with that hamlet. Tulchin had been the scene of unspeakable massacres during the Khmelnicky uprisings (1648–49). Reb Barukh chose to live there for a while, but not too long. Did he leave for the very same reasons that had made him come? *Because* of the memories? Or was it because of the Mitnagdim, the opponents of Hasidism, who made his life miserable with their constant attacks and slanders?

The fact is he returned home to Medzibozh, his grandfather's capital. There the Hasidim were masters, there they had nothing to fear from the Mitnagdim. From that point on, Medzibozh was linked not only with the Besht's name but with his own as well.

From visitors, disciples and chroniclers we know much about his life there. His home was not really what we would consider a palace, but for the Hasidim it was. He had *gaboim* and *shamoshim*, secretaries and servants, and displayed his riches especially on Shabbat and during holidays.

He had children, whom he loved – among them an ailing daughter, whom he loved the most. When medications were needed for her, he would personally journey to the big city.

In his home, as in that of his grandfather, women were not relegated to the kitchen or to secluded chambers. Was it Udil's influence? In Medzibozh women participated in festive meals and sat together with distinguished guests – something the holy Seer of Lublin objected to violently. One of their early disputes was on that subject. When the holy Seer was invited to Reb Barukh's Shabbat table, he was shocked to find the Master's wife and daughters there. Worse: they took part in the conversation.

An episode: One day, as Rebbe Barukh was saying grace, repeating three times the verse *Vena al tatzrikheni adoshem elokenu lo lidey matnat basar vedam* – 'May I not be dependent on other people's gifts' – his daughter Reisele interrupted him: 'But, Father,' she said, 'how can you say such a thing, do you not live from people's gifts? Do you really wish God to stop people from offering you money?' 'Only God gives,' answered Rebbe Barukh. 'But sometimes He uses messengers.'

He was hospitable and enjoyed entertaining his guests with stories, parables and songs. Before a fast he would offer them candy. A symbolic gesture: Yes, there are reasons for us to mortify ourselves, but sweetness too is part of life and willed by God.

Once he was surprised by Reb Moshe of Ludomir while he was quarrelling with his wife. 'Do not worry,' he told the visitor. 'It is just like the Almighty disagreeing with the Shekhina, His Divine

Presence – it is all for the sake of *Tikkun*, it is all meant to correct creation and shorten exile.'

It was in Medzibozh that Rebbe Barukh was seized by melancholy. We do not know what provoked it or when it was first noticed. Nor is it possible to describe accurately the attacks of morose languor. We only know that one day he was beset by them. They remain unexplained, inexplicable. Yet, how could anyone teach the Hasidic idea and not receive its message of joy? How could he claim to continue the Besht's mission and yield to sadness? How could Rebbe Barukh be a Hasidic Master and look at creation with anger?

Is this why he aroused such hostility among his peers – because he did not conform to the traditional Beshtian concept of the Tzaddik, whose task it is to guide and console, and to serve as an example? Rebbe Barukh differed from the others in many ways, and perhaps in all ways.

To begin with, he claimed to be their superior – no, more than that: their overseer. 'Rebbe Barukh is climbing to heaven . . . on our heads,' said Reb Sholem, the Maggid of Mezeritch's grandson.

True, Rebbe Barukh belittled other Hasidic Masters. The Besht's heritage was his alone, he maintained; he alone could spread it to Jewish communities in Podolia and beyond. He wished to be recognized as the one and only spokesman of the movement's Founder.

Modesty was surely not his major virtue. 'My soul,' he remarked, 'knows its way in Torah, all gates are open to me.' Once he told of a dream he had had: 'A number of Masters and scholars were sitting around a table presided over by Rebbe Shimon bar Yohai, who planted the fear of heaven in our hearts for not serving God as we should. We all began shivering. Then Rebbe Shimon bar Yohai noticed me. He rose and came over to me and placed his hand on my shoulder. "Barukh," he said gently, "you need not worry, I do not mean you – you are perfect."' Another time Rebbe Barukh was seen pressing the Zohar to his heart, saying, 'Rebbe Shimon bar Yohai, I know you, and you know me.'

At the same time, he liked to boast about his humility. Said he: 'If there are a thousand humble men in this world, I am one of them; if there are only two, I am one of them.'

Small wonder that many of his peers disliked him. He often quarrelled with them – he even had a dispute with the great Rebbe Shneur-Zalman of Lyady, who dared collect funds for ransoming prisoners in Reb Barukh's domain, in Tulchin. 'But this is an emergency,' Reb Shneur-Zalman argued. 'We must save those Jews!' 'If you are a Tzaddik,' Reb Barukh replied, 'save them with prayers, not with money.'

There was another reason, too, for their dislike. In those years disciples of the great Maggid of Mezeritch were already at work in hundreds of dispersed communities between the Dnieper and the Carpathian Mountains, revolutionizing Jewish life everywhere. They spoke to the forlorn and forsaken villagers in their own language, they shared their burdens and misery, they tried to turn imagination into a magic vehicle to spirit them away from misfortune. A small barrack was now formed into a sanctuary, simple words became litanies. These new Masters were successful because they lived *with* their followers, helping them cope with poverty through faith and faith alone. But this Rebbe insisted on being different. And he was.

Like the Rizhiner somewhat later, Reb Barukh dressed like a prince, behaved like a prince, spoke like a prince. He was the first Rebbe to introduce the external trappings of power and privilege into Hasidic lore. He was the first to stress the element of *malkhut*, of royalty, in the Tzaddik's role. His meals had to be royal feasts, his home a royal court.

A story: One day as Reb Barukh visited his brother, Reb Ephraim, he was struck by the poverty of his home – his candlesticks were made of clay and not of silver. 'Do not be sad,' said Reb Ephraim. 'The light is the same.' Shortly afterwards, Reb Barukh gave his brother a pair of silver candlesticks. But when he came to visit him next, they were not to be seen.

'Where are they?' he wanted to know.

'At the pawnbroker's,' said Reb Ephraim. 'I needed money.'

'And you don't mind?' asked Reb Barukh.

'No,' said his brother. 'I'll tell you how I look at it: I would rather be at home and have my silverware at a stranger's than the other way around.'

A hint of criticism? Maybe, though it would would seem out of character; Reb Ephraim, the elder brother, was a gentle, sweet, unassuming man who never offended anyone – and would not have sought to hurt his brother. So humble was Reb Ephraim that in his important book, *Degel machnei ephraim*, he contents himself with quoting the Besht and his immediate disciples and almost never speaks on his own behalf. Still, Reb Barukh must have envied him, for he once remarked, 'I have not written a book – thank God for that.'

He was suspicious of both the written word and the oral word. He was suspicious – period.

As he grew older, he became restless, moody; he felt a stranger everywhere – even in his own home. Uprooted, alienated, the king in him felt threatened. His obsession was that all men are strangers in the world. And that God Himself, in exile, dwells as a stranger in His own creation. One day he told his disciples, 'Imagine someone who has been expelled from his country. He arrives at a place where he has no friends, no relatives. The customs and the tongue of the land are unfamiliar to him. Naturally, he feels lonely, terribly lonely. Suddenly he sees another stranger who, like him, has no one to turn to – no place to go. The two strangers meet and become acquainted. They talk, and for a while stroll through the streets together. With a measure of luck, they may even become good friends. This is true of God and man; they are two strangers who try to become friends.'

What a depressing concept of man and his relation to God. No wonder that many Masters rejected it – and him. They could have fought him publicly on these grounds alone. Why didn't they? Out of respect for his grandfather? Yes, that too. But they respected the grandson as well. He had great charisma. They may not have agreed with his methods, but they could not fail to recognize his genuine qualities of leadership. Also, they were afraid – afraid of his sombre gaze, afraid of his dark outbursts of anger.

Anger became his particular sign, his distinction: the ability to be harsh, just as his peers were gentle. They blessed their followers; he insulted his. They sought to appease; he to annoy. However, his followers were not to be discouraged; they clung to him even more. They believed that the angrier he was, the kinder he was. They took his curses for benedictions – which only made him angrier.

Forever misunderstood, he tormented others – and himself. Why? Because of what was happening in the world, to the world? International politics left him indifferent. He did not mix into the affairs of Napoleon and the Czar, and he expected them to stay out of his. Because of what was then taking place inside the Jewish world? Possibly. The war between the Hasidim and their opponents surely affected him. But what interested him most was what was going on inside the Hasidic universe.

Like his grandfather, Rebbe Barukh understood that in order to improve the world, one has to improve oneself first. If God does not dwell in me, whose fault is it? Have I prepared for Him a dwelling place worthy of His glory?

Often Reb Barukh was beset by doubts. The Besht was so great, so intense, unique – and he, Reb Barukh, was the Besht's successor. Worse: The Besht was so majestic – and others pretended to take his place. How could Reb Barukh keep calm? Strange: the grandson's way differed so much from his grandfather's. Is this how the Besht would have expected his grandson to lead his community? With anger? In sadness?

We do not understand. No one seems to have tried to delve into the mystery. No attempt seems to have been made to explain his bizarre outbursts, his depressions. People chose to move away from him, rather than criticize him or judge him. Perhaps they did not dare antagonize the grandson of the Besht, the son of Udil, a Master who every morning wore the Besht's very own *tefillin*.

And yet, we must insist, he was a man of greatness. He had an intense inner life; he was endowed with a burning vision. Though he could have led a peaceful life filled with honours, he chose to reject the safe course of merely preserving a glorious heritage. Instead, he walked the perilous new path of self-interrogation. As the Besht's grandson, he could have kept what was given to him; he chose instead to risk everything and antagonize everybody. He despised the serene existence of the Tzaddik. He was constantly rebelling, not always knowing against whom or what. And even there we find him poignantly human.

Listen:

Rebbe Moshe of Savran came to spend Shabbat in Medzibozh. After services, Reb Barukh paced up and down the room singing *Shalom alekhem*, welcoming the angels of peace who come carrying the light of Shabbat and its serenity on their wings; then he recited with his customary fervour the prayer *Ribon kol haolamim* – 'Thank You, Master of the Universe, for Your generous gifts – those I have received and those yet to come . . .' Suddenly he stopped and said in a loud voice, 'Why am I thanking You now for gifts to come?' He repeated the question several times and, after a long silence, began to weep.

'Why is the Rebbe crying?' wondered Rebbe Moshe of Savran. 'Because of the question?'

'Yes,' said Rebbe Barukh.

'And . . . the answer? What is the answer?' asked the disciple.

'Here it is,' said Rebbe Barukh. 'We thank Him now for gifts to

come – in case we will not be able to do so when we receive them.'
And again he began to weep.

'Why is the Rebbe crying?' asked the disciple once more. 'Because
of the answer?'

'Yes,' said Rebbe Barukh, 'because of the answer. I think of the
future, which, God willing, may prove to be good to me – but what
if I will be unable to give God my gratitude? How could I live
without expressing my gratitude?'

Later he added, 'You see, the question is good – and so is the
answer. And both make me cry.'

But on another Shabbat, when he had a guest from Jerusalem, he
stared at him for a long while and then asked, 'Are you sad?'

'Yes,' said the guest, 'I am; I cannot help it. I have travelled too
much, I have seen too much, lived too much.'

'But it's Shabbat, my friend. You are not travelling now, nor are
you witnessing any suffering.'

'I am sad nevertheless,' said the guest.

'Then I order you to shake your sadness away!' And after a
silence, he added, 'Come, I'll teach you.'

One of his sayings: God and man's love of God are alike – for
they are boundless.

Another one: People are careful not to swallow live ants but are
ready to eat up their fellow men.

Also: Every person is a vessel taking into itself whatever its
owner pours into it: wine or vinegar.

The world looks brightly illuminated, he said, for those who
don't want it – and gloomy and dark to those who seek to possess it.

He also said: I am afraid of Cossacks – one is enough to frighten
me. Ten would frighten me even more – and a thousand, a thousand
times more. And yet, they frighten me less than the tiniest of sins
that I could commit.

'Say something,' pleaded the holy Seer of Lublin in the course of
a famous encounter. 'I am told everywhere that you talk so well.
Please, Rebbe, talk. Say something, anything. I would so like to
take your words with me – even one. You talk so well – won't you
talk to me?'

'No,' said Rebbe Barukh. 'I would rather be mute than talk
well.'

*

Rebbe Levi-Yitzhak of Berditchev, who loved peace – and to make peace – managed nevertheless to appear on Reb Barukh's blacklist.

Perhaps it had to do with the fact that Reb Levi-Yitzhak had sent two emissaries to report on Reb Barukh's way of life. Did he study Talmud? Did he observe all the laws of Torah? Was it true that he read other people's thoughts?

The emissaries brought back their report, and the answer was yes, to all three questions, even the last. Yes, Reb Barukh could read other people's secret thoughts – and he had proved it. The message he sent back with the emissaries was as follows: 'Go and tell the Rebbe of Berditchev that God sees and forgives. Not I – I see and don't forgive.'

Actually, this was not true: Reb Barukh forgave Reb Levi-Yitzhak. The two Masters had great affection and esteem for one another. And there was a beadle in Berditchev who could corroborate this.

Reb Barukh was told of a certain Mitnagged in Berditchev who, unfortunately, happened to be a good scholar; so he used his scholarship, naturally, to make Reb Levi-Yitzhak's life miserable. He would interrupt his lectures, ridicule his sermons; in short, he was unbearable, as only erudite Mitnagdim can be.

'Let him come to see me, and thereafter he will keep quiet,' said Reb Barukh.

Somebody informed the Mitnagged, who repeated Reb Barukh's remark in public. 'Good,' he said insolently. 'I shall go and see him. Who is he? What is he? What is his strong point?' 'The Zohar,' he was told. 'Good,' he said. And he began studying the Zohar – page after page, chapter after chapter, with commentaries and commentaries on commentaries – until one day he felt he was ready. And he went to Medzibozh equipped with a difficult passage of the Zohar, expecting, with this passage, to trap Rebbe Barukh right away. To his surprise he found the Master poring over the Zohar, open to the very page he had meant to confound him with.

'You seem astonished,' said the Rebbe. 'What puzzles you: that I study Zohar? Or that I made *you* study Zohar?' And without allowing the Mitnagged to reply, he continued, 'Usually you study Talmud, right?' 'Right.' 'And you know the Talmud?' 'Yes,' said the visitor.

And the Rebbe told this story: 'Do you know the legend about the light that shines above the child's head before he is born? This light enables him to study and absorb the entire Torah. But one

second before he enters into the world, the child receives a slap
from his personal angel; in his fright, he forgets all that he has
learned. Well, there is something in this legend that one fails to
understand. Why study if it is all to be forgotten? Do you know the
answer?'

The visitor remained mute.

'No?' said the Rebbe. 'Let me explain it to you. It is to teach
man the importance of forgetfulness – for it, too, is given by
God. If man were not to forget certain things, if he were to remember the time that passes and the approaching death, he
would not be able to live as a man among men. He would no
longer go to plough his field, he would no longer wish to build
himself a house or have children. That is why the angel planted
forgetfulness in him: to allow him to live. But tell me, what happens when the angel forgets ... to make you forget?' Rebbe
Barukh looked at his visitor and waited before continuing: 'If he
forgets – I can still do it for him.'

And because the erudite Mitnagged had used knowledge against
his fellow man, Rebbe Barukh punished him. The Mitnagged forgot
all that he had ever known and became a simple beadle in the
synagogue – where Reb Levi-Yitzhak could, from then on, speak
and lecture without fear of being disturbed.

Another story:

Rebbe Barukh's grandson, Yehiel, came running into his study,
in tears.

'Yehiel, Yehiel, why are you crying?'

'My friend cheats! It's unfair; he left me all by myself, that's why
I am crying.'

'Would you like to tell me about it?'

'Certainly, Grandfather. We played hide-and-seek, and it was
my turn to hide and his turn to look for me. But I hid so well that
he couldn't find me. So he gave up; he stopped looking. And that's
unfair.'

Rebbe Barukh began to caress Yehiel's face, and tears welled up
in his eyes. 'God too, Yehiel,' he whispered softly. 'God too is
unhappy; He is hiding and man is not looking for Him. Do you
understand, Yehiel? God is hiding and man is not even searching
for Him ...'

Weeping over God and man alike, Rebbe Barukh could not help
sinking into melancholy. Like other Hasidic Masters before and

after him, he knew that the secret of redemption lies in the union between Creator and creation. But what if Creator and creation were to remain strangers forever? Reb Barukh's despair was of an existential nature. Divine severity was less threatening to him than divine separation. Let God be our king, our father, or even our judge – but let Him not be estranged from us!

Perhaps that was the secret of Reb Barukh's anguish and anger: And what if he was wrong? And what if, due to man's foolishness, God were to hide His face forever? And what if the Besht and his allies were powerless to bring God and man closer together? And what if they were unable to protect the people of Israel from new and old dangers? And if the Besht was powerless – what could his grandson do? What was there left for him to do?

People came to him with pleas for heavenly intercession, with pleas for miracles – and he reacted with outbursts of rage: he was against miracles. When Prophet Elijah performed miracles on Mount Carmel, the people shouted, 'Adoshem hu haelohim – Look! God is God.' Said Rebbe Barukh, 'The Prophet was admirable and so were the people, for they did not shout: "Look! Miracles, miracles." But . . . "Look! God is God." They disregarded the miracles.'

But his followers wanted miracles. What could he do? Levi-Yitzhak of Berditchev chose to side with his people – against the Almighty. Not Reb Barukh. Hence his rage – at himself, at the situation in which he found himself. For his followers, who forced him to choose. For his peers – in order to provoke their anger. Yes, he wanted them to be angry, and to begin by being angry with him.

Then there was melancholy. Sadness. Despair. So great was his suffering that a famous jester, a shokhet named Hershele Ostropoler, had to be engaged to cheer him up. Poor, penniless Hershele had a biting sense of humour. Which was why he was forever being asked to leave his positions; he would invariably antagonize his employers. Hundreds of stories circulated about his sharp tongue and quick mind.

Once his wife complained, 'The children have nothing to eat; go get them some bread.' Hershele went to the marketplace with a whip in his hand, shouting, 'Who wants to go to Zhitomir for half the price?' Many people, to save half the fare, flocked to him instead of taking the coach. He made them pay and then said, 'Follow me.' He led them out of town, and farther. Halfway to

Zhitomir, the 'passengers' asked him, 'Hershele, where are the horses?'

'Who spoke of horses?' he said. 'I spoke of half fare . . .'

Later he told his wife, 'See? The important thing is to have a whip – if you have that, horses will come to you anyway.'

One night he was awakened by his wife: 'Hershele, wake up, listen. Thieves! There are thieves in the house.' 'Really?' said Hershele. 'If they find anything valuable, then *we* are lucky . . .'

One evening Reb Barukh told Hershele to light the candles, for it was dark in the room. The jester lit one candle. 'Hershele,' scolded the Rebbe, 'one candle is not enough. I cannot see.' Next day Hershele lit more than one, more than ten, more than thirty – he wasn't going to stop lighting candles. 'Hershele, Hershele,' scolded the Rebbe again. 'Are you going to blind me now?'

'I don't understand,' said the jester. 'Yesterday you were against darkness, now you are against light.'

And Reb Barukh burst out laughing. 'Hershele,' he said, 'you want to teach *me* when to be angry?'

With his stories and witty aphorisms, Hershele often made him laugh – and sometimes made him angry. For Hershele was irreverent in the classic manner of jesters. He told the Rebbe things the Rebbe did not wish to hear. So much so that at least one Hasidic source maintains that on one occasion Hershele went too far . . . and the Rebbe grew too angry . . . so angry that he ordered his followers to throw the jester out. And Hershele, brokenhearted and sick, never returned.

Hershele, too, was a tragic figure – as tragic and as secretive as his Master. Whatever it was the Rebbe wanted to achieve with anger, Hershele tried to achieve with laughter.

Again and again we come across this word, 'anger'. It dominated the Rebbe's last years. Once he explained his behaviour by pointing to the Zohar, which speaks of a certain anger that is 'blessed from above and from below', and that is named – Barukh. At his deathbed his followers found the Zohar open to that very page.

He had tried to find an explanation; his contemporaries had not. They did not really seem to resent his anger. Rather, they appear to have been puzzled. As for me, I try to understand him, and I love him. Others accepted his taste for luxury and power; I accept his anger. Surely, he wanted to teach us something about the Tzaddik, namely, that though the Tzaddik must be revered and feared, he must also be measured in human terms. The Tzaddik is human – and must be. No true greatness, no real holiness can be attained if it is at the expense of one's humanity. To deny one's weaknesses is but another weakness. The Tzaddik is no angel, no heavenly saint – the Tzaddik is simply more human than his followers, and that is why he is their leader.

Of course, that idea was introduced by the Besht; but Reb Barukh developed it. The Besht said: 'Once upon a time we tried to come closer to God through study, prayer, fasting, mortification and contemplation – but I propose to open a new way, a way that leads through love: love of God, love of Torah and love of Israel.'

Perhaps his grandson, Reb Barukh, wished to open up another, yet unknown way: one dominated by anger, by rage. He may suddenly have perceived that love alone – in a world without love, filled with violence and peopled with strangers – was not enough to assure the survival of his people. Perhaps he thought that a certain measure of anger, of rage, was necessary for the people of Israel. Hence his sadness, hence his despair: How can one not despair of a world in which rage is needed for redemption?

The key to his enigmatic behaviour may possibly be found in his excessive passion for *Shir-hashirim*, the Song of Songs. What is the Song of Songs? A love song? Yes, it is without a doubt – a sublime chant of love. But what kind of love? Unhappy love, heavy with melancholy and nostalgia. It is a song of endless waiting and faithfulness, it is majestic and moving but marked by tragedy: the couple remains separated, torn apart. God waits for Israel while Israel is waiting for God, who is looking for His Shekhina, who is following Israel, who suffers with God, and at times for God, and always because of God.

And yet – beyond sadness, beyond despair, there *is* love, and there always will be. Without such love, which transcends all other love, man's life would not be less tragic but less lofty and therefore empty and meaningless.

A romantic idea? Never mind. This was, after all, the beginning of the nineteenth century, at the very beginning of the Romantic movement, with its agonies and dreams, its tears and outcries.

Rebbe Barukh died in 1811 – leaving us his own Song of Songs, but not his rage. He took along his many masks but bequeathed to us a most precious gift: his passionate love for his people.

The more you study his sayings, his stories, his life, the more you discover beauty in the man himself. Suddenly you realize that more than his contemporaries – or ours – he grasped the awesome weight of certain questions. More than his peers – and ours – he understood that one must never avoid questions, as one must not turn one's gaze away from the abyss. Remember the story of the disciple and the fifty gates? One must go through the gates. And confront truth. And look into the eyes of despair – and never mind if you will remain prisoner of your own anguish. Alone . . . you probably will remain prisoner. So . . . don't be alone. A Hasid is never alone, even if the Tzaddik is.

There is beauty in the fact that Rebbe Barukh spoke of faith, not as opposed to anguish but as encompassing anguish. 'Faith and the abyss are next to one another,' he had told that young disciple. 'I would even say, one within the other. True faith lies beyond questions; true faith comes after it has been challenged.'

We have learned much from his tales but most importantly that love and anger are compatible, provided they are motivated by *Ahavat-Israel*, love for one's people and for mankind.

Granted, we are all strangers under the sun. Granted, God's ways are not always understandable – or bearable. Is that reason enough – ever – for us to abandon another human being, friend or not yet friend, to solitude, danger and death?

I find Rebbe Barukh beautiful. He left the splendour of his palace and the comfort of his faith to save a young man by helping him surmount his fear and doubt. I find Rebbe Barukh admirable. In order to help his disciple, he chose to open and close the gates *with* him, to confront the perils *with* him and finally, to approach the awesome abyss *with* him . . .

He risked not only his soul for someone else's, but also his faith for someone else's: that was his concept – and the Besht's too – of *Ahavat-Israel*. He was angry? Naturally he was. He was angry because he cared, because he was concerned, because he was present to anyone in need of human presence.

To the desperate young student he had said: 'I know there are questions that remain open; I know there is a suffering so scandalous that it cannot even have a name; I know that one can find injustice in God's creation – I know all that as well as you do. Yes, there are reasons enough for man to explode with rage. Yes, I know why you are angry. And what do I say to you? Fine. Let us be angry. Together.'

Moshe-Leib of Sassov

Ask the old Hasidim. Ask them to tell you what the great Tzaddik of Nemirov was known to do during the week preceding Rosh Hashana. They will tell you that in the early morning hours, when Jews everywhere rise to go and say their prayers of penitence – the *Selihot* – with special fervour, the Tzaddik of Nemirov had a way of disappearing. He would disappear and could be found nowhere. Neither in the synagogue nor in the houses of study nor at the *shtibl* nor – least of all – at home.

Where could the Rebbe be? Well, where *should* he be, except . . . in heaven? Is not a Rebbe inundated with requests and pleas on the eve of the solemn days of judgement?

Jews need a livelihood, they need peace, health, a few nice Jewish boys for their daughters . . . Jews wish to be honest and pious, but their sins are many, and Satan, with his thousand eyes, surveys the world from one end to the other, prying into everyone's life and tempting young and old, worthy and unworthy. Who is there to redeem a sinner if not the Rebbe? Who is there to help, if not the Rebbe? Clearly, he personally had to go to heaven to take care of things – everybody understood that.

But one day a Lithuanian Jew – a stubborn enemy of Hasidism – came into town. And when he heard the story, he laughed. You know how those Lithuanian Jews are: they know the Talmud and nothing else – nothing else exists for them. And Talmud to them means logic. And logically the Tzaddik could not go up into heaven, since Moses himself had to stop ten levels *below* heaven. Now, tell me: what is the use of arguing with Lithuanian logic?!

Still, they did try. They asked the visitor, 'And where do you think our Rebbe goes?'

'That is no concern of mine,' he answered, shrugging his shoulders, but secretly, he made up his mind to solve the mystery.

When the evening prayers were over, the Litvak slipped into the Rebbe's bedroom and hid under the bed, ready to spend the entire night there to see where the Rebbe went when the others ran to recite the *Selihot* in the synagogue.

Anyone else would have dozed off. But not a Litvak – no! He kept awake by concentrating on a complicated Talmudic passage.

Just before daybreak he heard the beadle as he went from house to house, from door to door, calling out: '*Shtet oiff zu Sliches* – it's late! Get up for *Selihot* services!'

The Rebbe needed no one to wake him; he had been lying in bed moaning for hours. Anyone who ever heard the Rebbe moan knew that the moans expressed all the woes and sufferings of his people; they were enough to make you burst into tears. But a Litvak's heart is as cold as stone. He lay still under the bed listening, while the Rebbe tossed in his bed.

Soon the Litvak heard the house come to life. A few whispers, the splash of water, doors opening and banging shut. Then, with everyone gone, silence reigned again, and all was dark, except for a faint beam of moonlight creeping in through the crack of one of the shutters.

The Litvak admitted afterwards that when he was left alone with the Rebbe in the dark and empty house, he was frightened. To be left alone with the Rebbe at dawn, just before *Selihot* – that's nothing to joke about. But a Litvak is a Litvak: obstinate beyond reason. So he lay there, trembling. Waiting.

At last the Rebbe got up. He washed his hands, his face. Then he went over to the closet, pulled out a bundle containing peasant's garments – and put them on.

And dressed like a peasant, the Rebbe left the room – with the Litvak trailing him like a shadow. The Rebbe stopped in the kitchen to pick up an axe, tucked it in his belt, and left the house. Now the Litvak was trembling even more, but he followed the old man nevertheless. His heart was pounding hard as he followed the Rebbe, who was making his way through the silent, unlit streets leading out of town. They came to a forest and the Rebbe kept on walking. After a few minutes, the Rebbe stopped at a young tree. The Litvak was astonished to see the Rebbe pull the axe out of his belt and start chopping away at the tree until he had felled it and split it into logs and kindling. Then he tied the wood into a bundle, threw the bundle over his shoulder, tucked the axe back into his belt and started back into town. At the end of a narrow road, there stood a wretched hut. He knocked at the window.

'Who is there?' a frightened woman's voice came from within.

'It's me,' answered the Rebbe with a thick accent, sounding like a peasant.

'Who are you?' asked the woman.

'Vassili,' the Rebbe replied.

'Vassili who? What do you want?'

'I've got some wood to sell – cheap, very cheap, almost for nothing. I saw no smoke rising from your chimney so I thought you could use some of my wood.'

And, without waiting for an answer, he entered the shack, while the Litvak hovered near the door. And the Litvak saw the inside of the hovel. Under ragged bedclothes, a sick woman was lying helpless.

'Wood?' she said. 'You sell wood? I have no money.'

'It doesn't matter,' said the Rebbe. 'I trust you. How much is it anyway? Six coppers? I trust you for six coppers.'

'But how will I ever manage to pay you? I'm sick, don't you see how sick I am?'

'Foolish woman,' said the Rebbe. 'I trust you – why don't you trust God in heaven? Isn't *he* worth six coppers?'

'And who will light the stove for me?' the sick woman groaned. 'I am a widow, my son is away at work – do I look like one who has the strength to get up and light a fire?'

'Don't worry,' said the Rebbe. 'I'll do it.'

And, stooping down to put the wood into the stove, he whispered the first *Selihot* prayer. And when the fire caught the kindling, he said the second prayer. And then the third. Then it was time to replace the lid on the stove.

And that's how a Litvak became the Rebbe's most devoted follower. And whenever a Hasid would tell how the Tzaddik of Nemirov would rise early on the solemn days of *Selihot* to ascend straight into heaven, the Litvak no longer sneered but said quietly, 'To heaven? If not higher.'

This classic Hasidic story, made famous by the great Yiddish writer and poet Y. L. Peretz, was inspired by a short and poignant tale told by the celebrated Master Reb Zvi-Hersh of Zhidachov.

But in *his* version the hero is not an anonymous Tzaddik of Nemirov but the legendary Reb Moshe-Leib of Sassov, protector of the poor and defender of the hungry, the woman is not Jewish but Christian, and the action takes place on a winter night, not before *Selihot*. Also, the man who surreptitiously follows the Rebbe is not a Litvak but another Rebbe – Reb Zvi-Hersh himself. As for the rest, the story is the same – as is the moral of the story: to help a poor old widow is more important than to ascend into heaven through prayer.

This is the very substance of Hasidism. The holy man must not necessarily look holy; he may appear as a peasant, a wanderer, a worker, a merchant. He must not necessarily stay within the covers of the Talmud, the Zohar, or the prayer book; he may – and indeed should – leave his house, leave his shelter, leave his study and his work, and go into the forest, and perhaps chop wood in order to come closer to God.

This concept of humanism – meaning, of absolute commitment to compassion and human warmth – nowhere attained a higher degree of realization than in Sassov. If Reb Moshe-Leib takes care of a sick woman, it is not to attract her to the Hasidic movement, but to give her faith in her fellow man; if the Master disguises himself as a peasant, it is to impress upon her that one need not be a Rebbe to be charitable. In Sassov, what matters is compassion.

Sassov – who doesn't know Sassov? The chroniclers of Hasidic geography have ranked Sassov among the foremost capitals of the Beshtian kingdom. And yet, like Medzibozh, like Kotzk, like Bratzlav, it was, and is, nothing but a village. Were it not for Reb Moshe-Leib, nobody would know its name.

Sassov is in the Ukraine – not far from Lvov. The first Jews settled there in the sixteenth century. In 1726, they obtained special privileges from Jacob Sobieski, son of King Sigismund III of Poland; their communal and religious institutions were all declared tax-exempt.

In 1939 the community numbered 1,500 souls. All perished in Belzec and Zlotchov. Today, Sassov looks like all Jewish small towns used to look. Only there are no more Jews. Except for Rebbe Moshe-Leib, whose memory remains linked to Sassov.

Who was he? Here, I must confess, my attitude towards him has undergone several radical changes. When I first discovered him, I was happy to have found a Rebbe who was . . . happy. I mean, really happy, totally happy with his lot. In him, I said to myself, I had found, at last, one great Master who was not involved in messianic conspiracies like the Seer of Lublin, who did not repress anguish like the Rebbe of Berditchev, who was not engaged in endless battles against despair, one who had not succumbed to melancholy like the Rebbe of Kotzk. Reb Moshe-Leib seemed to me full of true joy. His joy was neither subterfuge nor pretext nor vehicle – it was an end in itself. And I was grateful.

Later, I became . . . annoyed. The very serenity that had appealed to me earlier began to disturb me. How could he? I wondered.

How could he – the Master and friend of his followers – be happy when they were not? Could he have been blind to their woes? Could he have been that insensitive, that self-centred?

Then came the third stage. As I went over the texts and testimonies again and again I recognized my error: Rebbe Moshe-Leib, who seems so carefree and at peace with himself, was neither. And I began to love him.

A tale:

When Rebbe Moshe-Leib decided to go and study with Rebbe Elimelekh, he walked all the way from Sassov to Lizensk. Penniless and hungry, he refused to beg. If God wants me to eat, he said to himself, let Him worry about food; and if He doesn't want me to eat – how can I go against His will? His logic was perfect but his stomach remained empty. A day passed, then another. On the third day he decided that something was wrong: If God doesn't want me to eat, that means that He doesn't love me – but . . . if He doesn't love me, how can I love Him?

Then he went one step further: How do I know that He doesn't love me? Only because He doesn't feed me? Is food *that* important? If it were, I would be no better than an animal. Animals are hungry and I am hungry. The difference? *I* can endure, they cannot. You see, Moshe-Leib, he said to himself, hunger is more important than food. Think of all the overfed, overnourished princes and leaders who can eat and eat, and eat until the end of their lives – are they happy? No, they are not. They are not happy because they are not hungry. But you are, Moshe-Leib. As hungry as a lion – so what are you complaining about? Thank God for your hunger! Louder, Moshe-Leib! You have a strong voice, shout! Tell God how *grateful* you are – and not only how hungry you are.

And he did. And with his powerful voice, he shook the forest . . . and the heavens.

This episode reveals much about him. We learn that he loved to walk and shout, and to be in love . . . with God. That he was physically strong, that he sought fervour and attained it. We also learn that more frequently than not he was hungry and destitute. And – lastly – that he knew much about gratitude.

All these are essential elements in Hasidism. Most Masters taught their followers the necessity and the art of turning sadness into joy, evil into good and despair into hope. Instead of fighting melancholy, you must transform it into joy, into ecstasy.

Thus sadness, as a point of departure, may be stimulating – but it must never become an end unto itself. And hunger may, for a while, be stimulating – provided it is your own, not your fellow man's.

And never to be hungry at all is also a curse. Said Rebbe Pinhas of Koretz: Rather than possess what I desire, I prefer to desire what I possess. And Reb Mendel of Kotzk, echoing Reb Moshe-Leib's words, said: For having seduced Eve, the serpent was sentenced to forever crawl in, and eat, dust. What kind of punishment is that? asked the Master of Kotzk. Condemned to eat dust, the serpent would never be hungry – is that a punishment? Yes, answered the Kotzker. That is the worst punishment of all: never to be hungry, never to seek, never to desire anything.

Now – who was this peculiar Rebbe from Sassov? We know that he was born in 1744 in Brody – a city famous for its scholars and its fairs, and also for the connections the Baal Shem Tov had established there before his revelation. We know that he was learned in Talmud and Kabbala. That his parents were neither poor nor rich. That he married, probably twice, and had at least one daughter, Temerl, perhaps more – and at least two sons. And that he died in 1807 in Sassov.

He never met the Besht – and this is difficult to understand. When the Besht died, Reb Moshe-Leib was sixteen. Surely he must have heard about the great teacher and his new way of life. Why then did he not try to meet him? Or his successor, the great Maggid of Mezeritch? Instead, he became a follower of the Maggid's disciple, Reb Shmelke of Nikolsburg. By then he must have been in his early twenties. Why did he wait so long?

One reason – the most obvious one – has to do with his father's fanatic opposition to Hasidism. Martin Buber retells a curious legend: Young Moshe-Leib ran away from home to join Reb Shmelke, whereupon his father, Reb Yakov, became so enraged that he put aside a special whip for the day when his son would return. Misplaced – accidentally or by design – by a servant, the whip wasn't there when the day arrived. Reb Yakov became even more enraged: his son had returned and he could not even punish him! As for the son, he could not bear the sight of his father's frustration, so he went himself to look for the whip, found it and brought it to his father. At that moment, the father broke down, made up with his son *and* with Hasidism.

The story seems implausible, improbable. While that is true of many Hasidic stories, it is even more true of this one. It would make sense if the Master in the story were the Besht. But Reb Shmelke? Also, by then, Reb Moshe-Leib was no longer a child. Can you imagine his father punishing him with a whip? But what does it matter? As long as the story ends well, all is well. The father lost his anger and Hasidism gained a follower.

I think that Reb Moshe-Leib had a different reason for going to Nikolsburg. He was attracted to Reb Shmelke not as a Hasid but as a student. Reb Shmelke was considered one of the Talmudic giants of his time, and the best students flocked to his Yeshiva from all over the country.

That is why he went to him rather than to the Maggid of Mezeritch. Like Reb Shmelke, and the Maggid himself, he began as scholar and became Hasid only later.

He studied in Apta, Nikolsburg and Lizensk. At the court of Rebbe Elimelekh he was involved in an incident whose true nature has never been revealed. Some sources claim that the old Rebbe Elimelekh resented the young disciple's self-assurance. For example, Rebbe Elimelekh, in his discourse, would raise some scholarly question; and instead of waiting for the teacher to come forth with an appropriate answer, Moshe-Leib would rush in to offer his own. When this happened, Rebbe Elimelekh, Master of Masters and founder of a school, understandably would be miffed.

Moshe-Leib sought questions, he believed in them, but in his own way: first he had to find the answers. To his disciple, the holy Jew of Pshiskhe, he made the point that Maimonides, too, in his book *Guide for the Perplexed*, raises disturbing questions and offers reassuring answers; and that what people don't know is that he wrote the answers first; then and only then did he fill in the questions.

Another version of the incident in Lizensk: Reb Elimelekh became angry when the young disciple interrupted him in the middle of a sentence – but why was Reb Moshe-Leib so disrespectful? Because, says this more magnanimous commentator, Reb Elimelekh was saying something negative about someone – perhaps someone from the dissident school in Pshiskhe? – and Reb Moshe-Leib could not and would not listen to anything derogatory about *any* Jew.

His son once remarked: 'My father was lucky that the Torah does not command us to say evil things about our fellow man – for if there existed such a law, my father surely would have transgressed it.'

Another biographical anecdote:

In his youth, Reb Moshe-Leib associated with boys his own age, which was natural, except that they spent their energy not on Torah but on seeking pleasure. He would leave the House of Study in the evening and join them in taverns of ill repute, and stay with them until the early morning hours. But, warns Hasidic legend, do not jump to conclusions: his sole purpose was to save them all.

In fact, continues the legend, many, many years later, when he was already a celebrated Master in the Hasidic kingdom, one of his former companions came to Sassov out of sheer curiosity; he was eager to see who this Rebbe was who could attract so many followers. He recognized Moshe-Leib immediately and remembered the good times they had had together. What an actor, he thought, he manages to fool all these people. They don't know what we used to do – and where – once upon a time. But then, something happened to him. Watching and listening to Reb Moshe-Leib, he realized his mistake: Moshe-Leib had indeed fooled him, and his former associates, not *now*, but *then*. When he and the others were young and foolish and sinners, Moshe-Leib had already been a Tzaddik, a Just Man, in disguise, a hidden Rebbe, who had wanted to help them, to keep them from further degradation.

Another strange story: While studying under Reb Shmelke in Nikolsburg, Reb Moshe-Leib overheard a poor man talking to his friend about his miseries. He had a daughter who was an old maid; not only was she not beautiful, she was also not intelligent – actually the man used simpler and harsher expressions: she was ugly and stupid. No wonder no one wanted to come near her. No wonder that he, her father, was heartbroken. Reb Moshe-Leib, deeply affected by the man's woes, felt he had to do something. He sent for the local matchmaker and said to him, 'Go tell this man that I would like very much to marry his daughter.' The matchmaker tried to discourage him – in vain. Then he went to see the girl's father, who at first thought Reb Moshe-Leib was making fun of him. No, Reb Moshe-Leib was serious. A marriage contract was arranged, duly signed – and the wedding took place soon after. Only then did Reb Yakov, Reb Moshe-Leib's father, hear about it. He came running to Nikolsburg, quarrelled endlessly with his son and finally managed to persuade him to divorce his wife.

This anecdote rings true – or at least it does contain an element of authenticity. Reb Moshe-Leib was known for his quick impulses when someone else's suffering was involved. Even so – very little is known about that first marriage. Nor about his second one. He spent little time at home, wandering from Master to Master, from fair to fair, seeking opportunities to be helpful to any and all who needed help.

Remarried, he continued his studies. His father-in-law, a merchant and a practical man, was not pleased. He admonished Reb Moshe-Leib: 'You cannot live from Torah alone – you must provide for yourself and your family.' He gave him some money and sent him to a fair in the next town. Of course, Moshe-Leib chose to go to the local House of Study. That evening, when he returned home, his children greeted him, shouting: 'Papa, Papa, what did you bring?' He fainted. Later, he explained: 'Suddenly I told myself that one day, upon arrival in the other world, I would be asked the same question: "Moshe-Leib, Moshe-Leib, what did you bring us?"' Never again did his father-in-law send him to the fair.

His philosophy? He had none. All he desired was to be able to bring joy to the wretched, the poor, the orphans, the widows, the oppressed – and some measure of hope to those who were deprived of hope. How did he go about it? Not through emissaries or go-betweens; he himself went everywhere. He kept informed of all the sick children, all the unfortunate creatures in his region; he visited them all, comforted them all, shared their sorrow and their pain if he could do nothing more. For instance: the Rebbe had a list of all the poor and lonely widows in Sassov, and would go every morning simply to say 'Good morning' to every one of them. Often, he could be seen hugging and kissing Christian children because they were sick or sad, or simply because they needed comforting.

Do you wish to know, asked Reb Moshe-Leib of Sassov, whether whatever you are doing is right? Ask yourself whether it brings you closer to man. If it does not, then you are heading in the wrong direction – you are moving away from God. For even the love of God must be measured in human terms. One must love God *and* man and never act against man or without man – such was Hasidism as practised in Sassov.

'In the beginning God created heaven and earth.' What does that mean? In the beginning, said Reb Moshe-Leib of Sassov, man must know that all is God's creation, all men are His and all that they possess – or wish to possess – is His. How can He love them if they do not love one another?

Here is what happened one Yom Kippur eve:

The House of Study was packed with worshippers ready to intone the solemn and awe-inspiring prayer of Kol Nidre, but the

Rebbe was late. Where, but where could he be? What could be more important than to lead the holy community of Sassov into prayer – the most magnificent prayer of all? Curiosity turned into worry and then into fear: what could have happened to their Tzaddik? And what if Satan, in his cruelty, had succeeded in hurting his powerful opponent? Minutes went by, long endless minutes. The sun had almost set. Soon the time for this prayer would be over; it would be too late.

There was a woman among the worshippers who was worried about her infant: she had left him home all alone, thinking she would be back in an hour, immediately after Kol Nidre – and now, more than an hour had gone by. So she decided not to wait but to go home to her child.

To her surprise she found that her infant was not alone. A man was cradling her child, singing to him softly. Said the Rebbe, 'What could I do? As I walked past your house I heard a child crying – I had to stay with him.'

He had an exquisite sense of humour.

He was once seen giving away his last coins to a drunkard, who, of course, headed straight towards the next inn for another drink.

'Why aren't you more discerning?' someone asked the Rebbe. 'You give charity – that's understandable. But why waste your money on a drunkard?'

'God gave *me* money, didn't He?' answered Reb Moshe-Leib. 'Why should I be choosier than He?'

He once remarked: 'It is easier for a poor man to have faith than for a rich man. The poor man has nothing, so he must rely on faith; but the rich man does have other things – he doesn't need faith, or, at least that's what *he* thinks: so who is the poorer of the two?'

'When I present myself before the heavenly tribunal,' he once said, 'I shall ask to go to hell. After all, who is in paradise? The learned, the saints, the pious – and they don't need me.'

On another occasion he added, 'Should I end up in hell, I swear that I shall not leave it unless I bring everyone else along with me. And I shall say, "All my life I tried to free prisoners – why shouldn't I do it here too?"'

Mingling with common people, involved in their day-to-day problems, Reb Moshe-Leib wanted to be their friend more than their teacher. And he was. He spoke to the people in Yiddish, Polish, Hungarian; he understood them all.

His favourite area of activity was not the synagogue but the various markets, where he was a familiar figure. He felt he was more needed there, he could accomplish more. He would speak to forlorn villagers who had come to sell or buy – or simply to look around and *be* among people. When they were too busy to listen to him, he took care of their horses. So humble was he that when some coachman mistook him for a servant, he obeyed his orders instead of protesting.

Like the Besht, but unlike the great Maggid of Mezeritch, he was forever on the move, going from village to village, from tavern to tavern, seeking out broken hearts and wounded souls, jailed inn-keepers and faceless wanderers: he wanted to be their brother. And he was.

But how can you absorb so much pain? he was asked. How can you take in so much suffering from so many people? And he answered, If their pain is only *theirs*, then my work and my life are wasted. Their pain is also mine – so why shouldn't I try to alleviate it?

In the name of *Ahavat-Israel* he felt compelled to deal with the issue of human suffering in the most personal manner possible.

But what *is* Ahavat-Israel? What *is* love? Said Reb Moshe-Leib of Sassov: 'I feel I ought to tell the truth and confess that I learned its meaning from two drunkards. Yes, drunkards. I saw them sitting in an inn, drinking – and drinking silently. But from time to time they would stop for a brief exchange. "Are you my friend, Alexei?" asked the younger one. "Do you love me?" "Yes, Ivan, I do. I am your friend." They emptied another glass and dreamed their separate dreams in silence. Again the younger peasant turned to his companion: "Alexei, Alexei, are you really my friend? Do you truly love me?" "Yes, I am your friend," said the older peasant. They emptied another glass and another hour went by in silence. Again the younger peasant spoke up: "Tell me, Alexei, tell me the truth; are we friends? Do you love me as a friend?" Finally, Alexei got angry. "How many times must I tell you, Ivan, that I do?! Don't you believe me? Are you drunk? You are my friend and I am yours; and my heart is full of brotherly love for you. Must I go on repeating it all night?" At that point, Ivan looked at Alexei and shook his head sadly. "Alexei, Alexei," he said, "if you *are* my friend, if you *do* love me, then how come you don't know what is hurting me?" '

The moral of the story? Truth can be found everywhere, even on

the lips of drunkards, in the noisiest of taverns. Only it is preferable
to have studied first. Had Reb Moshe-Leib spent all his time in
taverns, he would have become not a Master but a drunkard.
Simplicity is an art; to acquire it is not simple. You must first learn
many complex and obscure lessons; only then can you master
simplicity. The peasant and the poet utter the same words; but
their meaning is not the same, for their experience has not been the
same; and their silence is not the same.

Another lesson: Learn to listen. Learn to care. Learn to be concerned, to be involved. The opposite of love is not hate but indifference; the opposite of life is not death but insensitivity. Ivan was
right: if Alexei did not know what was hurting him, he could not
really have been his friend.

Reb Moshe-Leib learned even from thieves. Here is a story he
told. 'One day,' he said, 'I was desperate. I needed money – I
needed it badly to ransom a Jewish innkeeper from jail. I knocked
at innumerable doors, I pleaded with countless merchants – in
vain. So I decided to give up and go home.

'As I was ready to leave, I was informed that a Jewish thief had
been arrested and jailed. I ran to see him. He had been beaten so
badly, his ribs were broken. He was in terrible pain. I recognized
him. "Why did you do it?" I asked. "I mean; why did you do it
again? Last time, you were caught and beaten – why did you start
all over again?" "I'll tell you: I needed the money." "And now?
Will you stop at last?" "No," said the thief. "I'll try again, and
again – until I succeed . . ." Well,' said Reb Moshe-Leib, 'if a thief
has the strength to go on trying – why shouldn't I?'

Listen to another of my favourite stories:

Rebbe Uri, the celebrated Seraphin of Strelisk, needed money to
marry off an old maid, orphan to boot. Where could he go? To
people who had money. The problem was, he didn't know any; he
knew only people who needed money – for themselves or for others.
One of them was his friend Reb Moshe-Leib of Sassov, who also
was running around the country collecting funds for beggars. He
went to see him. At first, the two remained quiet for several hours,
reflecting. Then Reb Moshe-Leib turned to his friend and said,
'Uri, my friend, I wish I could help you with money but I have
none. Still, there is something I can do for you: I shall dance for
you.' And he danced for his friend all night. Next morning, after
prayers, he told his friend: 'I must go. Wait for me.' He left and
returned two days later, with a considerable sum of money. 'Let

me tell you what happened,' he said. 'Years ago, I came into a strange city and was lucky enough to find a young boy who consented to be my guide. In return I promised him that I would come and dance at his wedding. Passing through Zlotchov after I left you, I heard music and singing. There was a wedding going on. Though I was not invited, I went closer – and recognized the bridegroom. I remembered my promise and kept it: I danced for the young couple and did my best to give them joy. When they heard my story – your story, Uri – they felt sorry for the poor old maid and they and their guests opened their hearts and their pockets. Here is the money, Uri, go and tell the girl that now it is her turn to rejoice.'

Concluded Reb Moshe-Leib, 'When somebody asks something impossible of me, I know what I must do: I must dance.'

From the encounter of the two Rebbes we thus learn that there is always *something* one can do for one's friends. What is Hasidism if not the belief that man must have faith in God *and* in people? You suffer? Pray to God but speak to your friend.

Remember the disciple who complained to the angry Master of Kotzk: 'Look, Rebbe! God created the universe in six days – and it's ugly!' 'Would you have done better?' snapped Reb Mendel. 'Eh, I think so,' stammered the forlorn disciple. 'Yes?' shouted the Kotzker Rebbe. 'Then what are you waiting for? Start working – right now!'

When it comes to helping someone in need, do not rely on prayer alone. Let the person in need pray, not you, your task is to help.

Said Rebbe Moshe-Leib of Sassov: We are told that the holy spark exists in all things – even in evil. Even in *apikorsut*, in atheism? What holiness can we ascribe to *apikorsut*? Imagine, explained Reb Moshe-Leib, a beggar meeting a wealthy man and asking for a contribution. 'I wish I could meet all your expectations,' says the wealthy man. 'But I cannot – and I shall tell you why. You are, after all, entitled to an explanation. I cannot help you because I believe in God and in His justice. If He had wanted you to have my money, He would have given it to you, not to me. Why do you expect me to oppose God's will?' Well, said Reb Moshe-Leib, when it comes to charity, be an *apikores*, do not use God as an excuse; help those who need help. If nothing else, pray with them; dance for them. There is always a way. And if there is none, invent one. If you accept the challenge, you will succeed.

When the legendary Reb Levi-Yitzhak of Berditchev fell ill, he wrote an urgent plea to his friend Reb Moshe-Leib of Sassov, asking that he keep him in his thoughts as he danced in honour of Shabbat. And because this was a special case, Reb Moshe-Leib wore special shoes that particular Shabbat. Witnesses later said that they had never seen him dance with such concentration – with such fervour.

Isn't all this rather simplistic? Is *this* the message of Hasidism? One dances, one sings, one tells a story – and one collects charity?

And here, I admit that one could feel irritated with our hero Reb Moshe-Leib. What made him so great? So he was a good dancer and an occasional baby-sitter. So he fraternized with Masters and coachmen alike, and was at ease with both. I am troubled. He was too good, too kind, too perfect. He never lost his temper, never became annoyed or upset. Forever loving, forever caring, forever giving – is such behaviour . . . human?

Other Masters became involved in messianic conspiracies and mystical struggles – what about him? They were tempted by despair – what about him? They confronted melancholy – what about him? They had problems, conflicts, crises – what about *his* conflicts, his crises?

My problem with Reb Moshe-Leib was that most tales about him – or by him – stress his joy, his warmth, his ecstasy; he seemed threatened by nothing, hurt by no one. Forever serene, at peace with himself and the world, forever singing and dancing and consoling and rejoicing – how could one not be disturbed by him?

Then I found a clue which made me revise my perception of the man. Perhaps he was not really as monolithic as he appeared. He too may well have been haunted by shadows but just didn't show it.

I came across a saying of his which startled me. *Ashre hagever asher teyasrenu ka*, says the Psalmist. 'Happy is the man who is chastised by God.' Reb Moshe-Leib translated it differently: Happy is the man who is chastising God, who is questioning him, and taking him to task for not fulfilling His obligations towards His people.

What? He too had quarrels with God – the God of love, the God of mercy? He too thought that the Creator was too severe with His creation? He too, like the Berditchever, turned his prayer into an argument with the Almighty?

Strange – it was out of character. But . . .

Then I found another clue:

Said the Tzaddik of Lentzne: 'Reb Moshe-Leib is a true miracle-maker for he *is* a miracle; his heart is at the same time entirely broken – and entirely whole.'

He was sad but few people knew it. He was so busy creating joy around him that nobody noticed the sadness within him.

Like most great Masters, he too carried a secret within himself. He would often meditate for hours – in total silence. Tears would flow from his eyes, his lips would move soundlessly, and he would be transported into another world.

His son Rebbe Shmelke tells of a childhood memory. He was five and went with his father to the Rosh Hashana services. 'I hid under his *tallit*,' said Reb Shmelke. 'And I heard him speak to the Almighty in Yiddish: "Master of the Universe – we have been praying and praying, waiting and waiting, and redemption has not come. Why not? We can bear it no more, Master of the Universe. Do you hear me? We have reached the end." '

A neighbour of his endured one tragic loss after another. All his children died in the year of their birth. Their mother one day asked Reb Moshe-Leib's wife, 'Rebbetzin, what kind of God is our God? He is not merciful but cruel; He takes back what He has given.' 'Don't say that,' answered the Rebbetzin, trying to console her. 'One must submit to His laws, one must say, His ways are inscrutable but just.' At that point Reb Moshe-Leib, who had heard the conversation from his study, appeared at the door and told the grief-stricken mother: 'And I am telling you *not* to accept His ways. My advice to you is to shout, to scream, to protest – do you understand me, woman? I want you to protest . . .'

Yes – there seems to have been another dimension to his personality. He too had obstacles to overcome, memories to cope with. His submission was not uninterrupted; his exuberance covered multiple layers of melancholy.

He too wanted to be alone. 'A man who does not keep an hour a day for himself is not human,' he once remarked. To be involved with other people's lives can become too absorbing: in order to give, man must *be*; and man's being is rooted in solitude. Yes – he too needed to be alone when he addressed God as defender of his people, and when he had to reveal his anguish to God, to God alone.

One of his remarks shows insights that later were to characterize the school of Pshiskhe. 'What is life?' he once asked. 'It is like walking on the razor's edge. On the one side there is the abyss – and on the other side as well. Yet you continue walking.'

And what happened to other great Masters also happened to Reb Moshe-Leib. He too saw the abyss – and he too transcended his own fear, his own pain, and put them in the service of others. He too continued to walk.

Towards the end of his life, he had two friends who never left his side; they were jesters. And when his sadness became unbearable, they would tell him funny stories to make him laugh – and then his laughter became unbearable.

At fifty-nine he fell ill. His physicians gave up all hope, and he knew it. His pain became more and more violent, excruciating. But he never complained. All he kept on saying was 'I do not wish to stop the suffering – that is impossible – I only wish to suffer *for* the people of Israel.' Not instead of, but for.

A strange yet characteristic incident took place at his funeral. A band of musicians in a carriage appeared out of nowhere at the cemetery; they sat there looking bewildered. The coachman explained, 'We don't know what happened. We were on our way to a wedding in Brody; suddenly the horses became wild and began running, running – and here we are. Whose funeral is this?' Among the musicians there was an old man who then cried out, 'What? Reb Moshe-Leib of Sassov? He died? Now I understand . . . years ago, we were at the wedding of two orphans whom he had brought together. He danced and we played – and he loved our melodies. He loved them so much that he said, "I would like this *Niggun* to be played at my funeral." So what are we waiting for, friends? Let us accompany the great Tzaddik with his *Niggun* – let us play, with more fervour, and more and more . . .'

Before we leave Sassov, let us take a minute to ask ourselves these last questions: Was Reb Moshe-Leib the forerunner of all those helpless men and women who, generations later, eternities later, continued to sing and rejoice even in the ghettos? Even in the kingdom of night? Even as they went into darkness? Was their *Ani Maamin*, their faith in the coming of the Messiah, a reverberation of his? Is joy possible – is faith possible – is hope permissible – when death is sovereign? Is joy the answer? Is memory the answer? Is there an answer?

How did Reb Moshe-Leib of Sassov, the symbol of compassion and love in Hasidism, put it? 'You who wish to find the fire, look for it in the ashes.'

—— *The Holy Seer of Lublin* ——

This is one of the most mysterious and troubling episodes in Hasidic literature – an episode that chroniclers and storytellers are still reluctant to explain, or even explore.

The year: 1814.

The place: Lublin. Inside the House of Study, Hasidim – old and young, students and peasants, innkeepers and travellers – participate in the traditional ceremony of rejoicing with the Torah.

They have come in their hundreds, and more, from beyond mountains and rivers; they have crossed many borders and overcome many obstacles to be here tonight.

Never have there been such crowds or such fervour. With their old Master, the holy Seer of Lublin in their midst, the weak forget their weakness, the old make light of their age. Tonight the poor are less poor, the sick forget their illnesses. Tonight all worries are forbidden.

Surrounding their Master, people sing and dance with frenzy. Like him, with him, they lift the Holy Scrolls higher and higher, as if to follow them – and follow *him* – and they do. He carries them away, far away. They trust him. No matter that they do not know the outcome or even the purpose of his secret plan. *He* does, and that should be enough, and it is. What matters is to be present. Hasn't he taught them that passion succeeds where reason fails? Tonight they are consumed by passion.

They all feel it now: this celebration is unlike any other. Every word reverberates in higher spheres, every impulse is echoed in invisible palaces up there in heaven, where Israel's fate is being determined – and mankind's too.

Just before the holiday the Seer had dispatched emissaries to friends and disciples, urging them to mark this Simhat Torah with particular emphasis. 'I have one favour to ask of you,' he told his old friend Reb Israel, the Maggid of Kozhenitz. 'Rejoice on this festive event, let yourself go, let your soul soar.'

And to his own community, gathered from all over the kingdom, he repeated over and over again, 'Drink and celebrate – it's an order. And if your ecstasy is pure enough, contagious enough, it will last forever – I promise you that.'

In spite of his age and his fatigue, he himself leads the assembly with astonishing vigour. It's as though his intention is to move the entire creation from darkness to redemption.

Yes, now it's clear to everyone: this holiday is destined to be special; man's future hinges upon it. Let Israel attain perfection through joy – and man will know no more anguish.

'*Sissou vesimkhou besimkhat Torah*,' orders the Master. And the Hasidim obey. They let go of their senses until they see nothing and nobody. And they fail to notice when the Master suddenly breaks away from the crowd and moves slowly, quietly, towards the door. Still unnoticed, he opens it, and retires into his private study. He stays there all alone, while down below, on *his* orders, the happy, exuberant Hasidim continue to celebrate.

No one knows what he did there – no one knows what really happened to him then. All we know is that at one point the Rebbetzin heard strange noises coming from the Seer's study – sounds like those of a child weeping. She rushed into the room and shrieked with fear. The room was empty.

Down below, they heard the scream. And for a second they remained frozen in silence. Then they heard the Rebbetzin crying, 'He told me to keep an eye on him – now he is gone, gone. He has been taken away.'

Taken away? By whom? Why? Where? The Rebbetzin didn't know. She claimed to have seen monstrously large hands pulling the Rebbe out the window – that was all.

Those who were there will never forget that night. Everyone ran into the street. The night was dark, opaque. Minutes went by. Nothing. The Rebbe? Swallowed by darkness.

Hours went by. Still nothing.

Suddenly, fifty feet away from the House of Study, a certain Reb Eliezer of Khmelnik heard a weak moaning in the shadows. Approaching, he saw a man lying on the ground, twisting with pain. 'Who are you?' asked Reb Eliezer.

'Yaakov-Yitzhak, son of Meitil,' whispered the man.

Reb Eliezer called out for help. The older Hasidim quickly conferred about who should carry their stricken Master – and how. Reb Shmuel of Karov held his head and heard him softly intone ancient poignant lamentations, repeating the words 'And the abyss calls for another abyss.'

Thus ended, prematurely, tragically, a memorable celebration which was meant to last beyond the night. Having put their Master to bed, the Hasidim, silent and distraught, returned to the House of Study. Defeated.

What had happened? Who had done what to the old Seer of Lublin? And what had *he* done . . . to whom? To himself? No one knows – no one will ever know.

Hasidic literature has shrouded this disturbing episode in secrecy. It is considered almost taboo. A strange conspiracy of silence has surrounded it ever since it took place.

Some sources refer to it cryptically as the Great Fall – *Hanefila Hagdola* – without entering into details. Usually they add the expression *keyadoua* – 'as everybody knows'. And, as usual, it means the opposite. Whenever Hasidic texts say *kayadoua*, it means that nobody knows. Or that nobody is supposed to know.

Most sources indicate that the Great Fall had important metaphysical or mystical implications. Why the Fall? Had the old Master *fallen* from his second-floor window? The window, according to testimony, was too narrow for a man his size to pass through. And also, empty bottles were left standing intact on the sill.

So the feeling persisted that the accident had some connection with the supernatural. Perhaps the work – or the vengeance – of Satan, who surely resented the holy Seer's messianic experiments, which no one may conduct with impunity.

At this time, as we shall see, the Rebbe of Lublin had been involved in perilous activities, trying to use Napoleon's wars to precipitate events – and he was punished. That was the general belief. Seeking and failing to achieve cosmic salvation, the Rebbe's quest had ended in personal catastrophe. The fact is that he never recovered. He stayed in bed for forty-four weeks. When he died, the entire Hasidic world went into mourning.

For he was one of its most dazzling and most secretive figures. His impact was felt throughout its communities from Galicia to the Ukraine. Some of the greatest Masters had been his disciples. How many? Some say sixty. Others, one hundred and twenty; and still others, four hundred. What does it matter? Hasidism is better known for its boundless fantasy than for its accuracy. All agree that Lublin was one of the most dynamic centres of the Hasidic movement.

Said Rebbe Naphtali of Ropshitz: 'The holy Seer is dead – and the world goes on? I don't understand.'

Said Rebbe Moshe of Ujhely: 'Our Master possessed all the

qualities and virtues of the Prophet Isaiah – except that he did not dwell in the Holy Land.'

Uri, the Seraphin of Strelisk, remarked, 'Lublin *was* the Holy Land: our Master's court was Jerusalem; his House of Study, the Temple; his private study, the sanctuary; and in his voice, the heavenly voice could be heard.'

And Rebbe Zvi-Hersh of Zhidachov said: 'As long as our holy Master was alive, we would gather around him and place our arms on each other's shoulders, and thus we were able to reach heaven. Now, with him gone, we have no longer the strength to look up. Even our dreams have changed.'

In order to understand Lublin and its messianic currents and undercurrents, we must look at the setting. Before we investigate the accident, we must get acquainted with the victim – and his times.

We are at the beginning of the nineteenth century. Nations wage wars and man is their eternal victim. Europe is upside down, churning in blood and fury. The era of Enlightenment has brought forth its own myths, its own prisons, its own darkness. Wars, wars, more wars. Frontiers, systems, loyalties come and go. The earth trembles. Priests change their style, kings lose their thrones, and sometimes even their heads, paving the way for other kings, other kinds of kings.

Napoleon has reached the Holy Land, has invaded Russia, and he dreams of world domination. Military conquest does not satisfy him; wherever his armies appear, they bring emancipation. But is this good for Jews? Or not?

In Eastern Europe, opinions are divided. Persecuted by fanatic Russian and Polish Jew-haters, the Jews feel just as threatened by Austrian liberals. They must opt for either spiritual or physical safety – the two seem to be incompatible.

Rebbe Shneur-Zalman of Lyady, the eminent Hasidic thinker and teacher, says: 'I prefer Czar Alexander; under his rule, we suffer – but we remain united and unblemished as Jews. Under Napoleon, it will be the opposite.'

Reb Mendel of Riminov, on the other hand, favours Napoleon, in whom he sees the incarnation of the legendary Gog and Magog, who will be defeated by the Messiah. But first he must be victorious. So some opponents and sceptics say that Napoleon's *second* military headquarters, headed by Reb Mendel, are in Riminov.

In the Hasidic universe, everyone's mind is set on the messianic dimension of the apocalyptic events. All these defeats and victories succeeding one another . . . all this blood being shed. Clearly, the end of the world is near. So why not take the initiative and hasten it? It could save Jewish lives; in fact, nothing else could save them. The Jews need the Messiah as never before. Since he is so near, why wait for him? Why not run *to* him?

Moreover, the times seemed ripe. The wars. The total upheavals. The *Chevlei Mashiah*: the pangs of messianic birth. All the symptoms, all the signs were there. That is why the three conspirators – Reb Mendel of Riminov, the Maggid of Kozhenitz, and the Seer of Lublin – worked on their plan so feverishly. They met secretly to compare notes and coordinate their activities. Often the Seer disappeared from Lublin, and no one would know where he had gone. In fact, he regularly went to Kozhenitz or to Riminov – for strategy sessions. They really believed that with their *kavanot* and *yikhudim*, with their words and deeds, they could influence events and developments on the battlefield.

Said Reb Mendel of Riminov: 'Let the blood flow from Pristik to Riminov – as long as it means that redemption is imminent.'

One Kol Nidre evening the Maggid of Kozhenitz opened the Holy Ark and exclaimed: '*Ribono shel olam*, Master of the Universe, please say *salakhti kidvarekha* – say that you have forgiven our sins. And send us the Redeemer. If you need a Tzaddik, Reb Mendel of Riminov is one. If you need a Prophet, the Seer of Lublin is one. If you need a penitent, I, Israel, son of Sarah of Kozhenitz, proclaim here and now that I am ready for sacrifice in the name of the living community of Israel.'

What, then, went wrong? Why hadn't the Messiah come? The three Masters, and their friends and allies, could not agree on tactics. That's why. Had they all supported Napoleon, he would have conquered the world, only to hand it over to the Messiah. The trouble was that except for Reb Mendel of Riminov, no one gave the French Emperor unqualified support. Legend has it that Napoleon knew this and came clandestinely to plead with the Maggid of Kozhenitz to win him over completely. He failed – and lost the war.

Another legend claims that one of the Seer's sons served in the Austrian army. Somehow – who knows how? – he was introduced to Napoleon at a military parade. And the Emperor told him, 'Tell your father that I am not afraid of him.' Such insolence could only lead to – Waterloo.

After Waterloo, following the Seer's plea, the three conspirators decided on Simhat Torah to make one last attempt to bring the Messiah. Again, had they rejoiced on that holiday, as only they could rejoice, the event might have occurred. But – *lo ikhshar dara* – the generation wasn't ready. The Maggid of Kozhenitz died a week before Simhat Torah, on the eve of Succoth, and the Seer had his famous Great Fall.

The accident caused great joy among his opponents, the Mitnagdim. But the Seer remarked, 'They are silly to overdo it. I can assure them that when I die, they will not be able to drink to the occasion – not even a glass of water.' Sure enough, he died on the ninth day of Av, which is a day of mourning and fasting. Even for Mitnagdim.

Who *was* the Seer?

From personal testimonies and recollections of disciples and followers, we possess enough material to piece together his biography and his portrait.

We know that Rebbe Yaakov-Yitzhak Horowitz was born in 1745 in a village near Tarnigrod in Poland. He grew up in the home of his grandfather, Reb Kopel, in Yusepov.

Three times married, he was the father of four sons and a daughter – and the author of three important books of commentaries.

Having had a solitary childhood, he was attracted to the young and vibrant Hasidic movement, first as disciple and then as Master. He settled in Lublin around 1800. Active in Jewish politics of the times, he fought unsuccessfully for the emancipation of the Jews, but successfully against their induction into military service.

Though founder of a school, he established no dynasty of his own. His disciples became leaders in their own right.

Tall, robust, tense, extremely perceptive, eloquent, he was unquestionably charismatic; he seemed always to be the centre of any gathering. He radiated wisdom, beauty and authority. He rarely said 'I' – rather, he said 'We'. He rarely ate in public. There was an aura of royalty surrounding him.

In his presence, one felt shaken, purified . . . transformed. What struck people most were his eyes – one larger than the other – which often took on a disquieting fixity when looking at someone. Hasidim were convinced that he was searching their inner depths. Nothing resisted his gaze, neither time nor space. He would go to the window and observe what was happening continents away, centuries before. It is said of him that he was able to trace one's soul back to Cain or Abel, and determine precisely how many times it had migrated since – and where.

His surname – the Seer – has remained his exclusively. Other Masters were endowed with powers, but none with his vision. In his early youth he prayed to God to take that vision away; he found it a burden. He saw too much, too far. But his plea was not answered.

Some legends maintain that for a period of three – or seven – years he chose not to lift his eyes from the ground, so as not to see the world. Others claim that for seven years he chose silence, in order not to use and abuse language.

Though he was accessible, generous and compassionate, there existed between him and his followers a barrier which prevented them from coming too close, from lifting the veil.

Serious, at times melancholy, he would nevertheless sit with his close disciples once a week and try to make them feel gay and happy. That was on Saturday nights, at the meal called *melave-malka*, during which Hasidim accompany the Queen Shabbat on her way to exile for another week. At that meal the Master would encourage his followers to speak up and entertain the audience.

The rest of the week he was often withdrawn, and even forbidding.

Listen to an anecdote: a Hasid who had just been received by the holy Seer was so enraptured that he told a friend of his, 'You know? The Rebbe of Lublin looks . . . looks like an angry lion.' 'Have you ever seen an angry lion?' asked the friend. 'As a matter of fact, no.' 'No? Then how do you know what an angry lion looks like?' 'Well – I didn't know. *Now* I do,' said the Hasid.

At the age of three, Yaakov-Yitzhak often ran away from *heder* – for which he was regularly punished by his teacher, until one day the *melamed* surreptitiously followed him into the forest – and heard him shout, '*Sh'ma Israel:* Listen, Israel – God is our God.' Only then did his teacher stop punishing him.

But his father wanted to know: 'Why are you wasting your time in the forest? Why do you go there!' 'I am looking for God,' said the three-year-old boy. 'Isn't God everywhere?' asked the father. 'And isn't He everywhere the same?' 'He is – but I am not,' replied the child.

At fourteen he went to Yeshiva, first at Zhulkova, where he studied under the renowned Talmudist Reb Moshe-Hersh Meisels, and then under the celebrated Reb Shmelke of Nikolsburg, in Shineve. There the regime was extremely rigorous. An average day meant fourteen hours for study, four hours for prayer, four for sleep, one hour for communal activity, a half-hour for meals and another half-hour for rest. Only the young Yaakov-Yitzhak was exempt from these rules.

For a while he led a marginal existence. Legend has it that he concealed his erudition. Only Reb Shmelke knew his true value and permitted him to go his own way. To fast, to seek solitude. To purify his mind and soul through *dvekut* – concentration, attachment – and prayer. When Yaakov-Yitzhak prays, remarked Reb Shmelke, the heavenly host of angels say Amen.

It was there, in Shineve, that he decided to close his eyes to the visible world and live the life of the blind: no solitude equals theirs. But later he had to open his eyes, for his solitude was threatened: he was getting married. And once again we stumble on a dramatic incident.

The marriage was arranged by Reb Shmelke and Yaakov-Yitzhak's grandfather, Reb Kopel. The girl? From a good family, naturally. Her father was a wealthy merchant from Krasnograd. The groom, when informed of the decision, agreed. How could he say no to his teacher and to his beloved grandfather? A date was set. Preparations began amid the usual excitement.

Many people came to attend the ceremony. Let us look in on them as they partake of the customary 'groom's meal' on the eve of the wedding. They sing, they play music, they laugh. The groom delivers a speech. Suddenly, he turns to his grandfather with a strange request: He would like to see the bride. General amazement. What? Now? Before the ceremony? Doesn't he trust his grandfather? But Yaakov-Yitzhak, nicknamed Reb Itzikl, quotes the Talmud: A man ought not to take a woman as his wife unless he has seen her first. Well, since the Talmud is on his side, the grandfather has no choice but to satisfy his whim. The bride is fetched from her chambers to meet her fiancé. Reb Itzikl lifts the veil – and begins to shiver. The bride leaves, and he is still shivering.

It's all right, people think; he has never seen a woman before, let alone his own. Only natural that he reacts this way.

When the meal is over and the guests have left, the groom turns to his parents and declares flatly, 'I am not going to marry her. Let us go away, far away, far from here – far from her. We are not suited to each other.'

You can imagine their reaction. 'What happened, Itzikl? All the time you said yes, now all of a sudden you say no. What has come over you?'

'Nothing,' says the groom. 'Only that I have seen her. That's enough. I don't like her; she is not for me.'

'How do you know?'

And Itzikl replies, 'I have seen her face, the face of a stranger.'

They implore him, they plead with him: to offend and shame a nice Jewish girl publicly is a sin, an outrage. Reb Itzikl is obstinate. Finally his father has an idea: marry her – and divorce her. And that is what he did. He married her and left as soon as the ceremony was over. He didn't even bother to wait until the next day. Or to change his clothes. He ran away. Where? Two versions: to Mezeritch or to Lizensk. From there he sent her a divorce.

To justify his behaviour, Hasidic legend tells us that he was lucky to have run away: she was not right for him. The proof? *Kayadoua* – as everybody knows – the girl later left her family and her people and married a Polish nobleman. And that was what he had seen at their first meeting.

The escape itself inspired many a Hasidic storyteller. Several versions offer variations on the same theme. One version: He ran away not knowing where he was going. He was tired, hungry and cold. He was picked up by coachmen who were on their way to Lizensk – or Mezeritch. Somehow, during a stopover at an inn, a beautiful woman tried to seduce him. He ran away – which made Rebbe Elimelekh call him Joseph Hatzaddik, the Just, after the Biblical Joseph.

Another version: On his way to Mezeritch – not Lizensk – Reb Itzikl loses his way as he crosses an immense, thick forest. Strong winds begin to blow. A snowstorm begins to rage. Frozen, tired, blind with fatigue and fear, Reb Itzikl feels close to death. He leans against a tree and recites the *Viddui*, the last confession before death.

Suddenly he stops in the middle, for the storm has subsided abruptly. The forest has become hospitable, and there does seem to be a way out after all. Reb Itzikl begins to walk. After a while, he comes upon a light. A house. No, a castle. A palace. He knocks at the door. No answer. He pushes the door open. It is warm inside. The castle seems empty, but it isn't. A woman appears. A beautiful woman – probably the most beautiful woman alive. She invites

him to come and sit next to her; her voice is soft and caressing –
never before has he heard anything like it.

'I am so alone,' she whispers. 'Come closer; I have been waiting
for you, for you alone.'

Reb Itzikl is seized by a violent temptation but it is fleeting. For
he immediately remembers: It is forbidden to remain alone with a
woman other than one's own. And then, God, too, is waiting. And
so he runs from the castle, away from the woman, away from
temptation. And then he realizes that it has all been an illusion.
There is no castle, no woman – only the forest.

When he arrived in Mezeritch, the great Maggid received him
with unusual affection: 'The other side – the evil impulse – tried to
get you. I am glad you won.'

Reb Itzikl stayed a while in Mezeritch. So poor was he that he
couldn't even afford challah for Shabbat. But to be close to the
undisputed leader of the movement was his reward. He learned the
principles of the Baal Shem Tov's new way of life, based on love of
man and love of God and lived in a constant state of exultation.
Ancient words came to life; human encounters offered new meaning. He observed the singular relations between Master and followers as they existed in Mezeritch: the disciple *chose* his Rebbe, to
whom he then owed absolute allegiance. He also learned the vital
importance of friendship in Hasidism. And of beauty. And sincerity.
Mezeritch was a laboratory of the soul: those who came as disciples
left as teachers.

The Maggid loved Reb Itzikl. Of him he said, 'A soul like his has
not been sent to us since the times of the Prophets.'

But like most of his friends who gathered in Mezeritch, the Seer
didn't stay there. In due time he moved to Lizensk, where he
became the protégé of Rebbe Elimelekh. There, too, he began by
leading an isolated life – far from his fellow students, bent on
silence and truth. And there an incident occurred which one must
remember as one explores the mystery of his Great Fall.

One day Reb Itzikl left Rebbe Elimelekh's House of Study and
went for a walk in the woods. He climbed a hill, then a mountain,
and sat down on a rock projecting over a precipice. There he
meditated on the meaning of life and the futility of man's endeavours. God is God and man is small – so small; Reb Itzikl felt
grateful to God for noticing man at all. I wish I could give Him
something, he thought. But I have nothing, I possess nothing. All I
can ever offer Him is myself. So he stood up, ready to throw

himself over the edge. Fortunately, it so happened that a certain Reb Salke was standing not too far behind him. He caught him in time and brought him back to Lizensk. Years later the Seer would often remind Reb Salke of the incident, and would add cryptically, 'Yes, Salke, we remember what you have done for us in Lizensk – that is why our love for you is not whole.'

How many years did he stay in Lizensk? This is not clear, though he did stay long enough to become Reb Elimelekh's favourite disciple. It was his task to take care of young, scholarly followers. To teach them, guide them – open them to Hasidic fervour. Thus the disciple became Rebbe and began attracting followers of his own – whereupon the old Rebbe Elimelekh felt hurt and betrayed. He asked Reb Itzikl to wait before establishing his own community. Too late. The first break in the life of the young movement could not be avoided. The Seer moved to Lanzhut, then to Rozvadov and finally to Lublin – the new centre, the youngest, the most dynamic in Hasidism.

As had happened in Mezeritch and Lizensk, an attempt was made in Lublin to intensify Jewish life – to reconstruct the Jewish world through simple prayers, simple stories. And human contact. People mattered more than doctrines.

Here the Seer's followers lived together, sharing possessions as well as dreams. They came here for the same reasons their forefathers had gathered in Jerusalem long ago: to be together, to participate in new experiences. Here one could forget one's misery, one's hunger; one's earthly problems mattered less or not at all. Close to the holy Seer, one found meaning in what seemed to have none. In Lublin one was again allowed to see Jewishness as a magnificent adventure.

In Lublin one learned that God is present everywhere and that man can talk to Him about all his problems – and not only about theology. And one also learned that the Rebbe must be available to every one of his followers and listen to their pleas on any level, and be their ally on any terms.

What was Hasidism if not an attempt to tear down everything that separated one man from another – and from himself? Hasidism tore down the walls that exist between God and man, creation and creature, thought and deed, past and present, reality and soul: the secret lay in oneness.

In Lublin the Hasid could dream again – without feeling guilty – of his own possibilities. To the lonely Jew, the Seer said, 'God, too, is alone – alone because of you.' To the melancholy Jew, he said, 'God too is sad – sad because of you.' To the poverty-stricken Jew, he said, 'It is up to you to alter your condition. You can defeat misfortune; invoke joy or create it, and things will change for you and others as well.' For this is basic to the Hasidic message: there is total interdependence between man and heaven; one affects the other.

Like other Masters, the Seer advocated passion and compassion, and enthusiasm, fervour – *hitlahavut* – fervour, above all. 'I prefer a passionate Mitnagged to a lukewarm Hasid,' he said. For absence of fire, absence of passion, leads to indifference and resignation – in other words, to death. What is worse than suffering? Indifference. What is worse than despair? Resignation – the inability to be moved, to let oneself go, to let one's imagination catch fire.

At that moment in Eastern Europe, when hundreds of Jewish communities felt abandoned by mankind and noticed by the enemy alone, this was a powerful, irresistible message.

Thus, by putting the emphasis on *Ahavat-Israel*, on its repercussions in higher spheres, on its redemptive quality, Hasidism kept alive many Jews who came close to giving in to shame and hopelessness. And it restored to the Jew the idea of joy.

This is why in less than fifty years the Beshtian movement swept through Eastern Europe's Jewish communities. The spark kindled between Kossov and Kitev now illuminated them all.

Which was good – and not so good. There were many Hasidim, and that was good. But there were many Tzaddikim, and that was less good. Soon they would begin quarrelling, and the movement would lose something of its original purity.

From Mezeritch and Lizensk came numerous Tzaddikim. They were active in the Ukraine, in White Russia, in Lithuania, in Hungary and, naturally, in Galicia. Suddenly it was so easy to be a Jew – a Hasidic Jew: all you had to do was to choose a Rebbe for yourself. He knew all the answers; his was the supreme authority.

The Seer, conscious of the perils inherent in success, referred to them occasionally: 'I prefer a rascal who knows that he is a rascal to a Tzaddik who knows that he is a Tzaddik.' He also said: 'Tzaddikim are sinners too, except that they don't know it. In the other world, they are led into hell – and they believe they're on a visit, or on a mission to help those who are there permanently, but then the gates are shut and they stay inside.' And repeating the last sentence, the Seer would laugh and say, 'Oh, yes, they stay inside.'

Except for Reb Barukh of Medzibozh, the Besht's grandson, the

Seer maintained cordial and even friendly relations with most of his illustrious contemporaries. He would visit them and they would visit him. His quarrels with Reb Barukh? The most notorious had to do with his attitude towards women. At the Shabbat meal the Seer would sit with his followers, while Reb Barukh would have his wife and daughters at the table. The Seer found this offensive. And yet, in other ways, he deferred to women, allowing them to dress elegantly and taking them to the door as they left his study.

Many Gentiles were attracted to him. One of them, the famous Prince Adam Czartoryski, was received with special warmth in Lublin. A Hasid wondered aloud, 'Why him and not me? I, at least, am a little bit of a Jew, while the Prince is not.' Answered the Seer, 'I prefer a Gentile who is a Gentile to a Jew who is only partly or half-heartedly Jewish.'

Like the Besht, he knew and loved nature, and brought it back into Jewish life. Everything in creation testifies on behalf of God's work, he said. All things are examples. Take a raven, for instance. He has three distinctive marks. One: he accepts no strangers into his circle; if he croaks so hoarsely and loudly, it is so as not to hear outsiders. Two: he is convinced that in the world of birds he alone exists — that other birds are nothing but ravens in disguise. Three: a raven does not tolerate loneliness; the moment he loses his way and breaks away from his companions, he goes from dark anguish to death.

In the spirit of Hasidism, the Seer urged his followers to encourage belief in two cardinal principles: *emunat-Tzaddikim* and *dibuk-haverim* — faith in the Master and fidelity to friends.

And he did love his followers, both collectively and individually. He would call each and every one of them *Yidele* — the affectionate diminutive for *Yid*, Jew. He listened to their sorrows and shared in their pain. More than in Mezeritch, more even than in Lizensk, the Rebbe in Lublin was an integral part of the individual Hasid's life.

Teacher, guide, friend — the Seer was also miracle-maker. In Lublin, miracles occupied the forefront. People came for miracles and found them. Innumerable legends speak of the Seer's powers. It was sometimes enough for the poor, desperate men and women to implore him to intercede on their behalf, and heaven would submit to his will. Lublin was the needy, the sick Jew's last recourse. When everything else failed, he went to the Rebbe. Financial disasters. Health problems. Doubts, crises, threats. The Seer had cures for every ailment.

I know all this may seem shocking, even revolting to the rationalists among us. But one must look at the overall situation of that time. Before judging, one must take into consideration the immense suffering Jews were subjected to. What they needed most was a reason to believe. The very possibility of believing was a miracle in itself. That was why Tzaddikim performed miracles. To spark the imagination. To inspire awe. To help souls open themselves to faith and hope. *Vayar Israel et hayad hagdola asher assa adoshem bemitzrayim* – and the Jews saw the miracles in Egypt; thanks to them, they could believe. What does the Tzaddik do? asked the Seer of Lublin. Through his prayer he reveals God's greatness. Miracles were meant to encourage man's faith in God – to make him feel that whenever man speaks, God listens. And that the laws of the soul are more important than those of nature.

Did the Seer have *ruakh-hakodesh*? Was he endowed with pro-phetic powers? His followers were convinced of it, and he himself never denied it. Indeed, he made a point of periodically issuing legal decisions based on his clairvoyance. An example: A woman was accused of adultery. Said he: 'Did anyone see her commit the sin?' 'No, but she was seen as she entered a room alone with a man.' 'Is that all?' said the Rebbe. 'Then I tell you she is innocent.' And he explained: 'I know that in your hearts there is a doubt; still, to protect a person, I am entitled to invoke my inner sight against your doubts.'

Such was the nature of all his miracles. He used them *for* the community; they were but means to an end – namely, to comfort and console, to encourage and uplift those lonely human beings who felt unworthy of God's attention.

He himself, incidentally, would sometimes utter remarks that led observers to assume that he did not take his miracle-making too seriously. That people believed in them was all right, but he was too intelligent, too lucid not to laugh at himself.

A story: Rebbe Levi-Yitzhak of Berditchev, his older friend and companion, admonished him one day for making a public display of his mystical powers: 'Is this what I taught you?' he asked. 'I am sorry you feel that way,' said the Seer. 'Just give me the order and I shall stop immediately.' 'No, no,' said the Berditchever, 'you may continue, you may.'

One of the Seer's younger sons, who had been present at the meeting, asked him later, 'Did you really mean it, Father? Were you ready to give up your *ruakh-hakodesh*, your prophetic gift?' 'Oh, no,' said the Seer, laughing. 'Thanks to my second sight, I knew in advance that he would *not* ask me to stop.'

*

'I dislike fools,' he said. 'Even if I should see, in the next world, a fool being invited into paradise and given every possible honour, I would run from street to street and shout, "Fools remain fools, no matter where they go, and I don't ever envy them." '

He also said: 'People go to Riminov to get sustenance and to Kozhenitz to get cures. But they come to Lublin to get the Hasidic fire.'

To a Hasid who complained that he suffered from impure, alien thoughts, he said: 'Alien? They are not alien – they are *yours*.'

A Hasid came to ask for permission to spend Shabbat with the Maggid of Kozhenitz. 'What kind of Hasid are you?' said the Seer. 'When I was a Hasid, I went to see all the Masters – and I didn't ask anyone's permission.'

A great scholar – and opponent of Hasidism – in Lublin, Reb Azriel Hurwitz, nicknamed *Der Eizerner Kop* – mind of iron – once had a friendly conversation with the Seer. 'I don't understand,' said he. 'I am more erudite than you, more learned and a better scholar than you, and yet people come to you and not to me. Why is that?'

'I don't know,' answered the holy Seer. 'Perhaps we ought to turn the question into an answer. You don't understand why people don't come to you, that's why they don't come. I don't understand why they *do* come, that's why they come.'

Another time, the same Reb Azriel said to him, 'Reb Itzikl, people call you Tzaddik, whereas both you and I know that you are not. Why not admit it publicly? If you do, people will go away.' 'Perfect,' said the Seer. 'Good idea.'

The following Shabbat, before the reading of the Torah, he ascended the *bimah* and declared: 'I want you all to know that I am not a Tzaddik; on the contrary, I am a sinner. I do not study enough, nor do I pray enough. I do not serve God the way I should. So – go and find yourself another Rebbe, one worthier of your trust.'

Naturally the reaction was unanimous: Our Master is even greater than we thought. He is the greatest of all – look at his humility.

Next, Reb Azriel suggested that the Seer do the opposite: that he state publicly that he was a true Tzaddik, so the people would resent his vanity and leave him alone. But the Seer refused, saying:

'I agree with you that I am *not* a Tzaddik – but I am not a liar either.'

In spite of their friendly arguments and Reb Azriel's open, relentless hostility to Hasidism and Hasidim, the Seer deeply respected his scholarship; he would even send the best of his disciples to study under him.

What he himself had to give was not learning, though he was learned, but the art of human relations, which, of course, goes beyond learning. He taught his followers not how to study but how to listen, how to share, how to feel, how to pray, how to laugh, how to hope – how to live. What the Besht had done for his followers, the Seer did for his: he gave them a sense of dignity. Simple innkeepers, city coachmen, villagers from afar came to Lublin once a year, and that was enough to make them feel part of the Jewish people. What Kant said of himself – that because of his books, people would no longer think as before – was, in a larger sense, true of the Seer. Once he entered the lives of his followers, they no longer lived as before. It is said that even his opponents fell under his spell: those who attended his Third Meals of Shabbat would sit down as opponents and get up as admirers.

And yet, he who gave so much to others was himself longing for change. He gave joy to others but rarely to himself. Often he would remark: 'Strange – people come to me sad and leave happy; whereas I . . . I stay with my sadness, which is like a black fire.' In moments of doubt he would groan, 'Woe to the generation whose leader I am.'

He sought joy with such intensity that he ignored other considerations. Said he: 'I prefer a simple Jew who prays with joy to a sage who studies with sadness.'

A notorious sinner in Lublin had free access to him, for the Rebbe enjoyed his company. To his Hasidim who cautiously voiced surprise, he explained, 'I like him because he is cheerful. When *you* commit a sin you immediately regret it; you repent for the pleasure you have felt. Not he. His joy continues.'

Once he asked, 'Do you know the real sin of our forefathers in the desert? It was not their rebellious behaviour, but their ensuing melancholy.'

To fight melancholy, he had, like Reb Barukh, a kind of clown, a court jester – Reb Mordechai Rakover – who would tell him jokes to make him laugh.

With the exception of Rebbe Nahman of Bratzlav, no other

Hasidic Master placed such emphasis on the concept of exuberance and celebration. In Lublin, Hasidim were urged to live not only in fear of God but also in fear for God and, above all, in joy with God.

Legend has it that Reb Mendel of Riminov, who wanted his followers to aspire to silence through quiet meditation, was shocked when he discovered the cheerful mood of Lublin. He looked at the Hasidim at services and uttered a simple *Na* – and all were struck with awe and fear. Whereupon the Seer uttered a simple *Ho* – and they happily resumed their singing and hand-clapping.

Exuberance, joy, celebration, enthusiasm, fervour, ecstasy: this is what the Seer of Lublin gave his disciples and followers – weapons against melancholy, sadness and despair.

Why was he himself haunted by sadness? Because of his tragic break with his teacher, Rebbe Elimelekh? No. He was melancholic before their first meeting. Because of his opponents *outside* the movement, the early Maskilim who preached emancipation? Or the militant Mitnagdim, who once, just before Rosh Hashana, drove him out of Lublin? Well – other Masters had similar and worse experiences.

But they, too, seem to have been subject to spells of depression. From the Besht to the Maggid, to Reb Levi-Yitzhak, to Reb Barukh, to Reb Elimelekh, to the Kotzker – all endured pain and anguish. The reasons were manifold. Mystically inclined, they constantly thought of the Shekhina suffering in exile, and if the Shekhina suffered, how could *they* not suffer with her? The Seer of Lublin said, 'A Hasid, like a child, should cry and laugh at the same time.' And he explained how he managed to combine the two when lamenting over the Shekhina's suffering every night at midnight: 'Imagine an exiled king who visits his friend; the friend is sad that the king is in exile, but still he is happy to be seeing him.'

There were other reasons for the Masters' melancholy. Most Hasidim came to the Rebbe to unburden themselves of their misery and anxieties. And the Rebbe listened – listened well. And empathized. And identified. Well, how long can one go on absorbing tales of woe and tears? Of hungry children and persecuted fathers? Week after week, day after day, hour after hour, the Rebbe would listen to the misfortunes of his people in the various small communities ruled by mostly merciless landowners. How could he stay immune? One morning he had to wake up with a broken heart.

But in the case of the Seer of Lublin, there were other elements, of a more personal nature, that affected his mood.

He survived both his Master, Rebbe Elimelekh, and his successor, Yaakov-Yitzhak, the 'Jew of Pshiskhe'. He had hurt the former and was hurt by the latter.

In truth, one fails to understand. Why had he been in such a hurry? Why hadn't he heeded Rebbe Elimelekh's pathetic pleas to wait and inherit his kingdom . . . later? Why had he inflicted such suffering on the old teacher? And why did he complain when the same thing happened to him? What the Seer had done to his Master, the Jew of Pshiskhe did to *his*. The Seer, too, felt rejected, betrayed. Rebbe Elimelekh had foreseen it. He had warned the Seer: 'You have no pity for my old age – or for yours.'

The break between Lublin and Pshiskhe was tragic for both leaders. There were no major differences between Lizensk and Lublin, but there were between Lublin and Pshiskhe. The young rebels claimed that Hasidism in Lublin had become too popular, too popularized; they rejected its emphasis on miracles and advocated instead a return to study, devotion, self-fulfilment – a return to the true source of their inspiration. Relations between the two groups grew bitter, angry. Intrigues, gossip, clannishness turned brother against brother, father against son. Several times the Jew of Pshiskhe came personally to plead with his Master not to reject him, not to condemn him. The wounds eventually healed, but the scars remained.

Before the Jew of Pshiskhe passed away, he said, 'I had the choice; it was to be either him or me. Since my prayers could save only one life, I preferred it to be his.'

When the Seer learned of his death, he wept and said, 'He will be our emissary in heaven to hasten the coming of the Messiah.' His disciples wept too, so much so that he had to console them. 'True,' he said, 'a great teacher died – but remember: God is alive; don't cry.'

His was the tragedy of the survivor. He felt alone, rejected by both his Master and his favourite disciple. He still had friends, followers, companions, particularly the Maggid of Kozhenitz and Reb Mendel of Riminov, his two co-conspirators. Together, the three Rebbes attempted to shake the laws of time and bring redemption. The story of that mystical conspiracy is among the most beautiful in Hasidic or messianic literature. It ended in failure. All three died in the same year. And the Seer – who could see so far and so deep – must have known from the beginning that the Messiah would not come, not yet, not before a long time. How could he help being sad?

On his deathbed, he wanted his wife – she was his third – to promise him not to remarry. She refused. He did not insist. He remained quiet, at peace. Then he began reciting *Sh'ma Israel* with increasing passion, his face aflame as never before.

And now, let us go back to that Simhat Torah evening in Lublin. What really happened? What caused the accident? Was it an accident? What kind of accident?

Why did the Seer leave the festivities? Why did he stop dancing? Why did he tell the Rebbetzin to keep an eye on him? Was he afraid? And if so – of what, of whom?

Was it a sudden attack of sadness, of depression? Was it his way of telling God, Either You save Your people or erase me from Your book? I no longer wish to go on living – unless You put an end to Jewish suffering?

Could it be that, having failed to bring the Messiah through joy, he thought of trying . . . despair?

Perhaps he realized suddenly that it was too early for real redemption. That the ruins of Jerusalem would not disappear so soon. His old Master was gone. His young disciple and successor was gone. His trusted companion, the Maggid of Kozhenitz, was gone. His allies and accomplices were disarmed. He must have felt lonelier than ever – more despondent than ever.

Perhaps he remembered the first time, in his youth, in Lizensk, when he had felt the irresistible urge to jump into the abyss and become an offering to God. To God – who had refused his gift of joy.

Could it also be that in a sudden flash of fear the Seer had a glimpse of the distant future when night would descend upon the Jewish people, and particularly upon its most compassionate and generous children – those of the Hasidic community? Was that why he strayed outside? To wait under the sombre sky, abandoned and shattered, to wait and wait through several generations, if necessary, for other victims of other catastrophes?

Lublin: the sanctuary, the centre for messianic dreamers. Lublin then, Lublin now.

Somewhere a group of Hasidim join a nocturnal procession. They sing and they dance as they come closer to gigantic flames that reach into the sky. After all, it's Simhat Torah and they must celebrate the eternity of Israel and wait for the Messiah, whose idea of eternity – but not of Israel – must be different from theirs.

Lublin, during the darkest hours, became a centre for torment and death. Lublin, an ingathering place for condemned Jews, led to the nearby concentration camps at Belzec and Majdanek. Lublin meant the great fall, not of one man, nor of one people, but of mankind.

And yet, and yet . . .

What do we learn from all this? We learn that the tale of Lublin survived Lublin, that the beauty of Lublin was mightier than Lublin. We learn that what the Tzaddik may do, the Hasid may not. The Master may come close to despair, his followers may not. Hasidism is a movement out of despair, away from despair – a movement against despair. Only Hasidism? Judaism too. Who is a Jew? A Jew is he – or she – whose song cannot be muted, whose joy cannot be killed by the enemy . . . ever.

Meir of Premishlan

On that particular night, Rebbe Meir was alone with his helper, Reb Arye, in his study. The Master was meditating. Reb Arye was saying psalms. It was snowing outside. The streets were empty. The town was asleep. At midnight, Rebbe Meir sighed and, as was his custom, sat down on the floor and quietly began to recite the lamentations over the destruction of Jerusalem and God's exile from one eternity into another.

It was cold in the room but the Rebbe did not feel it. He did not feel the cold because he was far away, wandering with sages and poets of long ago, with fallen princes and their children. He did not feel the cold because he was dreaming about redemption.

Hurry, God of Abraham, Isaac and Jacob. Your patience is no longer a virtue. Your children can bear it no longer. Look at us: we are tired, poor, helpless; do something – and if not for our sake, then for the sake of Your name!

For centuries and centuries Masters and disciples have repeated these litanies at the same hour, shedding the same tears – and with the same results, or rather, with the same lack of results. Would Rebbe Meir of Premishlan be more successful than they? Was he worthier than they? He knew the answer – he was humble enough to know it – and yet, like those before him and those after him, he said his prayers, wept and finally stood up, ready to retire. Tomorrow would be another day; more Jews would come and plead with him to intercede on their behalf, more Jews would place their faith in his powers.

Suddenly there was a knock at the door. Both Master and helper stopped reading, stopped breathing. Who could that be? Foe or friend? An evil emissary or his victim? 'Open,' said the Master to his helper. 'But Rebbe, we don't know who it is!' 'Open! It may be someone who needs help. A sick woman perhaps. A prisoner on the run. Do not waste time.' Reb Arye opened the door. A soldier stood outside, asking to be allowed in. He spoke Yiddish. 'I am hungry,' he said. 'Hungry?' asked Rebbe Meir. 'You said you are hungry?' He ran into the kitchen and returned with bread and milk. The soldier sat at the table and ate. 'Tell me,' said the Master, 'don't they feed you in the army?' 'Oh, yes, they do,' said the soldier. 'But their food is not for me. That is why I came here tonight. You see, Rebbe, I was taken into military service by the Czar years and years ago and I have forgotten everything I learned in my parents' home; everything, except that I am Jewish and that Jews eat kosher. So wherever I go with my unit, I seek out Jewish homes to get a proper meal.'

Visibly moved, Rebbe Meir went to the window and looked out at the snow covering the town. For a while he said nothing. Then he sighed and said, 'That the Messiah will come one day is certain; we all know that, don't we? But thanks to whom will he come? Thanks to Meir? No. Thanks to you, Reb Arye? No. He will come thanks to this soldier who goes around knocking on doors, reminding us of who we are.'

The longing for the Messiah, the poverty and loneliness of the Jew in exile, the compassion of the Master, the unknown visitor – many of the ingredients of the classic Hasidic story can be found in this one. Except that in most stories the unknown guest turns out to be the Prophet Elijah, or one of the thirty-six Just Men, whereas in this one it is simply a soldier who refuses to relinquish the only tie that binds him to his past, to his people.

Perhaps the reason for this difference lies in the Master himself: Rebbe Meir of Premishlan rarely indulged in messianic pursuits and mystical meditation; his constant preoccupation was to feed those who were hungry and reassure those who were afraid. He never claimed that he entertained relations with lofty personalities such as Rabbi Shimon bar Yohai or the Ari Hakadosh; he preferred to be with villagers and peasants and talk to them not about the secrets of creation but about everyday concerns and worries affecting them.

Thus, he was renowned and revered by followers of Beshtian Hasidism everywhere.

For Hasidism was – and remains – a universe in itself. Its Masters have opened many ways to the human heart and within the human soul. Some have advocated joy, others discipline. Some have expressed themselves through anger, others through friendship. Rebbe Barukh of Medzibozh and Rebbe Pinhas of Koretz, the Seer of Lublin and Rebbe Naphtali, the Jester of Ropshitz – each one had his trademark, his distinct seal, his specific colour. What about Rebbe Meir of Premishlan?

A warning: do not expect too much of him. Rebbe Meir of

Premishlan was the poor man's Rebbe; he made no startling discoveries, provoked no tumultuous upheavals in the world of the
mind or the soul, and conquered no important fortresses for the
Hasidic kingdom.

No revolutionary doctrine is attached to his name; no original
system bears his imprint. He seems just another Rebbe, another
Tzaddik – one of many. Simpler than some, wiser than others.

At first you love him but you do not admire him. You love him
for his human qualities; only later, imperceptibly, does your love
take on a measure of admiration as well.

For many years his main preoccupation was to ransom prisoners:
Pidyon shevuyim was his obsession. If one allows one's fellow men
to be in jail, one's own freedom is compromised: that is the substance of our tradition, a tradition that compels us to act, always,
and with every means, on behalf of prisoners everywhere.

Rebbe Meir: obsessed with freedom, he wandered from prison
to prison, a living link between prisoners and their families – between prisoners and the outside world. His simplicity was de-
ceptive. Wait until you hear about the way he made preparations
for his death; wait until you hear about his strange relationships
with other Masters; wait until you get acquainted with him. It will
not be easy – though it may seem so. No walls separate him from
his followers; no secret zone darkens his being. Just tell him that
you need him and he will receive you. Tell him that you are suffering and he will be your companion. Tell him you need a presence
and he will share your solitude without invading it. This may seem
unusual today, but in those days many Hasidic Masters treated
their followers in that way, with similar compassion.

Not much is known about his childhood. What is known – and
stressed – in various sources is that his grandfather was the 'Great
Rebbe Meir of Premishlan', the Besht's companion and friend. We
know that he was born around 1780 and that he died around 1850.

As we scan the decades and the events that filled them, we find
him with the Seer of Lublin as disciple, and with the Rizhiner as
friend, and with Rebbe Uri of Strelisk as opponent and adversary.
For a long time he refused to marry, until Rebbe Levi-Yitzhak of
Berditchev prevailed upon him to have a family. Since Rebbe Levi-
Yitzhak was the matchmaker, he could not refuse. And so he
married the daughter of Reb Itamar Hakohen, a renowned Kabbalist. They had one son and five daughters. The son became a
Rebbe and the daughters all married Rebbes.

His teacher was Rebbe Mordecai of Kremenets. His disciples

were Rebbe Shlomo Kliger, Reb Yoseph-Saul Natanson, and Reb Hayim of Sanz. He was their Rebbe and they would travel to Premishlan to consult with him about their communities or simply to spend Shabbat with him.

Rebbe Meir is generally described as a man of the people who was as much at ease with coachmen as with scholars. He had a biting tongue, a keen sense of humour and, in the true tradition of the Besht, an immense hunger for love.

Passionate and compassionate, he expressed his feelings and ideas with grace and simplicity: his sentences were short, to the point; and they somehow sounded aggressive to those in power, but soothing to those who were made to suffer by those in power.

Most of the legends about him deal with his ability to perform miracles. When words were sufficient, he found them; when they were not, he resorted to action; when action failed, he invoked miracles. When everything else fails, the Master must transform failure into victory, sadness into joy – and what is this metamorphosis if not a miracle?

He was no longer alone in doing this. Most Hasidic Masters had gained a reputation as Wonder Rebbes.

A story: One day he dispatched a special messenger with an urgent letter to be handed over personally to Rebbe Israel of Rizhin. So important and so secret was the message that the man was instructed to hide it in his shoe. When he arrived at the Rizhiner's court, he refused to discuss his assignment with anyone but the Tzaddik himself. After being admitted to the Rizhiner's private study, the emissary sat down on the floor, removed his shoe and took out the letter, which he respectfully handed over to the Master who symbolized the royalty of Hasidism. Rebbe Israel Rizhiner read the note and smiled. 'Meir has a question for you to answer,' Rebbe Meir had written. 'Since we shall soon celebrate the holiday of Shavuot, when we are supposed to eat *kreplach*, Meir thought he would ask your advice: How many is one supposed to eat? One? Not enough. Two? That is an even number and even numbers are unholy. Three? Two many – after all, one must not be a glutton. So what should Meir do?'

'Tell Rebbe Meir of Premishlan,' said the Rizhiner, 'to prepare one – but let it be as large as two.'

Another story:
In the town of Sutcheva there lived a man named Natan-Shimon

who, woe unto him, refused to acknowledge the holiness of holy Masters. And yet, he needed them. He had no children. He was sick. 'Why don't you go to Rebbe Meir of Premishlan?' his wife asked him. 'So many people go – why don't you?' 'I have no time to waste,' he answered. 'Well,' said she, '*I* went to see him. And he has a message for you: You were in Galatz last week, weren't you? You were there on business; but you did something bad there – and he knows what you did.' Natan-Shimon paled; he decided to go to Premishlan. Only he was ashamed to admit it publicly. Thus when friends asked him where he was going, he answered, to Lemberg. But when he arrived in Premishlan, Rebbe Meir sent him back angrily: Go home and tell all your friends that you are going not to Lemberg but to Premishlan to see Meir! The poor man had to obey.

Later, he became Rebbe Meir's fervent admirer. Since you live near the border, the Master told him, you may be able to help . . . one day.

And so it was to be. Natan-Shimon helped smuggle the Rizhiner from Russia into Austria. In fact, he carried him on his shoulders part of the way. They stopped at a checkpoint: 'Do not worry,' Reb Natan-Shimon told the Rizhiner Tzaddik. 'I know what to do. You just stay here and wait for me.' And he went inside the sentry house and invited the policeman to play a game of cards. Strange as it may sound, Reb Natan-Shimon, the Hasid, was an excellent player. Still, he managed to lose four hundred rubles and his partners were much too happy to bother going outside to look for illegal aliens. And so the Rizhiner reached Sadgora and there established his new court. All his life he remained grateful to the Tzaddik of Premishlan.

But who was Rebbe Meir? If you wish to know a Hasid, get to know his best friend and his worst enemy.

Rebbe Meir's closest friend was the Hasidic Master we just left in his palace in Sadgora, Rabbi Israel of Rizhin – who was all that Rebbe Meir was not: rich, famous and domineering. He behaved like a king, spoke like a king, and his symbols – both mystical and real – were those of a king. His court was luxurious, his costumes regal; he was surrounded by aides and servants, musicians and jesters. It is said that on his journeys he was escorted by a retinue that numbered a hundred. Eight white horses pulled his golden coach. He considered himself a descendant of King David and felt it proper and necessary to represent the concept of *malkhut Israel* – of Israel's immortal kingdom.

As for Rebbe Meir of Premishlan, he lived in a small house, at first with his parents, then with his wife, Malka, and their children. For a while he had to work as a tutor to support his family.

The Rizhiner ate from golden plates and used golden cutlery, whereas Rebbe Meir had hardly anything to eat. The Rizhiner had accumulated great wealth, whereas the Premishlaner distributed the little he had. How then is one to explain – or understand – the friendship between the two? What could have drawn them one to the other? Merely the fact that they were opposites?

One day they met on the road. The Rizhiner was travelling to attend a celebration and the Premishlaner to collect funds for charity. They stopped and looked at one another with some embarrassment and amazement. The Rizhiner felt he had to justify his expensive carriage and splendid horses: 'I need them,' he said. 'Should I happen to drive into the mud, I would need six strong horses to pull me out.' 'Not Meir,' answered the Premishlaner. 'Meir has only one horse, and it is weak and small and old; it can hardly pull him on a flat road – it would surely not be able to pull him out of the mud; therefore, my friend, Meir must be careful, very careful not to fall into the mud . . .'

He referred a man to the Rizhiner, saying, 'You need intercession in heaven; his is more valuable than mine. But do what Meir tells you. When you arrive in Sadgora, go to the palace. Ask to be admitted into the Rebbe's study. And there you must start singing a particular Sabbath song; sing it even if it is not Sabbath. You'll see: heaven will help you.'

So the man went to Sadgora, rushed to the palace and asked to see the Rizhiner, explaining that Rebbe Meir had sent him. The Master's aides were glad. The Rizhiner was going through a deep depression; any message from his friend Reb Meir would improve his mood. And true enough, when the man entered the Tzaddik's study, he started right away to sing a long, a very long, Sabbath song, with passion and fervour – as though he were singing it on Sabbath and not on a simple Wednesday. The Rizhiner reacted with laughter; he shook with laughter; and seeing him laugh, all his aides began to laugh too. Never had they laughed so hard; they could not stop laughing. At the end, the Rizhiner remarked, 'I don't know what Reb Meir wants from me and why he sent you to me; but you helped me and therefore you yourself have also been helped.'

On another occasion Rebbe Meir sent one of his Hasidim to go and see the Rizhiner with another one of his messages: Tell him, he said, that he has taken the high road whereas Meir is following the low road; but we shall both arrive at the same place – together.

What brought these two Masters together? Actually, let us turn the question around: Were they together? We are told of their close relationship, of the esteem and warmth they felt for one another; we are told of their lasting friendship – but not of their spending much time together. In fact, we are told the opposite: their contact was maintained through emissaries.

Still, they *were* friends. True friends. On what basis? Perhaps both believed in Hasidic pluralism. Both believed that there was more than one way to implement the Besht's principles and programmes. That study without prayer would be as sterile as prayer without study. That to emphasize meditation alone, compassion alone, miracles alone, nobility alone, would distort the image of both the Hasid and the Master. Nothing in creation is monolithic. Words contain silence, and silence exists only thanks to surrounding words. God needs man for His glory and man needs God for his memory. One can love the poor and be a Hasid, one can aspire to riches and be a Hasid; but one cannot be alone and be a Hasid. Both Premishlan and Rizhin constituted, each in its way, a protest against human solitude as opposed to, rather than integrated into, God's own solitude.

The despairing Jew, living marginally in his faraway village, had to ask himself some disturbing questions: Where is God in my life? Where am I in His? Does He hear me? Am I heard by Him? Is He my king, my father, my friend? Is He – could He be – my enemy? Worse: Is He – could He be – indifferent to the fate of His creation? Hasidism answers emphatically: No – God is not indifferent; God is an answer to indifference.

Yes, both Rebbe Meir and Rebbe Israel yearned to reach the same goal; and each needed the other to be able to follow his own road without ever losing sight of the road ahead.

In some places, men are one another's prisoners; in the Hasidic kingdom they were one another's companions. One man was not another man's boundary but, on the contrary, an opening unto other men. Thanks to Premishlan, Rebbe Israel felt freer to experience Rizhin; thanks to Rizhin, Rebbe Meir felt that Premishlan had its own merits. God dwelled in both places. For, according to the cardinal principle of the Besht and his disciples, *let atar panui minei* – no place in creation is devoid of God; God is everywhere.

At first, we are more attracted to Rebbe Meir than to the

Rizhiner. The reasons are obvious. Eastern European Jewry was enduring such misery that the very thought of a Rebbe living in luxury is – understandably – shocking. We naturally prefer the modest, unassuming, poor Rebbe Meir who lived with his people, on their level, sharing their poverty, their anguish, their sorrow, their thirst and their hunger.

But – wait a moment. First impressions may be misleading; they certainly bear checking. Are we sure that of the two Masters it was the Rizhiner who was excessively preoccupied with earthly matters? And what if it were the opposite? The Rizhiner had everything, therefore he did not have to think of food or rent money; he could devote all his time, all his energy to spiritual pursuits, to truth and justice and inner peace. As for Rebbe Meir, he had no time to spare for lofty excursions of the soul: he had to think of jobs and meals and rent for his followers ... And so is it not possible that the Rizhiner may have been more idealistic than his destitute friend? The Premishlaner thought of bread, the Rizhiner of redemption!

And yet, as we reflect upon their friendship, we like Reb Meir more than ever. Without judging the Rizhiner – who are we to pass judgement on a Master, especially one whom we love with all our heart? – we must come to the inevitable conclusion that when there are people going hungry, they must come first; their well-being must take precedence over all ideals – no, their well-being must become our ideal. The Messiah can wait and he should: first priority goes to the sick child who needs medicine; or to the desperate mother who needs to be consoled; or surely to the father who loses his mind when he is unable to feed, to preserve, his family.

I think that the Rizhiner knew this and that is why he clung to his friendship with Rebbe Meir, who reminded him of the other road, the small one, the neglected one. As for Rebbe Meir Premishlaner, he was too busy with his poor Hasidim to think about such matters.

Now – let us look at the third point of the triangle and examine his relationship with his fierce and outspoken rival, Reb Uri, the so-called Seraphin of Strelisk.

Actually they should have got along well, for they had much in common, more in common than Rebbe Meir had with the Rizhiner. Reb Uri, too, was penniless. He too worshipped in ecstasy – unlike the Rizhiner, who insisted on self-control and proper decorum. He too was forever on the road trying to rescue persecuted villagers and to ransom jailed innkeepers. But then, why the hostility between the two *poor* Masters?

There were at least two reasons. The first: Reb Uri resented the Premishlaner's boasting about his powers. The Seraphin believed that whoever is initiated into secret knowledge must keep it to himself; one must take care not to reveal too much to outsiders. And because Reb Meir used to tell people what he saw in heaven – or in the human heart and mind – the Seraphin went so far as to try to deprive him of his powers. To this end, he sent two of his trusted Hasidim to Reb Naphtali of Ropshitz to enlist his support. The two men arrived in Ropshitz on a Thursday and the Tzaddik received them warmly – so warmly that they could not say anything about Reb Meir; Reb Naphtali was doing all the talking. They returned the next day. Again he told them stories about his Masters, invited them to stay for Shabbat, and again not a word was said about Reb Meir. During Shabbat, the Tzaddik naturally spoke of and listened only to words of Torah. On Sunday, Reb Uri's two Hasidim returned, this time determined to tell Reb Naphtali openly and firmly what their Rebbe expected him to do about the Premishlaner. But again, Reb Naphtali did not allow them to say a word. Having spoken on and on about many things, he accompanied them to the door; there he stopped and said, 'Reb Meir's father, the late Reb Aaron-Leib, appeared to me last night and said, "I have left behind me a small flame, please, do not let it be smothered . . ." At that moment, a man announced: "Reb Meir is here!" The Premishlaner appeared seemingly out of nowhere, and angrily commented, "My father called me a small flame? No, Rebbe of Ropshitz! He left behind him a huge flame!"'

Reb Meir was left with his mystical powers and Reb Uri with his anger.

The second reason for the Seraphin's hostility had to do with . . . materialism.

Whereas Reb Meir forever pleaded with God on behalf of his Hasidim's physical and economical welfare, Reb Uri was concerned with their spiritual development only.

Like the Kotzker Rebbe, the Seraphin categorically refused to intercede with heaven to obtain improved health or material gain for his followers. You wanted him to pray for your soul? With pleasure. For your intellectual growth? No problem. For your share in paradise? Any time. But if you were left with no meat for Shabbat, no credit for clothing and no money for your children's education – you had better not count on the Seraphin of Strelisk!

There exist stories upon stories describing his stubborn refusal to help improve his community's material welfare. Eventually his followers no longer expected him to be their advocate in such earthly matters. They were content with what they had and they loved him for what he was – not for what he gave them concretely but for what he did to elevate their souls.

One day he stopped his morning prayer, turned to his Hasidim and exclaimed, 'Whoever, whoever wants money, let him come nearer! Let him put his hand in my pockets; he will find more money than he needs.' He repeated his invitation but no one came forward, first, because his pockets were empty, second, because in Strelisk money did not seem to matter to those who had none.

On another occasion, he justified his behaviour as he talked with a visiting Rebbe. The visitor wanted to know: 'Why aren't you taking care of your people's immediate needs?' 'Needs?' said Reb Uri. 'You said, "Needs"? Let us see whether my people need anything.' And, during services, he raised his voice and asked, 'Who wants me to get him wealth?' No one moved. 'Who wants health?' No one moved. 'Who wants security?' Still, no one moved. 'See?' asked Reb Uri. 'Now listen: Who wants fear of heaven?' All responded eagerly. 'And who wants fervour?' Again, all responded. 'Who needs Yirat-Shamayim – fear of heaven?' All needed, all wanted Yirat-Shamayim. In Strelisk, they needed nothing else.

Not so in Premishlan.

What Reb Meir's people needed above all was food for the body, a roof over the head, an assured livelihood. And the Premishlaner listened and responded with concern and understanding. Urgent everyday worries were important to him. He did not care much about his own poverty, but that of his fellow men touched him deeply. In this he followed in the footsteps of the Besht and the Maggid of Mezeritch. Just as the Besht was against deliberate self-mortification, the Maggid spoke up against imposed suffering. A small hole in the body turns into a large hole in the soul, the great Maggid had said. To diminish and despise your body is to sneer at God's creation, for the body, too, is part of it – it is in fact its most visible and tangible part. How would man perform His commandments were it not for his senses? Of course, the heart is at the centre of man's activities but in order for the heart to live, it needs a healthy body. And the body needs food, not prayer! How did Rebbe Israel Salanter put it? Your olam-haze is my olam-haba: your earthly needs are my spiritual concerns. What is Ahavat-Israel, the basic principle in Hasidism, if not a direct injunction to care for one another in the present? Said Rebbe Aharon of Karlin, 'I wish I could love the greatest Tzaddik the way the Almighty, blessed be His name, loves the greatest villain.' And this love is not abstract; it is immediate. And real. The love of God is linked to the love of man. One without the other leads to idolatry and inhumanity.

This was – and remains – the teaching of Beshtian Hasidism. Remember his three modes of love? *Ahavat-Hashem* – love of the Almighty; *Ahavat-Torah* – love of study; and *Ahavat-Israel* – love of Israel and mankind. At the time, this formulation of Jewish commitment was called an innovation – why? For centuries and centuries Jews were taught to love God and Torah and Israel – and many sacrificed their lives for that love. But what the Besht did was new indeed: he linked the three modes together in an unbreakable bond. Before him they were separate and divisible. In some circles, only Torah mattered. In others, only God existed. Or only man. The Besht was the first to proclaim for all to hear: The way to heaven leads through this world; the way to divine reward leads through human commitment; the way to God leads through your fellow man.

Fervour? Yes – later. Study? Yes – later. Ecstasy? Yes – later. Not on a hungry stomach. Not with a sick child at home.

But what if you cannot help it? What if you tried everything and misery is still dwelling under your roof? And what if your heart remains shattered? Then – only then – the Tzaddik will teach you how to overcome despair and attain ecstasy through joy and devotion. The difference between Rebbe Meir and Reb Uri of Strelisk? Reb Uri skipped the intermediary stages. He demanded and offered ecstasy right away.

Of course, Reb Uri himself set the example: before his morning prayer, he would bid farewell to his family. So all-consuming was his love of God that he was convinced each time he left that he might not see them again; that while praying in total communion with his Creator, he might die.

Rebbe Meir did not wish to die; he had no time for dying. He had other things to worry about: his helpless Hasidim who had to deal with the village lord and not with heaven, with today and not with eternity.

Of course, both he and his rival from Strelisk loved their poor followers – and they loved them with equal force and passion. But, Reb Uri went one step farther: he loved even their poverty – whereas Rebbe Meir considered poverty outrageous and disgraceful and fought it valiantly throughout his entire life.

When he was only a boy, he was already helping the poor. Every

Thursday he would go from house to house collecting money for the town's beggars. Once he returned home empty-handed. In desperation he went to the stable, took his father's only cow, sold it at the marketplace, and, of course, gave the money to the poor.

Then he remembered that the cow was his father's only source of income; he began to cry. He thought of his mother and cried even more. As he stood crying on the road, a man stopped and asked him why he was crying; Meirl told him the truth. 'Do not worry,' said the stranger. 'Here is money, go and buy another cow.' But Meirl's mother saw the substitution. 'What happened?' she asked her son. 'Where is *our* cow?' 'She disappeared,' said Meirl. 'Disappeared?' shouted his mother. 'How does a cow disappear?' 'Well, she did,' said Meirl. 'She became charity and went up into heaven . . .'

To a rich man who refused to give for charity, he once said:

'Before I was born, I was given twenty-five thousand rubles — but I refused to keep them. Already then I wanted to live in absolute austerity. "Take the money," my angel insisted. "It is yours and only yours. If you don't take it, it will stay here in heaven, whereas if you do, you may do something good with it." "All right," I said. "I have an idea. I shall take the twenty-five thousand rubles and divide them in five equal sums and entrust them to five Jewish merchants — so whenever I shall need money for unmarried daughters and imprisoned innkeepers, I shall know to whom to go . . . to claim my money." Well,' he said to the richer miser, 'you are one of the five. The money you have is not yours. If you refuse to help the poor — I shall take it back.'

'Why shouldn't I pray for money for my Jews?' he once asked. 'What do they do with their money? Gamble it away? No. Use it to get drunk? No. They feed their families, they give to charity, they pay tutors, they support Yeshivot — why then shouldn't I help them get money?'

On another occasion, a preacher asked for his permission to speak in Premishlan and earn some money thereby. He spoke, but nobody gave him anything. Later he sat in the Rebbe's study and saw people come in and put money on the table. 'I don't understand,' said the preacher. 'Why do they give you money but not me?' 'Simple,' said Rebbe Meir. 'We all influence our listeners to become more like us. You love money and therefore, after meeting you, they love it even more. I despise money and therefore they throw it away, and I am here to pick it up.'

Once he was asked by a disciple, 'Why do we put *maror* (bitter herb) on the table on Passover eve but not gold or silver? Why must we remember only the bitterness of our Egyptian bondage and not the wealth we took when we left the country?'

'I'll tell you why,' said Rebbe Meir. 'Much of the bitterness is still here – but the money is gone, oh, yes, gone for good.'

A storekeeper complained to him that a competitor had opened a shop too close to his. 'What do you want me to do?' asked the Premishlaner. 'Chase him away? And what will he do to feed *his* children, ha? Listen: have you ever noticed how the horse behaves at a pool of water? He stamps with his hoof in the water, right?' 'Right.' 'Do you know why he does that? I'll tell you why. When the horse drinks, he sees his shadow. So he thinks that another horse is drinking from the same pool and tries to chase him away. In so doing he stirs up the mud in the water and it becomes undrinkable . . . You'd better drink and let others drink: there is enough for all the storekeepers in the world!'

We must remember that poverty was considered a virtue in some Hasidic circles. Not only because it was there – and because there was not much they could do about it, except pray – but also because, on a higher level, they felt it was – do not laugh – good for the soul.

They were afraid that money corrupts both those who give it and those who receive it – and that more money engenders more corruption. Better therefore to live without it.

Still others felt that since poverty, too, was willed by God, why then should one reject it?

Just as Reb Nahum of Chernobyl felt sorry for darkness, Reb Meir was moved to pity for poverty.

Poor darkness, Reb Nahum would say. Everybody hates it. Everybody loves light and praises it at the expense of darkness . . . Well, said he, people are wrong. Between darkness and light the contest is unfair: darkness always loses – but only on the surface. When it yields to light, it does not disappear; it simply goes into hiding. Where? Inside light . . .

The same could be said of poverty. Everybody is against it – so somebody had to redeem it. Thus Reb Uri – like Reb Nahum of Chernobyl – often praised poverty.

Since poverty was a dominant factor in Jewish life in Eastern Europe, Hasidic Masters had to take a position on it. What could it have been? They had four options: One – to ignore it. Two – to accept it with resignation. Three – to rebel against it and defeat it. Four – to rebel against it by turning it into a virtue.

The Seraphin of Strelisk chose the last option, but Reb Meir of Premishlan would not. He saw in it a hostile presence to be disarmed and vanquished. That is why, in his lifelong battle against his 'enemy', he used miracles. So great was his compassion for his people that he even tried to force God's hand. He promised children to childless parents. He offered hope to hopeless farmers. He reassured lonely prisoners everywhere, telling them that God is present to all His creatures, that God listens – and more important, that God can be heard. Even in jail? Even in jail. Even in misery? In misery above all.

True, said Reb Uri. God *is* in misery – in exile – therefore we must do everything on *His* behalf. But what about compassion? Is not a Rebbe, as a human being, as a Jew, as a leader of men, duty-bound to show compassion towards his fellow man? Why did Reb Uri of Strelisk not show any pity for *his* followers? Is it conceivable that he – a pillar of Hasidism – was immune to pity? I do not believe so. The Seraphin of Strelisk was a man of deep feelings. He was possessed and consumed by compassion – but for whom? That is the question.

And that was the issue that divided the two Masters: Rebbe Meir of Premishlan maintained that since man is vulnerable and fragile, forever threatened and hurt, he, as the Rebbe, was duty-bound to feel sorry for his flock. Whereas Rebbe Uri asked: And what about God? What about the Almighty Master of the Universe, who views with sadness what has been going on inside His creation? Who will feel sorry for Him? God suffers because of us – God suffers with us – therefore how can I deny Him my love? My compassion? Condemned to solitude, God is invoked by people only when they need Him – when they want something; what about His demands, His needs? He has given so much – what does He get in return?

One may wonder whether Reb Meir's simplistic miracle-making was really to his taste. After all, he was both lucid and learned; he surely knew that there was much more to Beshtian Hasidism than dealing with the supernatural. Moreover, if he didn't, there were others who forced him to acknowledge it. Reb Uri of Strelisk was not his only antagonist. Reb Meir himself often mentioned his many adversaries, those Hasidic Rebbes and Tzaddikim who objected to his spectacular methods of helping his followers. Then why did he continue? He continued because the welfare of the poor Hasid mattered to him more than the opinion of other Masters. Still, he felt unsure. And what if they were right and not he? And what if he were wrong in using – and displaying – his secret powers?

He was human – profoundly human – and therefore prone to constant introspection and self-doubt.

Actually there remains little by him or about him to support my view, which is mostly intuitive, except for one aspect of his personality . . .

He rarely spoke about himself in the first person. Instead he would say: Meir believes, Meir thinks, Meir sees, Meir says . . . The word 'I' was almost banned from his vocabulary. Whether he addressed himself to God or to people, he would say: Meir implores you, Meir tells you, Meir asks you . . .

This form of speech must have been motivated, at least partly, by humility. Remember the friend who knocked at the window of Rebbe Aharon of Karlin? 'Who is it?' asked Reb Aharon. 'Don't you recognize my voice? We studied together at Mezeritch! It is I.' 'If you say "I", that means you have not studied enough; go back to Mezeritch. Only God may say "I".'

The other motivation is more complex, for it involves one's attitude not towards God but towards oneself. Since the origins of time, 'Who am I?' is the question of questions, the question human conscience cannot avoid. What is the nature of the 'I' one refers to? Obstacle or opening? Wall or gate? Sublimation or alienation? In the phrase 'I said to myself', who am I? The one who spoke or the one who listened? Who was Rebbe Meir of Premishlan: the character in his tale or its author? Where was Rebbe Meir when Meirl was thinking and pleading and observing and counselling on his behalf? One thing is clear: the miracles were performed by Meirl. Since the Rebbe did not really wish to change the laws of nature by making use of his powers and privileges – but since he did have to use them for the sake of the sick and the hungry – he invented someone to perform his miracles for him: thus Meirl did what Reb Meir would rather not do.

Psychologists may read into this play of words one thing, philosophers another. Both may be right. Or wrong. As for myself, I admire him even for things that may appear childish. Between Meirl and Rebbe Meir I choose . . . both.

The time has come for us to leave Premishlan – for he himself left it. And he did so in a striking and stirring manner.

One day Rebbe Hayim of Sanz came to see him. They talked for a long time; about what, no one knows. All we know is that, at the end of their conversation, Rebbe Meir turned to his guest and said,

'Rebbe of Sanz, you are a member of the great rabbinic court. Tell me: Don't you think that it is time for Meirl to leave these tight quarters and move into larger ones?' 'Oh, yes,' answered Reb Hayim of Sanz. He immediately realized his mistake and tried to retract his statement but it was too late.

The Premishlaner addressed similar questions to other celebrated Masters asking for their permission to depart from this world. Unfortunately their replies were not recorded. He dispatched a special emissary to inform his beloved friend Rebbe Israel of Rizhin that soon he would be left alone . . .

By then Rebbe Meir was an old man, at the end of his road, and he was no longer the same. He who had sought the company of people now avoided them, he who had given his life and his soul to help others now prepared himself to enter eternity alone. He was sick, tired and disconsolate. During the last week of his life, he let it be known to all his followers gathered under his roof that whoever wished to celebrate Shabbat without disturbance should go home. No one left. He insisted. He wanted everyone to go away. He would have liked to be left to himself and face the inevitable – alone. No one left. And Shabbat went by undisturbed.

That evening, after the last meal in the Rizhiner's palace at Sadgora, a strange incident occurred: the two candles on the royal table were flickering as usual when suddenly the Rizhiner gasped in pain and so did all those who were present. At that moment one of the candles went out.

And it was never lit again.

──── *Naphtali of Ropshitz* ────

It happened on Shabbat Hagadol, the Shabbat that precedes Passover, which is an important holiday, though ... a costly one. It
requires money, a great deal of money, to celebrate it the way it
should be celebrated. And the people of Ropshitz had none, or
almost none. There were but a few rich merchants; all the others
lived from day to day, worrying about every coin, every mouthful
that they brought back home. The men were constantly overworked; so were the women. Even the children were pale with
fatigue and hunger. That was the picture all year around – which
was bad enough. But the week before Passover it became even
worse. For at Passover, every Jew must consider himself free and
sovereign, free of worries and bonds, like a king.

So on this particular Shabbat, the Rebbe of the community – Rebbe
Naphtali – devoted his speech to the theme of *tzedakah* – charity.
He quoted parables, invoked the authority of Talmudic sages,
added argument to argument, asking those who were well off to
share with the have-nots, the victims of providence, the deprived
ones, so as not to embarrass them at the Seder, when through the
open door the Prophet Elijah would enter and be their guest of
honour.

On no other holiday is food that important – on no other holiday
is money that important.

Rebbe Naphtali explained, argued, pleaded, ordered. Never
before had he spoken with such ardour; never before had he put his
entire soul into every one of his words. For this was the time of
year when the poor felt even poorer. He had to bring them some
joy for the holiday. He had to succeed in convincing his congregation – he *had* to, at any price.

Back home, after services, he fell into a chair, exhausted. His
wife asked him how it went. Were there many people? Yes, many;
the place was packed. Did so-and-so attend? Yes. And such-and-
such? Also. Did you speak? Yes. Were you good? Yes, I believe so.
Did you succeed in convincing them? With a smile, Rebbe Naphtali
answered: 'I only half succeeded, and that isn't bad.' And as his

wife seemed puzzled, he explained: 'I convinced the poor to receive
– but not the rich to give.'

Original, picturesque, amusing, Rebbe Naphtali was a friend, a
peer, of the greatest – with a difference: he dared to antagonize the
holy Seer of Lublin, who disliked his sense of humour, and Rebbe
Mendel of Riminov, who distrusted his political views. He even
dared – albeit respectfully – to mock the founder of a school, the
revered Rebbe Elimelekh of Lizensk. He was Hasidism's *enfant
terrible*. Most Masters spoke of God; he discussed everyday down-
to-earth matters. Most Rebbes cried; he laughed. Better yet: he
made other people laugh. Most tended to take life seriously, if not
tragically; there were few things *he* took seriously. Laughter was
one of them. 'Why do you laugh while I am crying?' asked Rebbe
Mendel of Riminov. 'Because you are crying while I am laughing,'
he replied. For him, laughter performed a philosophical, quasi-
religious function. With him, laughter became an integral part of
Hasidic experience and its tales.

Another story:

The celebrated Rebbe Israel, Maggid of Kozhenitz, was said to
have such powers that he could be denied nothing in the higher
spheres. When the request was simple, he would close his eyes and
whisper a prayer. When the request was more difficult to fulfil, he
would include it in his thoughts during services. But the most
complicated cases he would take up late, very late, at night, surrounded by silence and solitude. For each midnight, sitting on the
floor, his forehead covered with ashes, he would mourn over the
destruction of the Temple, whose flames still seemed to flicker in
his eyes, and he would cry with such intense sorrow that it became
impossible – up there – not to lend him an ear. His tears would
open all the gates. And then, in the midst of his litanies, he would
quickly slip in an urgent plea for this man rotting away in prison,
or this other one with a dying wife – and all his wishes would be
granted. And he knew it. And he was pleased.

Only once did he encounter a refusal. On one particular night
his pleas were not accepted. His prayers were returned; his tears
had no effect in heaven. Unhappy, he demanded an explanation.
When he received it, he understood – and forgave.

For that same night Rebbe Naphtali of Ropshitz had been on the
road, on his way to Kozhenitz. In the inn where he had stopped
to rest, a wedding was in full swing; the men and women were
drinking and eating and singing. Only the bride was sad, terribly

sad. Rebbe Naphtali, who was travelling incognito, wanted to console her.

'Why are you sad?' he asked her.

'Because,' she answered, 'there is something missing in this wedding, something essential to make it festive and joyous. A jester! There is no jester here to make us laugh – that's why I am sad.'

'Is that all?' the Rebbe cried out. 'Then stop being sad! For the heavens, may they be blessed, have foreseen this possibility. They have sent me here tonight to dispel your sadness, for I am a *badkhan* by profession, a troubadour and jester – a wedding specialist!'

And he began to compose rhymes about the company, the inn-keeper, the Rebbe and the cantor, and he did it with so much talent, so much humour, that all the guests fell under his spell and responded by laughing loud and hard. And the bride, too, was amused. To make her even happier, he sang with great exuberance and told funny stories – and danced – and danced. All around the table the guests were shaking with laughter, and up there, in paradise, the sages and the saints, sitting around their Master and ours, interrupted their studies and listened, and laughed, and laughed. And the angels forgot their nocturnal missions and flapped their wings, and laughed, and laughed. And in the palace of the celestial tribunal, the judges stopped judging and sentencing, and they, too, could not resist laughter. The Supreme Judge Himself stopped receiving His servants' prayers and litanies, including the tears of the holy Maggid of Kozhenitz – for He, too, was listening to the funny stories of Rebbe Naphtali. And He, too, was laughing, He was laughing . . .

Later the Maggid of Kozhenitz would say to his friend and disciple, 'Naphtali, Naphtali, are you aware of your own strength? What I cannot accomplish with my tears, you accomplish with laughter!'

Rebbe Naphtali of Ropshitz was born in 1760 in Linsk, a hamlet in Galicia, the very same day that the Besht died in Medzibozh.

Simple coincidence perhaps? Hasidism denies coincidences. No event is isolated, no encounter deprived of meaning. Some disciples insinuated that, on a very high level, Rebbe Naphtali was the Besht's successor. It is quite possible, since the same could be said – and was – of all great Masters. Except that these particular two personalities had few traits in common: if the Besht was the perfect Master, Rebbe Naphtali was the perfect disciple.

His father, a noted Talmudist, served as local Rabbi and was rather hostile to Hasidism. Not so his mother; she was the one who turned little Naphtali into a Hasid. At thirteen, for his Bar Mitzvah, he went with her to the great Rebbe Mikhel of Zlotchov, a disciple of the Besht and a companion of the Mezeritcher Maggid. Rebbe Mikhel was the one who helped him put on the *tefillin* for the first time, remarking, 'I have just tied his soul up there; the knot will be a lasting one.'

Shortly thereafter Naphtali was engaged to the daughter of a wealthy Jew, a wine merchant from Brody. The marriage created a sensation – though less than the divorce that followed one year later. The reason? One day he came home and found his young wife primping in front of a mirror. 'Don't,' he said. 'I like you the way you are.' 'And the others don't count?' she answered. Troubled by such impudence, he fled from the house and took refuge with the Rebbe of Zlotchov, having already made up his mind to divorce.

When he remarried, a year later, he settled in Ropshitz as official Rebbe. Was he happier with his second wife? A witness, Rebbe Yekhezkel of Shineve, says no. And I quote: 'Rebbe Naphtali of Ropshitz had the rare and awesome powers to bring the Messiah, but couldn't use them – he was prevented by heaven; he was given as a wife a woman who disturbed him, bored him and annoyed him.'

She would often boast about her own erudition and piety, and remarked once that her father regretted that she was born a girl and not a boy, for then his son would have become the greatest of the great scholars alive. 'In this case I agree with your father,' said Rebbe Naphtali. 'I also regret that you were not born a boy.'

Was it because he spent so little time at home that she made his life miserable? Or was it, on the contrary, she who made him stay away so much? The fact remains that it was easier to meet him in other people's homes than in his own. Though he was the Rebbe of Ropshitz, and later also of his native town, where he inherited his father's position, he managed to assume and fulfil his official functions in both places – and at the same time roam around the capitals of the Hasidic universe.

He spent one year at the court of Rebbe Mordecai of Neskhiz. Then he spent some time with Rebbe Elimelekh of Lizensk, who at first refused to accept him as disciple: 'I don't want celebrities in my house,' he said. Crushed, the young Naphtali stretched out on the floor and began to shed bitter tears and even to spit blood. 'Is it my fault my father is a Rebbe?' he cried. The Tzaddik of Lizensk finally gave in.

But these were brief attachments. Others, more lasting, linked him to the Seer of Lublin, the Maggid of Kozhenitz and Reb Mendel of Riminov. He sought their company; he admired all three, and all at once, as though to contradict the Lizensker theories of exclusivity. He, Naphtali, of Ropshitz, demonstrated that one could have ties to more than one Master; that one could believe in more than one Tzaddik. He believed this so strongly that, while they were alive, he refused to serve as Rebbe himself.

All three died the same year: 1815–16. He himself died in 1827. In other words, his reign lasted but ten years. Time enough to leave a mark on the life, the ways, and the language of Hasidism.

Time enough, also, to attract and keep disciples such as Rebbe Hayim of Sanz and Rebbe Sholem of Kaminka. They could frequently be found in his kitchen . . . peeling potatoes. Reb Hayim would say about him: 'I never called him Rebbe, for I didn't learn anything from him. I couldn't. He was too profound for me. All I took from him . . . is *Yirat-Shamayim*, fear of heaven.'

Ten years – time enough to make himself enemies as well – both inside and outside the Hasidic movement. The Mitnagdim – the adversaries – made his life so miserable that he predicted their punishment: after their death they would all return reincarnated as dogs. Inside the movement, his principal enemy was Reb Shlomo-Leib of Lentsheno. But as Hasidic quarrels go, this one was neither too serious nor too fierce. He suffered but didn't show it. Answering his critics, he quoted the Biblical phrase 'And the Jews were jealous of both Moses and Aaron'; they resented Moses' solitude and Aaron's sociability. Impossible to please everybody.

Yet he had fewer adversaries, fewer rivals, fewer enemies than most Masters. Even among the Tzaddikim of faraway dynasties, his prestige was great. The Rizhiner praised his intelligence and so did the Premishlaner, and even the Pshiskher. He was invited to all the courts, to all the festivities; he earned his peers' loyalty by being loyal to them – all of them. He saw himself not as prince but as messenger, as link between the various Rebbes. If two Rebbes were rivals or enemies, that was no reason for Rebbe Naphtali not to befriend both . . . and he did. Most leaders sought his allegiance, for they considered him not only a valuable friend but also a man of wisdom. In Hasidic literature he is most often described as a wise man – wisdom is his trademark. 'Rebbe Naphtali is a *hokhem*,' other leaders would say.

A strange description, because he often did not act 'wisely' at all. He frequently got himself into trouble because of his humour – and he was always saved by his humour. He loved to tease the Masters he admired. When the Rizhiner paid him a compliment, expecting some words of protest – he did not protest. The Maggid of Kozhenitz, eternally ill, goes to the *mikvah*? Rebbe Naphtali slips into the Maggid's bed. Rebbe Elimelekh insists on remaining in his chambers for an hour of isolation between *Minha* and *Maariv*? Rebbe Naphtali hides under the Rebbe's bed. If that isn't enough, he dares to imitate him in public – leaning on his cane the way he does, frowning in concentration the way he does and even distributing blessings to followers in distress . . . the way he does.

Strangely enough, Rebbe Elimelekh – known for his temper – let him get away with it. 'Aha,' he said, 'I see you have learned my tricks.'

Rebbe Naphtali got away with worse offences, perhaps because they were not directed against any one Tzaddik in particular, but against all. He was, and yet was not, one of them. Other Rebbes attracted admirers by offering them miracles? He offered no miracles and wanted no admirers. He said, 'Rebbes usually pray that people should come to see them and be helped. I pray that they should be helped at home.'

And . . . he was forgiven. Forgiven his sceptical comments, his sharp remarks. Forgiven his way of gently mocking his own peers and their habit of taking money for their services. Invited to spend Shabbat at Vielipol, he asked a fee: twenty coins. They promised to pay – and didn't. They couldn't. So he demanded that the synagogue's chandelier be taken down and given to him. Did he need it? Or take it? Of course not; this was his way of refusing all fees. A visitor said, 'We are told that the universe was created six thousand years ago, yet astronomers claim that there exists one star which is visible once every thirty-six thousand years!' 'So what?' commented the Rebbe. 'God can be found in this mystery too. Look for Him – not for the star.'

He was forgiven everything – because of his humour. Furthermore, his wit was directed only at the Masters and never at the followers. He loved Rebbes and loved Hasidim. He wanted to be both – and to serve as bridge between them.

'For a long time I refused the role of leader,' said he, 'because a Rebbe must flatter his followers. I had thought of becoming a tailor, a cobbler, a street sweeper, a bath attendant, even a beadle. And then I realized that the tailor, too, must flatter his customers. And so must the beadle. And the cobbler. So . . . I might as well join the rabbinate.'

Even as Rebbe, he adopted an attitude of amused sobriety towards himself. One day he remarked: 'In the more distant provinces I am called Rebbe Naphtali of Ropshitz. In Ropshitz, where I am well known, I am referred to as the Rebbe of Ropshitz. But my wife, who knows me best, simply calls me Naphtali.' He himself preferred the surname Naphtali *der Belfer* – the tutor.

His very first sermon in Ropshitz made a stir. It is customary on Shabbat that the speaker take into account three principles: the speech must be true, brief, and linked to the Sidra (section of the Torah) of the week. 'Well,' he said, 'I confess I don't know what portion is being read this week. This is true, brief, and to the point.' End of speech.

His practical advice to preachers: Make the introduction concise and the conclusion abrupt – with nothing in between.

Another time he ascended the *bimah*, the podium. It was Shabbat Shuva, between Rosh Hashana and Yom Kippur. For what seemed a long time, he silently stared at the congregation. Then he said: 'What is man? A worm of the earth – and yet you fear his words.' And once more he came down from the *bimah* without another word.

His strong point, however, was not sermons but conversation. His sense of humour was direct, concrete, and showed a swift and sharp mind. Every one of his words hit home.

Even as a child, he baffled adults with his quick replies. A visitor, a friend of his father, turned to him one day and said: 'Naphtali . . . if you tell me where God can be found, I'll give you a golden coin.' Answered the child: 'And I'll give you two if you tell me where He cannot be found.'

A Hasid implored him to intercede in heaven on his behalf, saying, 'I study, I learn Torah day and night, and I do not make any progress; I still don't know it.' 'God didn't ask you to *know* His law, but to study it,' was the Rebbe's reply.

Another Hasid, wishing to repent, came to see him – with a story, the classic story about a friend who had committed all the sins enumerated by Torah: sins against God, sins against man, and against himself. But now the friend had seen the light, had repented, and would like to know what to do to expiate his sins. 'But he is timid and doesn't dare come himself. What advice would you give him?' 'He should come and say that he is speaking not for himself but for his friend,' was the Rebbe's tongue-in-cheek reply.

Once, while going around collecting funds to ransom prisoners, he arrived in a small village where there lived a Jew known for his money and for his unwillingness to part with it. Fearing the rhetorical talents of the Rebbe, this Jew hid in the hayloft under a huge bundle of hay. Knowing his man, the Ropshitzer went straight to the hiding place. Face to face with the embarrassed miser, he had this sublime word: 'The Talmud claims that to offer hospitality is a deed more important than welcoming the Shekhina. I never understood why; now I do. To welcome the Shekhina, Moses covered his face. You, when you receive guests, cover your entire body.'

He hated misers – he hated them almost as much as fools and hypocrites. Hypocrisy was to him the most degrading of sins; he loved to expose it. Nothing made him happier than to unmask self-styled ascetics who wanted only to impress others. 'Life is given to man to be lived,' he would say. 'To mutilate life is to offend its source; to choose suffering is to reject a gift both rare and irreplaceable. The path to paradise leads through the world of reality,' he maintained.

He, incidentally, displayed but a very qualified interest in paradise. He affirmed without the slightest hesitation, 'Better to go to hell with wise men than to paradise with fools.' The Seer of Lublin reproached him with attaching too much importance to intelligence. This is what he answered: 'Yes, it is true that the Torah orders man to be naïve, or whole – *tamim* – with God. Only, to be naïve, one must be *very* intelligent.' On another occasion he said: 'Three principal virtues enable man to comprehend and communicate truth. They are kindness, devotion and intelligence. Kindness alone leads to promiscuity; devotion alone comes close to stupidity; intelligence alone is conducive to crime. So it is essential that the three qualities be present together for man to benefit from them.' Well, he possessed them all. But above all, he was known for his wit and intelligence.

However, a question arises: What made him so clever? What exactly did his intelligence consist of? In his two posthumous collections we read his comments on Torah, we repeat his amusing anecdotes. We smile, we laugh – but we do not cry out in wonder. We are struck neither by the depth of his perception nor by his erudition. On the contrary, his metaphors, though brilliant, lack the anguish of a Kotzker saying and the fire of a Bratzlaver tale. Where is his famous *hokhma*, his wisdom, of which one speaks so much in Hasidic literature? In that he managed to serve several Masters at once without arousing their jealousy? Because he

enjoyed himself and enjoyed practical jokes? Because he possessed
common sense, a talent for practical living . . . and making friends?

We should like to know his own perception of *hokhma*. Unfortunately, it was either not formulated or not transmitted. Was it
wisdom? Shrewdness? Intuition? We do know this: that every time
his wisdom was mentioned he replied with some witty line – as
though to prove that he did not take it seriously. The word
provoked a strange reflex in his behaviour – a reflex seemingly
unrelated to the subject matter.

One day the Rizhiner said to him, 'You are considered a sage. So
tell us a story.' And Rebbe Naphtali obeyed. He told a story, a
terrible story, about how a long time ago he had deceived a notorious village miser by impersonating the son-in-law of Rebbe Meir
Ba'al Hanes, the famous miracle-maker of the second century.
Fooled, the miser gave him money, which he, the Ropshitzer, and
his companions, used to purchase some . . . *yash* – liquor. This is
wisdom? This is compassion? More surprising is the Rizhiner's
comment: 'I knew that you were a sage – but not like this!' And
both burst out laughing. What were they laughing about? At whose
expense?

It would appear that for the Ropshitzer – and the Rizhiner –
intelligence and wit were weapons to be used as defence. Rebbe
Naphtali loved to tell of his verbal exchanges and in particular he
liked to tell about the only three he had lost.

The first time he lost to his son, the future Rebbe Eliezer of
Dzikow. Seeing him play one day, Rebbe Naphtali scolded him for
wasting precious time, time he could have put to better use – to
study Torah, for instance. 'It's not my fault,' said the little boy.
'It's the fault of the *yetzer-hara*, the evil spirit. It's he who led me
into sin.' 'Well answered, son,' said the father. 'But you should
follow the example of the *yetzer-hara*; even he, by inducing you to
sin, obeys God's will. Why don't you do likewise?' 'For him it's
easy,' said the little boy. 'The *yetzer-hara* has no *yetzer-hara* to
talk him into disobeying God's will!'

The second time he was defeated by a little girl. He had met her
in a small village with perhaps ten Jewish men among its few
inhabitants. Still, it did have a synagogue and a cemetery. 'I don't
understand,' said the Rebbe to the little girl. 'Either the cemetery
or the synagogue is superfluous. If one of the ten men dies, there
will be no more services in the synagogue. If no one dies, what's
the cemetery for?' 'Don't worry,' said the little girl. 'The synagogue
will remain open. As for the cemetery, it's for visiting strangers.'

The third defeat was inflicted upon him by a coachman. It was on Simhat Torah eve. The Hasidim were rejoicing, celebrating – as one should – the presence and sanctity of the Torah by dancing to the point of drunkenness, by singing to the point of ecstasy. Suddenly the Ropshitzer saw in the middle of the crowd a coachman who was known for his primitive ways and his ignorance. 'What?' the Rebbe cried out. 'You participate in the festivity? You who never study Torah, you who obey its commandments so badly and so rarely? How does this festivity concern you?' And the coachman replied, 'Rebbe, Rebbe, if my brother arranges a wedding, a Bar Mitzvah or any other celebration, am I not allowed to participate?'

This anecdote, which seems cruel, damages him, not the coachman. Yet he himself told it – to show that the coachman was right, that the coachman had a better understanding of things than he.

For this complex and complicated Tzaddik was, in spite of appearances, profoundly humble – and sad. But his humility was hidden under arrogance and pride, just as his melancholy was covered with exuberance.

It is told that one night he was surprised by a visitor from his village who found him sitting on the ground, his face bathed in tears, lamenting the destruction of the Temple in Jerusalem. Yet, lest the visitor take him for a hidden saint, he began to indulge in self-glorification: 'Oh,' he said aloud, 'if the Jews of Ropshitz only knew the true qualities, the rare greatness of their Rebbe!' He wanted people to take him for a vain person, an actor, anything rather than a Just Man.

He loved to comment on the passage in Talmud in which God showed Moses *Dor dor vedorshav* – the men and women of all future generations and their leaders. 'Why,' he asked, 'did God not start with the leaders? This is why: because of the regression in history. The closer we come to our times, the less striking are the leaders. Imagine Moses resting his gaze on me. He would undoubtedly cry out, "What? Naphtali, too, is a Rebbe?" But since God would by then have shown him my contemporaries, Moses would understand: "All right, let it be. He, too, can be a leader . . . alas!"'

To understand him better, we must analyse his attachment to his favourite *mitzvah*: that of dwelling in the *succah*. Like the Berditchever, he said that his very soul was rooted in that commandment. Not one day went by without his mentioning something connected with Succoth, the Feast of the Huts, which lasts only one week. This attachment is symbolic. What is a *succah*? Half tent, half hut, a temporary refuge whose one side remains constantly exposed to rains and winds. It is small, modest and austere – it is meant to remind us of our life in the desert.

Rebbe Naphtali's obsession with Succoth offers the first clue to his hidden image. Only someone who dwells in the desert seeks a tent with such intensity. To rest. To breathe. To dream. What is the *succah* if not the Temple of Jerusalem before Jerusalem – the vision before fulfilment? Only a nostalgic and unhappy visionary would dream of dwelling year-round in his own private *succah*.

The Ropshitzer – sad? Unhappy? He whose gaiety was as legendary as was the Kotzker's melancholy? People saw his laughter but not the torment beneath it; he ranks among the most misunderstood figures in Hasidism.

That is what he wanted: not to be understood. Not to be pitied. He concealed his pain – and that was his wisdom. He laughed so as not to cry; he chose exhibitionism so as to hide his anguish, his lack of confidence in himself, in his own prayers, in his own words.

One Shabbat, surrounded by his followers, he delivered an impressive address. Everyone present listened with bated breath and rose with him to the highest spheres of mystical meditation. He tore away the veils, one after another and one and all could witness creation. After Shabbat was over, Rebbe Naphtali ran to his friend and teacher Reb Mendel of Riminov. 'I'm afraid,' he said, 'I'm afraid I spoke too well; I must have said things I shouldn't have . . .' Reb Mendel asked him to repeat the address, so he could judge for himself. And I like to believe that Rebbe Naphtali improvised another lecture on the spot.

Was he consoled? Comforted? If so, it didn't last long. It never did. From his early youth he lacked self-confidence, to the point of soliciting blessings from everyone, even from strangers. Before the Jew of Pshiskhe became known, Naphtali Ropshitzer asked for his blessings.

To his disciple Reb Yehuda-Zvi of Razdal he said, 'One day you will be Rebbe. You will have to offer blessings to people. So start with me.' The disciple refused. 'You are wrong,' insisted the Ropshitzer. 'You see, when I was your age, the great Levi-Yitzhak of Berditchev pleaded with me for the same favour, and I also refused. And I regret it to this day.'

Behind the visible Ropshitzer, there was another, invisible one. The first told stories, teased the great and amused them; the second, withdrawn in his own inner tent, lived in silence and torment, aspiring to attain some unattainable truth.

The first was active, militant, gay, exuberant – singing the praises of hope and life in the best tradition of the Baal Shem Tov. His very presence drove away sadness. With one funny remark he disarmed sadness; with one word he brought joy. No matter what the cost, the unhappy Jews in Galicia, who had nobody but their Rebbe in the whole world, needed to laugh, to rejoice, to hold on to existence. In this respect, the Ropshitzer performed a vital function: his combat against despair was a personal one. He didn't trust disciples or messengers; he came alone wherever communities in distress were in danger of giving in to resignation. His weapons? Song and laughter.

One evening of Simhat Torah the news arrived that his friend and disciple Reb Avraham of Ulanov had died. The Hasidim did not have the heart to go on with the festivities. But Reb Naphtali scolded them angrily: 'Are we not at war – at war with destiny, with the entire world? What does one do at the front when an officer falls? Does one run away? On the contrary, one closes ranks and fights even harder. So close your ranks and dance, dance, with more vigour than ever; dance like you have never danced before!'

On another occasion he remarked, 'What is a Hasid? Someone who possesses a precious key, a key that opens all the doors, even those that God keeps closed. And that key is . . . the *Niggun*, the song of joy that makes our hearts beat faster. The *Niggun* opens the gates of heaven, melancholy closes them.'

Dynamic, tireless, the visible Tzaddik participated in Hasidic life. He encouraged, he mediated, he entertained wherever his talents were needed. He visited all the courts to bring them closer to each other. Rather than repudiate the society surrounding him, he worked on it from the inside. He said, 'What is the difference between the Prophet and the Tzaddik? The Prophet unveils the future – and the Tzaddik the present. The Tzaddik's task is the more difficult.'

Yet he himself accomplished it. He was the wandering minstrel who brought smiles to poor children and memories to their old, tired grandparents. In the famous quarrel between Lublin and Pshiskhe, he vainly urged moderation. Though not publicly, he opposed the messianic conspiracy of his three friends; he was against suffering and war – against using them for any purpose, be it the most sacred of all.

The conspiracy failed, and the three Masters died in the same year. It was Rebbe Naphtali who saw to the holy Seer's burial. Dressed as a gravedigger, his clothes covered with mud, he buried him in Lublin, whispering. 'This is how one looks when one buries one's teacher.'

He always found the right word for every situation. But behind words, there are other words, inaudible, imperceptible words. And behind them, there is silence.

There was silence in Rebbe Naphtali.

This is a parable he loved to retell: One day the Czar, while inspecting his troops at the front, fails to notice an enemy soldier whose rifle is aimed at him. Fortunately for the Czar, one of his loyal soldiers pulls the imperial horse's reins and so averts tragedy. The grateful Czar says to his saviour, 'Tell me your secret wish and consider it granted.' 'Majesty,' says the soldier, 'my corporal is cruel; send him to another company.' 'Fool!' the Czar cries out. 'Why don't you ask to be made corporal yourself?'

Man's tragedy lies not in what he is denied but in his inability to formulate his desire. He demands too little; he is afraid to set his sights too high; his dreams drag in the dust and his words are empty. That may have been the realization that came to Rebbe Naphtali as he approached the end of his life.

Did he regret his past? Regret that he had not chosen another path? That is possible. Once upon a time, in his youth, he had sought truth in ascetic modes; he had rolled naked in the snow and he had practised prolonged fasting. He had given all that up – as a Hasid, he had to. Now it was too late to start all over again. The traveller had reached the end of his journey. The singer felt no further desire to confront his audience. The minstrel was tired. Now it was the *other* Ropshitzer who emerged and dominated.

Rebbe Naphtali went into seclusion. He stopped entertaining, stopped visiting Rebbes and receiving their disciples; he turned away from his own followers and retired into his own beloved, invisible and haunted *succah*. Surprisingly, and symbolically, he stopped speaking.

For months and months no word left his lips. To the questions of his son, Reb Eliezer of Dzikow, he opposed absolute silence. In the beginning he would explain by gestures that his muteness was due to fatigue, to exhaustion, and ought not be mystically interpreted. Later he stopped explaining altogether. He remained silent. Alone.

Then came the last day. The sick father and his son were alone.

'Speak, Father,' begs Reb Eliezer. 'Say something, one word.'
The old Master looks at him and says nothing. 'You can,' pleads
the son, 'I know you can. You can speak. Why don't you? Why
don't you want to speak, Father?'

The old Master stares at him for a long, long moment and then
replies in a hoarse, halting whisper: 'I . . . am . . . afraid. Do you
. . . understand? Do you understand, Eliezer? I. Am. Afraid.'

Afraid of what? Of whom? We shall never know.

The School of Worke

Worke: another kingdom, a new, enchanting Hasidic adventure – another aspect of Hasidic language, another face of the Hasidic movement.

Worke: a song both humble and powerful – a whisper with profound reverberations of communal life, intense and intriguing alike. Worke: a fervent but restrained prayer – full of ecstasy, but controlled ecstasy. Worke: a journey to the end of language – to the birth of silence.

Silence: that is the seal and distinction of Worke. Elsewhere, Masters and guides talk and make others talk, sing and move others to sing; they shout and are obeyed in this world and in the other. Not here, not in Worke. Here you will meet a silent Hasidism, meant to allow each and every disciple to meditate quietly, though with the Master and through the Master.

Listen to testimony given by Rebbe Berish of Biala:

'It happened during a Shabbat meal. Our holy teacher, the Tzaddik of Worke, was presiding. Lost in thought, he looked at us and at the twilight looming behind us, and said nothing; and we, at his table, listened and said nothing. For a while we could hear only the buzzing of flies on the walls; then we didn't even hear that. We heard the shadows as they invaded the House of Study and brushed the burning faces of the Hasidim; then we stopped hearing even them. Finally, we heard only the silence that emanated from the Rebbe united with our own; solemn and grave, but passionate and vibrant, it called for beauty and friendship. We had rarely experienced such communion. We lost all sense of time; we were living in another sphere, in another universe, where silence was the only language available to man. Then, all of a sudden, the Rebbe shook himself and asked that the *Birkat ha-Mazon* be recited – and that was the end of that.'

And the Rebbe of Biala concluded, 'Well, let me tell you: what a lesson, what a lesson I received that day . . . The Master submitted me to a severe and rigorous interrogation that made me shiver. I felt my heart ready to burst – and my arteries too. But I was lucky and the Almighty came to my rescue . . . I passed the test, I knew what to say. What a lesson, what a lesson . . .'

*

Actually, to do this the right way and really translate the spirit of Worke, perhaps we ought to bring back Worke in its own style and manner, namely, not with words but with silence.

But we have not yet reached Worke, we have not yet reached that level. We have just set out on our journey. And what do travellers with a long journey ahead of them do? They tell each other stories. So – let us tell each other stories.

The ones about Worke and its leaders are, naturally, endowed with wisdom, charm and depth, although the Masters of the school of Worke, in comparison to their predecessors, are less famous, less important. But then – why compare them at all? Hasidic legends are strikingly singular in that they deny analogies. Every Hasid is called upon to recognize his Master as the greatest – and he will be right. What Hasidism did was to restore to the individual Jew his ability to praise and admire and follow and trust and love. To feel less lonely, less vulnerable, less abandoned, the Hasid had to believe in the strength and wisdom of *his* Rebbe. Each Master was different, as were their followers, but their relationship to their followers was similar: every Rebbe responded to the same need, evoked the same response and told the same tale. There were many Rebbes and many more Hasidim, but all were taught to believe that life has meaning, that words are rooted in a memory older than our own, and that the Hasid's song contains the song of rivers and forests, clouds and fields; all were convinced that man and God are anything but strangers to one another.

In Hasidic terms, every person is unique – but the Rebbe is more so. The Besht was unique – as was his successor, the celebrated Maggid of Mezeritch, the architect and organizational genius of the new movement. And as were his disciples: Rebbe Shneur-Zalman of Lyady with his emphasis on learning and passion; Rebbe Aharon of Karlin with his contagious enthusiasm; Rebbe Levi-Yitzhak of Berditchev with his love, his all-consuming love for Israel; Rebbe Nahman of Bratzlav with his fiery imagination; Rebbe Mendel of Kotzk with his holy anguish. Each had his own vision, each elaborated his own method, each developed his own imprint. Again, it must be stressed, this derives naturally from the basic concept of Judaism: for man, God is one – and for God every human being is one, irreplaceable, never interchangeable: God and God alone may say 'I' – but we are all made in His image, we are all part of His 'I'. Thus all men, including those who oppose Him and contradict one another, meet in God.

Remember the four sons in the Passover Haggada? The Rasha – the wicked one – refuses the tale altogether; he says: *Ma haavoda hazot lackhem* – what is all this to you? What do I have to do with it – or you? The Haggada does not concern me.

And what is our response? We include him against his will! His very opposition to the Jewish tradition becomes part of the Jewish tradition.

How did the Rizhiner put it? If the Rasha, the wicked atheist, were to know that in opposing God he actually obeys Him, he would have a heart attack.

God is everywhere and in all things; this is the basic belief formulated in the Zohar and glorified in Hasidic texts. God dwells in all hearts – God is in everything that brings people together, but also in everything that tears them apart.

Hasidism, therefore, strove not only for harmony but also for variety: all dynasties are interrelated; Hasidism is a tree, and although the branches are separate, they are alive – only because the tree is alive.

Hasidism puts special emphasis on this approach.

Though Rebbe Elimelekh and Rebbe Zusia were brothers, they were different – and Hasidism might well not have been what it was had they been more alike. Was one greater than the other? Was the Tzaddik of Alexander more important than the Tzaddik of Ger? No – such comparisons are unwarranted. A Rebbe is to be compared to himself alone, which means: he is not always equal to himself, which means: he is human.

And necessarily different. Therefore, the leaders of the school of Worke were as essential to the growth and development of Hasidism as any other. True, they are less known. A matter of temperament or luck – or injustice? Some Hasidic Masters are more celebrated than others: Reb Mendel of Vitebsk is better known than Reb Wolfe of Zbarazh; the Shpoler Zeide is less influential today than his adversary Rebbe Nahman.

I confess that I am unable to discriminate among them – I love them all and, at various times, one more than the others. Much depends on my mood. Sometimes I need a Bratzlaver tale, sometimes I need a Rizhiner saying. I particularly love the modest Masters, the humble ones, those who didn't 'make it', not really; those who simply wished to be companions or disciples of great Masters and remained reserved and withdrawn; in other words I am fond of the Tzaddikim of the school of Worke, this small village near Warsaw which would have found no place in Hasidic history were it not for the fact that a certain Rebbe Itzhak of Kalish came to settle there.

Let us follow him there – it's worth while. We shall learn the importance of collective silence in Hasidism. Let us go to Worke and witness the metamorphosis of words into other words – and then into something else.

Worke represents an unknown area in Hasidism – unknown and unsung. No grandiose projects were undertaken there, nor were there any dramatic upheavals to cope with. Its two Rebbes – father and son – were not heroes of any spectacular movements – nor were they victims of any mystical mishap. Worke's originality lies in its modesty – and in the intensity of its particular form of communication.

Worke represents silence – Hasidic silence – which may sound like a contradiction in terms: somehow we do not imagine Hasidim silent; silence is not usually one of their virtues. But then Hasidism never claimed to resolve human contradictions – rather, it assumed they were there. You need an example? Come – let us go to Worke.

Its followers will teach us that silence too has its place in Hasidism. I hope you will find it as attractive as I do. The world has become increasingly noisy. Society has never used so many means to tell, report, investigate, explain, comment, articulate, reveal, expose and criticize; no generation has ever been more talkative – and no generation has managed to say less.

The Torah speaks of God hiding His face. 'I am glad it does,' said Rebbe Itzhak of Worke. 'I am glad that the Torah tells us that there are things we cannot understand – and never will. *Andersh wolt men es nisht oisgehalten* – Were it not for the Torah saying it, we would find it intolerable.'

Ancient sages have told us that it takes a person three years to learn how to talk – and seventy years how to be silent. Let us go to Worke: a poetic kingdom is waiting for us there.

Rebbe Menahem-Mendel, the angry old man of Kotzk, once said to Rebbe Mendel of Worke, son of Itzhak, 'You seem to have mastered the art of being silent – where have you learned it?' And Rebbe Mendel did not answer.

Clearly, silence can be traced back to the very origins of mankind. If God's word is eternal, so is His Silence. But before God spoke, before God did anything – what did He do? He waited? Yes, He waited. For His word to become creation – and for His creation to be expressed in words. God being both source and fulfilment of silence *and* language, there is no conflict between the two – on *His* level. The conflict exists only on the human level, where words form the human language and silence is a form of divine language – or a divine form of language, which is slightly different. For us, both represent a challenge and even a threat: the mystery of one matches that of the other. Adam listened before he spoke – and only God can listen and speak at the same time. For Him, both language and silence point to harmony, and no creation can be accomplished without them.

The theme of silence is rooted in the Bible itself. All those unfinished sentences, all those questions that remain unanswered: God asking Adam, *Ayekha*? – Where are you? – without even waiting for an explanation.

Hence the primary tension in him – and in us – between the human word and the silence of the world. The mystery of the one is matched by the elusiveness of the other. Both are dangerous, therefore attractive vehicles for men of faith, visionaries, poets.

As a child, I yearned for silence – the mystical silence that evokes faraway secrets and forbidden truth. My teachers taught me how to cleanse language and thought by refusing to indulge in language and thought, thereby hastening the coming of the Messiah. Let all men be silent, I thought, and man will be saved.

In Scripture, silence appears on every page, variously as theme, subject, action, illustration of human weakness or its ultimate dénouement.

Silence in man's relations to others, silence in man's attitude towards God, silence enveloping the word of God.

Vayomer Cain el Hevel achiv – and Cain spoke to his brother Abel ... And the text does not tell us what he said to him. As though Scripture wanted to let us know that Abel did not listen. And this is perhaps how we are to understand the meaning of the first murder of a man by his brother: one spoke and the other was silent – his silence denied language and was opposed to it; and this kind of silence cannot but end in death.

On that level, silence is sinful, for it means indifference. Why was Job punished? Because in Egypt, as one of Pharaoh's advisers, he chose prudently to remain neutral. He kept quiet. His silence made him an accomplice. Neutrality and silence favour the killer, always; never the victim.

We encounter the same idea in the tragic story of Nadav and Avihu, Aaron's two sons, killed together for having penetrated, desecrated the sanctuary. What was their sin? They were too ambitious, according to Talmudic commentators. They aspired to succeed Moses and Aaron and become Israel's new leaders. One day, Nadav is supposed to have said to his brother Avihu, 'When are these old men going to die and let us take over?' That is why they were punished. But there is something wrong with this explanation. We understand why Nadav deserved punishment; he had spoken with arrogance. But his brother had not; in fact he had said nothing – then why was *he* punished? The answer is: That is why. Because he said nothing. He should have protested; his silence made him an accomplice. Even Moses was punished because he failed to object when, in the land of Midian, he was referred to as *Ish mitzri* – the Egyptian.

But then, there are times when silence is interpreted as virtue. When he lost his two sons, *Vayidom Aharon* – Aaron remained mute. He suppressed his pain and his tears. And he is praised for not having spoken.

Before crossing the Red Sea, Moses turned to his people and shouted, '*Adoshem yilachem lachem veatem tachrishun?* – God will fight for you and you will be silent?' What did he want them to do? What could they have done? Fight? With what? No, the sentence has a different meaning. Saul Liebermann, the eminent Talmudic scholar, with his special sense of humour, would simply change the question mark into an exclamation point: God will fight for you, provided you keep quiet!

For God loves silence – or as Rabbi Eliezer of Worms put it: God *is* silence. After the tempest at Sinai, after the thunder and the lightning, there is silence – and that silence signifies that God is present, ready to be heard.

Silence can appease, it can carry melodies and dreams – but it can also open you to anguish and sadness, even to anger. In the Talmud we often meet sages who, in their final hour, do not hesitate to cry out, 'But why, why is the Almighty silent?' *Mi kamocha baelim adoshem* – Who among the gods can be compared to you? *Al tikre elim ki im ilemim ki roe beelbon banav veshotek*: Who is as mute as You, God, for You witness the shame and the sorrow of Your children and still You say nothing . . .'

Said one of the Masters in Worke, 'Isaac, son of Abraham, never lost his temper, never got angry – and that is fortunate, for his anger could have destroyed mankind. Instead, his silence saved the world.'

So – let us go to Worke and meet its founder, Rebbe Itzhak – or Reb Itzikl, as he was affectionately called.

A disciple and friend of several great Hasidic masters, Reb Itzikl shared in their greatness. He himself has been revered for his saint-liness, his knowledge, his humanity, his piety and his modesty.

In Hasidic chronicles we find facts and anecdotes, sayings and episodes that help us reconstruct his portrait.

We know that he was born in 1779 in Zaloshin, a small village near Kalish, in western Poland. His father was affectionately called Reb Shimon Baal-Rachmones: the charitable Reb Shimon. Married at the age of fifteen, Reb Itzikl settled in Zharik, where his wife's family lived.

We know that he was not happy. His wife made too many demands on his time; she treated servants too harshly; she seems to have lacked the sweetly subdued, resigned manner that, in those times, people considered a necessary virtue in a Jewish woman. So miserable was he that he solicited the advice of his first Rebbe, David of Lelov, who gently admonished him not to talk about it – not even to him. And so – he never mentioned it again.

Sources give varying accounts of how he earned his livelihood. In the beginning he was employed by Temerl, the famous woman benefactor whose place in Hasidic legend and lore is often as prominent as that of certain Masters. He was her 'regional representative' for a number of years. At one time the government gave him the concession for all local tobacco sales. This we know because we are told that he lacked the funds to pay for the concession. We also know that he owed a certain Reb Hersh Friedman ten thousand golden coins. Before becoming Rebbe he lived in a rented one-room apartment. Even after that, he lived in poverty. An eye-witness relates the following episode: One day, as Reb Itzikl was teaching his afternoon course at the House of Study, his wife came in and angrily interrupted him: 'You do nothing but teach,' she shouted. 'You do nothing but study, and there is nothing to eat at home.'

A scholar himself, he was an intimate friend of the first Rebbe of Ger and of the Kotzker, who were both renowned for their erudition. He was also close to the Rizhiner and to Rebbe Yehezkel of Kuzhmir. He travelled frequently. And whenever he went from Zharik to Warsaw he never failed to bring news or messages from their families to the Zharik girls who worked as servants in the capital city. Everybody knew that he was always in a hurry. In fact, he found it necessary to explain why: A Jew is always running, he said. Running *from* sin, running *to* study or pray; a Jew does nothing slowly; he lives fast.

Because of his business activities he had to learn Polish – and he did. He spoke it well, though not as well as Yiddish.

What else do we know? He suffered from insomnia; he would sleep twelve minutes, wake up to study and doze off for another twelve minutes . . . He was a disciple of more than one Rebbe. Rebbe David of Lelov was one of his teachers, as were the holy Seer of Lublin, Reb Bunam of Pshiskhe and Reb Mendel of Kotzk. He died at the age of seventy, in 1848, on the last day of Passover, having served for twenty years as head of the school of Worke. His two sons continued the dynasty of Worke – the elder as founder of the Amshinov line and the younger as the new Tzaddik of Worke.

In Lublin, he was included in the Seer's private *minyan*. Here is how it happened: When he was first introduced to the holy Seer, Reb Itzikl felt so intimidated that he couldn't utter a word. 'Are you studying?' the Seer asked him. 'I am,' said Reb Itzikl. 'Do you know?' 'I try,' said Reb Itzikl. 'Do you understand?' 'I try,' said Reb Itzikl. 'Have you come up with anything new?' 'No,' said Reb Itzikl. 'All I do is I repeat – I repeat the words and thoughts of our sages – that is enough for me. But today . . .' He stopped in the middle of the sentence and the Seer had to urge him to continue. 'Today,' said Reb Itzikl, 'I studied the question of witnesses who testify before a tribunal. And I do not understand.' 'What didn't you understand?' 'The Talmud stipulates that close relatives may not testify either for or against the defendant. And this I fail to comprehend. I understand why relatives ought not to testify on behalf of a defendant: they are biased. But why couldn't they testify *against*?' 'Excellent question,' said the Seer. 'And what is the answer?' And this is what Reb Itzikl replied: 'The Torah says, referring to the witnesses, V*eamdu shnei anashim* – Two persons, meaning two human beings, must testify. Well, a person who would be prepared to testify against a close relative is not human . . .' The Seer smiled. He enjoyed the question and the answer – and that is how he admitted young Reb Itzikl into his private *minyan*.

Unlike others, Reb Itzikl stayed in Lublin – or rather, Lublin stayed in him – even after he left it. We remember with sadness the break between the Seer and his favourite disciple, Reb Yaakov-Yitzhak of Pshiskhe. Lublin signified miracles, while Pshiskhe meant study. In Pshiskhe they said: 'Miracles? Ha! It's much more difficult for a Jew to be Jewish than to perform miracles.' Unlike many of his friends, Reb Itzikl chose not to take sides. He admired Pshiskhe and loved Lublin. He himself, as Rebbe, preferred not to impress his followers by dealing with the supernatural.

A story: While he was still working for Temerl, a man came to beg him for three hundred rubles. He needed money desperately to marry off his daughter, who was desperate to get married – she was over eighteen already. 'I cannot help you,' said Reb Itzikl, who was known never to send visitors away empty-handed. The Jew began to weep: 'If you don't help me, who will?' 'Well,' said Reb Itzikl, 'come back tomorrow.' Next day he gave him the three hundred rubles. 'But why did you wait a whole day?' asked the Hasid. 'Why did you let me worry?' 'I wanted to teach you,' answered Reb Itzikl, 'not to rely on men – only on God, on God alone.'

A sick man came to him in tears; the doctors had given him up. So Rebbe Itzhak set up a rabbinic court and 'sentenced' him to stay alive – and he stayed alive.

We don't know for sure how long he stayed in his position as regional representative for Temerl. What we do know is that he enjoyed it. He talked about it often with relish and humour. Once he observed an inspector doing his work with particular devotion, looking everywhere, checking everything. Reb Itzikl spoke to him. 'You know,' he said, 'perhaps your interpretation of the Torah is too strict; you need not interpret too literally the commandment Thou shalt not steal. You may, you know, yes, you may steal from time to time.' 'What?' said the overseer, who couldn't believe his ears. 'You advise me to steal?!' 'No,' said Reb Itzikl. 'You didn't understand. What I meant was that you may steal a minute here, a minute there, for study and prayer.'

In this connection one is reminded of Rebbe Naphtali of Ropshitz, who said, 'I read ten brilliant commentaries on the commandment Thou shalt not steal – I almost forgot that it also means simply: "You shall not steal."'

We don't know how Temerl, the business tycoon, felt about Reb Itzikl's ideas of labour relations. But we do know that she did not fire him. What is more, he took care of her interests even after he was crowned Rebbe – though not for long.

But perhaps he really did not want to become a Rebbe. Like many of his friends and teachers, he became Rebbe under protest. As they had, before him, he was forced to accept the crown of leadership. More than once, a Rebbe had to be coerced. But, as Reb Itzikl put it, a Hasidic Rebbe doesn't want to become Rebbe; but once he does, he remains Rebbe even in his sleep.

Reb Itzikl would have preferred to live his condition as Hasid and disciple. He would have preferred not to stay in any one place

– even his own – but to roam around the courts and centres of Hasidic Masters. And there were many.

For that was the glorious era in Hasidism – an era of heightened hope and exuberance: all things seemed possible within the star-filled movement that had by then reached its climax.

Capitals of study, centres for prayer and meditation, sanctuaries for dreamers and spiritual rebels; they could be found all over, between the Carpathians and the Dnieper; and each bore its particular seal, each developed its distinctive theme. The dream of the Besht, nourished in his mountainous retreat, had blossomed and spread.

Lublin and Pshiskhe, Kotzk and Rizhin, Riminov and Ropshitz, Premishlan and Strelisk: there wasn't a village where the Baal Shem Tov's call for hope and faith was not heard and transmitted from home to home, from heart to heart.

The world outside was caught up in its own destructive and/or liberating upheavals, but the Hasidic movement, drunk with God and transfigured by His mystery, continued to broaden the scope of its conquest and deepen the intensity of its message.

Hasidism had never known such glory. In Kotzk they were busy trying to lift the world by lifting the heavens. In Rizhin they were determined to reinstate the royalty of Jerusalem's kings and princes. In countless courts and centres, men young and old sang and danced, studied and prayed, and everywhere they created bonds to alleviate Jewish solitude, to fight Jewish suffering and dispel Jewish melancholy. There were scores of communities, each with its own customs and melodies, its schools and its Masters – there were so many Masters available that Reb Itzikl refused to be one of them. However this was not a question of preference but of election; he had to yield. And so he used his position, his title, his prestige to help, to reconcile, to appease.

And he was badly needed. Success provokes quarrels, jealousies, among Hasidim. You admire one Master? Then you must fight others. To believe in two Rebbes is bigamy, according to Rebbe Aharon of Karlin. Exclusivity is emphasized in most quarters. Surely that is not only wrong, it's dangerous, but that's how it is, and there is nothing you can do about it. Nothing? Well, you can try to fight it – and Reb Itzikl did. He tried to make peace between the diverse factions and groups, between dissidents and dissidents of dissidents. He spent much time and energy to bring unity to the Jewish people.

Not that he himself escaped the professional scandalmongers.

He too was slandered and vilified in old-fashioned rumour campaigns. What people said against him has not been recorded. We are told only that there were rumours.

An episode: One day he was told that one of those rumourmongers had appeared in Worke, questioning his followers about him in order to smear his name. The Rebbe called in the man and said, 'You wish to find out evil things about me – why do you go to others? I know more than they. Sit down and I will tell you worse things about myself than anyone can.'

It was characteristic that he did not lose his temper; that he did not protest. Nothing: he remained quiet, friendly, smiling, generous even with an enemy.

While he was still in Pshiskhe, some people tried to provoke him. To this end, they used a simple man, a man without manners, to engage him in conversation while he was praying. 'Could you give me some of your snuff?' the man asked. Reb Itzikl interrupted his prayer, gave him some tobacco and went back to his prayer. Three minutes later: 'Could you give me some more of your snuff?' Again Reb Itzikl complied and went back to his prayer. Two minutes later: 'Could I get some more?' Reb Itzikl smiled, gave him what he wanted – and went back to his prayer, which, because of the interruptions, lasted longer than usual. At the end – because eventually there was an end – he took off his prayer shawl and went over to the man. All those present were convinced that now he would reprimand him. No: Reb Itzikl was still smiling. He took his snuffbox from his pocket and handed it to the man, saying, 'I think you need it more than I; when I want some tobacco, I'll ask *you* for it.'

Legend has it that he owned a special vest, one he would wear every time he felt himself getting angry. By the time he had put it on, his anger would be gone. Then he would turn to his aide and say, Listen, *you* get angry – I cannot.

In this respect he was totally different from his great and terrible friend Reb Mendel of Kotzk, who elevated anger to the rank of theological principle. In Kotzk, people shouted and howled, shaking heaven and earth and tearing off all masks. In Worke, people meditated – and gathered strength.

There is a story about a Hasid of Worke who happened to arrive in Strelisk just as the followers of Reb Uri the Seraphin were in the middle of their services, singing loudly and shouting even more loudly.

'I understand, I understand,' commented the gentle visitor. 'You wish to obtain blessings for our people – so do we in Worke. But why are you using force? Have you tried kindness?'

Of his two disciples, who disagreed on everything, Rebbe Bunam of Pshiskhe said, 'Both are ascetics and pure; but while Mendel wants to scorch the world with his fire, Itzikl tries to illuminate it with his.'

To better comprehend the Masters of Worke, perhaps we ought to return, however briefly, to the Kotzker Rebbe – the solitary visionary who rejected all compromises, weaknesses and failings. Taking a position against the Hasidic establishment, he preached a return to sources, to the early hardships, the pioneering discoveries. The Kotzker felt that, sixty years after the Besht, it had become too easy to be a Hasid: people didn't study enough, didn't pray with enough devotion; they sacrificed truth for comfort and expediency. In Kotzk, he was going to change all that – and his followers trembled in anticipation. They were not many, but to him they were still too many. He disliked crowds; he considered them volatile and servile. He wanted an elite. 'If only I could gather ten men to climb to the top of the world and shout that God is God,' he would say. Ten? Ten times ten would have followed him. Anywhere. But he chased them away. And the more he chased them, the more they flocked to him to receive his knowledge and learn from him how to discern divine truth in human lies – or, better yet, divine truth in human truth.

For twenty years he lived in isolation and rage. Only three men were allowed into his study: the Gaon of Sochatchov, Rebbe Itse-Meir of Ger and Reb Itzikl of Worke.

When Reb Bunam of Pshiskhe passed away, his followers crowned the Kotzker as their new leader, although there had existed a greater affinity between Reb Itzikl and Reb Bunam. Both loved to travel; the Kotzker did not. Both were interested in secular matters; the Kotzker was not. Both saw themselves as part of society; the Kotzker did not. Both involved themselves in the material problems of their followers; the Kotzker did not. Both wished to change and enrich the world; the Kotzker aspired to escape from it.

But then why was the Kotzker chosen? *Because* he was different from the Master. This was how the disciples wanted to implement their late Master's ideas of rebellion. They applied them even to his succession: they elected someone who was *not* like him.

Reb Itzikl himself described the difference between Worke and Kotzk as follows: 'Reb Mendel,' he said, 'is an express train going nonstop to Leipzig, whereas I am an omnibus; I stop in many places and pick up many passengers, who are permitted to come and go as they please. You see, not everybody is capable of going straight to Leipzig!'

One day, Reb Itzikl returned from a visit to the celebrated Reb Mottel of Chernobyl. 'What did you see there?' the Kotzker wanted to know. 'Just one thing: the table at which the Besht used to sit and study.' 'That's all?' commented the Kotzker. 'That table is one hundred years old while we here study teachings that are six thousand years old . . .'

Both were right – both approaches were necessary. *Ele veele divrei elokim hayim*: God is everywhere – man is not; man is not even where he thinks he is.

Reb Itzikl and the Kotzker represented two opposing views in Hasidism, but they remained friends: both lived and worked *leshem shamayim*, for the sake of heaven.

The Kotzker yearned for solitude, Reb Itzikl opposed it. In Kotzk people believed that Kotzk was the centre of the universe; in Worke they learned that the universe has more than one centre. Every person is the centre of creation – every person is called upon to justify creation.

Form played no role in Kotzk; it did in Worke. The Kotzker was indifferent to things visible, tangible and concrete; only the ineffable attracted him. Reb Itzikl of Worke mingled with his followers, visited their homes, queried them about their worries and preoccupations, shared in their joys as well as in their sorrows; he even took part in the political activity of certain Jewish groups that were working to improve conditions for the Jews. He sometimes went to see influential politicians and social leaders to solicit their help. It is known that he asked for and obtained an audience with the influential Jewish philanthropist Sir Moses Montefiore. We even know where that meeting took place: in the so-called Green Inn near Lomza. What was his request? Better treatment for Russian and Polish Jews – for all Jews, but especially for Hasidim. He wanted permission for Hasidim to dress as they chose. And to obey the *Shulkhan Arukh*, which the authorities, according to rumour, intended to burn. And it is said that Montefiore told Reb Itzikl, 'If only the Jews could have their *own* little state, all Jews would be happier, and safer, everywhere.'

One day Reb Itzikl tried to convince an important Jew to go to the governor on behalf of the community. The Jew was afraid: How could he go alone? Then the Rebbe of Worke said, 'It is written in

Scripture that God told Moses, *Bo el Paaro*, come to Pharaoh. Come? He should have said: "*Go* to Pharaoh." But – when someone goes to intercede on behalf of his community, God is with him. God precedes him. God is there to meet him.'

Man is never alone. This idea, conceived by Judaism and glorified by Hasidism, dominated the mood in Worke. Even if man wished to be alone, he could not. Man cannot detach himself from his Creator. God is in His creation – God is present, God is presence. It is up to man to be present, too – present to God, to himself, and to his fellow man.

Unlike Kotzk, which provided the framework for Worke just as Pshiskhe did for Kotzk, and Lublin for Pshiskhe, Worke stressed the humanist implications of Hasidism. In Worke friendship was as important as study – even more important than the attachment to the Tzaddik.

Biglal Kamtza u-Bar-Kamtza nechreva Yerushalayim; remember the Midrash? Jerusalem was destroyed because of human hatred. There was a man who had a friend named Kamtza and an enemy named Bar-Kamtza. One day he organized a dinner and told his servant to invite Kamtza; the servant invited Bar-Kamtza instead. The host was furious, and after insulting Bar-Kamtza publicly, chased him out of his house. But Bar-Kamtza took revenge: he denounced the Jews to Rome and, as events unfolded, Jerusalem was ultimately reduced to ashes. 'I can understand the guilt of Bar-Kamtza,' said Reb Itzikl of Worke. 'But Kamtza? How can he be guilty since he wasn't even present at the dinner? *That* was his guilt,' commented Reb Itzikl. Kamtza's friend gave a dinner party to celebrate an occasion, and he – his best friend – did not attend? What kind of friend was he? All right, he wasn't invited; never mind! As a friend he should have come – even without an invitation!

Popular belief has it that true friendship can be ascertained only in times of need. Not so: there are Hasidim who maintain that only in happiness will you recognize your true friends. They alone will not be envious. You will usually find friends to feel sorry for you. But rare are those who will be happy simply because you are happy.

Said Reb Itzikl of Worke: 'The Talmud tells us that Rebbe Zeira lived long because he never rejoiced over the defeat of his colleagues. What kind of praise is this? Is it conceivable that a sage like Rebbe Zeira could rejoice over his friends' misfortunes? No, the text must be read differently: as long as his colleagues were unhappy, he was unable to rejoice.'

From his sayings and teachings, from anecdotes about him, we learn that the founder of Worke was modest, unassuming, simple, warm, often choosing to stay in the shadow, doing everything in his power to honour his teachers and then his companions. Though he was a Rebbe, he fled the limelight. Though he was a Rebbe, he behaved as a Hasid, endlessly searching for continuity and fidelity. After Rebbe Bunam died, he remained loyal to the Rebbe's son, Rebbe Avraham Mordecai, whereas most disciples followed Reb Mendel to Tomashov and then to Kotzk.

Rebbe Bunam's death occurred on a Friday evening, according to Hasidic tradition. A few days earlier the Master had been reciting *Maariv*, the evening prayer, in bed. His son, who was standing at his bedside, was surprised to hear him suddenly say the morning prayer. 'Father,' he exclaimed, 'it's still evening.' Without a word of reply, Rebbe Bunam then began to recite the afternoon prayer – *Minhah*. That was too much for Reb Avraham Mordecai; he lost consciousness and was carried into his chambers. When he came to, he ordered his friends to leave him alone, and forbade them to allow anyone into his room. 'You keep the door closed,' he told his servant, Reb Yiddel, 'even if they try to break it down.' A day went by. Another one. Three days went by. In the meantime Rebbe Bunam's condition worsened. People came to warn the son and take him to his father's bedside. He refused to let them in. Then his mother came to beg him: 'You must be there, your father is dying . . .' 'I cannot,' he answered. 'I don't have the strength.' She asked Reb Itzikl of Worke to plead with her son. He refused, saying, 'This matter is too serious; I have no right to interfere.'

Later, years later, when Reb Itzikl himself was on his deathbed, his son, Reb Mendel, withdrew into his private chambers and gave orders not to disturb him. He too felt he didn't have the strength to face the loss of his father. As for the Hasidim of Worke, they had to face the loss of their Master – and of their friend. Rebbe Itzikl was more than a friend; he was a brother to his disciples. Every person, he said, must see in the other a Sefer Torah – a Holy Scroll. Every human being is sacred; every creature deserves respect. Man's body itself reflects divinity. Once he scolded a Hasid who had mortified himself: 'You are selfish,' he told him; 'selfish and possessive.' 'I?' wondered the man. 'But I have nothing.' 'Precisely:

you have nothing and yet you behave as though you do; you punish your body – is it yours alone? It belongs to God, to God too.'

Another disciple told him of his custom to fast from Sunday to Friday. Reb Itzikl scolded him too: 'This is not the Hasidic way,' he said. 'But it was the Besht's way,' said the Hasid. 'Didn't *he* live in the mountains, didn't *he* fast from Sunday to Friday?' 'No comparison,' said Reb Itzikl. 'On Sundays the Besht left his family, taking with him food for the entire week – but he forgot to eat it. You go without food but you don't forget it; your mind is on food all week long.'

A woman in Worke misbehaved, and as a result, people ostracized her. He defended her, saying, 'If everything I hear about her is true, then she deserves pity, not insults.'

Ahavat-Israel cannot go hand in hand with self-hate, according to Worke. Dignity, respect and self-respect are principles to be adhered to. Why do we recite the *Viddui* – the confession – alphabetically? 'So we know when to stop,' said Reb Itzikl. 'To cry and moan endlessly is wrong; it is not the way that leads to God. Joy and gratitude are also part of life. *Banim atem laadoshem*, we are all God's children,' said Reb Itzikl: 'to forget it is the worst of sins.' Quoting the Song of Songs, which describes King Solomon sleeping in a bed made of gold, he wondered aloud, 'But how can one sleep in a bed made of gold? Read what follows,' said Reb Itzikl, answering himself: '". . . and the inside thereof was inlaid with love" – where there is love, one can sleep even on gold.'

Reb Itzikl's son, Reb Mendel, told the Rebbe of Kotzk that he had seen his late father in a dream: he was leaning on a cane, near a river. 'Yes,' said the Kotzker. 'And do you know what the river was? It was a river of tears – tears of all the Jews persecuted everywhere.'

True: all his life, Reb Itzikl tried to collect the tears of his tormented people. His son said of him, 'Throughout his life, my father would repeat over and over one verse of the Torah: *Veahavta* – and you shall love your God with all your heart, and you shall love, and you shall love . . .'

Yet, at the same time, Reb Itzikl displayed a marvellous sense of humour. Once he was told that thieves had broken into his son's store and had carried away much of his merchandise. On the following night they returned for what they had left. 'Poor thieves,' Reb Itzikl remarked, 'they didn't sleep two nights in a row . . .'

Why isn't hospitality included among the six hundred and thirteen commandments of the Torah? he wanted to know. 'I'll tell you why,' he said. 'If it were, people would force strangers not to go home but to come and eat with them, sleep with them, live with them . . . True hospitality means,' he said, 'to let your guests leave when they want to leave – and not later.'

His older son – a Talmudic scholar – would study aloud in his presence. 'Good, good,' the father would say, 'but you must want to study.' So his son studied harder. 'Good, good,' Reb Itzikl said, 'but you must want to study.' So his son studied even harder – until he neither slept nor ate, doing nothing but study. 'Good, good,' said his father, 'but you must want to study.' 'But I have been doing nothing else!' cried the son. 'Not entirely true,' said Reb Itzikl. 'One must want to study to study – and not to impress.'

The Kotzker asked him why he had hired a cynic as his private secretary. 'I'll tell you,' said Reb Itzikl. 'All private secretaries become cynical – so why wait?'

He used to say: 'One can be alone with people, one can fast while eating; and true silence can be obtained inside words.'

It is this silence that, under his younger son, Reb Mendel, was to become the emblem of Worke. He was called Reb Mendel der Schweiger – the silent one. He welcomed silence into Hasidism as a force both disturbing and creative.

In many ways, Reb Mendel, who was born in 1819, is more striking than his father. Philosophically he is closer to Kotzk than to Worke. He too seeks solitude; he too is fascinated by what remains unsaid, unseen, inaccessible.

At the age of three, he was introduced to Rebbe Bunam, who gave him a glass of beer. 'Do you like it?' 'Yes,' said the child. 'It tastes bitter but good.' 'He will be a Rebbe,' said Rebbe Bunam.

He married, but soon after left his business and his family and, together with a few friends, went to live in the forest. What they did there has not been revealed. Hasidic tradition has it that they indulged in certain mystical experiments with joy rather than mourning. They sang, they danced, they laughed, they played – but in appearance only. What they hoped to achieve we don't know. We do know, however, that they didn't achieve it – and that Reb Itzikl tried unsuccessfully to convince his son to return to a normal life.

Reb Mendel refused. When his father fell ill, instead of fasting and praying, he went from one inn to the next, drinking one *Lehayyim* after the other in the company of friends whom he called his bodyguards.

Rebbe Berish of Biala followed them secretly one evening. It was Shavuot eve, when one is supposed to spend the whole night in study and meditation. Well, Reb Mendel and his friends spent the night ... drinking. Reb Berish was indignant, but he contained himself. He watched the scene and waited. Reb Mendel and his friends continued drinking, and after a while Reb Mendel stood up and began talking quietly, almost in a whisper. Reb Berish couldn't hear a word but he saw Reb Mendel burst into tears. Later he begged the group to accept him as a member, and he was admitted but only after a long initiation period.

When Reb Itzikl died, his orphaned followers insisted on crowning Reb Mendel as his successor rather than his elder brother, Reb Yaakov-David of Amshinov. But Reb Mendel refused. Like his father, like the Kotzker and other great Masters, he wanted to follow rather than be followed, leave the title, the responsibilities to someone else. 'I am not a Rebbe,' he told the Kotzker; 'I don't feel that I am one.' 'It's not up to you to make that decision,' answered the Kotzker. 'Hasidim make the Rebbe, not the other way around.' 'No,' said Reb Mendel cryptically. 'I refuse to be a beggar.'

Was it a lack of self-confidence? Possibly. Excessive humility? Probably. 'The proof that vanity is bad,' he used to say, 'is that it can be found in mean people.' He was afraid of becoming a leader because leadership implied the possibility of vanity – if not vanity itself. He preferred to be away from crowds – not to show them his true face, not to allow them to come too close. God's command to Abraham: *Lech lecha* – go away, go to another land – is interpreted by Reb Mendel as *Lech lecha*, go towards yourself. This is how he explains the Talmudic expression 'Tzaddik-Hasid': an average man is ordered not to fool others while a Tzaddik-Hasid is called upon not to fool himself. 'From my father,' he said, 'I learned two things: not to tell lies, and not to be a fool.' Another version of the same idea: 'You cannot fool God,' he said; 'you cannot even fool people; you can only fool yourself.' To the Kotzker he said: 'What did King Solomon teach us? That man's intelligence is powerless without God.'

Like the Kotzker Hasidim, the followers of Reb Mendel of Worke are encouraged to accept that while life is not made of joy and ecstasy alone, and also contains fear and trembling, and anxiety and sadness – fear and trembling, anxiety and sadness, too, can lead to truth. And God. 'To avoid sin,' he once said, 'is easy, and even simple: when you lie in your bed, imagine that you are lying in your grave.'

Contrary to his father, he paid no attention to the routine worries of his followers. My father, he explained, interceded for them with kings; I plead on their behalf before the King of all kings.

And yet, Hasidim flocked to him in great numbers; they revered him, they loved him. He was strange? Surely he had his reasons. He did not talk? Silence too can become a link, a link stronger than the spoken word.

He *was* strange – he resembled the Kotzker, except that he went further than his father's friend. The Kotzker was angry – but present. He shouted. He admonished. He thundered. But he was there. Even when he was in his room, alone, he was there: his Hasidim felt his presence, his closeness. With Reb Mendel it was different. He was there – but not really, not entirely. He was present but not all the way.

He delivered no sermons, gave no courses, avoided offering commentaries on the weekly portion of Scripture, revealed no mystical secrets – in fact, more often than not he said nothing. People came to Worke simply to be silent. To discover living silence – the newest and most disturbing aspect of the Hasidic experience.

He would spend sleepless nights sitting around his table with fervent disciples. The silence would be overwhelming, total. Soon there was nothing else in creation but this silence, and soon it reached farther still, higher still. A primary force, it would grow more and more intense and pure and true. Time stood still, for it had not been disrupted by words. One morning, at sunrise, Reb Mendel shook his head and said in a clear resonant voice, 'Happy is the person who knows that the one is one – always one.'

Silence has virtues that words cannot have. He explained: 'Silence is good even if it is empty – not so with words. When they are empty, they remain empty.'

Once he quoted a passage from the Psalms – *Eenkha beseter raam* – God says: 'I shall answer you from inside thunder.' And Reb Mendel exclaimed, '*Brider Yidden*, brother Jews, *lomir dunnern shtilerheit* – let us all thunder silently.'

'These are the three principles I want you to follow,' he told his disciples. 'Learn how to kneel and stand erect; to dance and remain motionless; to shout and be silent – all at the same time.'

Other Hasidic masters have extolled the virtues and powers of silence, but none practised it as he did.

There were times when the Baal Shem Tov asked his disciples to contain their ecstasy – or their laughter – and keep quiet, and turn the absence of sound into something creative, and enter silence.

There were times when the great Maggid Reb Dov-Ber of Mezeritch would listen, listen to his disciples without offering them a
reply.

There were times when Rebbe Elimelekh of Lizensk would
withdraw, for hours or days, into a state of muteness.

There were times when Reb Levi-Yitzhak of Berditchev would
speak in whispers, so that no one could hear him. He too was
intrigued by silence. 'When the Messiah will come,' he once said,
'it will be given to man to understand not only the words of the
Torah but also the empty spaces between them.'

As for the Kotzker, he taught us that certain truths can be transmitted by words, others by silence, and still others cannot be communicated at all, not even by silence.

Yes – many Hasidic masters felt, at one point in their lives, the
compulsion to confront the problem – the mystery – of silence.
Rabbi Nahman of Bratzlav, for instance, demanded of his disciples
that they live one hour every day in solitude and silence. In his tales
we often meet characters – poets, orators and minstrels – unable or
unwilling to speak.

But no Master spoke of silence – no Master put silence into
words – as did Rebbe Mendel of Worke. With him, it became a
world to explore, a major theme to dwell upon, a way of life.

He loved to explain the Biblical verse *Vayishma adoshem et kol
hanaar* – And God heard the complaints of Ishmael in the desert.
He commented: 'There is no mention that Ishmael cried or even
moaned. This means,' he continued, 'that Ishmael, Hagar's tragic
son, cried silently – and that is why he was heard by God.'

The same, he felt, was true of Hannah, mother of the Prophet
Samuel, who prayed in silence – the highest form of prayer,
according to Reb Mendel. Once he spoke of Batya, Pharaoh's
daughter, who noticed the child floating on the Nile and saw him
crying. She *saw* him crying? Didn't she hear him? Can a child cry
inwardly? 'Yes – a Jewish child can,' said Reb Mendel of Worke,
'at times, a Jewish child must.'

One day he met Rebbe Eliezer, son of the Maggid of Kozhenitz,
to discuss an urgent matter. They withdrew into a room, sat down
facing one another, looked at one another for a long while but said
nothing. Then they opened the door. 'We have finished,' said Reb
Mendel to his Hasidim waiting outside.

Why this obsession with silence? Was it because Reb Mendel
distrusted the spoken word, too often and too successfully misused

by man? Was it that he longed for the silence that the Besht had absorbed in the Carpathian mountains before it was turned into tales and sayings, teachings and precepts? Was it something else, something more? Was his purpose not to withdraw from language but to amplify and deepen it with silence? Perhaps he meant to innovate, to invent, to create something new in Hasidism. Perhaps he felt that everything had been said: that he could only repeat what others had said before him. That he could never live up to his forerunners.

There is another possibility. His actions may have derived from higher, more spiritual impulses – perhaps even theological considerations. Since God dwells in silence, why not seek Him out there? Why not challenge Him there?

The nineteenth century witnessed new bloodshed and justified new fears. Outside the Hasidic kingdom, the world was preparing the abyss for future generations of Hasidim and their Masters. New wars were erupting, preparing the way for the most cruel of all. And God was silent? Satan howled and God did not respond? Evil spread throughout creation and the Creator said nothing? Since He remained silent, what could man possibly do?

One Passover evening, a week before he died, at the age of forty-nine, Reb Mendel was singing the Haggada – the beautiful story of our exodus from Egypt – when he stopped in the middle. He paused and then he whispered, 'In truth, there exist in this world Tzaddikim, Just Men, who possess the powers to bring the Messiah. But they choose not to use their powers. Why? I shall tell you why: Since God is silent, they choose to remain silent too.'

When divine silence is answered by human silence – it is tragic for both.

But then – where is hope to be found? The two silences *can* merge, *can* grow one through the other, one in the other. That is sufficient – that *must* be sufficient. One can purify and free the other, and that is sufficient, that *must* be sufficient.

For ultimately the choice is a limited one: We can answer God's silence with human words – or respond to God's words with human silence. But there too the road is not without obstacles: What if the silence of the one is the language of the other? How are we to know? Is it at all possible to know?

These are disturbing questions, especially for my generation. We have so far failed to decipher or even to confront God's silence in a universe empty of God – or worse: filled with God.

Now, in this generation, we have learned at least one lesson: that some experiences lie beyond language, that their language *is* silence. For silence does not necessarily mean absence of communication.

Imagine a great dancer motionless – for one hour – on stage; imagine a gifted painter staring intently – for one day – at the white canvas; imagine a forceful sculptor with her fingers riveted to the stone – her fingers becoming stone. Imagine them and you may be able to capture the evocative, descriptive silence of the artist.

For the poet, the artist, the mystic and the survivor, silence has many facets, zones and shades. Silence has its own texture, its own spheres, its own archaeology. It has its own contradictions as well. The silence of the victim is one thing, that of the killer, another. And that of the spectator, still another. There is creative silence, there is murderous silence. To a perceptive human being the universe is never silent – but there exists a universe of silence, and only perceptive human beings are aware of it.

Now – I confess that I feel close to Worke because of its silence – it symbolizes to me another universe, one that *was* dominated by silence. There, during the eternity of one night, endless nocturnal processions of men and women and children, crossing a continent in flames, went to meet their executioners and death – and God – silently whispering age-old prayers, the *Kaddish*, the *Viddui*, the *Sh'ma Israel*, and nothing else, as though they too had despaired of language.

More than the hunger of the hungry, more than the agony of the tormented, more than the flames over the mass graves, it is the silence of the victims that is haunting us – and will haunt us forever. The quiet, fearless Rebbe and his frightened community. The teacher and his disciples. The dreamers, the workers, the rich and the poor, the learned and the ignorant, they did not cry, they did not shout, they did not protest; they walked and walked into death and left their silence behind them. And if ever silence attained the level of absolute, it was then. It was there.

And so, let us go back – back to Worke – and stay there, lest we go mad, mad with pain and anguish and yearning.

I remember silence in Worke – I remember silence away from Worke.

And now we know what it was: an appeal, an outcry to God on behalf of his desperate people and also on His behalf, an offering to night, to heaven, an offering made by wise old men and quiet children to mark the end of language – the outer limits of creation – a burning secret buried in silence.

Afterword

It is only reluctantly that the teller of tales considers leaving these great Masters whom we have just encountered in their very own capitals of the Hasidic universe; their hold on him has never been stronger.

Such is the power of their legends; their intensity, their beauty stay with you and involve you — almost against your will, almost against your better judgement.

Somewhere, a Master spoke to one or many of his followers about their fears and doubts and what to do to alleviate them, and his message was heard then, and today, for their exchange is also about us; there is a curious immediacy to their stories, a timeless application to their sayings.

A Hasidic story is to be told, not studied. It is to be lived, not analysed. The anger of Rebbe Barukh, the compassion of Rebbe Moshe-Leib, the melancholy visions of the Seer of Lublin: they teach Hasidim how to live, not how to reflect.

A Hasidic story is about Hasidim more than about their Masters; it is about those who retell it as much as about those who experienced it long ago, in a time of both physical and spiritual hunger and solitude.

Rebbe Pinhas and his wisdom, the Besht and his warmth, Rebbe Naphtali and his humour: to their followers they appeared as kings, judges, prophets. There are intimations of royalty in their vocabulary: notables are 'appointed' to positions, Rebbes are 'crowned' and ascend 'thrones'.

How can the attraction they held for their contemporaries be comprehended today? They were as close to God as to those who were seeking Him. Though they differed considerably in their outlook, in their lifestyles, their education — some were more learned than others, more renowned than others — they were all endowed with mystical powers and they used them not to isolate themselves but rather to penetrate and enrich their communities.

They were inspired, and they inspired others. They communicated joy and wonder, and fervour too, fervour above all, to men and women who needed joy and fervour to live, to survive. These teachers brought warmth and compassion to followers in the

Ukraine, in Poland and in Lithuania. For Jews who felt abandoned, forsaken, there was always a Master somewhere who incarnated an irresistible call to hope and friendship.

Friendship, *Dibuk-haverim*, is a key word in the Hasidic vocabulary. For the disciple it is as important as *Ahavat-Israel*, love of people, is for the Master.

To follow a certain Rebbe means also to relate to his pupils and admirers. A Hasid alone is not a true Hasid. Solitude and Hasidism are incompatible. What was the Hasidic movement in its origins if not a protest against solitude? The villager left behind his farm, his daily misery and uncertainties, and went to spend the High Holidays, or a simple Sabbath, with his Master – not just to see and hear him and pray and study with him, but also to meet his fellow Hasidim, his friends. And over and over again, they would celebrate their reunion, their common faith and their dream.

And yet, and yet . . . all these great spiritual leaders and guides, who somehow, somewhere, managed to move so many others to joy and ecstasy, often seemed to struggle with melancholy, and at times even with darkest despair.

The holy Seer of Lublin, the famous Jester of Ropshitz, the Sage of Koretz, the wanderer from Zbarazh: what was this sadness they had to engage in combat – and why?

Intercessor rather than mediator (the Jewish tradition rejects the concept of intermediaries in the relations of man to his Creator), the Rebbe often is bound to feel inadequate: all these vigils, all these prayers, all these promises, all these appeals, yet the Messiah does not come. All these trials and sufferings, and heaven remains closed. And the Shekhina remains in exile. As do the people of Israel. What must one do to keep from losing hope, what can one do? Said Rebbe Aharon of Karlin: 'Either God is God and I do not do enough to serve Him, or He is not and then it is my fault.' Who is responsible for all the wars, the persecutions, the long nights of fear? Who is to blame for all the hatred, the torment, the massacres, the pogroms? Hunger, thirst, death: Who can acquiesce? Who can justify? The Master listens and listens to his followers' tales of woe and eventually cannot ignore the signs of approaching melancholy.

Every Master – whether in Mezeritch or Sassov, in Rizhin or in Premishlan – is vulnerable. The problem is inherent in his functions. He must go on listening to his followers. He must go on being available to them – always and in everything. He has no right to abandon those who believe in him. The Master is responsible for his Hasidim.

And so he controls himself. Surmounting all obstacles — rational doubts, irrational fears — he liberates in himself and in his followers a kind of joy that will be justified only retroactively. He combats sorrow with exuberance; he defeats resignation by exalting faith. He attempts to create happiness so as not to yield to the sadness around him. He tells stories so as to escape the temptations of irreducible silence.

To express my admiration and my love for all these Hasidic Masters whose portraits I have tried to draw is repetitious. But then, repetition is part of the Hasidic tradition.

Naturally, I stressed some themes more than others. I probably spoke too much of certain Rebbes and not enough of others — Rebbe Shneur-Zalman deserves a volume to himself — but there too, I only did what the Hasid in me has always done — and what all Hasidim are still doing. Hasidism has never claimed to oppose subjectivity.

In retelling these tales, I realize once more how much I owe these Masters. Sometimes consciously, sometimes not, I have incorporated a song, a suite, an obsession of theirs into my own fables and legends. For me, the echoes of a vanished kingdom are still reverberating. And I have remained the child who loves to listen.

While listening I see myself with my grandfather at various 'courts'. We laugh with the Rebbe of Ropshitz, we tremble in the presence of the Seer of Lublin, we dance with Rebbe Moshe-Leib of Sassov. Somewhere, a Master is singing, and we feel compelled to join him and learn his song.

Elsewhere, in a novel, I imagined a man who one day finds himself sharing a cell with a madman. After a while, he realizes that slowly, inevitably, he too is losing his mind. Having been exposed to madness, he will in time become its victim. And so, in order not to go mad, he sets out to cure his mad fellow prisoner. The hero of my tale did not know, could not know that he was only following in the steps of Rebbe Nahman of Bratzlav, Rebbe Pinhas of Koretz, Rebbe Mendel of Worke and their peers whom I have evoked in this volume.

Did I say that the teller of tales would soon leave his old Masters? In truth, he will not. For even if he wanted to, he could not; they surely would not willingly recede into the shadows of his burning memory.

More than ever, we, today, need their faith, their fervour; more than ever, we, today, need to imagine them helping, caring — living.

Glossary

AGGADA: Parables, commentaries, legends, proverbs and fables, most often deriving from Biblical texts, expounding on their complexities and constituting one of the aspects of Talmud and Midrash. Whereas Halakha enjoins conformity by tracing guidelines to a way of life, Aggada, less severe and less coercive, and even at times and as circumstances require mischievous or poetic, awakens thought, meditation or prayer, and brings into focus the foundations of a system of ethics and faith.

ALIYAH (literally 'Ascent'): Usual meaning is emigration to Israel.

BAAL SHEM (literally 'Master of the Name'): Title attributed since the Middle Ages to men who know the true name of beings and things, recognize their secret and can act upon them, through them. By naming the forces, such a man masters them; his knowledge is power. Were he to use this power to attain immediate or profane gains, he would be nothing more than a miracle-maker. But if he chooses to bring the names closer to the Name, and unite beings and things with God, he becomes Master of the Good Name, Baal Shem Tov.

BEADLE: The equivalent in the synagogue to a church sexton.

BEIT MIDRASH (literally 'House of Study'): In order not to interrupt meditation and discussion on the sacred Word, the rabbinical academies chose to remain there for services rather than move to the Beit Knesseth, the assembly house (synagogue). The two 'Houses' often became one, or at least were made to adjoin, with services extending into study and study culminating in prayer. 'At the house of prayer and study' is a frequently recurring expression in Hasidic texts.

According to Aggada, the first Beit Midrash was founded by Sem on the morrow of the Deluge. When Isaac was freed of his bonds and left the altar, that is where he retired to study.

THE BESHT, or Rebbe Israel Baal Shem Tov (1700–1760): The founder of the Hasidic movement.

DAYAN: Judge of the rabbinical tribunal, arbiter.

DIN: Judgement, legal decision; *midat hadin*: divine rigour and severity.

FRANK, JACOB (1726–91): Last of the 'great' would-be Messiahs. A disciple of Shabtai-Tzvi, he tried to 'rehabilitate' Christianity for the Jews, ultimately converting amid great pomp in the Warsaw cathedral with Emperor Augustus III as his godfather. Later he spent thirteen years in prison for heresy. Retired to the Rhineland with his daughter Eve, famous for her beauty, he taught and practised the 'rehabilitation' of sexuality by unrestrained indulgence in its every form.

GAON OF VILNA, or Rabbi Elijah ben Salomon Zalman (1720–97): The most exalted rabbinical figure of Eastern European Jewry, a man of outstanding moral stature and quasi-encyclopedic learning. The unchallenged master of Halakha, he also had a profound knowledge of Kabbala. Leader of the Mitnagdim, he vehemently opposed the Hasidic movement and vigorously fought its expansion in Lithuania.

GOG AND MAGOG: The opponents of the Messiah. In the great eschatological battle against the righteous host, they are to head the forces of evil. In rabbinic literature, the rebel people who rise up against God and His anointed.

HAGGADA: *See* AGGADA.

HALAKHA (literally 'walk, way, rule'): That which in Talmud and rabbinical literature concerns itself with the ritual, social and economic life of the community and the individual. Like the texts of Aggada, with which they overlap, the texts of Halakha are generally based on Biblical exegesis. They constitute the basis of an ample body of laws regulating every aspect of the life of a practising Jew.

HASID (literally 'fervent, pious'): One who acts out of love, with tenderness. Derived from *hesed*, grace, one of God's attributes complementing *din*, strict justice. God's grace calls forth the fervour, the piety of man, his love for God and all His creatures.

In the Psalms, Hasid (plural, Hasidim) often denotes the faithful, the lover of God. In the Talmud (Pirke Aboth, V, 13–16), Hasid is 'he who says: what is mine is yours and what is yours is yours; he who is slow to anger and quick to relent; he who enjoys giving and likes others to give' – and again, 'he who, even before he prays, turns his heart to God – for at least one hour' (Ber. 30b) – and even 'the Hasidim among the Gentiles will have their share in the world to come' (Toss. Sanh. 13; Mishne Torah, Melakhim 11).

In the second century BC a Jewish sect, the Hasidim or Assideans, 'valiant men whose hearts were bound to the Law', fought with the Maccabees against Antiochus Epiphanus. But refusing all compromise on religious law and unwilling to become involved in politics, they broke away from the Hasmonean dynasty after victory had been achieved. The Talmud refers to them as 'the Hasidim of yore'.

In the thirteenth century of the Common Era, there flourished in the

Rhineland an important school called the Hasidim of Ashkenaz, the Holy Men of Germany; they created a trend of thought that found wide acceptance. Their major work, the *Sefer Hasidim*, the Book of the Devout, rooted in Jewish mystical tradition, stresses the majesty of God but also the mystery of oneness, elaborating a veritable philosophy of history and man's relationship to man, emphasizing the importance of silent piety, of prayer, and of a system of ethics based on renunciation of earthly matters, spiritual serenity, total love of one's fellow man culminating in the expression of the fear and the love of God in 'the joy that scorches the heart'.

HEDER: An elementary religious school of the type prevalent in Eastern Europe, often situated in a single room in the teacher's home.

HILLEL AND SHAMMAI: Respectively president and vice-president of the Sanhedrin in the first century BC. They are the last and best known of the 'couples' of rabbis whose opinions challenge and complete one another. The School of Shammai, more concerned with principles and ultimate goals, was the more severe, the more rigorous of the two; the House of Hillel, mindful of the lessons of the past, leaned towards a gentler approach.

KAVANA (literally 'intention'): Spiritual concentration on prayer or the religious act to prepare for *dvekut* – compliance with the Divine Will. The Talmud stresses the need of directing one's thoughts towards God, not only while praying but also while obeying the Commandments. The 'mystics' of the Middle Ages, and later the Hasidim, insisted on this form of contemplation, and composed *Kavanoth*, 'prayers – or poems – of intention', to prepare and assist in the transition into ritual service.

LAMED VAVNIK: 'The world,' says the Talmud, 'must not contain fewer than thirty-six Just Men' who have been allowed to contemplate the Divine Presence. It is thanks to them that the world subsists. Popular imagination took hold of these Lamed Vavnik (the numerical value of the letters *lamed* and *vav* is thirty-six), gave them a background of poverty and obscurity and described them as leading hidden lives, revealing their qualities and powers only in cases of need, when the survival of the community, the people, or the world is at stake.

LURIA, ISAAC, also referred to as the Ari, the Holy Lion of Safed (1534–72): He was born in Jerusalem, lived in Cairo and died in Safed; one of the most mysterious, complex and popular masters of Kabbala. His strictly oral teachings owe their dissemination to notes taken by his disciple Hayim Vital. His thoughts on *Tzimtzum* (the withdrawal of God into Himself to leave room for human groping and error); on the *Shevirat Hakelim*, the 'broken vessels' of Primary Light whose sparks subsist even in the infernal regions; on the *Tikkun* (the 'bridging' of gaps, the in-gathering of sparks, 'restoration' as a historical objective);

on the Messiah in chains awaiting the redemption of our every deed, all strongly influenced Hasidism.

MAARIV: Evening service, also called *Arevit*, recited daily after nightfall and named after one of the opening words of its first prayer.

MAGGID: A popular preacher. The Maggid became a characteristic feature of the Russian and Polish Jewish communities. It was mainly by means of these wandering preachers that Hasidism was spread in the eighteenth century.

MASKIL: A title of honour for a learned man.

MELAMED: A teacher who supervised the single-room *heder*.

MEZUZAH (literally 'doorpost'): A small tubular case, usually of metal or wood, containing a tightly rolled piece of parchment inscribed with verses 4–9 of Deut. 6 and 13–21 of Deut. 11 on one side, and *Shaddai* (a name applied to God) on the other, the latter visible through an aperture in the case. The mezuzah is traditionally attached to the right doorpost of the Jewish home. The great philosopher-legislator of the Middle Ages, Moses ben Maimon (Maimonides), expressed its meaning this way:

'By the commandment of the mezuzah, man is reminded, when entering or departing, of God's Oneness, and is stirred into love for Him. He is awakened from his slumber and from his vain worldly thoughts to the knowledge that no thing endures in eternity like knowledge of the "Rock of the World". This contemplation brings him back to himself and leads him unto the right path.'

MIDRASH: From a Hebrew verb meaning to expound, to interpret, to deduce; specifically to expound the precepts and ethical dicta of Scriptures; in fact, a large body of Talmudic literature that developed during the Tannaic and Amoraic periods (second century of the Common Era).

MIKVAH: Ritual bath for immersion to wash every uncleanness.

MINHAH: The second of the two statutory daily services. It is recited any time during the afternoon until sunset and corresponds to the daily 'evening' sacrifice in the Temple.

MINYAN: The ten male Jews required for religious services.

MISHNAH (literally 'study'): Compendia of tradition compiled in Palestine *c.* 200 CE.

MITNAGDIM (literally 'adversaries'): They opposed the 'new Hasidic sect', judging it revolutionary, dangerous, heretic.

QUEEN SHABBAT: The Sabbath is welcomed as a bride and a queen and the end of the Sabbath is marked by the festive meal *melave-malka* – 'accompanying the Queen'.

RABBI: Literally 'master' or 'teacher'.

REB: Mr.

REBBE: Term used for Hasidic leaders and spiritual guides. The Rebbe or Tzaddik is not necessarily a halakhic scholar and teacher, but guides his followers by virtue of his spiritual power and holiness.

SHABBAT: The Sabbath, the weekly day of rest, observed from sunset of Friday until nightfall Saturday.

SHABTAI-TZVI (1626–76): The most prestigious of the false Messiahs. Born in Smyrna, well versed in Talmud and practical Kabbala, he wandered from Salonika to Jerusalem, enticing crowds and attracting wrath, teaching a doctrine in which are evident elements of the school of Luria. In 1665 he proclaimed himself Messiah. The news spread like wildfire and aroused indescribable enthusiasm and exultation in the Jewish world; people everywhere prayed for 'our Master, the Anointed of the Lord'; some even sold their property, expecting an imminent miraculous departure for the Holy Land. In 1666 he expressed the wish to meet the Sultan so as to request recognition of his sovereignty over the Land of Israel. Instead he found himself in prison. Then, one day, the Sultan summoned him; we don't know what took place, except that soon thereafter Shabtai-Tzvi converted to Islam – only to be exiled to Albania, where he ended his days in obscurity.

Yet the most fervent among his disciples saw in his conversion but another step in a divine pattern; his cult subsisted until the twentieth century in the East, and at least one hundred years in the West, where he provoked controversies and suspicions, heresy and excommunications.

SHAVUOT: Holiday in late spring, commemorating the gift of Torah at Mount Sinai.

SHEKHINA: The Divine Presence. Tradition has it that the radiance of the Shekhina with its many blessings accompanies those who are pious and righteous.

SH'MA ISRAEL (literally 'Hear O Israel'): A liturgical prayer, prominent in Jewish history and tradition, recited daily at evening and morning services, 'you will say them when you lie down and when you rise' (verse 7, Deut. 6); it brings together three passages of the Pentateuch, all expressing Israel's ardent faith in and love of God. The important place it holds in Jewish consciousness has made it into a veritable 'profession of faith' that is repeated by the dying man and the martyr.

SHIMON BAR YOHAI (second century of the Common Era): Famous Master whose teachings are frequently quoted and expounded in the Talmud. He was condemned to death for having criticized the Roman occupiers but succeeded in escaping. With his son, he took shelter in a cave, where he spent thirteen years. There are numerous legends woven around this period in his life: it was said that he explored the mysteries of Kabbala during his reclusion and laid the foundations of the Zohar. To this day, there are considerable numbers of faithful who visit his grave in Meron, near Safed, on the thirty-third day after Passover, the anniversary of his death.

SHOKHET: One trained and ordained to perform the ritual slaughter used to supply kosher meats.

SHTETL: A very small town.

SHTIBL: House of Prayer of Hasidim, usually extremely small with only one or two rooms.

SHULKHAN ARUKH: A compendium of Jewish law compiled in the sixteenth century CE by Joseph Caro.

SIMHAT TORAH: Festival of the Law in the autumn; the last day of Succoth celebrating the end of the yearly cycle of reading the Torah.

SUCCAH: A temporary, wooden hut covered with branches, in which all meals are taken during Succoth.

SUCCOTH: Feast of Tabernacles; begins four days after Yom Kippur.

TALLIT: Prayer shawl.

TALMUD (literally 'learning'): Mishnah plus Gemara, the commentary on the Mishnah produced in rabbinical academies from c. 200–500 CE.

TANYA: The basic work of the HaBaD movement within Hasidism which produced the school of Lubavitch. Authored by the founder of HaBaD, Rebbe Shneur-Zalman of Lyady (1747–1813), the Tanya consists of two parts: the first shows the way to 'those who are neither perfect Just Men nor evil outcasts', in other words those who may, through study, prayer and meditation, attain the love of God; the second, the Book of Unity and Faith, is a commentary on the Sh'ma.

TEFILLIN: Phylacteries; two leather cases which are bound by straps attached to the forehead and the left arm during the morning prayer.

TORAH (literally 'teaching'): Can refer to the Pentateuch, or to all of Scripture, or to all revelation, written or oral, in Judaism.

TZADDIK: Just Man, ideal of moral, social and religious perfection, he is a man 'who lives by his faith', and to whom God responds. In the Hasidic movement the Tzaddik rapidly became an institution, but though a 'spiritual model', when exposed to temptation, he was not always able to resist, going as far as to proclaim himself intermediary between his disciples and God, presiding over veritable courts and founding dynasties.

YOHANAN BEN-ZAKKAI, also called Rabban, our Master: One of the key figures in the elaboration of the Talmud. In order to protect the continuity of studies, he fled a Jerusalem occupied by Vespasian and founded the Academy of Yavneh, which succeeded the Sanhedrin and guaranteed the survival of the tradition. After the destruction of the Temple, Rabbi Yohanan Ben-Zakkai compiled all that was known of sacrificial ritual, down to the smallest details, in expectation of messianic restoration. At the same time he stressed the important place held, in the absence of the Temple, and to this day, by study of the holy texts and the synagogal cult.

ZOHAR: The 'Book of Splendour', principal work of Kabbala, esoteric commentary on the Pentateuch, traditionally attributed to Shimon bar Yohai.

SYNCHRONOLOGY

Synchronology

ISRAEL BAAL SHEM TOV (THE BESHT) (1700–1760)	1700 One thousand European Jews emigrate to the Holy Land.
DOV-BER OF MEZERITCH (THE MAGGID) (1704–72)	
ELIMELEKH OF LIZENSK (1717–86)	1720 In Lowicz (Poland), the clergy decides to prohibit the building of new and the restoration of old synagogues.
	1727 First Jews naturalized in American colonies.
PINHAS OF KORETZ (1728–91)	1730 Founding of the first synagogue in New York.
AHARON OF KARLIN (THE GREAT) (1733–72)	
WOLFE OF ZBARAZH (–1802?)	1738 Public execution in Stuttgart of Joseph Susskind Oppenheimer (Jud Süss).
LEVI-YITZHAK OF BERDITCHEV (1740–1809)	
MOSHE-LEIB OF SASSOV (1745–1807)	1745 Empress Maria Theresa orders the expulsion of Jews from Bohemia and Prague.
THE SEER OF LUBLIN (1745–1815)	
	1750 Stringent anti-Jewish legislation adopted in Germany: limitation on marriage and increased taxation.

IN THE WORLD AT LARGE	IN THE ARTS
1700–1721 The 'Great Northern War'. Russia, led by Peter the Great, Poland and Denmark fight against Charles XII of Sweden for supremacy in the Baltic.	
1701–14 War of the Spanish Succession.	1715 Pope translates the *Iliad* into English.
	1726 Swift's *Gulliver's Travels*.
1733–5 War of the Polish Succession.	1733 J. S. Bach's B-Minor Mass.
1740–48 War of the Austrian Succession.	1740 Hume's *Treatise on Human Nature*. 1742 Handel's *Messiah*.
	1748 Montesquieu's *Spirit of the Laws*.

1753 British Parliament rejects a proposed law granting certain civic rights to Jews.

BARUKH OF MEDZIBOZH
(1757–1811)

Major trial of Polish Jews accused of ritual murder. (More than twenty such trials took place in Poland alone between 1700 and 1760.)

NAPHTALI OF ROPSHITZ
(1760–1827)

BUNAM OF PSHISKHE
(1762–1827)

1763 The twenty-five-year-old philosopher Moses Mendelssohn receives the first prize of the Prussian Academy of Sciences for an essay on metaphysics.

1764 'Council of the Four Lands' dissolved. Polish Jews are left without any central organization.

NAHMAN OF BRATZLAV
(1772–1810)

1772 The Mitnagdim, gathered in Vilna, excommunicate the 'new sect', the Hasidim.

1775 Pius VI's edicts condemn the seven thousand Jews of Rome to misery and public disgrace.

YAAKOV-YITZHAK OF PSHISKHE
(THE JEW) (1776–1813)

ITZHAK OF WORKE
(1779–1848)

1779 Lessing publishes his apologia of Judaism: *Nathan der Weise*.

IN THE WORLD AT LARGE	IN THE ARTS

1756–63 Seven Years War. Russia, Austria, France and others against Prussia and Great Britain.

1759 Public debate in Lemberg between Frankist renegades and prominent rabbis.

1759 Inauguration of the British Museum.
Hayden's First Symphony performed.
Voltaire's *Candide*.

1760 Beginnings (in England) of the Industrial Revolution.

1762–96 Reign of Catherine II (the Great) of Russia. In the name of the Englightenment she encourages art, education and letters, and instigates political and social reforms – yet she does nothing to abolish serfdom.

1762 Rousseau's *Le Contrat Social* and *Émile*.
Gluck's *Orfeo ed Euridice* performed.

1764–95 Reign of Stanislas II (Poniatowski), last king of Poland. The country is dismembered by Russia, Austria and Prussia during the first (1772), the second (1793) and the third (1795) partitions. Having no country left to govern, he resigns in 1795.

1771 First publication of *Encyclopaedia Britannica*.
1772 Diderot publishes last volume of *Encyclopédie*.
1774 Goethe's *Werther*.

1772 First partition of Poland.

1775–83 American War of Independence.

1778–9 War of the Bavarian Succession.

1779 Lessing's *Nathan der Weise*.

MEIR OF PREMISHLAN
(1780–1850)

1781 First Jewish Free School opened in Berlin, marking the breakthrough of Jewish *Aufklärung*: Enlightenment.

1784 Beginning of publication in Berlin of *Hameassef* (The Gatherer), devoted to rationalist Judaism.

MENAHEM-MENDEL OF KOTZK
(1787–1859)

ISRAEL OF RIZHIN
(1796–1850)

AHARON OF KARLIN
(1801–72)

1812 Napoleon's invasion of Russia brings about the emancipation of its Jews.

IN THE WORLD AT LARGE	IN THE ARTS
	1781 Kant's *Critique of Pure Reason*.
	1785 Mozart's *The Marriage of Figaro*.
1789–99 The French Revolution.	
1793 Second partition of Poland.	1790 Goya's *Caprichos*, works of social satire. Goethe's *Faust*.
1793–4. The Reign of Terror. Robespierre massacres opposition; Marie Antoinette is guillotined.	
1794 Polish national uprising led by Thaddeus Kosciusko crushed by combined Russian and Prussian armies.	
1795 Third partition of Poland. Russia, Prussia and Austria absorb the last Polish territories.	
1796 Napoleon Bonaparte embarks on a series of victories.	
	1797 Chateaubriand's *Essays on Old and Modern Revolutions*.
1799 Napoleon and his army reach the Holy Land.	
	1800 Schiller's *Maria Stuart*.
	1807 Byron publishes his first poems; Fichte, his *Sermons to the German Nation*; Hegel, his *Phenomenology of the Mind*.
	1808 Beethoven's Pastoral Symphony.
1812 Napoleon invades Russia.	
1813 Battle of Leipzig – Napoleon defeated.	
1814–15 Congress of Vienna ends wars of Napoleonic era.	
1815 Waterloo. Napoleon defeated and exiled.	

1815 Pius VII reinstitutes the Inquisition. The constitution of Poland – finally formulated – denies civic rights to Jews.

MENDEL OF WORKE
(1819–68)

1819 Beginning of movement 'Wissenschaft des Judentums' in Germany; it will expand to all of Western Europe.

1824 Mass persecution of Jews in Russia.

1840 Jews accused of ritual murder in Damascus.

1842 More persecutions of Russian Jews; their children are forced into military service for twenty-five-year stretches.

1845 Jews are expelled from Basel.

1847 A Jew becomes a member of the British Parliament: Baron Lionel of Rothschild.

IN THE WORLD AT LARGE	IN THE ARTS

IN THE WORLD AT LARGE

1815 The Holy Alliance is signed by all European rulers except the King of England, the Pope and the Sultan. Alexander I is the most active sponsor of this agreement, which allies Christian principles with politics and which generally represents a reactionary policy against liberal ideas.

IN THE ARTS

1820 Keats publishes his major poems, the *Odes*; Shelley, his *Prometheus Unbound*.

1825–55 Reign of Nicholas I of Russia is marked by autocracy and repression of all liberal tendencies.

1827. Heine's *Das Buch der Lieder*.

1830 Victor Hugo's *Hernani*.

1831 Stendhal's *Le Rouge et le Noir*.

1838 Dickens' *Oliver Twist*.

1843 Kierkegaard's *Fear and Trembling*.

1848 Revolutions in Austria, Prussia, Hungary, Italy, Prague ... all of Europe is in an uproar.

1849 Dostoevsky arrested for his political activities, condemned to death, but pardoned by the Tsar and sent to prison.
Tolstoi tries to establish a school for peasants at Yasnaia Polyana, his family's estate.

1850 Balzac's *La Comédie Humaine*.

1859 Darwin's *Origin of Species*.

Baltic Sea

R. Niemen

Gdynia

Gdansk (Danzig)

R. Narew

R. Vistula

Bialystok

FIRST CENTRES OF HASIDISM

- Principal centres
- Major towns
- Provinces

| 0 | 100 | 200 miles |
| 0 | 100 | 200 | 300 km |

Warsaw

Worke • Ger

Kozhenitz
Kotsk

Pshiskhe
Lublin

Opatov (Apt)

Lizensk
Tomasho

Ropshitz
Lwov
(Lemberg)

GALICIA

Baltic Sea

RUSSIA

LITHUANIA

Kovno

Vilna

Minsk

PRUSSIA

Warsaw

Pinsk

Lublin

VOLHYNIA

UKRAINE

Cracow

Kiev

Lwow (Lemberg)

R. Dnieper

GALICIA

PODOLIA

AUSTRIA

R. Dniester

Poland in 1772

Poland in 1815

TURKEY

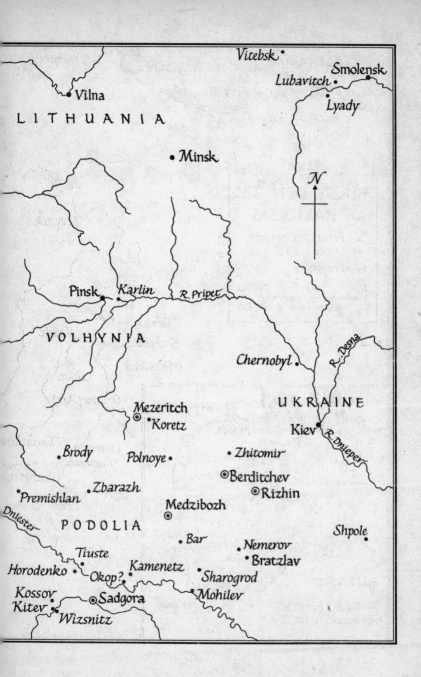

MORE ABOUT PENGUINS, PELICANS AND PUFFINS

For further information about books available from Penguins please write to Dept EP, Penguin Books Ltd, Harmondsworth, Middlesex UB7 0DA.

In the U.S.A.: For a complete list of books available from Penguins in the United States write to Dept DG, Penguin Books, 299 Murray Hill Parkway, East Rutherford, New Jersey 07073.

In Canada: For a complete list of books available from Penguins in Canada write to Penguin Books Canada Ltd, 2801 John Street, Markham, Ontario L3R 1B4.

In Australia: For a complete list of books available from Penguins in Australia write to the Marketing Department, Penguin Books Australia Ltd, P.O. Box 257, Ringwood, Victoria 3134.

In New Zealand: For a complete list of books available from Penguins in New Zealand write to the Marketing Department, Penguin Books (N.Z.) Ltd, P.O. Box 4019, Auckland 10.

In India: For a complete list of books available from Penguins in India write to Penguin Overseas Ltd, 706 Eros Apartments, 56 Nehru Place, New Delhi 110019.